X3D: Extensible 3D Graphics for Web Authors

In Praise of X3D

There will be no problem understanding these concise, clear, comprehensible background concepts for readers new to Extensible 3D (X3D). There are many notes and examples that compare X3D to Virtual Reality Modeling Language (VRML) features. Don Brutzman and Leonard Daly clearly and thoroughly illustrate each logical concept and feature of X3D with diagrams, tables, code snippets, screenshots of 3D objects/environments, and example scenes, while making use of the very latest specifications and implementations. Their approach contributes greatly to an easy and in-depth understanding of the X3D language. This book is the ultimate introductory guide to X3D!
—Dr. Vladimir Geroimenko, University of Plymouth, School of Computing Communications and Electronics, Plymouth, UK

This book is required reading for anybody interested in Web3D. The authors are well known and respected in the X3D community as pioneers. Their writing style is concise and engaging, set at an appropriate level to encourage understanding, and uses the concepts being introduced. Their "Hints and warnings" sections provide added value above what is available from X3D specification documents. Hard to achieve in a reference manual!
—Professor Nigel W. John, School of Computer Science, University of Wales, Bangor

How many times have we heard "The ISO specification is hard to read, do you have something more approachable?" This book is the answer. It provides a detailed explanation of each node in the Immersive profile and gives many reusable examples. After reading this book you'll be well prepared to develop your own X3D content.
—Alan Hudson, President Web3D Consortium, Yumetech Inc.

This is a much-needed book about the X3D standard and X3D content development. The book follows the structure of the X3D standard specifications which helps readers understand and apply the X3D standard. It can also be used as a reference material in virtual reality and graphics-related courses.
—Professor Denis Gracanin, Virginia Polytechnic Institute & State University

X3D: Extensible 3D Graphics for Web Authors

DON BRUTZMAN
Naval Postgraduate School, Monterey, California, USA

and

LEONARD DALY
Daly Realism, Los Angeles, California, USA

AMSTERDAM • BOSTON • HEIDELBERG • LONDON
NEW YORK • OXFORD • PARIS • SAN DIEGO
SAN FRANCISCO • SINGAPORE • SYDNEY • TOKYO
Morgan Kaufmann Is an Imprint of Elsevier

Publisher: Denise E. M. Penrose
Publishing Services Manager: George Morrison
Senior Project Manager: Brandy Lilly
Assistant Editor: Michelle Ward
Cover Image: Christian Greuel/Planet 9
Text Design: Frances Baca
Composition: SPI India
Illustration: Graphic World Illustration Studio
Copyeditor: Graphic World Publishing Services
Proofreader: Graphic World Publishing Services
Indexer: Graphic World Publishing Services
Interior printer: Hing Yip Printing Co. Ltd.
Cover printer: Hing Yip Printing Co. Ltd.

Morgan Kaufmann Publishers is an imprint of Elsevier.
500 Sansome Street, Suite 400, San Francisco, CA 94111

This book is printed on acid-free paper.

Library of Congress Cataloging-in-Publication Data
Application submitted

ISBN-13: 978-0-12-088500-8
ISBN-10: 0-12-088500-X

For information on all Morgan Kaufmann publications,
visit our Web site at www.mkp.com or www.books.elsevier.com

Printed in China
07 08 09 10 11   5 4 3 2 1

Dedication

We dedicate this book to our families,
with grateful thanks for their patient support and love.

—Don Brutzman and Leonard Daly

Contents

CHAPTER 2

Geometry Nodes, Part 1: Primitives 37

CHAPTER 3

Grouping Nodes. 65

CHAPTER 9

Event Utilities and Scripting 249

Preface

A journey of a thousand miles begins with a single step.
—Chinese proverb

1. Goals

Welcome! This book describes Extensible 3D (X3D) Graphics, the open international standard for 3D on the Web. X3D is used for building 3-dimensional models, both simple and sophisticated. X3D can show animated objects from different viewpoint perspectives, allowing user insight and interaction. X3D models can be further combined and connected to build sophisticated 3D virtual environments running across the Internet.

The primary goal of this book is to show Web authors how to build and connect X3D models. Another goal is to teach students the essential principles of Webcapable 3D graphics. Because X3D scene-graph concepts are easily understood from the perspective of creating Extensible Markup Language (XML) documents, this material has been successfully used to teach 3D to students with or without prior programming experience. Finally the book should serve as a handy reference for X3D authors, explaining both the broad principles and specific details of X3D scene construction.

2. Motivation

More than 30 years of innovative research, theoretical mathematics, and application-development effort have made 3D graphics an exciting field that produces amazing results and frequent surprises. The heart of the 3D community is the Special Interest Group on Graphics (SIGGRAPH), which is one of many professional societies making up the Association for Computing Machinery (ACM). SIGGRAPH can be found online at *www.siggraph.org*. The classic text for this subject area is *Computer Graphics, Principles and Practice* by James D. Foley, Andries van Dam, Stephen K. Feiner, and John F. Hughes (Addison-Wesley, 2nd Edition, 1997). Hundreds of other books about

3D graphics are also available, covering a wide spectrum of technical and practical topics.

Nevertheless, for most Web authors and software programmers, 3D graphics remains a complex niche technology that is not easily mastered and not often used. For many people, 3D is best known from movies or computer games. It is something "special" created by others, and viewed only in movie theaters, by DVD playback, or by locally installed computer-game programs. 3D scenes are typically created only by small teams of experts who have worked hard to achieve programming mastery using expensive professional application tool kits.

Enabling Web authors to independently create and compose 3D objects has been difficult for the same reasons, because such graphics have almost always been produced by highly trained programmers and animators using specialty 3D software packages. Unfortunately, because most 3D software packages are created using proprietary commercial products or computer programming languages, users can only rarely combine diverse 3D models and interact directly with them. This challenging state of affairs has prevented 3D graphics from becoming a commonly authored form of multimedia.

Rather than creating yet another technical niche, X3D is designed for interchange and interoperability that allows authors to build simple or sophisticated 3D models of interest. X3D collects the most common 3D techniques and provides common-denominator graphics capabilities that map satisfactorily to many industry approaches (which often vary more in style than in substance). Thus translators and converters can import and export X3D scenes both to and from many other 3D graphics formats, allowing easier 3D interchange. This approach allows the various specialty tools to do what they are good at, noncompetitively, while making 3D models available for composition together in an effective, efficient way. Thus X3D can enable 3D graphics to transition from isolated islands of functionality to become a first-class media type used in web pages and documents everywhere.

According to the International Standards Organization (ISO), Extensible 3D Graphics (X3D) is the "ISO standard that defines a royalty-free run-time system and delivery mechanism for real-time 3D content and applications running on a network." Supported X3D file-format encodings enable the construction of interactive, animated, 3D virtual environments that stably incorporate the latest advances in graphics hardware capabilities, file compression, and data security. Networking is optional, allowing X3D scenes to work compatibly over the Internet via http servers, on local disk drives or CDs, and even as standalone email and chat attachments.

Because licensing restrictions for all of the underlying contributions in the X3D standards are royalty free, X3D technologies can be used freely without fear that they will "time out" or become unusable as a result of corporate-profitability concerns or one-sided policy changes. An open process guided by the nonprofit Web3D Consortium has consolidated 12 years of work and achieved full certification from ISO as an International Standard. Thus X3D models can be used and improved by individuals, companies, government agencies, and educators without fear that the underlying technology might eventually become unavailable.

The 3D graphics community is highly technical, artistic, sensitive, and motivated, usually all at the same time. Many X3D authors and users already hope that bringing

3D graphics to the Web can make all kinds of models more widely available, thus making 3D graphics a useful part of everyday life. Building compatible X3D models for the Web is a worthy effort, showing progress that steadily grows with each passing day.

Hopefully this book will help you learn the fundamentals of X3D, master the techniques needed to show others your work, and bootstrap the Web into the third dimension. Good luck with your efforts!

3. Reader background

Prior experience in 3D graphics programming or XML authoring is helpful but not required to use this book. The creation of X3D scenes is presented with an emphasis on XML so that content production might appear familiar to Web authors. Many examples are developed as part of the book, and many more are available online.

4. Software support

A free Java-based authoring tool designed especially for X3D is available on the Web site: X3D-Edit. This scene-graph editor has been used to produce all of the book examples. X3D-Edit has been tested under Windows, Macintosh, and Linux operating systems. Features include tooltips for each X3D node and field in multiple languages: English, Chinese, French, German, Italian, Portuguese, and Spanish. Models and tooltips have also been tested satisfactorily using other XML-based tools.

Authored X3D scenes are viewed using separate browser plugins, usually installed into the local Web browser. Multiple X3D viewer plugins and applications are provided on the support Web site and online.

5. Book structure

5.1. Typographic conventions

The following typographic conventions are observed in this book.

- Definition terms are identified using *italics*.

- Source content is shown using a `fixed-width font`.

- Null or absent nodes are represented as NULL.

- Empty arrays may be represented as empty square brackets [ ].

- Empty string values may be represented as empty double-quote marks, either `" "` or `&quot; &quot;`.

5.2. Chapter organization

5.2.1. Introductory chapters

This preface describes the structure of the book. Chapter 1 is the in-depth Technical Overview, which describes the architectural principles governing how X3D works. Topics include scene-graph structure, file encodings, the Extensible Markup Language (XML), various related ISO specifications, and the underlying technical detail common to all X3D components and nodes.

5.2.2. X3D Component chapters

Each of the subsequent chapters cover the primary nodes provided by each component in the X3D Immersive Profile. The layout of each chapter is organized consistently in order to best support clarity of presentation. Chapter structure follows.

The Concepts section discusses shared usage issues, abstract node-type interfaces, and the common fields shared by nodes presented in the chapter. Each node is explained using both XML syntax (for .x3d files) and ClassicVRML syntax (for .x3dv files). Each of the fields is then described in detail, emphasizing allowed values and the types of functionality provided. Usage hints and warnings emphasize lessons learned and problems to avoid.

Each chapter concludes with a summary of the key ideas covered, a list of related nodes and concepts, and a brief preview of the next chapter.

5.2.3. Examples

Working example scenes are provided for each node. First modeled by masters students at the Naval Postgraduate School, the Kelp Forest exhibit of Monterey Bay Aquarium provides a common theme for most of the examples in the book. These example X3D scenes are designed to illustrate specific features of X3D.

The best approach to learning this material is to load each scene in and X3D browser, view it, and verify that it works as described, and then modify values for various nodes and fields to confirm your understanding of the concepts discussed.

6. Chapter descriptions

This book is designed to be read in order. Each chapter builds upon previous chapters with only occasional forward referencing. The ordering of chapters provides a clear path to learn how to build increasingly sophisticated 3D worlds.

6.1. Chapter topics

The chapters are organized by function and ordered as follows:

1. **Technical Overview.** General introduction of the fundamentals of 3D, including scene graphs, events, node reuse, file structure and encodings, components and profiles, and conformance.

2. **Geometry Nodes, Part 1: Primitives.** The basic primitive shapes: Box, Sphere, Cylinder, Cone, and Text.

3. **Grouping Nodes.** Collecting and positioning objects in the 3D world using Inline, LOD, Group and StaticGroup, Switch, Transform, and Anchor.

4. **Viewing and Navigation.** How to view and navigate in the 3D world with Viewpoint and Navigation Info.

5. **Appearance, Material, and Textures.** Adding colors, shininess, and transparency using Material, or adding image-file textures using PixelTexture, ImageTexture, MovieTexture, TextureTransform, TextureCoordinate, and TextureCoordinateGenerator.

6. **Geometry Nodes, Part 2: Points, Lines, and Polygons.** Geometric creations that are more advanced than the basic shapes, including Coordinate, Color, PointSet, LineSet, IndexedLineSet, IndexedFaceSet, ElevationGrid, and Extrusion.

7. **Event Animation and Interpolation.** Making objects move, twist, wiggle, and shake with TimeSensor and the interpolation nodes: ScalarInterpolator, Position-Interpolator, PositionInterpolator2D, ColorInterpolator, OrientationInterpolator, and CoordinateInterpolator.

8. **User Interactivity Nodes.** Allowing users to interact with the world by connecting TouchSensor, PlaneSensor, CylinderSensor, SphereSensor, KeySensor, and StringSensor nodes.

9. **Event Utilities and Scripting.** Event type conversion, improved animation using the event-utility nodes BooleanFilter, BooleanSequencer, BooleanToggle, BooleanTrigger, IntegerSequencer, IntegerTrigger, and the author-programmable Script node.

10. **Geometry Nodes, Part 3: Geometry2D Nodes.** Flat geometry can be helpful for building 2D constructs that face the viewer. Planar nodes include Polypoint2D, Rectangle2D, TriangleSet2D, Polyline2D, Circle2D, Arc2D, ArcClose2D, and Disk2D.

11. **Lighting and Environment Nodes.** Lighting and scene background effects are accomplished using DirectionalLight, PointLight, SpotLight, Background, TextureBackground, Fog, and Sound.

12. **Environment Sensor and Sound Nodes.** User activity in the environment can be detected and processed by using LoadSensor, Collision, Billboard, ProximitySensor, and VisibilitySensor.

13. **Geometry Nodes, Part 4: Triangles and Quadrilaterals.** Fundamental low-level geometry creation using triangles: TriangleSet, TriangleStripSet, TriangleFanSet, IndexedTriangleSet, IndexedTriangleStripSet, and IndexedTriangleFanSet.

14. **Creating Prototype Nodes.** Probably the most powerful extension feature in X3D is the ability to define new reusable nodes, known as prototypes. Prototype declarations are combinations of already-existing nodes and (option-ally) other prototypes. Prototype instances can then be used like any other X3D node. External prototype declarations allow authors to collect reusable prototype definitions together in a single file that can be accessed by other scenes.

15. **Metadata and Information Nodes.** Metadata includes background information describing the makeup of the X3D scene itself. Nodes of interest include WorldInfo, MetadataSet, MetadataDouble, MetadataFloat, MetadataInteger, and MetadataString. This chapter is provided online.

6.2. Appendices

Several appendices provide supplementary information.

*   Description of resources available online

*   Help: X3D/VRML examples

*   X3D scene authoring hints

6.3. How to use this book

X3D has many capabilities, so there is a lot to learn. Chapter 1, Technical Overview, provides a thorough background study of how X3D works. Each of the following chapters presents a set of related X3D nodes, each providing new functionality.

You will learn best if you load and test each example using X3D-Edit or another authoring tool. Usually, you need to modify nodes and field values to fully observe how the displayed scene might change. Do not worry about breaking things. A common occurrence in 3D graphics is that a problem or bug actually turns out to be a feature!

Chapters 2–6 provide the essentials of X3D scene graphs and are essential reading. Chapters 7–9 explain animation and interaction and are best read together. Because X3D is consistently designed, readers can skip around among the chapters if they wish. This is especially helpful when building new parts of a specific project.

The suggested sequence for proceeding through the chapters depends on the reader. Guidelines follow.

*   **Web authors and X3D students.** First, read just the Section 1 Introduction in Chapter 1, Technical Overview, then skip ahead to Chapter 2. Follow the chapters in order. Read the other Chapter 1 sections later when you are ready to learn more about the technical underpinnings and design rationale of X3D.

*   **Experienced 3D programmers.** Read Chapter 1, Technical Overview, first to see how X3D differs from (and is similar to) the technologies that you are already familiar with. Gain familiarity with Chapters 2–6 for scene-graph fundamentals, and then Chapters 7–9 for animation and scripting. The remaining chapters can be followed in any order.

*   **Experienced X3D authors.** Read the descriptions of both the XML and ClassicVRML encodings in Chapter 1, Technical Overview, so that you understand the syntax of both file formats. They are functionally equivalent. You can then read the rest of the book in any order and use it as a ready reference manual. You may find the sections providing hints and warnings especially helpful.

Feedback from readers is encouraged and welcome. Errata and improvements are posted on the book's Web site.

Contributor List

Many talented individuals contributed unselfishly to the technologies and capabilities described in this book. In particular, we want to thank the following people:

Dr. Michael Aratow (Web3D Medical Working Group); Christian Bouville (France Telecom), Len Bullard (independent consultant); Timothy Childs (RoundUP Productions), David Colleen and Christian Greuel (Planet 9 Studios); Dr. David Duce (Oxford Brooks University, Oxford, United Kingdom), Miriam English (miriam-english.org); Dr. Pablo Figueroa (Universidad de los Andes Colombia); Dr. Vladimir Geroimenko (University of Plymouth, United Kingdom); Rob Glidden (Sun Microsystems), Rick Goldberg (Aniviza); Dr. Julian Gomez (Polished Pixels), Barb Helfer (Capital University, Columbus, Ohio); Alan Hudson, Justin Couch, and Stephen Matsuba (Yumetech Inc.); Dr. Nigel John (University of Wales, Bangor, United Kingdom); Robert Lansdale (Okino Graphics), Braden McDaniel (endoframe); Tony Parisi, Keith Victor, and Dave Arendash (Media Machines); Dr. Nicholas Polys and Dennis Graconin (Virginia Tech); Dr. Richard Puk (Intelligraphics Inc.); Dr. Mark Pullen (George Mason University); Sandy Ressler (NIST); Larry Rosenthal (Cube3.com); Dr. Cristina Russo dos Santos (European Patient Office); Peter Schickel, Holger Grahn, Cecile Muller, Herbert Stocker, and Brian Hay (Bit Management); Hyunju Shim (University of Florida, Gainesville); John A. Stewart and Sarah Dumoulin (Communications Research Centre Canada); Chris Thorne and Viveka Weiley (Ping Interactive Australia); Neil Trevett (nVidia and Khronos); Rita Turkowski (Web3D Consortium); Joe D. Williams (HyperMultiMedia); Mitch Williams (3D-online); Jeff Weekley, Don McGregor, Curt Blais, and Terry Norbraten (Naval Postgraduate School); several dozen NPS graduate students, and the many contributors who have worked on X3D.

About the Authors

Don Brutzman is a computer scientist and Associate Professor working in the Modeling Virtual Environments & Simulation (MOVES) Institute at the Naval Postgraduate School in Monterey, California, USA.

He is one of the original participants involved with Virtual Reality Modeling Language (VRML) since this community effort began in 1994. He is a founding member of the nonprofit Web3D Consortium, serving on the Board of Directors. He cochairs the X3D and X3DEarth Working Groups and leads a variety of X3D technical development efforts. He also serves as the Web3D Consortium liaison to the World Wide Web Consortium (W3C) Advisory Committee and the Open Geospatial Consortium (OGC). He has been teaching VRML and X3D since 1996.

Dr. Brutzman's research interests include underwater robotics, real-time 3D computer graphics, artificial intelligence, and high-performance networking. He is a member of the Institute of Electrical and Electronic Engineers (IEEE), the Association for Computing Machinery (ACM) Special Interest Group on Graphics (SIGGRAPH), and the American Association for Artificial Intelligence (AAAI). Dr. Brutzman directs numerous related research and development projects as part of the Extensible Modeling and Simulation Framework (XMSF).

A retired submarine officer, Dr. Brutzman holds degrees from the U.S. Naval Academy in Anapolis, Maryland, and the Naval Postgraduate School.

Leonard Daly is President of Daly Realism, an Internet Consultant working in 3D graphics and e-business, based in Los Angeles, California, USA.

He is secretary of the X3D working group, managing and contributing to the X3D specification development and ISO approval process. He has been working in 2D and 3D computer graphics since 1980 and with the X3D/Virtual Reality Modeling Language (VRML) community since 1997. He was founder and Treasurer of the Los Angeles VRML User's Group (LAVUG). He was the organizer and lead presenter of X3D courses at SIGGRAPH Conferences (2002 and 2003) and the Web3D Symposium (2000, 2002, and 2003).

Mr. Daly's primary research interest is in large interactive networked systems with real-time 3D graphical plus audio interfaces. He is a member of the Association for Computing Machinery (ACM) Special Interest Group on Graphics (SIGGRAPH) and has served on the nonprofit Web3D Consortium Board of Directors. He holds a Bachelor of Science in Mathematics from Harvey Mudd College.

Technical Overview

When we mean to build, we first survey the plot, then draw the model.
—William Shakespeare, Henry IV Part II Act 1 Scene 2

1. Introduction

Building and interacting with 3D graphics is a "hands on" experience. There are many examples in this book to teach you how X3D works and to assist you in building your own projects. However, before creating your own Extensible 3D (X3D) graphics scenes, you should understand the background concepts explained here.

The book has an accompanying website at X3dGraphics.com. All examples plus links to other reference material and software are available on the website.

This chapter presents the ideas needed to understand how an X3D scene graph works. This information is used throughout the following chapters and is especially helpful when creating your own X3D scenes. This book assumes that you are interested in learning more about 3D graphics—prior knowledge is helpful, but not required. This chapter is best for people who already have some knowledge of 3D graphics and are ready to learn more of the technical background about how X3D works.

X3D uses a scene graph to model the many graphics nodes that make up a virtual environment. The scene graph is a tree structure that is directed and acyclic, meaning that there is a definite beginning for the graph, there are parent-child relationships for each node, and there are no cycles (or loops) in the graph. Each node has a single parent, except for the X3D root at the top (which has no further parent). The scene graph collects all aspects of a 3D scene in a hierarchical fashion that properly organizes geometry, appearance, animation, and event routing.

X3D is built on the Virtual Reality Modeling Language (VRML), which was first approved as an international standard in 1997. X3D adds Extensible Markup Language (XML) capabilities to integrate with other World Wide Web technologies.

X3D design features include validity checking of content, componentized browsers for faster downloads, flexible addition of new hardware extensions, a lightweight Core Profile, and better script integration compared to VRML. Numerous (more than 2000) example scenes demonstrate most 3D and animation aspects of these scene-graph specifications, and demonstrate syntax checking during autotranslation to VRML encodings. The web3d.org members-only website provide a challenging conformance and performance suite for demonstrating exemplar high-end content. Both XML-based and VRML-based file formats are valid ways to encode the information in an X3D scene. The relative benefits of each are explained and compared in this chapter.

If you are interested in learning how to author X3D scenes right away, you can skim (or even skip) this chapter and read Chapter 2, Geometry Nodes, Part I: Primitives. The background information contained here is not immediately necessary, because the authoring tools take care of headers and structure automatically. The X3D-Edit authoring tool is available to help you build scenes, available free on the book's website.

2. Concepts

This chapter begins with historical background on the development of X3D, presents a brief look at the X3D specifications, and then provides a detailed overview of how the X3D scene graph works. Relevant X3D concepts include scene-graph structure, file encoding, field and node types, and extensibility via profiles and components.

2.1. Historical background: VRML, ISO, and the Web3D Consortium

X3D is a scene-graph architecture and file-format encoding that improves on the VRML international standard (formally listed as ISO/IEC 14772-1:1997 but frequently called VRML 2 or VRML97). X3D uses XML to express the geometry and behavior capabilities of VRML. VRML is well known as a highly expressive 3D interchange format that is supported by many tools and codebases. In addition to expressing diverse geometry renderings and animation behaviors, X3D allows program scripting (in ECMAScript or Java) and node prototyping, which together provide excellent support for scene-graph extensions and new language functionality defined by authors.

The VRML effort began in 1994 when Mark Pesce and Tony Parisi called for the creation of a markup language for 3D graphics on the Web. Several candidates were considered through an open competition, and eventually OpenInventor by Rikk Carey and Paul Strauss at Silicon Graphics Inc. (SGI) was selected as the best basis for creating such a language. Originally called the Virtual Reality Markup Language, VRML 1.0 was quickly produced using an informal, open, consensus-based working-group effort. Several years later, a somewhat restructured (and much improved) VRML 2.0 successfully passed the rigorous scrutiny necessary for approval as International Standard 14772-1:1997, becoming known as VRML97.

To protect VRML as an open 3D-graphics standard, and further encourage the continuation of open development, more process and support was needed than a simple mailing list and web server. A broad cross-section of business companies, academic institutions, government agencies, and individual professionals joined together to form the nonprofit Web3D Consortium. This combination of friendly cooperation, hard work, formal organizational support, and an enthusiastic community have remained the hallmark of VRML and X3D evolution throughout many development cycles.

Despite intermittent industry engagement over the past decade, VRML has persisted and remains the most widely supported nonproprietary 3D-scene format in the world. VRML has now entered its third generation as X3D. Many lessons have been learned and many successful new capabilities have been integrated into this evolving international standard. X3D 3.0 was formally approved by the International Standards Organization (ISO) as ISO/IEC 19775 in 2004. Since that milestone, annual specification updates continue to track the cutting edge of industry capabilities. The Web3D Consortium (www.web3d.org) actively supports many working groups and an active community of interested users. Authors, developers, professionals, and enthusiasts continue to add to the long list of capabilities in X3D. Web3D Consortium membership is open to both organizations and individuals.

2.2. X3D browsers

X3D browsers are software applications that can parse (read) X3D scenes and then render (draw) them, not only showing 3D objects from varying viewpoints but also enabling object animation and user interaction. Sometimes referred to as players or viewers, X3D browsers are often implemented as plugins that work as an integrated part of a regular hypertext markup language (HTML) web browser (such as Mozilla Firefox or Internet Explorer). X3D browsers can also be delivered as standalone or embedded applications that present X3D scenes for user viewing.

Figure 1.1 shows a representative example of the software architecture typically used in a browser. The descriptions in this paragraph follow the blocks in a counterclockwise order (starting at the upper left). X3D scenes are usually files that are read (or written) by the browser. Parsers are used to read the various file-format encodings available. Nodes are then created and sent to a scene-graph manager, which keeps track of defined geometry, appearance, locations, and orientations. The scene-graph manager repeatedly traverses the scene-graph tree of X3D Nodes to draw output image frames at

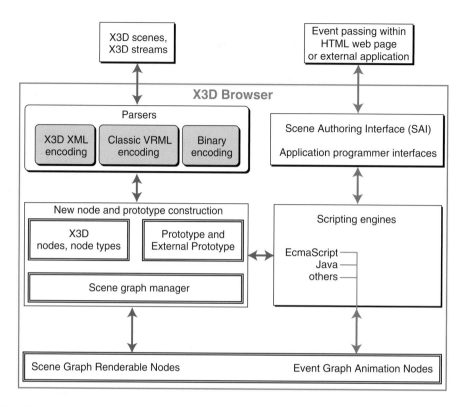

Figure 1.1. Example software architecture for an X3D browser.

a rapid rate. This process rapidly redraws precisely calculated perspective-based images as the user's point of view and objects of interest change. The event graph also keeps track of all animation nodes, which are computationally driven to generate and pass value-change events into the scene graph. Events received by the scene graph can change any aspect of the rendered image. Further extending the animation nodes are scripts, which can send or receive events and also generate (or remove) geometry in the scene. Scripts encapsulate programming code from other languages, usually either ECMAScript (formerly known as JavaScript) or Java. The Scene Authoring Interface (SAI) defines how these application programming interfaces (APIs) work, allowing authors to create scripting code that can work across different operating systems and different browser software. Finally (ending at the upper-right corner of the diagram), HTML web pages and external applications can also be used to embed X3D plugin browsers, which appear to users as live, interactive 3D images on the page.

The internals of different browsers vary. Nevertheless, the goal for all is to provide a consistent user experience for each X3D scene. That is one of the greatest strengths of X3D: defining how a software browser ought to draw 3D images and interact with users, rather than trying to tell browser-building programmers exactly how to write their high-performance software. This balance works well because authors can simply focus on building good X3D models (rather than difficult, nonportable software programs) and have confidence that the X3D scenes will work wherever they are displayed.

This approach is sometimes summarized by the slogan "content is king," because achieving interoperability and consistency among X3D scenes is considered more important than the idiosyncracies of any single programming approach. The overall approach also works well because the software programmers who build X3D browsers (an immensely capable but notoriously opinionated group!) can compete on implementation performance and conformance, independently choosing which programming approaches work best, all while agreeing on consistently achieving X3D scene interoperability. Best of all, legacy X3D scene content doesn't "rust" or get bugs. Instead, good content can remain valid and useful indefinitely, without modifications, even as browsers continue to change and improve year after year.

An example scene and corresponding browser snapshot image are provided in the last section of this chapter.

2.3. X3D specifications

The X3D specifications are a highly detailed set of technical documents that define the geometry and behavior capabilities of Classic VRML using the Web-compatible tagsets of XML. Scene graphs, nodes, and fields (in X3D terminology) correspond to documents, elements, and attributes (in XML terminology). As part of the Web3D Consortium, the X3D working Group has designed and implemented the next-generation X3D graphics specification (www.web3D.org/x3d). Lots of feedback and modifications by an active user community improved these results throughout the review process.

It is particularly important to note that XML benefits are numerous: XML has customized metalanguages for structuring data, is easily read by both humans and computer systems, has validatable data constraints, and so on. XML is license free, platform independent and well supported (Bos 2001). Together these qualities ensure that the VRML ISO standard has been extended to functionally match the emerging family of next-generation XML-based Web languages. X3D is now part of that Web-compatible information infrastructure.

The original VRML specification was written to stand alone as a single document. While this made for a simpler reference document, the result was not easily modifiable. Growing from VRML97 to X3D 3.0 took many years of work. Because the X in X3D stands for Extensible, there are now multiple specification documents that govern the coherent evolution and diverse capabilities of X3D. Each can be developed and extended independently, allowing annual updates that document the stable growth of X3D.

It is interesting that the primary functionality of nodes and fields in X3D graphics are specified in a technology-neutral way that is independent of any particular file encoding or programming-language binding. The X3D Abstract Specification remains the governing reference on how the X3D scene graph works. In this way, each file-format encoding and language binding is expected to remain interoperable, compatible, and functionally equivalent with the rest.

Each of these specification documents has been developed through an open, collaborative process by volunteer working-group members in the nonprofit Web3D Consortium. Many of these participants are industry experts who are supported by their companies. Each year, proposed new functionality is implemented (at least twice), evaluated, and specified in formal draft specifications that go to the ISO for final review and ratification. Because all X3D development, implementation, and evaluation is done within the Web3D Consortium process, the overall process is relatively rapid for production of an International Standard. The annual update cycle keeps this work in step with commercial-product development and the always-growing capabilities of the 3D-graphics industry.

The various file encodings and language bindings consistently implement the common-core functionality of the X3D Abstract Specification. The Humanoid Animation (H-Anim) specification is also supported. Figure 1.2 (the honeycom diagram) illustrates how these specifications relate to each other.

The World Wide Web Consortium (W3C) Document Object Model (DOM) is another language-neutral API designed for processing XML documents. It uses string-based

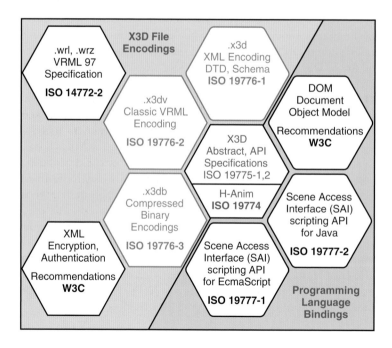

Figure 1.2. The family of X3D specifications includes multiple file encodings and programming-language bindings, all mapping to the same common functionality defined by the abstract specifications.

accessor methods to get and set both element and attribute values. It can also be used to build and modify X3D scenes that are written in the XML encoding. However, because string-based DOM performance is usually too slow for the demands of real-time, interactive 3D graphics, DOM is rarely used directly in combination with a rendering X3D browser. Nevertheless, DOM and other XML-related APIs can be quite useful for creating, reading, or modifying X3D scenes separately from an X3D browser.

Two more W3C Recommendations apply: XML Signature for digital signatures and XML Encryption. Together they are part of the XML Security area, and are compatible with the .X3db Binary Encoding. This rich set of functionality allows authors to reduce file size, optionally reduce geometric complexity (using either lossless or lossy algorithms), digitally sign content to prove ownership, and encrypt content to protect the source document.

Table 1.1 lists the pertinent specifications currently used in X3D and this book. They are available online (www.web3d.org/x3d/specifications), with X3D-Edit, and on the website accompanying this book. Installing the specifications on your working computer and referring to them in combination with this book is a good way to become familiar with the many details and options available in X3D.

Someday additional programming language bindings (perhaps for C++ and/or C#, perl, and so on) might be added to the X3D specification. Although this kind of work requires significant expertise, producing such an addition to the 19777 specification series of API language bindings is a relatively straightforward matter. The well-defined nature of X3D extensibility requires that all functionality align with already-standardized X3D Abstract Specification. The precise objects and methods of any new API are likely to resemble the similarly structured ECMAScript and Java language bindings. This means that the most difficult work (i.e., defining compatible 3D functionality) is already done, and any new language bindings merely have to define how they will implement well-specified X3D capabilities. Last but not least, any such programming-language interface must be independently implemented in at least two browsers before specification approval.

All of the X3D specifications are freely available in electronic form, updated online. Paper hardcopies or CDs can also be purchased directly from ISO. Serious X3D authors are advised to keep a copy of the specifications easily available to refer to when tricky questions arise. Copies of the X3D specifications, X3D tooltips, and other help files are linked on X3dGraphics.com for your convenience. Although this kind of reading can be difficult at first, the effort is worthwhile. Asking questions online about specification details is a good way to learn more. Perhaps someday you will even find yourself proposing an improvement to the X3D specifications on a Web3D mailing list. A large, friendly community of interest posing questions and solutions has made it possible for X3D to grow steadily since 1994.

2.4. Scene graph

Knowing some of the theory behind X3D is helpful. Scene graphs are a model-centric approach. Model geometry, size, appearance, materials, relative locations, and internal

Specification Number	Document Title	Description
ISO/IEC 14772	The Virtual Reality Modeling Language: Part 1 with Amendment 1 and Part 2, Known as VRML97	VRML 2.0 after formal specification review. Added EAI API. Superceded by X3D, which replaced EAI with SAI.
ISO/IEC 19774	Humanoid Animation (H-Anim)	Abstract definitions for H-Anim functionality, includes VRML encoding.
ISO/IEC 19775-1 & ISO/IEC 19775-1/Amendment 1	Extensible 3D (X3D)–Part 1: Architecture and base components	X3D Abstract Specification. Defines scene-graph functionality including nodes, components and profiles.
ISO/IEC 19775-2	Extensible 3D (X3D)–Part 2: Scene access interface (SAI)	X3D Abstract Specification of principles and semantics for SAI API.
ISO/IEC 19776-2 & ISO/IEC 19776-1/Amendment 1	Extensible 3D (X3D) encodings–Part 1: Extensible Markup Language (XML) encoding	XML encoding syntax for .x3d files.
ISO/IEC 19776-2 & ISO/IEC 19776-2/Amendment 1	Extensible 3D (X3D) encodings–Part 2: Classic VRML encoding	VRML encoding syntax for .x3dv files.
ISO/IEC 19776-3	Extensible 3D (X3D) encodings–Part 3: Binary encoding	Binary encoding syntax for .x3db files.
ISO/IEC 19777-1	Extensible 3D (X3D) language bindings–Part 1: ECMAScript	SAI functionality and syntax for script code written in ECMAScript.
ISO/IEC 19777-2	Extensible 3D (X3D) language bindings–Part 2: Java	SAI functionality and syntax for script code written in Java.

API, application programming interface; EAI, external authoring interface; H-Anim, humanoid animation; SAI, scene access interface; VRML, virtual reality modeling language; X3D, Extensible 3D; XML, Extensible markup language.

Table 1.1. X3D Specifications Summary Table

relationships are expressed as a directed acyclic graph (DAG). Data functionality is collected in nodes, which contain field parameters. Field parameters may contain simple-datatype values or further nodes. This approach allows program-independent, logical structuring of model data. The inclusion of viewpoint definitions makes it easy to add different user viewing perspectives.

It is interesting that scene graphs have been used by many 3D-graphic APIs, including OpenInventor and Java3D. Scene-graph concepts were derived from the notion of display lists, used in early 3D graphics. Scene-graph design is well suited for equivalent model representations as source code or file content. Thus, learning X3D can be valuable, because it provides an introductory path for many approaches to 3D graphics. Web authors and students do not need a programming background to get started.

Several 3D browsers render and animate scene graphs in a straightforward way. Starting at the root of the tree, the scene graph is traversed in a depth-first manner. Traversal of transformation nodes modifies the location and orientation of the current coordinate system (i.e., the current relative reference frame). Traversing appearance or material properties modifies the rendering parameters for subsequent geometry. Traversing geometry nodes renders polygons. Traversal of USE nodes (instance references) can efficiently redraw previously created structure without compromising the acyclic nature of the DAG tree.

Behaviors are an essential aspect of scene graphs. A *behavior* is defined as changing the value of some field within some node of the scene graph. This usually means generating numbers to animate the size, shape, position, or orientation of an object. Behaviors are powerful and general, because any parameter in the scene graph is usually manipulatable in one way or another. Data producers (such as sensor nodes monitoring the user, linear-interpolation functions, or scripts) are connected to other 3D nodes in the scene graph via ROUTEs. Thus a **ROUTE** passes events, which are time-stamped behavior values, produced by the field of one node and sent to the field of another node. This technique is presented in Chapter 7, Event Animation and Interpolation.

Behavior ROUTEs make up an event-routing graph that connects nodes and fields within the encapsulating scene graph. One way to visualize these relationships is print out a hardcopy of a pretty-print HTML version of a scene (landscape printing is usually best), and simply draw ROUTE lines from each target node to each destination node. Then annotate the beginning and end of each line with the name and data type of the source and target fields. The result is a copy of the event graph superimposed on the scene graph. This is an excellent learning technique for understanding behavior relationships within an X3D scene.

Taken together, the rules governing this animation-behavior framework are commonly referred to as the *X3D event model*. More rules regarding parallelism are provided in the X3D specification for browser builders. Nevertheless these special cases are not often a worry for X3D authors.

The overall design of X3D to augment the geometry of a scene graph with interpolators, animations, and behaviors is an excellent architectural example of a declarative simulation. The defining scene declares the various implicit interrelationships between objects, and the actual simulation sequence of events is determined simply by userprovided interactions and by author-defined timing of event production. Resultant behavior typically remains unaffected by differences in processor speed on different viewing computers, because animated events are synchronized with wall-clock time rather than processor-clock time. Addition of scripting nodes can further integrate explicit step-by-step imperative algorithms, compatibly operating imperatively (for short time intervals) within the declarative scene-graph framework.

Declarative simulations are powerful. The author can focus on the constraints and relationships between different parts of the scene graph, and desired behaviors emerge from those connections. This is much different (and usually much simpler) than writing an imperative program using a graphics programming language, in which every detail (draw this triangle, draw that triangle) must be directed and handled exhaustively. Experienced 3D-graphics programmers are often pleasantly surprised at the power and capability of X3D, packed into a much simpler modeling methodology.

2.5. File structure

The X3D scene graph is usually presented in a file, using either the .x3d XML encoding or the .x3dv Classic VRML encoding. The same-graph structure is well defined and remains consistent in each encoding. Each encoding imposes its own requirements on the syntax and layout of the common representation of information.

The top-level structure of X3D files is:

- File header

- X3D header statement

- Profile statement

- Component statement (optional, multiple)

- META statement (optional, multiple)

- X3D root node (implicit in Classic VRML encoding)

- X3D scene graph child nodes (multiple)

Each structural file element is described in more detail in the following sections.

2.5.1. File header

The X3D file header contains the primary setup information about the X3D scene. There are no renderable nodes in this portion of the file. The header contains required and optional information about the scene capabilities. The file header comprises the following statements: XML and X3D headers, profile, component, and meta.

Table 1.2 shows the proper definitions for a file that includes the Immersive profile, multiple components, and example meta tags. The .x3d XML encoding is similar to XHTML in that most of the header information is contained in a `<head>` tag. Complete details are provided in example scene, HeaderProfileComponentMetaExample.x3d. The following sections contain information on each part of the file header.

2.5.2. X3D header statement

The X3D header statement identifies the file as an X3D file. The specific format and position is encoding dependent. The information in the header statement is the X3D identifier, X3D version number, and the text encoding. X3D uses the (universal text format UTF-8) character encoding, which supports essentially all electronic alphabets for different human languages. The allowed versions of X3D include 3.0 and 3.1.

```
<?xml version="1.0" encoding="UTF-8"?>
<!DOCTYPE X3D PUBLIC "ISO//Web3D//DTD X3D 3.1//EN"
        "http://www.web3d.org/specifications/x3d-3.1.dtd">
<X3D version="3.1" profile="Immersive"
 xmlns:xsd="http://www.w3.org/2001/XMLSchema-instance"
 xsd:noNamespaceSchemaLocation=
   "http://www.web3d.org/specifications/x3d-3.1.xsd">
     <head>
       <component name='DIS' level='1'/>
       <component name='Geospatial' level='1'/>
       <component name='H-Anim' level='1'/>
       <component name='NURBS' level='4'/>
       <meta name='filename'
         content='HeaderProfileComponentMetaExample.x3d'/>
     </head>
     <Scene>
        <!--Scene graph nodes are added here-->
     </Scene>
</X3D>



#X3D V3.1 utf8
PROFILE Immersive
# No HEAD statement is provided in ClassicVRML Encoding
COMPONENT DIS:1
COMPONENT Geospatial:1
COMPONENT H-Anim:1
COMPONENT NURBS:4
META "filename" "HeaderProfileComponentMetaExample.x3d"
# Scene graph nodes are added here
```

Table 1.2. Comparison of XML (.x3d) and ClassicVRML (.x3dv) header syntax

The XML encoding matches general XML header requirements, starting with the `<?xml?>` declaration. Thus all .x3d scenes must first be well-formed XML: properly formed open, close, and singleton tags, single- or double-quoted attributes, and so on. There are two available XML-based mechanisms to further validate the correctness of the .x3d file. Each is optional but recommended. A Document Type Definition (DTD as indicated by a DOCTYPE statement) and an XML Schema reference. Schema information appears in the document root `<X3D>` tag. Version number is a required part of the X3D root declaration in all encodings.

```
<?xml version="1.0" encoding="UTF-8"?>
<!DOCTYPE X3D PUBLIC "ISO//Web3D//DTD X3D 3.1//EN"
    "http://www.web3d.org/specifications/x3d-3.1.dtd">
<X3D profile="Immersive" version="3.1"
    xmlns:xsd="http://www.w3.org/2001/XMLSchema-instance"
    xsd:noNamespaceSchemaLocation=
    "http://www.web3d.org/ specifications/x3d-3.1.xsd">
```

The character-encoding is identified in the `<?xml?>` declaration and Universal Text Format (UTF-8) is the most commonly used. The X3D identifier and version number are also included in the optional (but recommended) DOCTYPE and Schema references. Using a later version number in the DOCTYPE or Schema reference than the X3D root node requires is allowed, because each new version of X3D maintains backwards compatibilty.

For the ClassicVRML encoding, the header is as follows.

```
#X3D V3.1 utf8
```

This must be the first statement in a ClassicVRML encoded X3D file. Unlike the XML encoding, no external validation references are provided, because browsers are assumed to be capable of properly parsing the VRML-based scene syntax.

Like comment statements, header information is generally not available for run-time access after an X3D scene has been loaded into memory and begun running. Persistent information (such as metadata) can be stored within the scene using the strictly datatyped, persistent metadata nodes.

This book is based on ISO/IEC 19775 Parts 1 and 2, ISO/IEC 19775 Amendment 1, ISO/IEC 19776 Parts 1 and 2, ISO/IEC 19776 Parts 1 and 2 Amendment 1, and ISO/IEC 19777 Parts 1 and 2. These are known collectively as X3D 3.0 and X3D 3.1. The version number of X3D changes with each amendment release of the specification. The X3D 3.0 specification was approved by ISO in 2005. X3D 3.1 was approved in 2006, correcting some minor problems in X3D 3.0 and adding significant new functionality.

As additional amendments are developed and approved, the X3D version number is incremented accordingly. The Web3D Consortium and ISO continue working to produce extension updates, completing an amendment about every 18 months. As this book goes to press, amendment 1 (X3D version 3.1) is approved, amendment 2 (X3D version 3.2) is undergoing formal review, and proposed amendment 3 extensions are undergoing collaborative Web3D working-group implementation and evaluation.

2.5.3. Profile statements

There are a number of profiles defined for X3D. Each profile is targeted for a common market or commonly used set of functionality. Profiles exist in order to enable browser builders to achieve intermediate levels of support for X3D, rather than trying to implement a large specification at once. Profiles also assist authors, because they can target their created scenes to use the functional vocabulary supported in a given profile. This means that content is well defined and more likely to be widely portable. Profiles help conversion programs translate between different file formats. Finally, profiles help extend the reach of X3D to smaller, lightweight devices such personal digital assistants and cell phones.

The minimalist X3D profile is called Core. It includes only the basic X3D definitions (such as ROUTEs) and the metadata nodes, but does not include any geometry, appearance, or animation capabilities. The Core profile is a base level so that an author can specify the special functionality required for a virtual environment using component statements. Several intermediate profiles are also provided: Interchange, Interactive, CADInterchange and Immersive. The CADInterchange profile is designed to support web export and interoperability for computer-aided design (CAD) formats using X3D. An MPEG-4Interactive profile (similar to the Interactive profile) has been approved for use with Motion Picture Experts Group (MPEG-4) audio, video, and multimedia content.

The Full profile includes everything defined in all related X3D specifications. It provides a means for referring to every X3D component without naming any of them.

Typically each profile is a superset of the preceding profile, shown in Figure 1.3 (known as the "onion-layers" diagram). Details about each profile follow.

Core: The Core profile is not designed for regular use. Rather, it provides the absolute minimal definitions required by an X3D browser (essentially just the metadata nodes). Advanced authors can build minimally defined scenes by explicitly specifying the component and levels required in the scene.

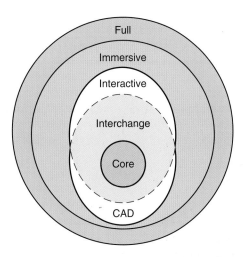

Figure 1.3. Multiple X3D profiles providing increasing sophistication allow more efficient browser support for lightweight content.

Interchange: This is the base profile for exchanging geometric models between various 3D applications. It is designed to be easy to export and import. All of the basic geometry (including primitives, triangles, and polygons), appearance (material and texture), and keyframe animation nodes are included in this profile.

Interactive: This profile is slightly bigger than the Interchange profile, and adds most of the nodes necessary for users to interact with a scene.

MPEG-4Interactive: This profile was designed specifically for the MPEG-4 multimedia specification's need for 3D graphics definitions, and is an appropoximate match to the Interactive profile. It is not discussed further in this book.

CADInterchange: This is a specialized profile that supports the import of CAD models. It includes most (but not all) nodes from the Interchange profile and includes a handful of new nodes for CAD. The details of this profile are not addressed in this book.

Immersive: This profile most closely matches VRML97. The Immersive profile includes everything defined in Interactive plus several advanced capabilities and a number of new nodes: 2D geometry, environmental effects, event utilities, and so on. It is a superset of VRML97, but without the extra functionality of VRML specification ISO/IEC 14772/Amendment 1.

Full: This profile includes all nodes defined in the X3D specification and further extends the Immersive profile. The Full profile incorporates all X3D capabilities including Distributed Interactive Simulation (DIS), Humanoid Animation (H-Anim), GeoSpatial, Non-Uniform Rational B-spline Surfaces (NURBS) and other advanced components.

A profile statement is required in all X3D scenes. The format of the profile statement depends on the file encoding. The Classic VRML file encoding uses a profile statement format of `PROFILE Immersive` while the XML file encoding embeds the information in a `profile="Immersive"` attribute in the document's root X3D tag.

The approval of new nodes as a part of annual amendments means that most profiles can continue to evolve. The Core profile is always expected to remain at the minimum possible set. The Full profile is always the total of the capabilities provided in a particular version of X3D. Changes for each major or minor version number (for example 3.0, 3.1, or 3.2) always correspond to well-defined profiles.

2.5.4. Component statements

Each of the preceding profiles is made up of a collection of components. Each component is divided into levels that describe increasing capability. Every X3D node is part of a single component, and has the same or better features at each succeeding component level.

As an addendum to a profile declaration in a scene file, the component statement informs the browser that a scene needs further support for functionality at the specified component at the specified level. Components at a specific level usually do not need to be listed in the header of a scene, because they are usually included in the scene's declared profile. In some cases, however, defining component details is useful. Adding component statements provides authors finer-grained control of the browser support needed to support the scene.

Normally an author's request for a given node capability in a browser is made as part of the encompassing profile statement. Nevertheless, there are two main reasons for using the component statement to provide further additions to the supported profile.

1. The stated profile does not support one or more of the nodes included in a scene. The browser may not support Full profile, or the author may prefer to allow a lighter-weight browser to handle the content running on the user's machine.

2. The author is constructing a minimal environment for the scene, perhaps as part of a library or collection of complementary objects. By specifying a lower profile along with a few necessary components, more browsers may be able to present the scene. Similarly, more parent scenes can include the child scene without requiring a higher profile.

There are 24 components in X3D 3.0, each with multiple levels. In 2005, X3D version 3.1 added four more, providing a total of 28 components. Table 1.3 lists the various components and corresponding levels provided by each of the profiles.

Thus, in most cases, it is simply a good practice to pick a sufficient profile that covers all of the nodes in a scene. Immersive, Interactive, and Interchange are the most commonly used profiles. One authoring option is to specify the Full profile for every scene, but that isn't always a practical solution, because browser support for the Full profile is often limited. This situation is commonly encountered when working with components outside the Immersive profile, such as the GeoSpatial or H-Anim nodes. (Note: these advanced nodes are not discussed in this book.)

2.5.5. Meta statements

Meta statements provide information about the X3D scene. These annotations are frequently used to provide author, copyright, reference, and other information. Each meta statement contains a name-value pair, that is, the name of the metadata item and the corresponding content for that one piece of information. Name-value string pairs are quite powerful and can be used to capture nearly any type of information.

The head and meta statements are directly patterned after the Extensible Hypertext Markup Language (XHTML). This approach simplifies conventions for use and maximizes consistency for web authors.

The meta statements contained in the header are not typed, meaning that each name content value is a string. Meta tags can only appear in the scene header, and are different than the various metadata nodes, which are only allowed to appear within the scene itself.

Example file newScene.x3d provides a number of default meta tags. It is the default scene used by X3D-Edit. Use it as a starter when beginning a new scene, and change the file name and meta values to record information about the work. Excerpts follow in Figure 1.4, including further references about defining metadata values consistently.

Components	Interchange Profile Supported Levels	CAD Interchange Profile Supported Levels	Interactive Profile Supported Levels	Immersive Profile Supported Levels	Full Profile Supported Levels
CADGeometry (X3D 3.1)		2			2
Core	1	1	1	2	2
Cube map environmental texturing (X3D 3.1)					3
Distributed interactive simulation (DIS)					1
Environmental effects	1		1	2	3
Environmental sensor			1	2	2
Event utilities			1	1	1
Geometry2D				1	2
Geometry3D	2		3	4	4
Geospatial					1
Grouping	1	1	2	2	3
Humanoid animation					1
Interpolation	2		2	2	3
Key device sensor			1	2	2
Lighting	1	1	2	2	3
Navigation	1	2	1	2	2
Networking	1	1	2	3	3
NURBS					4
Pointing device sensor			1	1	1
Programmable shaders (X3D 3.1)					1
Rendering	3	4	2	3	4
Scripting				1	1
Shape	1	2	1	2	3
Sound				1	1
Text				1	1
Texturing	2	2	2	3	3
Texturing3D (X3D 3.1)					2
Time	1		1	1	2

CAD, Computer-aided design; NURBS, non-uniform rational B-spline; X3D, Extensible 3D.

Table 1.3. X3D Profiles, Components, and Corresponding Support Levels

```
<head>
  <meta name='filename' content='*enter FileName
    WithNoAbbreviations.x3d here*'/>
  <meta name='description' content='*enter description here,
    short-sentence summaries preferred*'/>
  <meta name='author' content='*enter name of original author here*'/>
  <meta name='translator' content='*if manually translating
    VRML-to-X3D, enter name of person translating here*'/>
  <meta name='created' content='*enter date of initial version *'/>
  <meta name='translated' content='*enter date of translation here*'/>
  <meta name='revised' content='*enter date of latest revision *'/>
  <meta name='version' content='*enter version here, if any*'/>
  <meta name='reference' content='*enter reference citation or
    relative/online url here*'/>
  <meta name='copyright' content='*enter copyright information here*
   Example: Copyright (c) Web3D Consortium Inc. 2007'/>
  <meta name='drawing' content='*enter drawing filename/url here*'/>
  <meta name='image' content='*enter image filename/url here*'/>
  <meta name='movie' content='*enter movie filename/url here*'/>
  <meta name='photo' content='*enter photo filename/url here*'/>
  <meta name='keywords' content='*enter keywords here*'/>
  <meta name='permissions' content='*enter permission statements or
    url here*'/>
  <meta name='warning' content='*insert any known warnings, bugs or
    errors here*'/>
  <meta name='url' content='*enter online url address for this file
    here*'/>
  <meta name='generator' content='X3D-Edit,
    http://www.web3d.org/x3d/content/README.X3D-Edit.html'/>
  <meta name='license' content='../../license.html'/>
  <!--Additional authoring resources for meta-tags:
  http://www.w3.org/TR/html4/struct/global.html#h-7.4.4
  http://dublincore.org/documents/dces
  http://vancouver-webpages.com/META
  http://vancouver-webpages.com/META/about-mk-metas2.html
  Additional authoring resources for language codes:
  ftp://ftp.isi.edu/in-notes/bcp/bcp47.txt
  http://www.loc.gov/standards/iso639-2/langhome.html
  http://www.iana.org/numbers.html#L
  -->
</head>
```

Figure 1.4. Example meta tags in newScene. x3d.

Metadata produces big dividends over time, particularly if different or competing versions of a scene are available. Think of meta tags as a way to communicate with others about the scene, to help yourself keep track of content in the future, and to support library archive tools that keep track of many example scenes. Meta tags are used throughout the examples provided with this book for just such purposes.

2.5.6. Scene graph body

Following the head of the X3D document is the scene. Putting together a scene graph is the focus of the rest of this book.

To further explain the technical fundamentals underlying the X3D nodes that make up the scene graph, field types and node types are presented next.

2.6. Field types

The data for each node is stored in the fields of the node. Fields can contain a single value or multiple values for each data type. All fields are built from the fundamental X3D data types for boolean, integer, single-precision floating point, double-precision floating point, and strings. Simple field types may have one or multiple values, and can further be arrays of such values. Field types are also provided for a singleton node (SFNode) and arrays of nodes (MFNode). There are restrictions or structures placed on some of the elements in various fields.

The X3D field-naming convention starts with two letters designating a single-valued field (SF) or multiple-valued field (MF). Next comes the name of the data type of the field, for example, SFString, MFVec3f, and so on. In the XML encoding, no square brackets are needed. The type names are consistent for both text-based encodings (XML and ClassicVRML). In the Classic VRML encoding, an additional requirement is that multiple-valued fields (MFs datatypes) must be enclosed in square brackets. For example, a 4-tuple SFRotation field value is expressed as "0 1 0 1.57" in .x3d files or [0 1 0 1.57] in .x3dv files.

For the node-definition tables appearing throughout the book, a specific notation is used. Default values are listed as typed literal values from the specification. Ranges of values are listed using standard mathematical notation: A square bracket means that the range includes the bounding value, while a parenthesis means that the range does not include the bounding value. For example [0,1] means all numbers between 0 and 1, including 0 and 1. Similarly, (0,1] means all numbers between 0 and 1, including 1 only. As another example, $[0, +\infty)$ means all non-negative numbers (zero inclusive).

Individual string values are enclosed in quotation marks. If array values are *n-tuples* (meaning arrays with 2, 3, or 4 numbers), the value is quoted with spaces separating the data elements (for example, `translation="0 0 0"`). Multiple-valued data-type arrays contain zero or more copies of the single-value data type. Note that commas can only appear between each n-tuple field value, not within them. The uninitialized value for multiple-valued data-type arrays is always the empty list, which is an array containing no elements.

Table 1.4 lists abbreviations, names, and example values for each simple field type.

Field-type names	Description	Example values
SFBool	Single-field boolean value	true or false (X3D syntax), TRUE or FALSE (ClassicVRML syntax)
MFBool	Multiple-field boolean array	true false false true (X3D syntax), [TRUE FALSE FALSE TRUE] (ClassicVRML syntax)
SFColor	Single-field color value, red-green-blue	0 0.5 1.0
MFColor	Multiple-field color array, red-green-blue	1 0 0, 0 1 0, 0 0 1
SFColorRGBA	Single-field color value, red-green-blue alpha (opacity)	0 0.5 1.0 0.75
MFColorRGBA	Multiple-field color array, red-green-blue alpha (opacity)	1 0 0 0.25, 0 1 0 0.5, 0 0 1 0.75 (red green blue, varying opacity)
SFInt32	Single-field 32-bit integer value	0
MFInt32	Multiple-field 32-bit integer array	1 2 3 4 5
SFFloat	Single-field single-precision floating-point value	1.0
MFFloat	Multiple-field single-precision floating-point array	−1 2.0 3.14159
SFDouble	Single-field double-precision floating-point value	2.7128
MFDouble	Multiple-field double-precision array	−1 2.0 3.14159
SFImage	Single-field image value	Contains special pixel-encoding values, see Chapter 5 for details
MFImage	Multiple-field image value	Contains special pixel-encoding values, see Chapter 5 for details
SFNode	Single-field node	\<Shape/\> or Shape {space}
MFNode	Multiple-field node array of peers	\<Shape/\>\<Group/\>\<Transform/\>
SFRotation	Single-field rotation value using 3-tuple axis, radian angle form	0 1 0 1.57
MFRotation	Multiple-field rotation array	0 1 0 0, 0 1 0 1.57, 0 1 0 3.14
SFString	Single-field string value	"Hello world!"
MFString	Multiple-field string array	"EXAMINE" "FLY" "WALK" "ANY"
SFTime	Single-field time value	0
MFTime	Multiple-field time array	−1 0 1 567890

Table 1.4. X3D Field Types

Field-type names	Description	Example values
SFVec2f/SFVec2d	Single-field 2-float/2-double vector value	0 1.5
MFVec2f/MFVec2d	Multiple-field 2-float/2-double vector array	1 0, 2 2, 3 4, 5 5
SFVec3f/SFVec3d	Single-field vector value of 3-float/ 3-double values	0 1.5 2
MFVec3f/MFVec3d	Multiple-field vector array of 3-float/ 3-double values	10 20 30, 4.4 −5.5 6.6
VRML, Virtual reality modeling language; X3D, Extensible 3D.		

Table 1.4. (Cont'd.) X3D Field Types

2.7. Abstract node types

A major improvement in the design of the X3D language over VRML97 is the addition of strong typing of nodes, making the object-oriented nature of X3D nodes much more consistent. The X3D specification accomplishes strong node typing in two ways, first by defining field interfaces for child-node content and second by defining required simple-field attributes corresponding to each functional type of node. Although this aspect of the X3D architecture is not usually evident to authors, good language design leads to more predictable models and more consistent behavior. Strictly defined node typing gives the following benefits to X3D nodes implementing the same node type:

- Allowed child-node content is identical

- Simple-type field attributes are identical and have consistent default values

- Validation capabilities are improved

- Common APIs are the same

- Definitions and operations are easier to remember and adapt

New nodes (defined either by author prototypes or in future versions of X3D) with matching node types con be substituted for other nodes correctly and consistently. Thus, node types directly support Extensibility, the X in X3D.

Script programming uses node types and is covered in Chapter 9, Event Utilities and Scripting. Application programming interfaces (APIs) are more important when you are learning how to program X3D scene graphs directly. That is a big subject, suitable for another book. Most scene content preparation goes into the production of files, so file encodings are discussed in the next section.

2.8. File encodings: XML, ClassicVRML, and Compressed

There are three available encodings that can be used to format X3D files. In each case, the functionality of the displayed X3D scene remains consistent and independent of the encoding used. This is quite valuable, because any X3D encoding for a single given scene can be treated as visually and functionally equivalent. This is the same principle previously illustrated by Figure 1.2: an X3D scene renders and behaves consistently at run time, regardless of the file format (or programming API) used to create it.

The first file format is XML, which is plaintext and uses the .x3d filename extension. The second is also plaintext and based on the Classic VRML syntax of curly brackets and square brackets, using the .x3dv filename extension. The third is the compressed-binary format, which includes both geometric polygon/property compression as well as binary-data compression, using the .x3db filename extension. Gzip compression of .x3d or .x3dv files is another allowed approach, appending .gz as an additional extension to the original filename and extension, but the .x3db compressed binary encoding provides superior results.

X3D files that refer to other files (by using Inline and Anchor nodes) can legally refer to linked X3D scenes that have been saved with a different encoding than the master scene. Thus, .x3d, .x3dv, and .x3db file references are all legal in any combination of scenes. Hopefully all three encodings are supported by each user's browser as well.

Some browsers also support VRML97, which uses the .wrl filename extension for plaintext files and .wrz/.wrl.gz for gzip-compressed files. Nevertheless, it is good practice to upgrade VRML97 scenes to X3D for maximum compatibility and interoperability. Multiple VRML97-to-X3D translators are provided on the book's website.

2.8.1. Extensible Markup Language (XML) encoding: .x3d files

XML encoding is one of the biggest improvements in X3D. This section describes the benefits of using an XML encoding as the file format for X3D.

XML-based files are usually called XML documents. Figure 1.5 shows an example of an XML document fragment.

Each element (sometimes referred to as a tag) is surrounded by angle brackets. Elements that contain other elements start with an opening tag (no slash) and finish with an ending tag (leading slash). Standalone elements that have no child elements can either finish with a trailing slash, such as `<Sphere radius="10.0" solid="true"/>` or simply a matched pair of opening and closing elements, such as `<Sphere radius="10.0" solid="true"></Sphere>`. Intervening whitespace between elements is usually insignificant, so source-file formatting and layout is flexible. These simple XML rules for structuring data provide a lot of descriptive power.

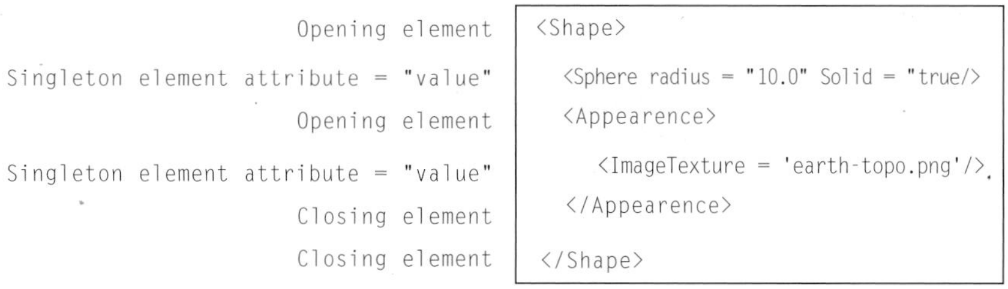

Opening element	`<Shape>`
Singleton element attribute = "value"	`<Sphere radius = "10.0" Solid = "true/>`
Opening element	`<Appearance>`
Singleton element attribute = "value"	`<ImageTexture = 'earth-topo.png'/>`
Closing element	`</Appearance>`
Closing element	`</Shape>`

Figure 1.5. XML documents have a consistent tree structure for elements, attributes, and values.

2.8.1.1. XML motivations

There are many reasons to use XML. Foremost is that XML is the basis of nearly every data language used on the World Wide Web. If 3D graphics are to become a "first-class citizen" on the Web, embedded in Web pages and interacting with clients, servers, and users of every type, then it is clear that an XML encoding is necessary; the .x3d encoding of X3D scenes provides that capability.

"XML in 10 Points" originally by Bert Bos (2001) (available at www.w 3. org /XML/ 1999/XML-in-10-points) provides an excellent overview of XML benefits and potential. An adapted summary follows.

1. *Structured data.* XML is a set of rules for designing text formats to structure data. XML is not a programming language.

2. *Similar to HTML.* Like HTML, XML makes use of tags (words surrounded by angle brackets) and attributes (of the form `name="value"`). HTML defines the functionality of each tag for presentation purposes, but XML is more general and allows for the definition of rules to govern tag and attribute names, relationships, and semantics that may be customized by the cognizant application.

3. *XML is text, but is not meant to be read.* Programs that produce structured data often store that data on disk, using either a binary or text format. One advantage of a text format is that it allows people to look at the data without the program that produced it. Text formats also allow developers to debug applications more easily. Rules for legal XML are strict, and prevent propagation or use of broken XML files. The *draconian parse* rule requires an application to stop and report any errors.

4. *XML is verbose by design.* Because XML is a text format and uses tags to delimit data, XML files are usually larger than comparable binary formats. That was a conscious decision by the designers of XML. The advantages of a text format are evident (see point 3), and the disadvantages can usually be compensated at a different level.

5. *XML is a family of technologies.* Numerous XML-support languages (themselves written in XML) extend the functionality of XML consistently for many uses. XLink describes hyperlinks. XPointer is a syntax for pointing to any specific part of an XML document. The Cascading Stylesheets (CSS) language is applicable to XML as it is to HTML. The Extensible Stylesheet Language for Transformations (XSLT) is used for rearranging, adding and deleting tags and attributes. The DOM is a standard set of string-based function calls for manipulating XML (and HTML) files from a programming language. XML Schemas help developers precisely define the structures of specialty XML-based formats.

6. *XML is new, but not that new.* Development of XML started in 1996 and has been a W3C recommendation since February 1998. Before XML there was Standard Generalized Markup Language (SGML), developed in the early 1980s,

an ISO standard since 1986, and widely used for large documentation projects. The development of HTML started in 1990. The designers of XML simply took the best parts of SGML, guided by the experience of using HTML, and produced something that is no less powerful than SGML and vastly more regular and simple to use.

7. *XML leads HTML to XHTML.* One important XML application is a document format: W3C's XHTML, the successor to HTML. XHTML has many of the same elements as HTML. The syntax has been changed slightly to conform to the rules of XML. A document that is "XML-based" inherits its syntax from XML, which restricts and strengthens it in certain ways.

8. *XML is modular.* XML allows you to define a new document format by combining and reusing other formats. To eliminate name confusion when combining formats, XML provides a namespace mechanism. XML Schema is designed to mirror this support for modularity at the level of defining XML document structures, making it easy to combine two schemas to produce a third schema that covers a merged document structure.

9. *XML is the basis for Semantic Web.* XML provides an unambiguous syntax for W3C's Resource Description Framework (RDF), a language for expressing metadata (that is, information about information). To communicate knowledge, whether in XML/RDF or in plain English, both people and machines need to agree on what words to use. A precisely defined set of words that describes a certain area of life (from "shopping" to "mathematical logic") is called an *ontology.* RDF, ontologies, and the representation of meaning so that computers can help people do work are all topics of the Semantic Web Activity.

10. *XML is license free, platform independent, and well supported.* By choosing XML as the basis for a project, you gain access to a large and growing community of tools (one of which may already do what you need!) and engineers experienced in the technology. Opting for XML is a bit like choosing Structured Query Language (SQL) for databases: You still have to build your own database and your own programs and procedures that manipulate it, but there are many tools available and many people who can help you. Because XML is license free, you can build your own software around it without paying anybody. The large and growing support means that you are not tied to a single vendor. XML is not always the best solution, but it is always worth considering.

As an example case in point, the use of XML provided multiple major benefits in the development of the X3D-Edit authoring tool. Because the X3D tooltips are captured in XML, they are automatically embedded in the interface and are available as separate HTML web pages. Multilingual support means that tooltips are provided in Chinese, English, French, German, Italian, Portuguese and Spanish. The HTML pretty printer uses XSLT to read and redisplay .x3d scenes. Similarly, separate stylesheets can convert .x3d scenes into equivalent ClassicVRML .x3dv or VRML97 .wrl files. The example-scene catalogs are produced automatically by a Java program and a multidocument XSLT stylesheet that can automatically and rapidly produce hundreds of HTML pages. Another XSLT stylesheet even converts Extrusion crossSection fields into 2D plots using Scalable Vector Graphics (SVG). Future work will probably produce X3D scenes from server-based data and make X3D library archives automatically accessible via Web services. Many new opportunities are available because of the XML encoding for X3D.

2.8.1.2. XML design for X3D

A lot of work went into mapping the VRML scene graph into XML, producing the X3D XML encoding, and creating .x3d files. The following design patterns governed the construction of X3D's XML tagset.

- X3D nodes are expressed as XML elements.

- X3D simple-type fields are expressed as XML attributes. Default values can be safely omitted from .x3d model documents.

- DEF and USE names for nodes are captured as attributes and given XML types ID and IDREF respectively. This ensures that only one DEF ID is allowed per scene, and also ensures that all USE IDREF values only refer to an already-defined DEF ID name.

- Parent-child relationships between X3D nodes are captured as corresponding parent-child relationships between XML elements.

- Because contained nodes are themselves X3D fields of type SFNode/MFNode, the name of the field relationship is listed in a containerField attribute. Default containerField values for each node are correct in most cases, so overriding containerField values is infrequent. This approach makes the X3D tagset terser, easier to read, and less prone to error.

- Only X3D simple-type fields with accessType initializeOnly or inputOutput are saved as XML attributes. Other native fields that have accessType inputOnly or outputOnly are transient and only named when used with ROUTE connections. Thus no attributes exist for fields such as isActive, set_value or value_changed.

- Prototype definitions are explicitly declared using ProtoDeclare/ProtoInterface/ProtoBody and ProtoInstance elements and name attributes. New XML elements are not produced for newly defined prototypes. This approach eliminates many potential errors, and ensures strong validation checking of parent-child relationships for all nonprototype X3D nodes in all scenes.

- 'field' elements are used for defining Script and ProtoInterface fields. 'fieldValue' elements are used to provide overriding default values for fields during ProtoInstance creation.

- X3D node types are defined as XML Schema complexType definitions. These match the X3D interface hierarchy, capture strong typing of node relationships, and collect common attributes shared among node types. These features also provide functional consistency between scene-graph content and the X3D Scene Authoring Interface (SAI) application programming interface (API).

Together these design rules have provided excellent results. The classical scene graph first developed as part of VRML97 is now fully elaborated in XML in ways that make sense for both languages. Furthermore, X3D graphics now become much more compatible with Web-based technologies. New capabilities such as server-side 3D and animation driven by Web services or chat also become feasible. As shown by the rapidly growing number of X3D scenes and software applications, this progress in deploying 3D content as a first-class interactive media type is a significant development for the World Wide Web.

2.8.1.3. *XML validation*

The original XML Recommendation by the World Wide Web Consortium (W3C) mandates default rules for "well-formedness" of XML documents. These rules also apply to .x3d scenes and include proper syntax for elements (corresponding to X3D nodes) and attributes (corresponding to X3D fields). Thus, even without prior knowledge of X3D constructs, these rules enable XML tools to detect a large number of potential syntax problems in documents.

After well-formedness checking, XML validity provides even stronger forms of error checking for XML documents. Special validation rules are provided to the XML processor that define the vocabulary of elements, attributes, and allowed parent-child relationships. One such set of rules is a DTD, and another is an XML Schema. DTDs provide strong checking of elements but weak checking of attributes, because attribute values are treated as simple text strings. XML Schemas provide strong checking of both elements and attribute values, and are defined using an object-oriented internal design that supports consistent extensibility.

Two primary mechanisms are provided for validating XML scenes: the X3D DTD and the X3D Schema. An X3D scene in the .x3d format, which is an XML document, can include references to either the DTD or the Schema (or both, preferably). Such validation capabilities are provided automatically in many XML-capable applications, making the production and modification of 3D content much less error-prone than in the past.

In addition, two stylesheets written in XML Stylesheet Language for Transformations (XSLT) are provided. The stylesheets convert .x3d files into VRML97 (X3dTo Vrml97.xslt) or Classic VRML (X3dToX3dvClassicVrml.xslt) encodings. These paired stylesheets also apply many X3D-specific consistency rules to provide extensive correctness checks. The X3D-based quality tests go beyond XML validation to provide hint, warning, and error diagnostic messages about the X3D scene graph, thus providing even more quality control of authored scenes. Detecting errors while authoring is invaluable, because scene-graph problems can otherwise go unnoticed until the scene fails for a user (who deserves a zero-defect result).

Table 1.5 shows which validation checks are provided with each mechanism. X3D-Edit (provided with this book) provides DTD and X3dToVrml stylesheet support. X3D Schema validation is also highly recommended and catches most authoring errors.

Scene graph validity checks	X3D DTD	X3D Schema	X3DToVrml stylesheets	Xj3D, Flux open-source browsers
Legal node (element) names	X	X	X	X
Legal field (attribute) names	X	X	X	X
Correct X3D profile/component level, matching nodes in the scene			X	X
Allowed parent-child relationships between nodes	X	X	X	X
All DEF attribute names are unique and properly named, all USE attribute names exactly match DEF names	X	X	X	X
All USE elements are only referenced after their corresponding DEF elements are defined			X	X
Properly overridden containerField value matches an allowed child-node field name			X	X
Legal field values are provided for attributes that match the defined simple type (SFInt32, MFFloat, etc.)		X	X	X
Mismatched interface names, types, or accessType values among Prototype, Script, field, fieldValue, and IS/connect definitions			X	X
Malformed MFString values for a URL field			X	X
Only ROUTE to/from DEF node names	X	X	X	X
Only ROUTE to/from legitimate target field names				X
URL, Uniform resource locator; VRML, virtual reality modeling language; X3D, Extensible 3D.				

Table 1.5. Capabilities Comparison for Validation of X3D Scene Graphs

Browsers (such as Xj3D) often provide excellent debugging feedback. These can be the most authoritative tools to debug the operation of an X3D scene. Unfortunately, most browsers suffer from (at least) two common pitfalls: error messages are often vague or misdirecting, and errors are often not caught until the scene is delivered to the user. Better error checking during scene production is preferred by most X3D authors, to ensure their efforts to build great content aren't rendered useless. It is a good authoring practice to frequently check scenes with a strictly validating browser while creating them.

It is worth considering the big picture in this context. In 1975, Dr. Niclas Wirth wrote a book entitled *Algorithms + Data Structures = Programs*. Since then, several decades of software-engineering theory and effort have been devoted to algorithm-related issues, especially structured and object-oriented programming. However, studies have shown that a surprisingly large amount of development and debugging time is usually spent on reading and verifying (or recovering from errors in) input data. The pertinent expression for this situation is preventing "garbage in, garbage out" (GIGO). Since the original development of SGML and advent of XML, much more work has been devoted to structuring, describing, and strengthening data. This practical emphasis on standards and best practices for structured data, in addition to all the work on structured programming, is an exceptionaly productive trend that continues to provide big payoffs. The importance of data integrity and preventing garbage in, garbage out cannot be overestimated.

Building X3D scenes using the XML-based .x3d encoding and gaining the benefits of strong validation is the best way to author 3D graphics for the Web.

2.8.2. ClassicVRML encoding: .x3dv files

As discussed earlier, VRML has been quite successful since it was first named an international standard in 1997. The ClassicVRML encoding is for the X3D alternative files that use the same "squiggly and square bracket" format used for describing a scene graph. All of the functionality of X3D is fully supported, regardless of which encoding is used to save an X3D file.

The ClassicVRML encoding for X3D matches the syntax for VRML97, with two expected differences: All of the new X3D nodes are also supported, and the first-line header changes as follows.

```
#VRML V2.0 utf8
```

becomes

```
#X3D V3.0 utf-8
```

For the ClassicVRML encoding, comment statements begin with a # character. A node's field values and children nodes are surrounded by curly brackets. Multiple-field (MF) values must be surrounded by square brackets if more than one value is present in the array. Fields with default values (such as a radius of 1 for a Sphere) can be omitted. DEF names precede a node's definition, and USE nodes replace a node's definition. The following example illustrates these rules.

```
# two simple shapes
DEF MyExample Transform {
translation 0 10 0
children [
  Shape {
    Sphere { radius 3 }
  }
```

```
Shape {
  USE SomeOtherBox # declared earlier in the scene
  }
 ]
}
```

Some other rules are worth mentioning. Whitespace is generally ignored when not with quotation marks (meaning within SFString and MFString fields). All text after a # comment character is ignored, so subsequent node or field definitions must start on a new line. ProtoDeclare and ExternProtoDeclare constructs are represented by PROTO and EXTERNPROTO, respectively. ProtoInstance has no corresponding term in Classic VRML, instead the name of the prototype is used solely by itself (just like a predefined X3D node). Empty node definitions are represented by NULL. There are no ClassicVRML equivalents for the X3D and head elements in the XML encoding nor is there a corresponding scene element. The XML-based profile, component, and meta elements are respectively represented as PROFILE, COMPONENT, and META statements in the ClassicVRML encoding.

One significant syntax change from VRML97 to X3D nomenclature is field accessType naming, as shown in Table 1.6.

Note that while the names for accessType values changed between VRML97 and X3D, the functionality remains unchanged. One troublesome accessType restriction in VRML97 has been relaxed: Script nodes can now define fields with accessType="inputOutput" in X3D.

Maintaining backwards compatibility with preexisting VRML97 content and authoring-tool exporters is an important design requirement for X3D. Because the creation of 3D models can be time consuming and expensive, most authors do not want to re-create or convert work that is already complete. Thus the ClassicVRML encoding ensures that legacy content remains available. Retaining the VRML97 approach as ClassicVRML (with the corresponding addition of new X3D nodes) also helps existing software tools upgrade to X3D capabilities more easily.

The ClassicVRML syntax does have some drawbacks. Any text editor can be used to create such files, but few provide VRML-aware shortcuts or special support.

VRML97 Name	X3D Name	X3D Specification abbreviation
eventIn	inputOnly	[in]
eventOut	outputOnly	[out]
field	initializeOnly	[ ]
exposedField	inputOutput	[in,out]
VRML, Virtual reality modeling language; X3D, Extensible 3D.		

Table 1.6. Naming Conventions for accessType Values

Mismatched brackets or unpaired quote marks can be difficult (and sometimes maddening) to debug or isolate. Misspelled node or field names, bad values, and any number of other errors are not caught until run time. The threat of "garbage in" is always lurking. Thus all .x3dv scenes need to be tested as thoroughly as possible by an author before they are distributed to other users.

All of the examples in this book are provided in both .x3d and .x3dv form (as well as a pretty-print .html version of the .x3d form). It is a benefit of using XML source for the master versions that all of the .x3dv versions are produced automatically by converting the .x3d originals, guaranteeing consistency among the different forms of each example. Because it is encoded as XML, the .x3d version has numerous advantages, including ease of translation. Nevertheless, the ClassicVRML syntax is fully functional, precisely specified, and will doubtless remain in use for a long time. Some authors still prefer it.

Many good VRML 2.0 (VRML97) books have been published over the past decade, and the examples and explanations within them are still quite usable, though they are not up to date with all of the new features in X3D. In addition to presenting new nodes in X3D, this book compares both syntaxes while emphasizing the benefits of XML.

2.8.3. Binary encoding: .x3db files

The primary goals for the X3D Binary Encoding are smaller X3D files, faster scene loading at run time, and network streaming of 3D data. Numerous technical requirements are derived from these goals. Applied design efforts have shown that all three of these goals can be accomplished simultaneously. Two basic kinds of size-reduction techniques are used in combination: information-theoretic compression to minimize data duplication (similar to zip/gzip) and geometry-based compression, in which polygons, colors, interpolators, and so on are combined, compressed, and rearranged.

Although some of this work is still undergoing technical improvements, a draft X3D Binary Encoding specification standard is approved by the Web3D Consortium. X3D compression algorithms include the Fast Infoset (FI) standard for XML-based compression of .x3d documents. Both lossless and lossy techniques are provided, allowing authors to either maintain identical results (compared to the original) or produce visually acceptable substitutions. Lossless compression is always the default setting, although some highly detailed scenes benefit from the removal of extraneous polygons or insignificant digits. The primary two technologies currently used are ISO-standard FI data reduction of .x3d XML-based encodings, and (optionally) a large number of patented Java3D geometric-compression algorithms. Sun Microsystems Inc. has provided a royalty-free license for use of the Java3D compression technology to be applied in X3D scenes. Other options are available using XML-based security standards for authentication (digital signature) and encryption. Unlike many other approaches, all of this technology can be used for X3D without licensing fees. Thus X3D use is royalty free.

Figure 1.6 is an example algorithm that shows how all these technologies are - combined to produce .x3db files. Optional steps are outlined using dashed lines. Note that by using the Web design principle of least constraints, implementations may use other algorithms as long as the transformation converting one form to another form produces consistent and interoperable results.

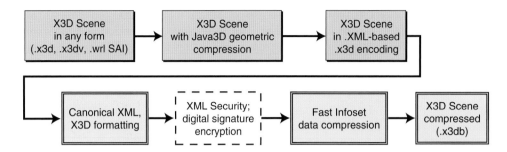

Figure 1.6. Processing chain to start with any X3D content, apply geometric compression (if desired), add XML security features (if desired), and produce .x3db compressed binary encoding.

Most remarkable about this work is that so many optimizations can be performed in combination. Typical file-size reductions range from 10%–25% of the original, consistently beating gzip reduction. Parsing speedups when reading data at run-time often run 5–10 times faster, which can be a significant improvement for large (multimegabyte) scenes.

The following list of requirements is taken from the original Request for Proposals by the Web3D Consortium to define an X3D binary encoding with compression. It lists the many capabilities achieved.

1. *X3D Compatibility*. The compressed binary encoding shall be able to encode all of the abstract functionality described in X3D Abstract Specification.

2. *Interoperability*. The compressed binary encoding shall contain identical information to the other X3D encodings (XML and ClassicVRML). It shall support an identical round-trip conversion between the X3D encodings.

3. *Multiple, separable data types*. The compressed binary encoding shall support multiple, separable media data types, including all node (element) and field (attribute) types in X3D. In particular, it shall include geometric compression for the following.

   • *Geometry*—polygons and surfaces, including NURBS

   • *Interpolation data*—spline and animation data, including particularly long sequences such as motion capture (also see Streaming requirement)

   • *Textures*—PixelTexture, other texture and multitexture formats (also see Bundling requirement)

   • *Array Datatypes*—arrays of generic and geometric data types

   • *Tokens*—tags, element and attribute descriptors, or field and node textual headers

4. *Processing Performance*. The compressed binary encoding shall be easy and efficient to process in a run-time environment. Outputs must include directly

typed scene-graph data structures, not just strings which might then need another parsing pass. End-to-end processing performance for construction of a scene-graph as in-memory typed data structures (i.e., decompression and deserialization) shall be superior to that offered by gzip and string parsing.

5. *Ease of Implementation.* Binary compression algorithms shall be easy to implement, as demonstrated by the ongoing Web3D requirement for multiple implementations. Two (or more) implementations are needed for eventual advancement, including at least one open-source implementation.

6. *Streaming.* The compressed binary encoding will operate in a variety of network-streaming environments, including http and sockets, at various (high and low) bandwidths. Local file retrieval of such files shall remain feasible and practical.

7. *Authorability.* The compressed binary encoding shall consist of implementable compression and decompression algorithms that may be used during scene-authoring preparation, network delivery and run-time viewing.

8. *Compression.* The compressed binary encoding algorithms will together enable effective compression of diverse datatypes. At a minimum, such algorithms shall support lossless compression. Lossy compression alternatives may also be supported. When compression results are claimed by proposal submitters, both lossless and lossy characteristics must be described and quantified.

9. *Security.* The compressed binary encoding will optionally enable security, content protection, privacy preferences and metadata such as encryption, conditional access, and watermarking. Default solutions are those defined by the W3C Recommendations for XML Encryption and XML Signature.

10. *Bundling.* Mechanisms for bundling multiple files (for example X3D scene, Inlined subscenes, image files, audio file, etc.) into a single archive file will be considered.

11. *Intellectual Property Rights (IPR).* All technology submissions must follow the predeclaration requirements of the Web3D Consortium IPR policy in order to be considered for inclusion. To date, the Web3D Consortium has only accepted royalty-free (RF) technologies for use in Web3D standards.

Streaming requirements include incremental loading of large geometry and interpolator data, incremental modifications for scene behaviors, and scene subgraph replacement to permit progressive improvements in level-of-detail fidelity. Some of these capabilities are already provided in X3D. For example, proper design of related X3D scenes allows an author to use the Inline node to selectively load scenes of increasing complexity. This approach allows a simple viewing experience to be quickly delivered and to interact with the user while additions to the scene continue to download in the background.

Though not yet in widespread use, binary encoding is expected to significantly increase the size, performance, and security of X3D scenes that can be effectively used over the Web. This is an important capability to check for in new X3D products.

The Xj3D open-source browser provides the primary test implementation of .x3db scenes, with other commercial X3D browsers expected to add this functionality as they continue to build out their supported X3D feature sets.

2.9. Hello World example using X3D-Edit and an X3D browser

A good example can help illustrate the many concepts presented here. Many computer languages are compared by showing a Hello World program that provides a simple example of how the language works. The following example, HelloWorld.x3d, uses the X3D-Edit authoring tool to display the X3D scene graph and produce both .x3d and .x3dv versions.

Figure 1.7 shows the X3D-Edit display. Tables 1.7 and 1.8 show the XML (.x3d) and ClassicVRML (.x3dv) encodings, respectively.

X3D-Edit is available free for any use and included in the online distribution for this book. It is written in Java and runs on all major operating systems. An autoinstaller simplifies initial setup. Features include explanatory popup tooltips for all nodes and fields, DTD-based validation checking, and multilingual versions of tooltips. VRML97 import/export and browser-based, pretty-print HTML display are also provided.

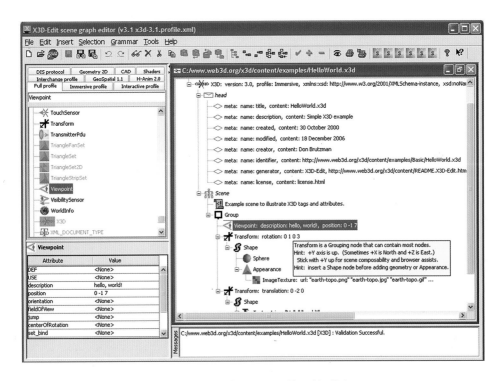

Figure 1.7. X3d-Edit is an XML-based Java application for creating and launching X3d scenes.

```xml
<?xml version="1.0" encoding="UTF-8"?>
<!DOCTYPE X3D PUBLIC "ISO//Web3D//DTD X3D 3.0//EN"
    "http://www.web3d.org/specifications/x3d-3.0.dtd">
<X3D profile="Immersive" xmlns:xsd="http://www.w3.org/2001/
    XMLSchema-instance"
    xsd:noNamespaceSchemaLocation="http://www.web3d.
    org/specifications/x3d-3.0.xsd" version="3.0">
  <head>
    <meta name="filename" content="HelloWorld.x3d"/>
    <meta name="description" content="Simple X3D example"/>
    <meta name="url" content="http://www.web3d.org/x3d/
        content/examples/HelloWorld.x3d"/>
    <meta name="generator" content="X3D-Edit,
        http://www.web3d.org/x3d/content/README.X3D-Edit.html"/>
  </head>
  <Scene>
    <!-Example scene to illustrate X3D tags and attributes.->
    <Group>
    <Viewpoint description="hello, world!" orientation="0 1 0 1.57"
        position="6-1 0"/>
    <NavigationInfo type='"EXAMINE" "ANY"'/>
    <Shape>
      <Sphere/>
      <Appearance>
        <Image Texture url='"earth-topo.png" "earth-topo-small.gif"
          "http://www.web3d.org/x3d/content/examples/earth-topo-
            small.gif" '/>
      </Appearance>
      </Shape>
      <Transform rotation="0 1 0 1.57" translation="0 -2 1.25">
      <Shape>
        <Text string='"Hello" "world!"'/>
        <Appearance>
         <Material diffuseColor="0.1 0.5 1"/>
        </Appearance>
      </Shape>
      </Transform>
  </Group>
  </Scene>
</X3D>
```

Table 1.7. Example HelloWorld scene using XML (.x3d) syntax

```
#X3D V3.0 utf8
#X3D-to-ClassicVRML XSL translation autogenerated by X3dToVrml197.xslt
#http://www.web3d.org/x3d/content/X3dToVrml197.xslt
PROFILE Immersive
META "filename" "HelloWorld.x3d"
META "description" "Simple X3D example"
META "url"  "http://www.web3d.org/x3d/content/
   examples/HelloWorld.x3d"
META "generator" "X3D-Edit, http://www.web3d.org/x3d/content/README.
   X3D-Edit.html"
# Example scene to illustrate X3D tags and attributes.
Group {
  children [
    Viewpoint {
      description "hello, world!"
      orientation 0 1 0 1.57
      position 6-10
  }
  NavigationInfo {
    type ["EXAMINE" "ANY"]
  }
  Shape {
    geometry Sphere {
  }
    appearance Appearance {
      texture ImageTexture {
      url ["earth-topo.png" "earth-topo-small.gif"
      "http://www.web3d.org/x3d/content/examples/earth-topo-small.gif"]
    }
   }
  }
  Transform {
    rotation 0 1 0 1.57
    translation 0 -2 1.25
    children [
      Shape {
      geometry Text {
        string ["Hello" "world!"]
      }
      appearance Appearance {
```

Table 1.8. Example HelloWorld scene using ClassicVRML (.x3dv) syntax

```
        material Material {
          diffuseColor 0.1 0.5 1
        }
      }
    }
  ]
}
]
}
```

Table 1.8. (Cont'd.) Example HelloWorld scene using ClassicVRML (.x3dv) syntax

The best way to learn X3D is by using it, so now is a good time to install an X3D viewer and X3D authoring tool on your computer. Almost all of the examples in this book were created using X3D-Edit. Loading, modifying, and improving (or breaking!) examples is a great way to make all of these capabilities part of your repertoire.

3. Summary

3.1. Key ideas

X3D has a long history of successful development, starting with the Virtual Reality Modeling Language (VRML) as early as 1994, adding the tremendous capabilities of the Extensible Markup Language (XML), and integrating many additional technologies along the way.

Building scenes is more like creating a Computer-Aided Design (CAD) model or authoring web-page content than programming. Using the .x3d encoding lets XML validation ensure that scene content is free of syntax errors, enabling authors to focus on the 3D models of interest. This is more productive for authors than worrying about how to achieve consistent results in different hardware and software environments.

A lot of technical detail is summarized in this chapter, but it is mostly background information about how X3D actually works. New X3D authors can skip ahead and learn how to create scenes without needing to know the underlying details. Periodic review of this chapter later can be quite helpful while mastering X3D.

3.2. Next chapters

Each of the following chapters explains a different set of nodes that together can be used to make up the X3D scene graph.

Chapter 2 (Geometry Primitives) shows how to construct simple geometric shapes to build a basic X3D scene. Chapter 3 (Grouping Nodes) shows how to group different shapes together and move them to different locations in virtual space.

Reference

Bos, Bert, and W3C Communications Team, *XML in 10 points*, web page, November 2001. Available at www.w3.org/XML/1999/XML-in-10-points.

Geometry Nodes, Part 1: Primitives

Dorothy in Oz: "Toto, I've a feeling we're not in Kansas anymore."
—L. Frank Baum, Wizard of Oz, 1939

1. What this chapter covers

The heart of Extensible 3D (X3D) graphics is geometry, especially three-dimensional (3D) geometry. X3D supports a wide range of geometry types from basic triangles to complex extruded shapes (think of mathematical Play-Doh). This chapter examines the simple shapes.

The many geometry nodes included in X3D are covered in four parts. This first part (Chapter 2, Geometry Nodes, Part 1: Primitives) covers concepts pertaining to the basic primitive shapes and text. The second part (Chapter 6, Geometry Nodes, Part 2: Points, Lines, and Polygons) covers the fundamental building-block nodes for creating arbitrary shapes, often used by modeling tools. The third part (Chapter 10, Geometry Nodes, Part 3: Geometry2D Nodes) presents simple planar constructs that can be used for signs, diagrams, etc.

The last part (Chapter 13, Geometry Nodes, Part 4: Triangles and Quadrilaterals) covers the advanced nodes that construct shapes using the most low-level constructs.

Many different kinds of geometry are available in X3D. This chapter covers the primitive geometric objects available: Shape, Box, Cylinder, Cone, Sphere, Text, and FontStyle. Shape is presented first because it is the parent node that holds any one of the various geometry nodes. These basic nodes are easy to author and master, allowing you to quickly begin constructing simple 3D scenes.

2. Concepts

Geometry nodes are the objects that actually get drawn when an X3D scene is rendered. Usually they consist of polygons, most often triangles, produced by the geometry nodes defined in the X3D scene. Lines, points, and 2D shapes can also be drawn. These are covered in the later geometry chapters: Chapter 6 for points, lines, and polygons; then Chapter 13 for triangle-based nodes.

The Shape node bundles a geometry node with an Appearance node. Appearance defines the color, material properties, or texture image to be applied. Materials add special effects to a color such as transparency, shininess, or luminosity. Textures are rectangular 2D images that are wrapped around the geometry, thus providing special rendering capabilities. These topics are covered in Chapter 5, Appearance, Materials, and Textures.

2.1. Purpose and common functionality

Each Shape node is located in the current scene-graph coordinate system based on cumulative parent Transform and grouping nodes. The Shape node, in combination with any one of the geometry nodes, provides the following capabilities:

- Define 3D (and sometimes 2D) objects that are easily drawn and viewed.

- Pair each geometric definition with a corresponding appearance, allowing the browser to compute and render sophisticated shapes.

- Optionally hold bounding-box dimensions that indicate the maximum size and extent of the defined geometry.

Figure 2.1 shows the example GeometryPrimitiveNodes.x3d, which presents a single scene demonstrating each of these simple geometry nodes. Note that default values are filled in here for clarity—ordinarily authors can omit them. It is a good authoring practice to explicitly insert default values for emphasis when they are critical to node definition. Other, more persistent ways to identify such values are to include them in comments or in a metadata node. In any case, entering default values for emphasis is optional, and the default values might even be stripped out later if filtered through a file optimizer.

Figure 2.2 shows an X3D rendering of the five primitive geometry nodes, side by side, using the default node values presented in the GeometryPrimitiveNodes.x3d scene.

Figure 2.1. Scene graph of GeometryPrimitiveNodes.x3d scene.

a

b

Figure 2.2. a. Screen snapshot of GeometryPrimitiveNodes.x3d scene. **b.** Screen snapshot of GeometryPrimitiveNodes-White.x3d scene.

This scene includes usage of the Transform node to position each Shape at a different location. Transform is covered in Chapter 3, Grouping Nodes.

By default, X3D worlds have a black background. For ease of readability, most examples for this book are presented with a white background. This is done with a Background node, specifically `<Background skyColor="1 1 1"/>`. The Background node is described in Chapter 11, Lighting and Environment Nodes.

Common characteristics of geometry nodes are described in the following sections.

2.2. Common fields

A large variety of geometry nodes are available in X3D. For this reason, there is no single common geometry node type except X3DGeometryNode, which does not require any common field definitions from a language-design perspective. By definition, geometry nodes implement the X3DGeometryNode type as a marker interface to permit strong type checking during scene-graph construction. As a result, only a single X3DGeometryNode (plus a single Appearance node) are allowed to exist inside each Shape node.

Most of the primitive geometry nodes included in this chapter have boolean fields to indicate whether certain parts exist, such as whether end caps are applied to a Cylinder. Parts that are turned off in this fashion are not rendered, nor are they used for intersection tests such as camera-to-object collision detection.

There are several common fields that are consistently defined and applied as appropriate to various geometry nodes. Most of these fields are presented in Chapters 6 and 13, on polygonal and triangular geometry nodes, respectively. For the primitive geometry nodes presented in this chapter, a single common field pertains: solid.

2.2.1. solid

The solid field describes whether geometry is viewable from one or both sides of the polygons. The field signature is shown in Table 2.1. The naming here is deceptive: the term solid is meant to indicate whether the geometry resembles some real-world object (such as a board or rock) that typically cannot be viewed from the inside. Thus, `solid="true"` means that only the outside of the geometry is visible, while `solid="false"` means that the inside is also visible.

Interestingly, polygons in 3D graphics have two independent sides. A triangle might be visible from one side and not the other, or it might be visible from both sides. This capability is known as *backface culling* and is often used to reduce the number of polygons

Type	accessType	Name	Default	Range	Profile
SFBool	initializeOnly	solid	true		Interchange

Table 2.1. Field Signature for solid

drawn by the 3D-graphics rendering engine. After all, there is no point in drawing triangles that are not visible. Reduced rendering cost is why the solid field defaults to `"true"`, so authors must be on their guard to avoid positioning viewpoints at locations inside these nodes. If the current view is somehow navigated inside a solid geometry, the shape becomes invisible, because only the undrawn sides of the polygons are facing the viewer.

Within a browser, the algorithm that determines which side is inside and which is outside depends on computations involving normal (perpendicular) vectors to each polygon. Normal directions are determined using the right-hand rule with the ordered definition of points. This process is covered with more detail in Chapter 13, Geometry Nodes, Part 4: Triangles. For primitive geometry nodes, normal determination is computed automatically and is not a feature that authors need to worry about.

2.3. Abstract node types

Abstract node types are used to ensure that common nodes have identical signatures. This is a good object-oriented design practice that helps to ensure that interoperability and extensibility are strictly maintained among the various nodes in the X3D scene graph.

Although authors usually do not need to pay much attention to abstract node types, it does help to understand the consistency of node relationships within X3D.

2.3.1. X3DShapeNode type

X3DShapeNode is the base node type for all Shape nodes. Because there is only one Shape node in X3D, the field signature for this abstract node type matches that shown for the Shape node.

2.3.2. X3DGeometryNode type

X3DGeometryNode is the base node type for all of the various geometry nodes. Although there are many common fields shared among the geometry nodes, there are not any fields that are common among all of them. Thus the only field that can be guaranteed to exist for an X3DGeometryNode is an optional metadata child node.

2.3.3. X3DFontStyleNode type

X3DFontStyleNode is the base node type for the FontStyle node. There are many fields for FontStyle, but other variations on this node might not need any of the same fields. Thus the only field that can be guaranteed to exist for an X3DFontStyleNode is an optional metadata child node.

2.4. Hints and warnings

The naming of the solid field can be confusing. Remember that solid implies that an object is ordinarily impenetrable, not that 2-sided polygons are somehow more rigid than 1-sided polygons. For most authors the safest choice is changing from the default value to `solid="false"` so that both sides of the geometry are rendered, guaranteeing that both the inside and outside of each polygon are always visible.

Only one Appearance node can be assigned to the polygons in a single piece of geometry, and that Appearance affects both sides of each polygon if `solid="false"`. If you need different colors or textures for each side, it may be possible to use slightly smaller geometry on the inside and separate Appearance nodes, with each geometry collected under separate Shape nodes. In this special authoring case, the outer geometry can safely be set with `solid="true"`. Also note that the inner geometry needs `solid="false"` for 2-sided rendering, unless you use the constructs in the advanced geometry chapters to invert the orientation of the geometry so that normals point inward. Future versions of X3D will likely include a 2-sided material node.

3. Node descriptions

3.1. Shape node

The Shape node contains both the geometry and appearance for individual 3D objects. Thus, an X3D scene often consists of many Shape nodes. Each Shape associates a single geometry node with a corresponding Appearance node. Shape, Appearance, and Material nodes (covered in Chapter 5) can each be reused efficiently by applying a DEF name to the first occurrence and then utilizing a USE copy with the same name in subsequent instances.

Appearance nodes are also containers, collecting material nodes that define object color, texture nodes that define images, and other special nodes that affect the visual appearance of the associated geometry. Appearance nodes are covered in Chapter 5, Appearance, Material, and Textures. The precise interactions between geometry nodes and appearance are determined by the lights available in the scene, described in Chapter 11, Lighting and Environment Nodes.

The Shape node is fundamental to all X3D scenes and is included in all profiles except Core. Shape implements the X3DBoundedObject interface (defined in Chapter 3) and has the fields defined in Table 2.2. Node syntax is shown in Table 2.3.

Shape nodes can be placed at the top level of a scene and under any grouping node. Only one geometry node and one Appearance node are allowed within each Shape. Both the geometry and Appearance are optional. Of course, if no geometry is included, no visible objects are rendered.

A combination of Shape and Transform nodes can be used to create interesting composite objects. For example, a simple dumbbell can be produced using one long, thin Cylinder node for the bar and two short, wide Cylinder nodes for the weights. Simple furniture can often be constructed from a combination of primitive geometry nodes. Your imagination is very important! Beginning authors often put together geometry nodes in creative ways to construct interesting new objects.

3.1.1.   Hints and warnings

If a model has multiple moving parts, then each part is usually modeled as separate geometry, each within a separate Shape. It is perfectly fine to have lots of piecemeal

Type	accessType	Name	Default	Range	Profile
SFNode	inputOutput	geometry	NULL	[X3DGeometry Node]	Interchange
SFNode	inputOutput	appearance	NULL	[X3DAppearance Node]	Interchange
SFVec3f	initializeOnly	bboxCenter	0 0 0	$(-\infty, \infty)$	Interchange
SFVec3f	initializeOnly	bboxSize	−1 −1 −1	$[0, \infty]$ or −1 −1 −1	Interchange
SFNode	inputOutput	metadata	NULL	[X3DMetadata Object]	Core

Table 2.2. Field Definitions for Shape Node

XML Syntax (.x3d)	Classic VRML Syntax (.x3dv)

`<Shape DEF="MyShapeNode"`
`bboxCenter="0 0 0"`
`bboxSize="-1 -1 -1">`
`  <Box DEF="SingleGeometryNode"/>`
`  <Appearance`
`  DEF="SingleAppearanceNode"/>`
`</Shape>`
	`DEF MyShapeNode Shape {`
	`geometry DEF SingleGeometryNode`
	`                    Box {}`
	`appearance DEF SingleAppearanceNode`
	`                    Appearance {}`
	`bboxCenter 0 0 0`
	`bboxSize -1 -1 -1`
	`}`

Table 2.3. Node Syntax for Shape

Shapes that are grouped together to make up an aggregated visual object. Grouping and transformation (repositioning, rotating, and scaling size) are described in Chapter 3.

Look for common shapes that can be DEFed and then reUSEd, because this polygon-reduction technique can boost performance in large scenes. Give the first instance of a Shape a DEF name, then USE that same name in further occurrences. To reuse geometry while giving it a different color, first DEF the geometry node with a name and then USE that same geometry name inside another Shape with a different Appearance node. Similarly, DEF and USE either copies for shared Appearance or Material nodes can give multiple related geometry nodes the same rendering.

DEF-node definitions are required to appear before USE-node copies. This X3D specification rule allows the scene graph to be more efficiently loaded and constructed in a single parsing pass by a browser.

If no geometry node is provided, no object is drawn. If no Appearance node is provided, then the default values for a Material node (light grey) are provided for the geometry.

3.2. Box node

A Box is a basic six-sided rectangular parallelepiped. The width, height, and depth dimensions (*x*, *y*, and *z*) can have any positive, nonzero values. The geometry produced has six faces, twelve edges, and eight vertices with opposite faces parallel. The Box node produces geometry that is centered at the local origin.

Figures 2.3 and 2.4 show a schematic drawing of a Box node and an example screen image.

The Box node is in all profiles except Core. The node has the fields defined in Table 2.4. Node syntax is shown in Table 2.5.

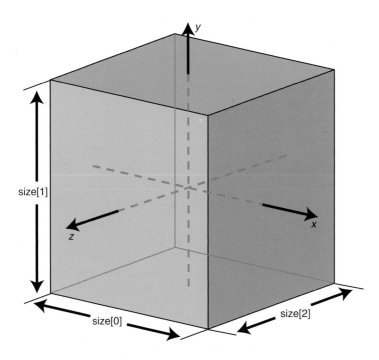

Figure 2.3. Definition of size dimensions for a Box.

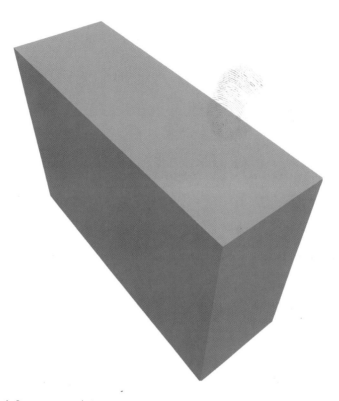

Figure 2.4. Example Box screen snapshot.

Type	accessType	Name	Default	Range	Profile
SFVec3f	initializeOnly	size	2 2 2	(0, ∞)	Interchange
SFBool	initializeOnly	solid	true		Interchange
SFNode	inputOutput	metadata	NULL	[X3DMetadataObject]	Core

Table 2.4. Field Definitions for Box Node

XML Syntax (.x3d)	Classic VRML Syntax (.x3dv)

`<Box DEF="MyBoxNode`
`size="1 1 1"`
`solid="true"/>`
	`DEF MyBoxNode Box {`
	`size 1 1 1`
	`solid TRUE`
	`}`

Table 2.5. Node Syntax for Box

Box nodes are perhaps the most commonly used primitive. Although a Box may often have more sides than are needed or visible in a model, it is easy to construct, and a few extra hidden polygons are not computationally expensive to render. A Box can also provide a quick approximation of a 2-sided quadrilateral when one of the three size dimensions is small. For example: `<Box size="2 0.001 2"/>` is quite flat and must be rotated to be seen.

3.2.1. size

The size field defines the x, y, and z dimensions of the Box, each respectively aligned with the x, y, and z axes of the local coordinate system. Note that all values must be greater than zero. Each size value is the length of a side, so if a Box remains centered at the origin, then half of each size component extends on either side of the origin.

3.2.2. Hints and warnings

Because size is an initializeOnly field, simple-geometry dimensions cannot be changed after creation. This is an intentional limitation that permits browsers to apply further polygonal optimizations at load time. To animate the size of primitive geometry, modify a parent Transform node's scale field instead.

A Box can be used to represent simple 2D rectangles, but this approach adds a few unneeded polygons to the scene, and the Box then must be viewed directly from one side. The Rectangle2D node can be used as described in Chapter 10, Geometry Nodes, Part 3: Geometry2D Nodes.

3.3. Cone node

Cone is another primitive geometry node. Each cone has a circular base with a perpendicular axis that is centered along the local y-axis. The actual number of polygons used to polygonalize the Cone is decided by the browser rather than the author. Each Cone produces geometry that is centered at the origin of the local coordinate system.

Figures 2.5 and 2.6 show a schematic drawing of a Cone node and an example screen image.

The Cone node is in all profiles except Core, beginning with the Interchange profile. The node has the fields defined in Table 2.6. Node syntax is shown in Table 2.7.

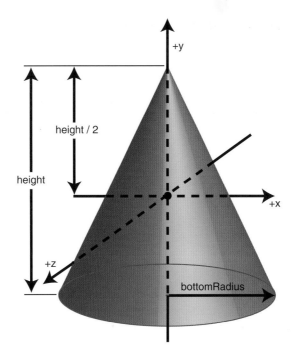

Figure 2.5. Definition of height and bottomRadius dimensions for a Cone.

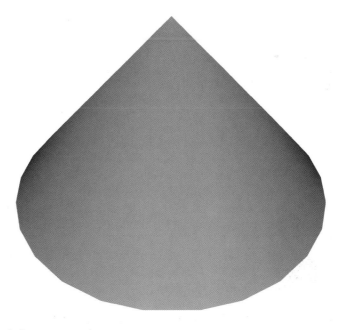

Figure 2.6. Example Cone screen snapshot.

Type	accessType	Name	Default	Range	Profile
SFFloat	initializeOnly	bottomRadius	1	(0,∞)	Interchange
SFFloat	initializeOnly	height	2	(0,∞)	Interchange
SFBool	initializeOnly	bottom	true		Interchange
SFBool	initializeOnly	side	true		Interchange
SFBool	initializeOnly	solid	true		Interchange
SFNode	inputOutput	metadata	NULL	[X3DMetadataObject]	Core

Table 2.6. Field Definitions for Cone Node

XML Syntax (.x3d)	ClassicVRML Syntax (.x3dv)
```<Cone DEF="MyConeNode" bottomRadius="1" height="2" bottom="true" side="true" solid="true" />```	```DEF MyConeNode Cone { bottomRadius 1 height 2 bottom TRUE side TRUE solid TRUE }```

Table 2.7. Node Syntax for Cone

Cones can model many objects. Cones make good 3D arrowheads and can point to other objects of interest. Sometimes cones with transparency and emissiveColor are used to indicate a beam of energy, or even to emphasize the presence of a Spotlight by outlining the conical Spotlight's otherwise-invisible boundaries. Surprisingly creative examples are possible. Further information about Spotlight can be found in Chapter 11, Lighting and Environment Nodes.

3.3.1. bottomRadius and height

The bottomRadius and height fields are the size of the circular base and the vertical axis of the Cone. Both must be greater than zero and are measured in meters.

3.3.2. bottom and side

The bottom and side fields determine whether each part of the Cone is visible. Because these are boolean (SFBool) fields, the bottom and side of the Cone are either visible or invisible.

3.3.3. Hints and warnings

One way to produce a flat circle is to define a Cone with a tiny height value (to minimize vertical offset) and set the side field to false. Flat circles can also be created with the end caps of a Cylinder. The resultant circle may be one-sided or two-sided depending on the solid field. An alternative approach is to use either a Circle2D or Disk2D node, described in Chapter 10, Geometry Nodes, Part 3: Geometry2D Nodes.

Use a parent Transform rotation to orient a Cone in the desired direction. The Transform node is covered in Chapter 3, Grouping Nodes.

Because all of the Cone fields are initializeOnly, none can be changed after initial creation. To animate the size of a Cone primitive, modify a parent Transform node's scale field. To change whether the side or bottom is displayed, alternate versions of the same Cone can be successive children of a grandparent Switch node (each with a Shape as the intermediate parent node, because geometry can only appear inside a Shape node). An authoring tool or run-time animation (such as IntegerTrigger or Script node) can then modify the Switch node's whichChoice field to select the desired version of the Cone. The Switch node is discussed in Chapter 3, Grouping Nodes. Run-time animation concepts are presented in Chapters 7 through 9.

3.4. Cylinder node

This node is a capped right-angle cylinder with the central axis oriented along the local y-axis. The actual number of polygons used to create the Cylinder are decided by the browser, and most browsers do a good job at providing well-rounded circular sides. Each Cylinder produces geometry that is centered at the origin of the local coordinate system.

Figures 2.7 and 2.8 show a schematic drawing of a Cylinder node and an example screen image.

The Cylinder node is in the Interchange profile, meaning that it is in all profiles except the Core profile. The Cylinder node has the fields defined in Table 2.8. Node syntax is shown in Table 2.9.

Each Cylinder has three parts: bottom, side, and top. Each part is included depending on the corresponding boolean (SFBool) value.

3.4.1. radius and height

The radius and height fields define the lengths of the circular radius and the central axis of the Cylinder. Each must be greater than zero and (like all other linear X3D dimensions) are measured in meters. Browsers generate numerous flat polygons to approximate a smoothly cylindrical surface. If your browser offers a "wireframe" mode of rendering, temporarily select it to inspect the construction of the geometry nodes.

As with the other primitive geometry nodes, the overall dimensions of a Cylinder are chosen to approximate the size of a unit Sphere.

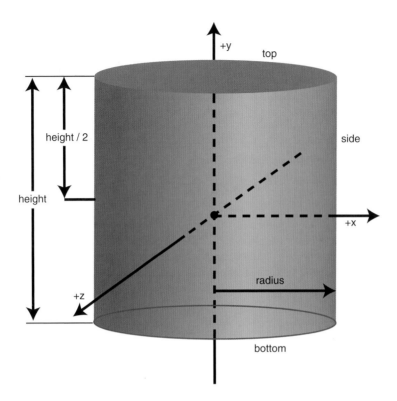

Figure 2.7. Definition of height and radius dimensions for a Cylinder.

3.4.2. bottom, side, and top

The bottom, side, and top fields determine whether each part of the Cylinder is visible. Because these are boolean (SFBool) fields, the end caps and side can either be visible or invisible.

3.4.3. Hints and warnings

If y-axis vertical alignment is not desired, create a parent Transform rotation to orient a Cylinder in the desired direction. Also see the hints for Cone node, because the same techniques can be used to selectively animate the visibility of different parts of a Cylinder. Translation, rotation, and scaling are covered in Chapter 3, Grouping Nodes.

3.5. Sphere node

A Sphere is the simplest node to define, because usually only the radius is declared. Spheres are common objects. As with other primitive geometry nodes, a Sphere can be defined with

Figure 2.8. Example Cylinder screen snapshot with top="false".

Type	accessType	Name	Default	Range	Profile
SFFloat	initializeOnly	radius	1	(0,∞)	Interchange
SFFloat	initializeOnly	height	2	(0,∞)	Interchange
SFBool	initializeOnly	bottom	true		Interchange
SFBool	initializeOnly	side	true		Interchange
SFBool	initializeOnly	top	true		Interchange
SFBool	initializeOnly	solid	true		Interchange
SFNode	inputOutput	metadata	NULL	[X3DMetadataObject]	Core

Table 2.8. Field Definitions for Cylinder Node

solid="true" to avoid drawing the interior surfaces, or solid="false" to draw the inside polygons and allow viewing from within.

Figures 2.9 and 2.10 show a schematic drawing of a Sphere node and an example screen image.

The Sphere node is in the Interchange profile. The node has the fields defined in Table 2.10. Node Syntax is shown in Table 2.11.

XML Syntax (.x3d)	ClassicVRML Syntax (.x3dv)

``
<Cylinder DEF="MyCylinderNode"
  radius="1"
  height="2"
  bottom="true"
  side="true"
  top="true"
  solid="true" />
``
	``
	DEF MyCylinderNode Cylinder {
	  radius 1
	  height 2
	  bottom TRUE
	  side TRUE
	  top TRUE
	  solid TRUE
	}
	``

Table 2.9. Node Syntax for Cylinder

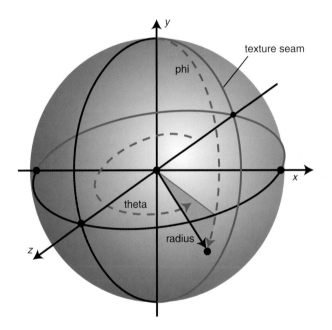

Figure 2.9. Definition of radius dimension for a sphere.

The process of subdividing curved shapes into polygonal approximations is known as *tesselation*. Modern browsers do not skimp on the triangles, often with noticeably superior results to the blockier geometry rendered by older browsers. An X3D browser is free to tesselate a Sphere as finely or coarsely as it chooses.

3.5.1. radius

The radius value must be greater than zero and is measured in meters. The default value of radius="1" meter is typically referred to as a unit sphere.

Figure 2.10. Example screen snapshot of a sphere.

Type	accessType	Name	Default	Range	Profile
SFFloat	initializeOnly	radius	1	(0,∞)	Interchange
SFBool	initializeOnly	solid	true		Interchange
SFNode	inputOutput	metadata	NULL	[X3DMetadataObject]	Core

Table 2.10. Field definitions for Sphere Node

XML Syntax (.x3d)	Classic VRML Syntax (.x3dv)

`<Sphere DEF="MySphereNode"`
`  radius="1"`
`  solid="true"/>`
	`DEF MySphereNode Sphere {`
	`  radius 1`
	`  solid TRUE`
	`}`

Table 2.11. Node Syntax for Sphere

3.5.2. Hints and warnings

Partial spheres can be constructed, but only by obscuring parts of the Sphere with other geometric objects (such as a Box or Cylinder). Creating hemispheres is a more advanced authoring technique usually reserved for IndexedFaceSet or the various triangle nodes.

3.6. Text node

The Text node generates readable text strings in the X3D world. The resulting object is 2-sided and planar (meaning flat, with no 3D depth). By default each text string is orientated vertically in the xy plane beginning at $z = 0$ of the local coordinate system. The formatting of the displayed text is primarily controlled by the FontStyle node, described in the following section. Multiple text strings may be supplied, so that each individual string is shown as a separate line in the text display.

The Text node is in the Interchange profile. The node has the fields defined in Table 2.12. Node syntax is shown in Table 2.13.

Type	accessType	Name	Default	Range	Profile
SFNode	inputOutput	fontStyle	NULL	[X3FontStyleNode]	Interchange
MFString	initializeOnly	string	[]		Interchange
MFFloat	inputOutput	length	[]	$[0, \infty)$	Interchange
SFFloat	inputOutput	maxExtent	0.0	$[0, \infty)$	Interchange
SFBool	initializeOnly	solid	false		Interchange
SFNode	inputOutput	metadata	NULL	[X3DMetadataObject]	Core

Table 2.12. Field Definitions for Text Node

XML Syntax (.x3d)	ClassicVRML Syntax (.x3dv)

```<Text DEF="MyTextNode"```
``` length=" "```
``` maxExtent="0.0"```
``` string='"some" "text"'```
``` solid="false">```
``` <FontStyle DEF="MyFontStyle"/>```
```</Text>```
	```DEF MyTextNode Text {```
	``` length []```
	``` maxExtent 0.0```
	``` string ["some" "text"]```
	``` solid FALSE```
	``` fontStyle DEF MyFontStyle FontStyle {}```
	```}```

Table 2.13. Node syntax for Text

3.6.1. string

The text to be displayed is specified in the string field. This field supports an array of strings. Each string is displayed according to the parameters in the FontStyle node. A complete description of all available effects is contained in the description for that node.

3.6.2. length

The length field contains an array of floating-point numbers that specify the length of each element of string in the local coordinate system. If the length of an individual string is shorter than its specified length, the string is stretched (either by scaling or expanding the spacing) to fit the length. If the length of an individual string is longer than its specified length, the string is compressed (either by scaling or decreasing the spacing) to fit the length. A value of 0 (either explicitly specified or implied by omission) uses the inherent length of the string element.

3.6.3. maxExtent

The width of all of the text strings is controlled by the field maxExtent. If the longest string is bigger than maxExtent (as measured in the local coordinate system), then all strings are compressed to maxExtent. If the length of the longest string is less than maxExtent, then this field has no effect. The length of the longest string is measured in the direction of character advance (see FontStyle for more details).

3.6.4. Hints and warnings

When a Text node has an associated TouchSensor, clicking on the geometry associated with Text can be difficult. It is easier on the user if you create a transparent, noncollidable flat Box that extends beyond the text in the x and y directions. Make both the Shape nodes containing the Text geometry and the transparent Box (or rectangle) associated with the text clickable. An example scene showing this technique is ClickableTextWithTransparentBoxOutline.x3d. TouchSensor is presented in Chapter 8, User Interactivity Nodes.

Remember that text is flat along a 2D plane that is placed in the 3D scene. Thus orientation is important. If the orientation is incorrect, users will not be able to see the text.

X3D has no built-in definitions for 3D text, which is a string that also has a depth component. If essential, 3D-text characters must be built separately (with some difficulty) using Extrusion or IndexedFaceSetSet nodes.

3.7. FontStyle node

The FontStyle node defines the size, font face, layout, and style used in a parent Text node. Thus, FontStyle does not produce rendered geometry by itself, and can only appear as the child of a Text node in a scene graph. The family, style, spacing, and size fields specify the details of the desired font.

The FontStyle node is in the Interchange profile. The node has the fields defined in Table 2.14. Node Syntax is shown in Table 2.15.

Type	accessType	Name	Default	Range	Profile
MFString	initializeOnly	family	" SERIF "		Interchange
MFString	initializeOnly	justify	" BEGIN "	[" BEGIN " | " END " | " FIRST " | " MIDDLE " | " "]	Interchange
MFString	initializeOnly	style	" PLAIN "	[" PLAIN " | " BOLD " | " ITALIC " | " BOLDITALIC " | " "]	Interchange
SFString	initializeOnly	language	" "		Interchange
SFBool	initializeOnly	horizontal	true		Interchange
SFBool	initializeOnly	leftToRight	true		Interchange
SFBool	initializeOnly	topToBottom	true		Interchange
SFFloat	initializeOnly	size	1.0	(0, ∞)	Interchange
SFFloat	initializeOnly	spacing	1.0	[0, ∞)	Interchange
SFNode	inputOutput	metadata	NULL	[X3DMetadataObject]	Core

Table 2.14. Field definitions for FontStyle node

XML Syntax (.x3d)	Classic VRML Syntax (.x3dv)
```<FontStyle DEF="MyFontStyleNode"` `family='"SERIF"'` `justify='"BEGIN"'` `language=" "` `style='"PLAIN"'` `horizontal="true"` `leftToRight="true"` `topToBottom="true"` `size="1.0"` `spacing="1.0"/>```	```DEF MyFontStyleNode FontStyle {` `family ["SERIF"]` `justify ["BEGIN"]` `language " "` `style ["PLAIN"]` `horizontal TRUE` `leftToRight TRUE` `topToBottom TRUE` `size 1.0` `spacing 1.0` `}```

Table 2.15. Node syntax for FontStyle

The default FontStyle field values produce text that is left justified, horizontal (goes from −x to +x), then vertical (goes from +y to −y). The FontStyle node completely controls the orientation, direction of characters, direction of lines, line spacing, font face, and font styling ("BOLD", "ITALIC", "BOLDITALIC" or "PLAIN").

The default operation of the FontStyle node defines a plain serif font (typically Times Roman) with horizontal left-justified English text, characters running from left to right with vertical spacing at 1 meter, and lines of text running from top to bottom in the local coordinate system. The large number of parameter fields are needed to properly support Web Internationalization (I18N) rendering of text.

The family, style, spacing, and size fields specify the details of the desired font. Properly chosen values (usually the defaults) can generate the desired layout results.

As with the other primitive nodes in this chapter, none of the fields of FontStyle can be modified once they have been defined. The font characteristics are set during initialization so that the computationally expensive task of building text polygons is only performed once during loading and not repeatedly during operation.

Thus, the Text node layout characteristics can only be changed at run-time by replacing the FontStyle node. Such a task is not hard, but it does require the author to provide some specialty scripting code. This technique is described in Chapter 9, Event Utilities and Scripting. It is also used in the following example, taken from the National Institute of Standards and Testing (NIST) X3D Conformance Suite. ConformanceNist example scene [Appearance, FontStyle, driver.x3d] provides clickable panels on the top, bottom, left, and right that modify different FontStyle field parameters and display the corresponding text result.

FontStyle provides extensive control for the layout of text in the X3D scene. Figure 2.11 shows default field values (leftToRight="true" topToBottom="true"). Figure 2.12 shows the same text with different FontStyle field values indicated by the green boxes. Figure 2.13 shows two lines of text (string='"Hello" "X3D"') using default layout with no FontStyle node.

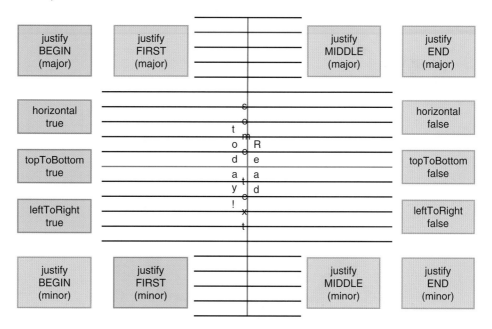

Figure 2.11. Example scene demonstrating the effects of varying FontStyle node parameters. Green boxes indicate selected values.

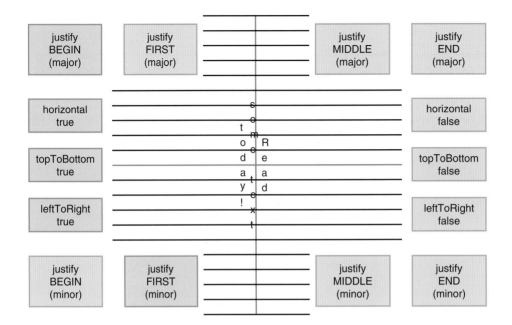

Figure 2.12. The same scene with <FontStyle leftToRight="true" horizontal="false" topToBottom="false" justify="'MIDDLE' 'MIDDLE'"/>. Green boxes indicate selected values.

hello
X3D!

Figure 2.13. An example of the Text node showing two lines of text.

3.7.1. family

The font family or face is specified with the family field. Any valid font name can be specified for this field. If a font selection is not available on the user's system, then it is skipped and the next element is considered. If no matching fonts are found, then the default value of `"SERIF"` is used. There are three values for the font field that are always supported: `"SERIF"`, `"SANS"` and `"TYPEWRITER"`. Chosen fonts are typically Times Roman for `"SERIF"`, Helvetica or Arial for `"SANS"`, and Courier for `"TYPEWRITER"`.

Note that the quotation marks and uppercase characters are always required for specifying each font-family name.

3.7.2. justify

The justify field determines whether the Text string starting position (0 0 0) is at the beginning, end, or middle.

Two string values are provided for defining the major and minor axis alignments. If `topToBottom="true"`, then the first value sets horizontal alignment and the second value sets vertical justification (for multiple-string outputs). If `topToBottom="false"`, then the alignment priorities are reversed.

3.7.3. language

Language-specific rendering techniques and characters are identified with the language field. If language is not specified, then English is used. Support for languages other than English is usually a browser-specific feature.

Language codes consist of a primary code and a (possibly empty) series of subcodes. Two-letter primary codes are reserved for language abbreviations, and include en (English), fr (French), de (German), it (Italian), nl (Dutch), el (Greek), es (Spanish), pt (Portuguese), ar (Arabic), he (Hebrew), ru (Russian), zh (Chinese), ja (Japanese), hi (Hindi), ur (Urdu), and sa (Sanskrit). Many other languages are also supported. Any two-letter subcode is understood to be a country code (for example, fr-ca for French Canada). Further reference information regarding language codes can be found at (RFC1766, www.ietf.org/rfc/rfc1766.txt) (ISO3166 or www.oasis-open.org/cover/iso639a.html).

3.7.4. style

A single font style is specified using the style field. The four specified candidates are PLAIN, BOLD, ITALIC, and BOLDITALIC. An empty style field is equivalent to PLAIN. Although not defined in the X3D specification, specialty browsers may feature additional style choices.

3.7.5. size and spacing

The size and spacing fields determine how much distance each line of text (each element of the field string in the parent Text node) uses. The size field specifies the height of the letter I as measured from the baseline (bottom of the letter) to the top of the letter. The spacing field is a multiplicative factor to size that determines the distance between the lines. A spacing value of 0 allows no space between successive lines of text, causing each line of text to have the same baseline. Spacing values less than approximately 1.3 may cause the geometry created by descending characters (for example, lowercase g) to intersect with geometry from the line below. The actual amount of spacing provided is specific to each font.

3.7.6. horizontal, leftToRight, and topToBottom

The horizontal field specifies whether the direction of the displayed text string characters is horizontal (`horizontal="true"`) or vertical (`horizontal="false"`). The leftToRight field determines whether text direction is left-to-right (true) or right-to-left (false). The topToBottom field determines whether text direction is top-to-bottom (true) or bottom-to-top (false).

3.7.7. Hints and warnings

It is interesting that browsers interpreting the FontStyle node may choose any means to generate and display the text. Text strings are not always rendered by turning the font characters into polygonal geometry. Systems may choose instead to render the text as a 2D image and then insert the image texture in place of polygonal text geometry.

3.7.8. Parameter combinations

Tables 2.16 through 2.21 adapted from the X3D Specification show all of the various combinations the justify, left to right, and horizontal field parameters, that can be used to vary text direction.

justify Enumerant	*leftToRight* = "true"	*leftToRight* = "false"
FIRST	Left edge of each line	Right edge of each line
BEGIN	Left edge of each line	Right edge of each line
MIDDLE	Centered about X–axis	Centered about X–axis
END	Right edge of each line	Left edge of each line

Table 2.16. Major Alignment, *horizontal* = "true"

justify Enumerant	*topToBottom* = "true"	*topToBottom* = "false"
FIRST	Top edge of each line	Bottom edge of each line
BEGIN	Top edge of each line	Bottom edge of each line
MIDDLE	Centered about Y–axis	Centered about Y–axis
END	Bottom edge of each line	Top edge of each line

Table 2.17. Major Alignment, *horizontal* = "false"

justify Enumerant	topToBottom = "true"	topToBottom = "false"
FIRST	Baseline of first line	Baseline of first line
BEGIN	Top edge of first line	Bottom edge of first line
MIDDLE	Centered about Y-axis	Centered about Y-axis
END	Bottom edge of last line	Top edge of last line

Table 2.18. Minor Alignment, *horizontal* = "true"

justify Enumerant	left To Right = "true"	topToBottom = "false"
FIRST	Left edge of first line	Right edge of first line
BEGIN	Left edge of first line	Right edge of first line
MIDDLE	Centered about X-axis	Centered about X-axis
END	Right edge of last line	Left edge of last line

Table 2.19. Minor Alignment, *horizontal* = "false"

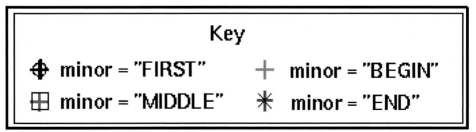

Table 2.20. *horizontal* = "true" layout result (taken from X3D specification)

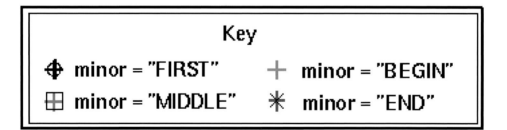

Table 2.21. *horizontal* = "false" layout result (taken from X3D specification)

4. Summary

4.1. Key ideas

Most rendered geometry in X3D is polygonal in nature. Authors create objects by specifying the detailed size and shape parameters of different geometric forms. This chapter examines primitive geometry nodes that are simple to define.

This chapter covers the Shape node and the simplest geometry nodes: Box, Cone, Cylinder, Sphere, Text, and FontStyle.

4.2. Related nodes and concepts

The advanced geometry chapters present a wide variety of other renderable objects: Chapter 6 covers Points, Lines, and Polygons; Chapter 10 covers Geometry 2D nodes; and Chapter 13 covers Triangle-based nodes. Chapter 5, Appearance, Material, and Textures, describes how to apply colors, shading, and imagery to these shapes.

When constructing exceptionally large scenes, such as buildings or cities, using more precise shapes that give better control of polygonalization may result in better overall performance.

4.3. Next chapter

The next chapter shows how to group different shapes together and move them to different locations. Chapter 5 shows how to modify object appearance by applying Material and ImageTexture nodes.

Grouping Nodes

A Working Group is a technical committee that researches and proposes solutions to specific technical problems relating to X3D.
—Web3D Consortium

1. What this chapter covers

This chapter covers the basic X3D nodes needed to organize objects in an X3D world: Inline, Group and StaticGroup, level of detail (LOD), Switch and Transform.

An Inline node loads one X3D scene into another. Grouping nodes can collect other nodes to make more sophisticated objects. LOD and Switch selections allow alternate geometric forms to replace one another, depending on the needs of the scene. Transformations include changes in position, orientation, and scale, which move the location of nodes away from the local center.

Several other grouping nodes are covered elsewhere. Anchor, Billboard, and Collision are in Chapter 4, Viewing and Navigation.

2. Concepts

Getting started in a new language is a "bootstrap" process—you have to help yourself along. There is usually quite a bit of basic information you must learn before you can produce even simple results. However, the information in these early chapters is enough to build and connect interesting X3D scenes. Modifying example scenes helps you learn how to build your own scenes.

2.1. Purpose and common functionality

Large complex X3D objects are most easily understood by breaking them into subcomponent objects. The relationship between these various subcomponent models is maintained by grouping them together. X3D provides six nodes for the purpose of grouping. These nodes are designed to contain other nodes. Each grouping node is a parent to zero or more children nodes. Thus, the collection of nodes in an X3D scene can be represented as a treelike graph structure, in which grouping nodes provide most of the connecting branch points.

Bringing multiple nodes together in a group can achieve several objectives. Grouping nodes can:

- Structure diverse pieces of content together in a sensible way

- Collect subgraphs of related nodes for easier authoring and animation

- Maintain a common coordinate system, where objects are more easily positioned and oriented relative to each other

- Make it easy to label, copy, and render aggregated collections of nodes via DEF and USE

Clear definitions of relative coordinate systems are essential to ensure that geometry is placed in the right location and oriented in the right direction. After first describing coordinate systems, this chapter presents related node types, which define fields common to various grouping nodes, and then the X3D grouping nodes themselves, which are essential in all X3D scenes.

2.2. Units of measurement and coordinate systems

In order for different X3D worlds to work together, scenes must utilize consistent measurement units. The default authoring conventions are to use seconds for time intervals, meters for coordinate measurements, radians for angle measurements, and red-green-blue (RGB) (values each ranging 0, 1) for colors. Radian measurements typically range from $[0, 2\pi)$ which corresponds to $[0°, 360°)$.

SFTime values can be relative or absolute numbers of seconds. Duration values are simply the number of seconds. The notion of "no time provided" or "stop" is represented by a time value of one (-1). Absolute values for time are measured in seconds elapsed since January 1, 1970, 00:00:00 GMT. Time values are stored as double-precision floating-point values, so the precision of time values used in X3D animation is excellent.

X3D uses a Cartesian coordinate system in which three coordinate values (x, y, and z) are sufficient to uniquely define any point in space. It arbitrarily defines a root origin for all coordinate systems in the virtual environment. The coordinate system is defined using right-handed orthogonal axes, with +x going from left to right, +y going from bottom to top, and +z coming out of the user's screen. "Right handed" refers to the ordered orientation of these three mutually perpendicular axes: the positive x, y, and z axes can be pointed to (in order) by the thumb, index finger, and middle finger of the right hand. Try this yourself—it can be a helpful habit when authoring X3D scenes to check the proper direction of translations and orientations by using your right hand.

Coordinates within the virtual environment specified by each scene are always relative to the local-origin location (0 0 0). The topmost parent scene implicitly determines the location of the root origin. Subsidiary inlined scenes can be translated (i.e., locally positioned) relative to that origin. In this way, consistent locations and relative positioning can be provided throughout a collection of X3D scenes.

Angular rotations are expressed in radians, using the right-hand rule, with thumb pointing along the positive direction for the axis of interest and the other fingers curling in the direction of positive rotation. When viewing the origin point from default viewpoint location (0 0 10), the x- and y-axes match typical 2D Cartesian axes with the x-axis to the right and y-axis up. Thus the default line of sight is along the negative z axis, as shown in the following figures.

When building 3D models that are intended to be animated and work together, good authoring practices have shown that these default coordinate-system directions are best applied so that a model's +x-axis is forward/North, +y-axis is vertical/up, +z-axis is right-hand side (RHS)/East. In this way, inlined models can be animated consistently when changing relative position or orientation. For example, an inlined automobile initially points in the correct direction. Figures 3.1 and 3.2 illustrate these relationships.

Geographic coordinates include a variety of systems for defining latitude and longitude on the Earth's surface. Although beyond the scope of this book, they are defined in the X3D Geospatial Component and can align with many other Geographic Information Systems (GIS) data formats. Continued Web3D Consortium efforts on the X3D Earth project promise to provide even greater interoperability in the future.

As a language-design consideration, note that X3D does not attach "unitType" labels everywhere, because that approach can cause unexpected mismatch errors and makes both scenes and software inefficient. Instead, the convention is to simply keep all units consistent for all values throughout all scenes.

Even so, using nonmeter measurements is sometimes desirable when the underlying measurement data is provided in a different set of units (feet, millimeters, fathoms, etc.) and the author wants to keep those original values unmodified for documentation or validation purposes. In those cases, wrapping a Transform as the overall parent node can rescale the child content to meters, reposition it to a proper origin, and rotate everything to match default coordinate-axis directions.

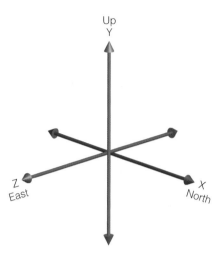

Figure 3.1. Default *x-y-z* coordinate axes for X3D scenes.

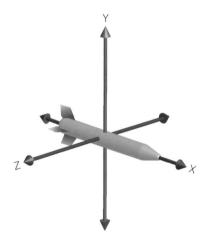

Figure 3.2. Aligning objects with the x-axis is a good practice that promotes consistent reusability.

Rotations are specified by defining the axis of rotation as an *x-y-z* vector of unit length, and then rotating about that axis by a specified number of radians. The axis of rotation is defined by specifying the point on a directed line from the origin. Any rotation can also be modeled as a nested combination of individual rotations about the *x-*, *y-*, and *z*-axes respectively. This representation is a close variation on quaternions which are mathematical constructs for rotation that are used widely throughout the field of 3D graphics.

2.3. Coordinate system details

In order to consistently define the locations, sizes and directions of 3D objects, we must strictly define and observe coordinate-system conventions. Thus it is important to understand the basic definitions governing coordinate systems.

2.3.1. Which way is up?

X3D matches most 3D graphics and engineering systems by following a right-handed Cartesian coordinate system. Figure 3.3 illustrates the default (x, y, z) orientation.

These are the default directions for each axis, with the origin in the center of the screen at (0 0 0). Note that the positive x-axis is horizontal and the positive y-axis is vertical, just as most people are accustomed to when plotting 2D functions on a graph. The positive z-axis comes straight out of the screen. Thus, in X3D worlds, y is up.

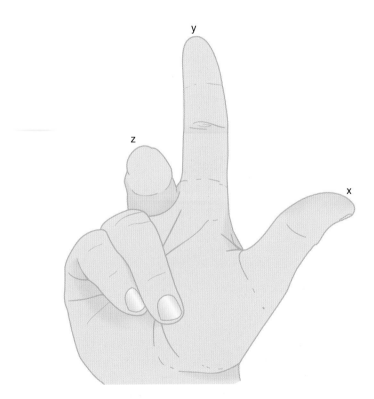

Figure 3.3. The right-hand rule governs the relative order of the x-, y-, and z-axes. The first three fingers of your right hand should be able to align with each axis, in that order.

This relationship is fundamental and frequently repeated. When a new coordinate system is defined relative to another, the local origin is redefined as (0 0 0) in the local coordinate space, even though it is located at a different position. The Transform node defines the relative offsets between parent and child coordinate systems. Each Transform node has a translation field to define the desired location change between one relative origin and another. Similarly, a rotation field defines relative orientation, and a scale field defines relative scaling.

2.3.2. "Right-hand rule" rules!

If you hold your right hand in front of Figure 3.3, you can align your thumb with the +x-axis, index finger with the +y-axis, and middle finger with the +z-axis. However, if you try the same thing with your left hand, you will find that you cannot align the same three fingers in order with the same (x, y, z) directions. This confirms the right-handed nature of the X3D coordinate system.

This book also follows the "right-hand rule" (RHR) whenever rotating geometric structures. This convention not only determines the ordering of (x, y, z) coordinates but also the direction of rotation when reorienting shapes, and even the directionality of normal (perpendicular) vectors.

Figure 3.4 shows how the thumb can point along an axis with the fingers curling in the direction of positive rotation. This approach can be used to compute the rotation about an axis pointing in any direction. Rotation values vary from 0 to 2π radians,

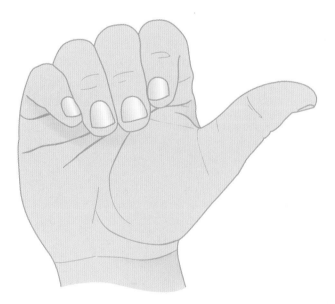

Figure 3.4. Right-hand rule for orientations provides the direction of positive rotation about an axis.

corresponding to 0° to 360°. Negative values specify a rotation in the opposite direction. Angle values with an absolute value greater than 2π are simply considered multiple rotations and are equivalent to the corresponding value modulo 2π.

2.3.3. Orientation

An author frequently needs to rotate shapes to align them in the proper direction. Placing objects in the right place is always a combination of translation and rotation, repeated for each Transform node in an X3D scene. In addition to Transform, several other X3D nodes (such as Viewpoint, CylinderSensor, and SphereSensor) have a rotation or orientation field of type SFRotation. Each SFRotation field determines an arbitrary direction axis (through a unit x-y-z vector) and an angular-rotation value in radians about that axis.

Interestingly, any single arbitrary rotation can be decomposed into a set of 3 separate rotations about the x-, y-, and z-axes respectively. The order of rotation is important. A good authoring practice for learning about rotations is to use nested Transforms that each only rotate about one axis at a time. Note that each child coordinate system is rotated relative to the coordinate system of its parent transform nodes.

Many 3D authoring tools provide good support for computing orientation values.

2.4. DEF and USE

DEF and USE names are the X3D mechanism for efficiently defining and copying a node, multiple nodes, or even groups of nodes. Copied nodes require far less memory and computation because they need only be created once. This efficiency can greatly improve rendering performance when extensively used in large scenes.

When a node is given a DEF name, that name is an identification label that is unique in the file. The DEF name must start with a letter and can contain letters, numbers, and the special characters underscore, hyphen, and period. DEF names must not include whitespace or other special characters. Uppercase and lowercase alphabetic characters are considered strictly different; therefore, DEF names are case sensitive.

USE names refer back to a node with a DEF name. These references allow faster and more efficient rendering of graphics objects. Note that the actual DEF node name definition must be located in the scene graph before any USE references. This permits X3D browsers to read and load a scene graph in a single pass, avoiding undefined references and thereby yielding faster parsing and loading. This performance boost not only helps when users first load a scene, but is also valuable when further subscenes are loaded within a parent scene. Authors also must be careful with animation of the fields of a DEF node, because this will equally affect all of the USE copies.

When authoring large scenes, using descriptive DEF names improves clarity and helps document a model. CamelCaseNaming is a good way to accomplish this: capitalize each word, never use abbreviations, strive for clarity, and be brief but complete. Avoiding underscore characters improves readability, because pretty-print HTML versions of scenes usually hyperlink these names, and underlined hyperlinks hide underscore characters from the user. ROUTE statements that connect one node's field to another node's field are much more understandable when the purpose and type of the node are evident in the DEF names themselves. Examples provided with this book strive to provide useful examples of good naming practices. ROUTE connections are covered in Chapter 7, Event Animation and Interpolation.

A good rule of thumb is that a proper DEF name can be sensibly used in a sentence. For example, "The fraction_changed field of the SpinningBoxClock TimeSensor node is ROUTED to the set_fraction field of the SpinningBoxInterpolator node." Although a bit long winded, such sentences provide a clear and sensible explanation for a given behavior.

2.5. Abstract node types

As described in Chapter 1, frequently occuring field definitions in related X3D nodes are usually collected together as node types. Node types define common characteristics among similar nodes. Consistent typing provides uniform interfaces for functionally similar X3D nodes, thus allowing substitution and interchangeability when appropriate.

It is worth noting that node types were not defined in the original VRML97 design. The VRML97 scene graph is largely object-oriented and reasonably consistent internally, however, so the designers of X3D were able to capture and extend that consistency. Well-defined node types and families of similar nodes are the result.

Abstract node types are templates, which means that they are not instantiable as actual objects. They ensure that related nodes and node types always share some common fields. Thus the abstract node definitions are not used by name in the X3D scene graph itself, but are built into the functional definitions of actual nodes instead. Understanding the substitution capability of nodes with identical node types helps authors understand which combinations are possible when constructing a scene. Node types are also important when designing new nodes and extensions, a topic covered in Chapter 14, Creating Prototype Nodes.

Three node types for grouping nodes are described in the following sections: X3DChildNode, X3DBoundedObject, and X3DGroupingNode.

2.5.1. X3DChildNode type

The X3DChildNode type is common to most X3D nodes. It simply indicates that such a node may be used in children, addChildren, and removeChildren fields of an X3DGroupingNode. Table 3.1 lists field definitions for X3DChildNode.

Type	accessType	Name	Default	Range	Profile
SFNode	inputOutput	metadata	NULL	[X3DMetadataObject]	Core

Table 3.1. Field Definitions for X3DChildNode Type

It is interesting to note that all nodes (not just grouping nodes) can contain a metadata node that may describe it. Metadata nodes can also add relevant descriptions about themselves by containing a child metadata node.

2.5.2. X3DBoundedObject type

The X3DBoundedObject type provides bboxCenter and bboxSize fields that define a bounding box surrounding a Group node's children, oriented within the current coordinate system. This information is optional, and is treated as a hint if provided. Bounding boxes are sometimes used in advanced applications, especially when determining object visibility or working with collision detection between objects. Table 3.2 lists field definitions for X3DBoundedObject.

Type	accessType	Name	Default	Range	Profile
SFVec3f	initializeOnly	bboxCenter	0 0 0	$(-\infty, \infty)$	Interchange
SFVec3f	initializeOnly	bboxSize	−1 −1 −1	$[0, \infty)$ or −1 −1 −1	Interchange

Table 3.2. Field Definitions for X3DBoundedObject Type

2.5.2.1. bboxSize

Bounding-box size (bboxSize) is usually automatically calculated, but can be specified in a scene as an optimization or constraint. The default value for bboxSize="−1 −1 −1", an intentionally impossible size. This special default value serves as a flag indicating that no bounding-box value has been computed for the contained geometry.

2.5.2.2. bboxCenter

Bounding box center (bboxCenter) is the position offset from origin of local coordinate system for the provided bounding box. This is helpful for off-centered geometry that might benefit from a similarly off-centered bounding box approximation.

2.5.2.3. Hints and warnings

Bounding boxes are not drawn and have no predefined visual representation.

Note that bounding box values are hints only. Some viewers or tools may choose to recalculate or ignore them.

2.5.3. X3DGroupingNode type

The X3DGroupingNode type implements the X3DChildNode and X3DBoundedObject interfaces. All nodes of type X3DGroupingNode can include children nodes, Metadata nodes and bounding-box information.

Type	accessType	Name	Default	Range	Profile
MFNode	inputOutput	children	[]	[X3DChildNode]	Interchange
MFNode	inputOnly	addChildren	[]	[X3DChildNode]	Interactive
MFNode	inputOnly	removeChildren	[]	[X3DChildNode]	Interactive
SFVec3f	initializeOnly	bboxCenter	0 0 0	$(-\infty, \infty)$	Interchange
SFVec3f	initializeOnly	bboxSize	−1 −1 −1	$[0, \infty)$ or −1 −1 −1	Interchange
SFNode	inputOutput	metadata	NULL	[X3DMetadataObject]	Core

Table 3.3. Field Definitions for X3DGroupingNode Type

2.5.3.1. *children*

The children field is the collection of all child nodes under a grouping node. Usually the parent-child relationship is implicit in the X3D encoding: child XML tags (tags within other tags) correspond to children X3D nodes. In the Classic VRML encoding, the field name children and square brackets [] are wrapped around this array of nodes. Usually the order of children does not matter unless a DEF and USE relationship exists.

All X3DGroupingNodes use children as the name of the contained child nodes. This consistency improvement changed some previous names defined under VRML97, specifically level for Switch children and range for LOD children.

2.5.3.2. *addChildren, removeChildren*

One of the best things about X3D is that it is flexible—an author can change nearly any part of the scene graph at run-time. The addChildren and removeChildren fields are used to ROUTE node changes to a grouping node's children. Advanced scripting techniques permit the addition or removal of grouping-node children.

Further table occurrences of addChildren and removeChildren are omitted in this book when children is shown as one of the contained fields.

2.5.3.3. *Hints and warnings*

Note that two VRML97 nodes used different names for the children field: Switch used choice and LOD used level. All X3D grouping nodes consistently use children as the field name.

2.5.4. X3DInfoNode type

The X3DInfoNode type allows any supporting node to contain Metadata nodes.

Type	accessType	Name	Default	Range	Profile
SFNode	inputOutput	metadata	NULL	[X3DMetadataObject]	Core

Table 3.4. Field Definitions for X3DInfoNode Type

2.5.4.1. Hints and warnings

Note that while only a single metadata node is allowed as the immediate child, use of a MetadataSet node as that child's Metadata node can collect multiple descriptive metadata nodes together. A metadata node also may be the parent for another metadata node.

2.5.5. X3DUrlObject abstract interface

The X3DUrlObject abstract interface is implemented by all nodes that include a url field for addressing data on the web. This includes the AudioClip, ImageTexture, and Inline nodes.

All url fields may include multiple addresses, each listed as a separate string value. Note that this is different from HTML, which only allows one address per field. Each address is attempted in order until a successful retrieval is achieved (or else no successful retrievals occurred).

The Uniform Resource Name (URN) concept is a superset of the URL concept. A URN allows a special resolution mechanism to be invoked to locate a resource, allowing a resource to be located on the local machine or locatable through a special address to be located using the URN along with platform-specific identifiers.

URNs are used by Universal Media for easy access to the media installed on the local computer or available online. More information on Universal Media including access and a downloaded version is available on the book's web site.

Type	accessType	Name	Default	Range	Profile
MFString	inputOutput	url	[]	[URN]	Interchange or Interactive
Interchange profile supports file://protocol and relative URLs. Interactive profile supports file://and http://protocols, relative URLs and URNs.					

Table 3.5. Field Definitions for X3DUrlObject

3. Node descriptions

3.1. Group and StaticGroup nodes

Various objects of the world can be collected together in the scene graph with the Group node. The children of this node are other root-level nodes. The Group node is used to collect related objects into a single parent in the scene graph hierarchy.

The Group and StaticGroup nodes are in the Interchange profile. These nodes both have the fields defined in Table 3.6. Node syntax for Group and Static Group are shown in Table 3.7.

Example scenes Group.x3d and StaticGroup.x3d in Figure 3.5 provide simple examples of how to use Group and StaticGroup, superimposing a Box and a Sphere.

Type	accessType	Name	Default	Range	Profile
MFNode	inputOutput	children	[]	[X3DChildNode]	Interchange
SFVec3f	initializeOnly	bboxCenter	0 0 0	(−∞,∞)	Interchange
SFVec3f	initializeOnly	bboxSize	−1 −1 −1	[0,∞) or −1 −1 −1	Interchange
SFNode	inputOutput	metadata	NULL	[X3DMetadataObject]	Core

Table 3.6. Field Definitions for Group and StaticGroup Nodes

XML Syntax (.x3d)	ClassicVRML Syntax (.x3dv)
```<Group DEF="MyGroupNode" bboxCenter="0 0 0" bboxSize="-1 -1 -1"> <Shape/> </Group>```	```DEF MyGroupNode Group { bboxCenter 0 0 0 bboxSize -1 -1 -1 children [Shape {}] }```

Table 3.7. Node Syntax for Group and StaticGroup

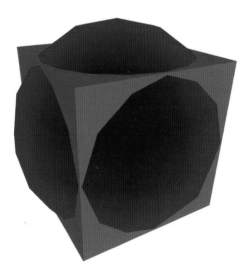

Figure 3.5. Screen snapshot of superimposed Box and Sphere, grouped together.

When there are no animation changes expected for any of the children of a Group node, a StaticGroup node can be used instead. StaticGroup behaves the same as Group when constructing the scene graph. The main difference is that none of the children of a StaticGroup node can change. Neither their state nor structure can be modified once they are incorporated into the scene graph at load time. These children cannot be independently animated, added, removed, or otherwise modified.

Because of this stability, the StaticGroup node allows the X3D browser to perform various optimizations to the internal node structure. These optimizations may make some contained data unavailable for ROUTE modification during the running of the world. Whatever optimizations might be performed depend solely on the browser, which remains responsible for providing consistent output results regardless of how the underlying content might be changed.

3.2. Transform node

The Transform node is a grouping node that defines a coordinate system for its children. Note that the root of a scene graph is located in default world coordinates shown at the beginning of this chapter. Thus each Transform node can translate, rotate, or scale (i.e., resize) each of its children relative to the parent coordinate system. In this manner authors are able to locate and orient objects correctly in relation to each other.

The Transform node is in the Interchange profile and has the fields defined as shown in Table 3.8. Node syntax is shown in Table 3.9.

Transform is a workhorse node that is frequently used in every nontrivial scene. As expected from the discussion on coordinate systems, the primary fields used are translation, orientation, and scale.

Example Transform.x3d in Figure 3.6 demonstrates use of Transform nodes for simple translations and rotations of primitive geometric shapes.

Type	accessType	Name	Default	Range	Profile
SFVec3f	inputOutput	translation	0 0 0	$(-\infty,\infty)$	Interchange
SFRotation	inputOutput	rotation	0 0 1 0	$[-1,1]$ $(-\infty,\infty)$	Interchange
SFVec3f	inputOutput	center	0 0 0	$(-\infty,\infty)$	Interchange
SFVec3f	inputOutput	scale	1 1 1	$(-\infty,\infty)$	Interchange
SFRotation	inputOutput	scaleOrientation	0 0 1 0	$[-1,1]$ $(-\infty,\infty)$	Interchange
MFNode	inputOutput	children	[]	[X3DChildNode]	Interchange
SFVec3f	initializeOnly	bboxCenter	0 0 0	$(-\infty,\infty)$	Interchange
SFVec3f	initializeOnly	bboxSize	$-1-1-1$	$[0,\infty)$ or $-1-1-1$	Interchange
SFNode	inputOutput	metadata	NULL	[X3DMetadataObject]	Core

Table 3.8. Field Definitions for Transform Node

XML Syntax (.x3d)	ClassicVRML Syntax (.x3dv)
| ```
<Transform DEF="MyTransformNode"
    translation="0 0 0"
    rotation="0 0 1 0"
    center="0 0 0"
    scale="1 1 1"
    scaleOrientation="0 0 1 0"
    bboxCenter="0 0 0"
    bboxSize="-1 -1 -1">
    <Group/>
</Transform>
``` | ```
DEF MyTransformNode Transform {
    translation 0 0 0
    rotation 0 0 1 0
    center 0 0 0
    scale 1 1 1
    scaleOrientation 0 0 1 0
    bboxCenter 0 0 0
    bboxSize -1 -1 -1
    children [Group {}]
}
``` |

Table 3.9. Node Syntax for Transform

3.2.1. translation

The translation field provides the position (x, y, z, typically in meters) of children relative to the origin of the local coordinate system, which is the origin of the coordinate system defined by the parent of this Transform node. The top-most coordinate system (defined at the root of the scene graph) is arbitrarily set to position (0 0 0).

3.2.2. rotation

The rotation field provides the orientation (x-, y-, z-axis, and then angle in radians) of children relative to local coordinate system. The top-most coordinate system (defined at the root of the scene graph) is arbitrarily defined as a right-hand rule, y-axis-up system. The example Transform nodes in Figure 3.6 rotate child geometry about various axes to make the scene more interesting. Looking at one of the example transformations, `rotation="1 0 0 -0.707"` rotates the Cone by −0.707 radians (−45°) about the x-axis.

3.2.3. center

The center field provides a position offset from origin of local coordinate system, applied prior to rotation or scaling operations.

3.2.4. scale

The scale field provides a nonuniform x-y-z rescaling of the child coordinate system, adjusted by center and scaleOrientation. This is a good way to convert child geometry size to match the scaling in the rest of the scene (typically in meters).

3.2.5. scaleOrientation

The scaleOrientation field provides a preliminary temporary rotation of the coordinate system prior to scaling. This feature allows nonuniform scaling of children around arbitrary orientation axes.

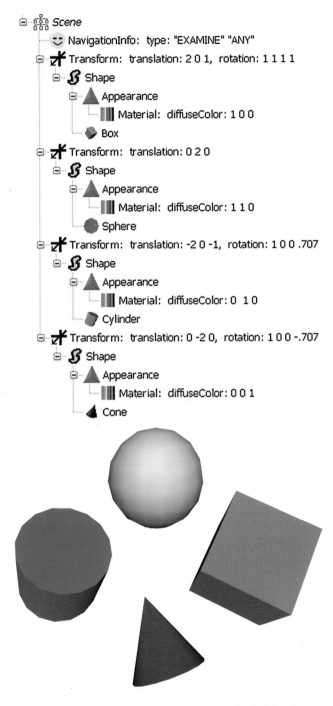

- Scene
  - NavigationInfo: type: "EXAMINE" "ANY"
  - Transform: translation: 2 0 1, rotation: 1 1 1 1
    - Shape
      - Appearance
        - Material: diffuseColor: 1 0 0
      - Box
  - Transform: translation: 0 2 0
    - Shape
      - Appearance
        - Material: diffuseColor: 1 1 0
      - Sphere
  - Transform: translation: -2 0 -1, rotation: 1 0 0 .707
    - Shape
      - Appearance
        - Material: diffuseColor: 0 1 0
      - Cylinder
  - Transform: translation: 0 -2 0, rotation: 1 0 0 -.707
    - Shape
      - Appearance
        - Material: diffuseColor: 0 0 1
      - Cone

Figure 3.6. Transform nodes are used to translate, rotate, and scale Shape nodes. Each Transform creates a new local coordinate system for children nodes.

3.2.6. Order of translation, rotation, scaling, and center operations

The ordering of various Transform operations is crucial and is applied consistently in order to prevent ambiguity. For example, rotating an object about its center and then translating the spun object by the translation distance is quite different than translating the center off by certain distance, and then rotating about that long-radius distance from the origin. These contrasting results are illustrated in Figure 3.7.

Transformation operations in X3D are much more expressive than the simple example in Figure 3.7. The default operations make no change, being equivalent to identity operations if not overridden by new field values. When computing a Transform, the following order is performed when converting an initial point, P, to a new point, P'.

1. Reverse center offset to set up for properly centered scaling and orientation operations

2. Reverse scaleOrientation, then scale operation, then forward scaleOrientation to regain the orientation of the initial coordinate frame

3. Rotate to final direction of new coordinate frame, then forward center offset to regain initial origin

4. Translate to final location of new coordinate frame

Figure 3.8 provides a strict definition from the X3D Specification that again describes the order of these operations, applied to each point affected by a parent Transform node.

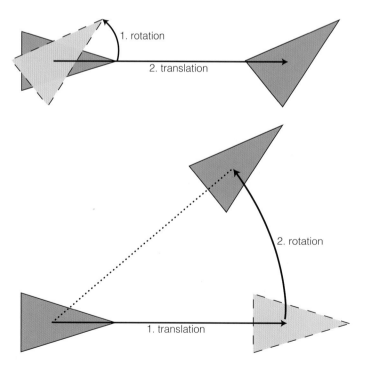

Figure 3.7. Order of operations is significant for translation and rotation.

Note that matrix operations are performed right to left, successively modifying point P until it is transformed into point P'.

Given a 3-dimensional point, P, and Transform node, P is transformed into P' in its parent's coordinate system by a series of intermediate transformations. In matrix transformation notation, in which C (center), SR (scaleOrientation), T (translation), R (rotation), and S (scale) are the equivalent transformation matrices,

$$P' = T \cdot C \cdot R \cdot SR \cdot S \cdot -SR \cdot -C \cdot P$$

The following Transform node:

```
Transform {
    center C
    rotation R
    scale S
    scaleOrientation SR
    translation T
    children [...]
}
```

is equivalent to the nested sequence of:

```
Transform {
    translation T
    children Transform {
        translation C
        children Transform {
            rotation R
            children Transform {
                rotation SR
                children Transform {
                    scale S
                    children Transform {
                        rotation -SR
                        children Transform {
                            translation -C
                            children [...]
                        }
                    }
                }
            }
        }
    }
}
```

Figure 3.8. X3D Specification excerpt that defines the order of sequential operations making up a Transform.

Note that linear, nonuniform scaling of an object is possible through application of the scaleOrientation field. Objects are first rotated into a scaleOrientation coordinate system, then scaled, and then finally moved back into the Transform coordinate frame.

It is helpful to know that, although these operations seem quite complex, they are carefully defined to provide extremely fast performance when implemented by X3D graphics software and hardware.

3.2.7. Hints and warnings

The order of operation is first scaleOrientation and scale, then center and rotation, then translation.

Arbitrary rotations can be decomposed into individual rotations about the local (x, y, z) axes. Similarly, multiple parent-child rotations without corresponding translations, scaling or offsets can be composed into a single rotation.

It may be easier conceptually to split multiple operations within a single Transform into individual transform nodes. A simple set of 3D arrows for the x y z axes can be drawn at each stage to show the intermediate results. Two example code snippets follow in Table 3.10.

3.3. Inline node

Inline is an X3DGroupingNode that can bring in nodes from another X3D scene by loading it. The external scene being inlined is retrieved via the first successful address in a list of addresses provided in the uniform resource locator (url) field.

The Inline node inserts the contents of the specified file into the scene graph. It allows more complex worlds to be built from smaller, simpler components. The url field specifies the world to load. The Inline node must reference a valid X3D file that does not exceed the profile, component, and level restrictions specified in the parent X3D scene. For example, an X3D file that declares itself to be Immersive can load an X3D file that declares itself to be Interchange (a lower profile), but not the other way around.

```
<Transform scale= '2 2 2'>
  <Inline DEF ='CoordinateAxes'
    url='"CoordinateAxes.x3d"          ·
"http://www.web3d.org/x3d/content/examples/Basic/course/
                    CoordinateAxes.x3d"'
<Transform position = "1 1 1" rotation = "0 0 1 0.78" scale ='2 2 2'>
  <Inline DEF= 'CoordinateAxesNSEW'
    url='"CoordinateAxesNSEW.x3d"
       "http://www.web3d.org/x3d/content/examples/Basic/course/
                    CoordinateAxesNSEW.x3d"
  '/>
</Transform>
```

Table 3.10. Nesting Transform Operations

Although Inline contains another scene subgraph, it is somewhat different from the grouping nodes, because the author of the parent scene cannot directly provide or remove children nodes of an Inline node. Thus Inline does not have addChildren or removeChildren fields, and does not implement the X3D Grouping Node type.

The Inline node is in the Interactive and Immersive Profiles. The Immersive Profile provides full support for the load field, though it may be optionally supported under the Interactive Profile as well. The node has the fields defined in Table 3.11. Node syntax is shown in Table 3.12.

Example scene Inline.x3d in Figure 3.9 provides a simple example of how an Inline node can load the contents of an entirely different scene (the Monterey Bay Aquarium Kelp Forest model) into a new scene.

3.3.1. Uniform resource locator (url) field

The X3D url field is more powerful than the HTML hypertext reference (href) field because more than one address can be specified where the target content is available.

Type	accessType	Name	Default	Range	Profile
SFBool	inputOutput	load	true		Immersive
MFString	inputOutput	url	NULL		Interactive
SFVec3f	initializeOnly	bboxCenter	0 0 0	$(-\infty, \infty)$	Interchange
SFVec3f	initializeOnly	bboxSize	−1 −1 −1	$(0, \infty)$ or −1 −1 −1	Interchange
SFNode	inputOutput	metadata	NULL	[X3DMetadataObject]	Core

Table 3.11. Field Definitions for Inline Node

XML Syntax (.x3d)	ClassicVRML Syntax (.x3dv)

```<Inline DEF="MyInlineNode"```
 ```url='"HelloWorld.x3d"```
 ``` "http://www.web3d.org/x3d/```
 ```   content/examples/Basic/```
 ```   HelloWorld.x3d"'```
 ```load="true"```
 ```bboxCenter="0 0 0"```
 ```bboxSize ="-1 -1 -1"/>```
	```DEF MyInlineNode Inline {```
	 ``` url ["HelloWorld.x3d"```
	 ``` "http://www.web3d.org/x3d/```
	 ``` content/examples/Basic/```
	 ``` HelloWorld.x3d"]```
	 ``` load TRUE```
	 ``` bboxCenter 0 0 0```
	 ``` bboxSize -1 -1 -1```
	 ```}```

Table 3.12. Node Syntax for Inline

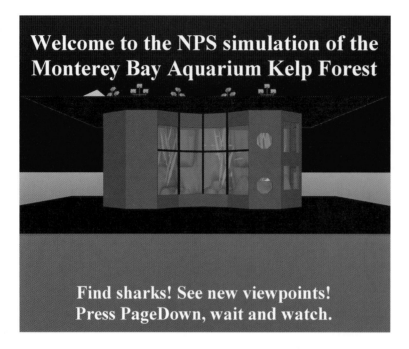

Figure 3.9. An Inline node can load an entirely separate scene into the current scene, adding new geometry to prior geometry.

This means that both relative and absolute addresses can be referenced by the author, providing greater reliability for retrieval of the desired content.

The url field is of type MFString. Each element refers to the address of an X3D file. The browser incorporates the content of one of the url-addressed scenes into the scene graph. Normally the browser tries each address in the order listed in the url field; however, initial values in that order may be skipped by the browser because of cache or network considerations.

The initial url value is that of the X3D file containing the Inline node. Typical usages of multiple entries in the url field are to support multiple copies of the desired world. A relative address may be resolved either locally on the user's disk or locally on a server, depending on where the parent scene is retrieved from. The three-part example in Table 3.13 refers to the local copy of the file, the primary web-based copy, and the secondary web-copy.

Note that MFString fields can have multiple values, so be sure to separate each string in the MFString array by quotation marks. This is tricky when using the XML encoding, because quotation marks might also be used to delimit the beginning and end of the url attribute. XML encoding for the quotation character (") is " (an XML character entity). Thus two examples are provided for the .x3d encoding; all three examples are equivalent.

3.3.2. load

The loading of the inlined content is controlled with the load field. The default value `load="true"` indicates that the browser is to load the content as soon as the url is

Encoding	Equivalent url Syntax Examples for Inline

.x3d	`url='"someScene.x3d"`
	`"http://www.site1.org/someScene.x3d"`
	`"http://www.site2.org/someScene.x3dv"'`

.x3d	`url=" &quot;someScene.x3d&quot;`
	`&quot;http://www.site1.org/someScene.x3d&quot;`
	`&quot;http://www.site2.org/someScene.x3dv&quot;"`

.x3dv	`url ["someScene.x3d"`
	`"http://www.site1.org/someScene.x3d"`
	`"http://www.site2.org/someScene.x3dv"]`

Table 3.13. Comparative Syntax for Example urls

resolved and the file parsed. If instead the value is `load="false"`, then the url is not resolved and the file is not parsed. Resetting this value from false to true initiates the functionality of Inline url parsing and processing.

3.3.3. Hints and warnings

Values can only be ROUTEd into (or out of) an Inline scene when IMPORT and EXPORT links are defined on each side. See Chapter 7, Event Animation and Interpolation for further details on IMPORT and EXPORT mechanisms.

Another advanced technique for routing events into predefined content is to use a prototype via ExternProtoDeclare and ProtoInstance definitions. This approach is covered in Chapter 14, Creating Prototype Nodes.

3.4. LOD node

LOD stands for Level Of Detail. The LOD node permits a single model to have multiple representations that include high-resolution detail (when seen up close) and adequate lower-resolution detail (when seen from a distance). LOD provides an important capability for making overall performance scalable when many scenes are composed together.

The LOD node is in the Immersive profile. The Immersive profile provides full support for the load field. The node has the fields defined in Table 3.14. Node syntax is shown in Table 3.15.

Example LOD.x3d in Figure 3.10 shows how two different forms of geometry can be used as LOD range from the viewer to the origin varies.

LOD measures current camera-to-object distance to switch among contained child levels. LOD range values go from near to far (as child geometry gets simpler for better

Type	accessType	Name	Default	Range	Profile
SFVec3f	initializeOnly	center	0 0 0	$(-\infty, \infty)$	Immersive
MFFloat	initializeOnly	range	[]	$(-\infty, \infty)$	Immersive
SFBool	initializeOnly	forceTransitions	false		Immersive (version 3.1)
SFInt32	outputOnly	level_changed		$[0, \infty)$	Immersive (version 3.1)
MFNode	inputOutput	children	[]	[X3DChildNode]	Interchange
SFVec3f	initializeOnly	bboxCenter	0 0 0	$(-\infty, \infty)$	Interchange
SFVec3f	initializeOnly	bboxSize	−1 −1 −1	$[0, \infty)$ or −1 −1 −1	Interchange
SFNode	inputOutput	metadata	NULL	[X3DMetadataObject]	Core

Table 3.14. Field Definitions for LOD Node

XML Syntax (.x3d)	ClassicVRML Syntax (.x3dv)

```<LOD DEF="MyLODNode"```
 ``` center="0 0 0"```
 ``` range="8 16"```
 ``` forceTransitions="false"```
 ``` bboxCenter="0 0 0"```
 ``` bboxSize="−1 −1 −1">```
 ``` <Group/>```
 ``` <Group/>```
 ``` <WorldInfo info="nonrendering```
 ``` node"/>```
 ```</LOD>```
	```DEF MyLODNode LOD {```
	 ``` center 0 0 0```
	 ``` range [8 16]```
	 ``` forceTransitions FALSE```
	 ``` bboxCenter 0 0 0```
	 ``` bboxSize −1 −1 −1```
	 ``` children [```
	 ``` Group {}```
	 ``` Group {}```
	 ``` WorldInfo {info```
	 ``` "nonrendering node"}```
	 ```]```
	 ```}```

Table 3.15. Node Syntax for LOD

overall rendering performance). Thus the highest-resolution version of a model will be the first child, and subsequent children will have decreasing resolution. For *n* range values, an LOD node must contain *n+1* children levels.

Note that only the currently selected child level is rendered, but meanwhile all levels continue to send and receive events. In this way intermediate models can stay synchronized with the current state of the scene. So, for example, if a virtual tree with multiple levels of detail is being animated to fall in a virtual forest, the LOD node con-

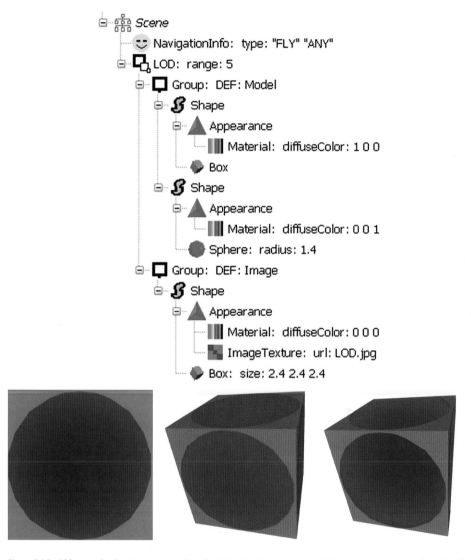

Figure 3.10. LOD example showing scene graph, substitution texture image, substitution images covering a box when the viewpoint is farther away, and high-fidelity geometry when the viewpoint is close to LOD center.

tinues to send and receive animating events to all of its children, regardless of whether a viewer is nearby to see it or which level is selected for display.

3.4.1. center

The center field is the position offset from origin of local coordinate system from which LOD computations are calculated.

3.4.2. forceTransitions

Ordinarily browsers are allowed to optimize when LOD transitions occur, treating the range array as a hint. If `forceTransitions="true"` then child-node transitions are required to occur at the viewer-to-LOD range values specified. This can be helpful for animating special effects and for testing transition ranges. This field is new to X3D 3.1.

3.4.3. level_changed

Browsers report the activation of each level (starting with child 0) by sending an outputOnly SFInt32 event named level_changed. This event can be helpful when synchronizing different animations. This field is new to X3D 3.1.

3.4.4. range

The range array provides camera-to-object distance transitions for each child level, in which range values are provided in order from near to far. Thus, the selected child of the LOD depends on how far the current camera position is from the center of the LOD. This relationship is illustrated in Figure 3.11 and then explained in more detail.

The range array provides camera-to-object distance transitions for each child level, in which range values are provided in order from near to far. The ranges must be ordered from closest (smallest value) to furthest (largest value). The provided ranges are just hints to the browser, unless `forceTransitions="true"` is set.

There must be one fewer range value than there are children of the LOD node. If there are insufficient ranges, then the extra children are ignored. If there are too many range values, then the last child level is repeated as many times as needed. If a child node is empty, then the browser is allowed to automatically choose a level (child node) that maintains a constant display rate.

If there are n ranges $(r_0, r_1, r_2, ..., r_{n-1})$ ordered so that $r_{i-1} \leq r_i$, then the ranges partition the distance from the center $(0, +\infty)$ as follows: $(0, r_0), [r_0, r_1), ..., [r_{n-1}, +\infty)$. If the children nodes are labeled L_i for $0 \leq i \leq n-1$, and d is the distance from the local

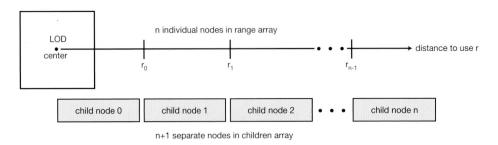

Figure 3.11. LOD range values determine the camera-to-object distances where corresponding selection of child-node transitions occur.

center of the LOD node to the current viewpoint, then the displayed LOD level is computed as follows:

$$L_{displayed} = L_0, \text{ if } d < r_0$$

$$L_{displayed} = L_i, \text{ if } r_{i-1} \leq d < r_i, \text{ for } 1 < i < n-1$$

$$L_{displayed} = L_{n-1}, \text{ if } d \geq r_{n-1}$$

Each time a different node is activated, a level_changed event can be ROUTEd to another part of the scene if desired. When `force_transitions="true"` then this displayed-child transition always occurs at the exact camera-to-object distance specified in the range array. Events and ROUTE operations are described in Chapter 7, Event Animation and Interpolation.

3.4.5. Hints and warnings

For n range values, an LOD node must have $n+1$ child nodes. Each range value is the recommended transition distance between one version of the model and the next. Because each child node can itself be a grouping node, each child can be of arbitrary complexity.

If the geometry is intended to disappear once it is outside a certain range, add a `<WorldInfo info='null node'/>` as a nonrendering final child. This is an excellent authoring practice for improving performance in large scenes.

Nodes contained inside an LOD node are now called 'children' fields in X3D, rather than 'level' fields as in VRML97, in order to maintain consistent naming of children among all GroupingNodeType nodes.

Browsers are not required to switch precisely at the LOD range values, because the range values are hints that may be further optimized depending on current frame rate. In fact, some browsers might always display the highest-fidelity model if the frame rate is sufficiently high. If precise control is needed for selecting LOD children, perhaps even as a simple animation, then employ a combination of Switch and ProximitySensor (or IntegerSequencer) nodes instead.

Events are still ROUTEd into (and out of) all animation-based child nodes, regardless of which LOD children level might be active at a given time.

The behavior of the level-changed field is not well-defined when on LOD node has multiple DEF/USE copies, because each different LOD is likely to be at a different range from the viewer (and thus at a different level). Apply DEF/USE to children instead.

3.5. Switch node

Switch is a Grouping node that only renders one (or zero) child at a time. Like the other X3DGroupingNodes, Switch can contain zero or more X3DChildNodes as children.

The Switch node is in the Immersive profile and has the fields defined in Table 3.16. Node syntax is shown in Table 3.17.

Type	accessType	Name	Default	Range	Profile
SFInt32	inputOutput	whichChoice	−1	[−1,∞)	Immersive
MFNode	inputOutput	children	[]	[X3DChildNode]	Interchange
SFVec3f	initializeOnly	bboxCenter	0 0 0	(− ∞,∞)	Interchange
SFVec3f	initializeOnly	bboxSize	−1 −1 −1	[0,∞) or −1 −1 −1	Interchange
SFNode	inputOutput	metadata	NULL	[X3DMetadataObject]	Core

Table 3.16. Field Definitions for Switch Node

XML Syntax (.x3d)	ClassicVRML Syntax (.x3dv)

<pre><Switch DEF="MySwitchNode"
   whichChoice="−1"
   bboxCenter="0 0 0"
   bboxSize="−1 −1 −1">
   <Group/>
    <Group/>
   <Group/>
</Switch></pre>
	<pre>DEF MySwitchNode Switch {
	   whichChoice −1
	   bboxCenter 0 0 0
	   bboxSize −1 −1 −1
	   children [
	     Group { }
	     Group { }
	     Group { }
	   ]
	}</pre>

Table 3.17. Node Syntax for Switch

The Switch node allows the scene author to switch one at a time among various sets of children nodes. Switch is used for animating geometries, providing customized level of detail, and maintaining scene optimization at run time. Unlike the LOD node, the choice of which child node to use is directly controlled by the author and the user through the initial setting (and subsequent animation events) that change whichChoice. Either one or no child node is displayed by the Switch at any given moment.

Similar to the LOD node, note that all levels of a Switch node continue to send and receive events even though only the currently selected child is rendered. In this way, all scene subgraph models can stay synchronized with the current state of the overall world.

Figure 3.12 shows an example Switch node holding four different geometric shapes as children. Use X3D-Edit to change the value of whichChoice and then view a different child.

3.5.1. whichChoice

The whichChoice field is the index of active child choice, counting from 0 for the zeroth child. The default value whichChoice="−1" means no selection from the children, and thus no rendering, and whichChoice="0" means to select the initial child.

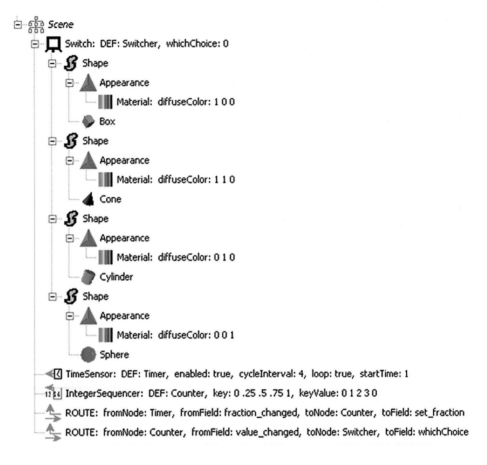

Figure 3.12. Switch node example holding four different geometric shapes as children. Only one child of the Switch is rendered at a time, depending on the value of the whichChoice field.

(*Continued*)

3.5.2. Hints and warnings

The default value for `whichChoice="-1"`, which means none of the children are rendered. Be sure to change whichChoice when first authoring a new scene or else the Switch effectively hides all children.

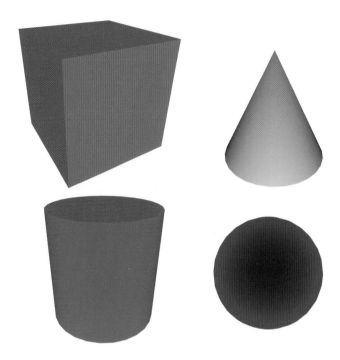

Figure 3.12. (Cont'd.)

The value of whichChoice cannot exceed the number of children nodes available. Because `whichChoice="0"` is the zeroth node in the children array, whichChoice ≥ (number of children available) causes a run-time error.

Contained nodes are now called 'children' fields in X3D, rather than 'choice' fields as in VRML97, to maintain consistent naming among all GroupingNodeType nodes.

Because each child node can itself be a grouping node, each switchable child can be of arbitrary complexity.

Authors can temporarily hide test geometry under an unselected child of a Switch. This is accomplished by wrapping a parent `<Switch whichChoice="-1"></Switch>` around children nodes can hide them from rendering. This is a good alternative to "commenting out" nodes in the source document, because they are easily restored for testing. It is also a good practice to keep comments and test geometry in scenes even after testing is complete, so that they might help with further debugging at a future date, if necessary. If the test geometry is particularly large or might otherwise use lots of memory by loading a big ImageTexture file, however, then commenting may be preferable for performance reasons.

Events are still ROUTEd into (and out of) all animation-based child nodes, regardless of which children choice is active.

4. Summary

4.1. Key ideas

This chapter describes how Grouping nodes are used to collect and select various other nodes. These principles are fundamental to the well-behaved design of an effective scene graph.

4.2. Related nodes and concepts

The Billboard and Collision nodes are simply viewpoint-aware grouping nodes. Billboard keeps child geometry aligned to face the current user viewpoint, making affected objects easier to see. The Collision node detects whether the near end of the view frustrum has intersected with child geometry, issuing an output event if true. Billboard and Collision are covered in Chapter 4, Viewing and Navigation.

Uniform resource locator (url) addresses are used whenever external-resource files or addresses are needed. Anchor is another X3DGroupingNode that has special semantics for linking shapes to other Viewpoint nodes, websites and other X3D scenes. The Anchor node includes additional uses for url to indicate local viewpoint. Anchor is presented in Chapter 4, Viewing and Navigation.

4.3. Next chapter

Chapter 4 introduces viewing and navigation capabilities for inspecting and exploring an X3D scene.

Viewing and Navigation

But the eyes, though they are no sailors, will never be satisfied with any model, however fashionable, which does not answer all the requisitions of art.
—Henry David Thoreau, 1849

1. What this chapter covers

This chapter looks at the nodes that allow users to view, explore, and navigate Extensible 3D (X3D) worlds: Viewpoint, NavigationInfo, Anchor, Billboard, and Collision.

This chapter assumes that you understand the X3D coordinate system, understand the basic structure of an X3D scene graph, and can group nodes together.

2. Concepts

It is sometimes helpful to think of X3D scenes as being fixed in 3D space: each object is positioned and oriented exactly where it is placed by the author. Viewing an X3D scene is then a matter of moving the user viewpoint throughout and around this geometry. Effective and intuitive movement is known as *user navigation* through the scene.

The most exciting benefits of 3D graphics often come from looking at scenes from various interesting viewpoints, navigating effectively from place to place, and then interacting with various scene components to trigger interesting behaviors. The X3D nodes that support these viewing and navigation behaviors are easily authored, provide rich capabilities, and are an integral part of every scene.

2.1. Purpose and common functionality

Viewing and navigation nodes are essential to providing an effective 3D experience for users. These nodes provide the following capabilities:

- Viewing a scene from different vantage points that reveal aspects of interest, document key locations, or help to tell a story.

- Navigating changes in the user's viewpoint effectively by moving from place to place in an intuitive manner.

- Making geometric objects selectable so that users can transport to another viewpoint, launch into another scene, or receive other web content.

- Taking advantage of viewpoint location for interactive techniques such as user-facing billboard rotations and terrain following.

Detailed concepts and node-type descriptions are provided next, followed by detailed descriptions of each node.

2.2. Viewing model

A scene author typically places several viewpoints in each scene in order to allow easy navigation. Often each item of interest is given a special viewpoint so that it can be seen clearly. Sometimes viewpoints themselved are animated, providing a carefully prepared exploration or an "over the shoulder" view of the action as seen from the perspective of a scene actor.

The first Viewpoint node in an X3D model typically shows all the primary aspects of the scene at a glance. Just like the initial topic sentence in a story, it provides a first impression and can present the big picture.

Maneuvering in sequence from viewpoint to viewpoint is easily accomplished through the PageUp and PageDown keys. Authors can usually produce a good guided tour around larger scenes through careful definition and ordering of viewpoints. Viewpoint descriptions help make clear the intended purpose of each view, and indicate valuable additional information that provides the viewer with clues about what is being seen.

The Viewpoint List is the browser's collection of all viewpoint descriptions, provided in the order they are defined in a scene. Selecting a description typically takes the user to that viewpoint. A new feature being added to X3D is the addition of ViewpointGroup nodes to collect nested submenus of related viewpoints within the Viewpoint List.

2.3. Navigation model

The browser normally allows users to change the mode by which they navigate, view, and observe the loaded 3D scene. A variety of different modes are possible, each suited to different types of scenes and interactions.

A user might fly through space, walk along the ground, examine an individual object, decide to look at a specific point, or simply be guided automatically by a previously rehearsed animation. Transitions may be smooth changes in viewpoint direction or immediate, that is, a *jump cut*. The user may pass through different geometric objects, or may need to navigate around them in order to pass.

Parsimonious definition of viewpoints and clumsy support for appropriate navigation leads to "lost in space" difficulties, in which the user finds little of interest and misses the action of importance. Authors need to consider what is important in the scene, and then create interesting Viewpoint nodes along with appropriate NavigationInfo type(s). Enabling proper navigation through the scene can greatly assist users who are new to an X3D world, keeping their attention on the most interesting objects and relevant behaviors.

2.4. Collision detection and terrain following

Under certain conditions, X3D supports camera-to-object collision detection. When the currently bound NavigationInfo type is set to WALK, FLY, or NONE, the viewing camera is blocked from passing through collidable geometry. The user must navigate differently to get around obstacles, not simply walk or fly through them. When authors want to keep track of when collisions occur, perhaps to trigger additional responses, the Collision node can generate events indicating when child geometry has been collided.

A special form of collision detection occurs when walking above geometry simulating a floor or terrain. This mode is triggered when the currently bound NavigationInfo node has type WALK selected. When properly oriented, a simple box-shaped *avatar* represents the user's virtual body and places the viewpoint at an appropriate distance above the ground. Allowances are also provided regarding how high an avatar can step above obstacles placed in the path. In this manner, gentle hills and steppable stairs can be traversed while other walls and barriers remain insurmountable. Terrain-following techniques are an excellent way to strongly guide user navigation in a virtual world.

2.5. Abstract node types

2.5.1. X3DBindableNode type

Bindable nodes have special functionality: only one node of each type (Viewpoint, Background, and so on) can be active at a time. The X3DBindableNode type implements the X3DChildNode interface, meaning that such nodes can appear among grouping node children arrays. X3DBindableNode is the base type for all bindable children nodes, including Background, TextureBackground, Fog, NavigationInfo, and Viewpoint.

Each set of bindable nodes has its own stack that allows only one node of each type to be active at a given time. The operation of a stack is similar to a load of plates at a cafeteria sitting on a spring-loaded tray. Selecting one of the nodes in the stack brings it to the top and binds it, meaning that it is now the active node. The remaining nodes are pushed down by one. Deselecting a node (via a `set_bind="false"` runtime event) takes it off the stack. Changing a node's position on the stack is often referred to as popping (bringing it to the top of the stack) or pushing (sending it back down the stack).

The fact that only one node in a binding stack is active at a time makes sense when one considers the types of nodes that observe this kind of behavior. Only one Viewpoint at a time can be active, because only one view is drawn at a time. Similarly, only a single NavigationInfo node needs to be active at a given time because it is not possible to simultaneously fly and walk (or rotate, or do nothing) all at the same time. Separate binding stacks are provided for each node type, so changing a Viewpoint does not directly affect the current NavigationInfo. When no nodes are present on a binding stack, the default values for the given bindable node are used.

The following figure shows a complicated sequence of binding and unbinding events. It is an example contrived to provide full detail about how such operations can proceed. In general, however, such attention to detail is not necessary: Simply binding the node of interest, when needed, usually gets the job done.

Similar operations can occur for the other bindable nodes (NavigationInfo, Fog, Background, and TextureBackground). This example is intentionally more involved than most viewpoint operations in order to show the possible variations in detail. Events and animation are described in Chapter 7, Event Animation and Interpolation; and Chapter 8, User Interactivity Nodes.

The following outline provides a detailed explanation of the sequence of binding events at times t_0 through t_8, presented in Figure 4.1.

- t_0. The initial loading of the scene has first `<Viewpoint DEF="View1"/>` active and bound to the top of the binding stack. Other viewpoints are off the binding stack. If no viewpoints are provided in the scene, then the default `<Viewpoint position="0 0 10"/>` defined in the X3D Specification is used.

- t_1. When the user selects View2 from the viewpoint list, it receives a `set_bind="true"` event and goes to the top of the binding stack. View2 also issues an `isBound="true"` event, and View1 issues an `isBound="false"` event as it moves down the stack.

- t_2. Similar to the previous transitions in step t_1, View3 receives a `set_bind="true"` event and responds with an `isBound="true"` event, while View2 issues an `isBound="false"` event and pushes View1 further down the stack.

- t_3. View3 receives a `set_bind="false"` event, triggering a corresponding `isBound="false"` event and dropping off the stack completely. Because View2 is the next node on the binding stack, it pops to the top to become the active Viewpoint node. View2 also issues an `isBound="true"` event.

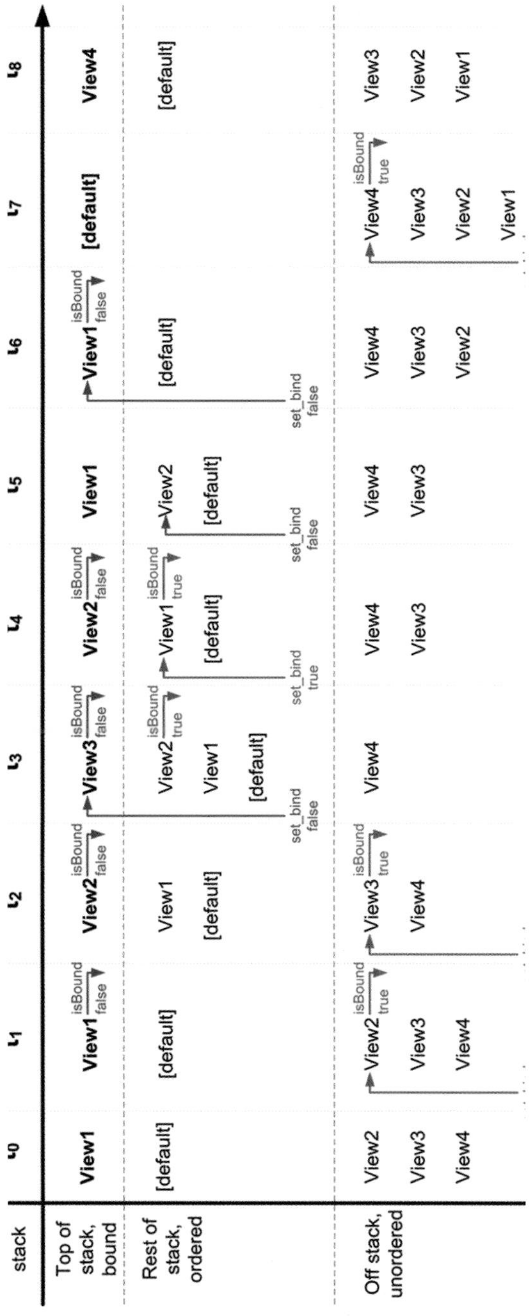

stack	t0	t1	t2	t3	t4	t5	t6	t7	t8
Top of stack, bound	View1	View1 — isBound false	View2 — isBound false	View3 — isBound false	View2 — isBound false	View1	View1 — isBound false	[default]	View4
Rest of stack, ordered	[default]	[default]	View1; [default]	View2 — isBound true; View1; [default]	View1 — isBound true; [default]	View2; [default]	[default]		[default]
Off stack, unordered	View2; View3; View4	View2 — isBound true; View3; View4	View3 — isBound true; View4	View4	View4; View3	View4; View3	View4; View3; View2	View4 — isBound true; View3; View2; View1	View3; View2; View1

set_bind events: false (t3), true (t4), false (t5), false (t6)

Figure 4.1. Binding node operations: set_bind events control whether bindable nodes go to the top of the stack or pop off the stack.

- t_4. The user now selects View1 from the browser's viewpoint list, so View1 receives a `set_bind="true"` event and sends a corresponding `isBound="true"` event. View2 is no longer bound, and is pushed down the binding stack.

- t_5. If View2 receives a `set_bind="false"` event while on the binding stack but unbound, and as a result, it is taken completely off the binding stack.

- t_6. View1 is now removed off the binding stack via a `set_bind="false"` event, leaving no other defined Viewpoint nodes on the stack.

- t_7. With no Viewpoint nodes remaining on the stack to bind, default viewpoint values are used: `<Viewpoint position="0 0 10"/>`. The user then selects the previously unbound View4 from the viewpoint list.

- t_8. View4 remains as the bound viewpoint with no further viewpoints remaining on the stack.

Fields available to all X3DBindableNode types follow in Table 4.1. Events for these fields are sent when a user selects a new Viewpoint node. An author can set new values or read changing values by defining ROUTE connections that move events through the scene. Those topics are covered in Chapter 7, Event Animation and Interpolation.

2.5.1.1. set_bind

Setting set_bind to true makes this node active, and setting set_bind to false makes this node inactive. Thus setting `set_bind="true"` (or false) performs a binding-stack pop (or push) that enables (or disables) the affected node. As with all accessType inputOnly fields, modifying set_bind is accomplished by using a ROUTE to send a value to the target bindable node.

2.5.1.2. bindTime

The bindTime event sends the time at which a node is bound or unbound.

2.5.1.3. isBound

With isBound, an event whose value is true (i.e., a true event) is sent when the node becomes bound, and an event whose value is false (i.e., a false event) is sent when the node becomes unbound (usually because another node has been bound).

Type	accessType	Name	Default	Range	Profile
SFBool	inputOnly	set_bind			Interactive
SFBool	outputOnly	isBound			Interactive
SFTime	outputOnly	bindTime			Interactive
SFNode	inputOutput	metadata	NULL	[X3DMetadataObject]	Core

Table 4.1. Field Definitions for X3DBindableNode

2.5.1.4. Hints and warnings

Binding is tricky. Authors cannot necessarily guarantee the ordering of binding nodes, because they can be bound (and unbound) at run-time through user actions. This means that unbinding a node may have unforeseen results. When constructing change mechanisms for binding nodes, the best strategy is to focus on binding the particular node that is needed. Usually the other binding nodes stay out of the way and the desired goal is accomplished.

3. Node descriptions

The viewing and navigation algorithms are closely related. A good match between Viewpoint nodes and NavigationInfo nodes is necessary to achieve effective viewing by users. Other nodes described in this chapter are also closely dependent on the viewpoints and navigation.

3.1. Viewpoint node

The Viewpoint node is used to define locations and directions for viewing an X3D world. The X3D browser may provide a user interface to the list of Viewpoint nodes in order to ease navigation through (and viewing of) the scene. The Viewpoint node provides viewing controls for position, orientation, and field of view. All of these controls are based in the local coordinate system and are subject to the operations of any Transform parents of the Viewpoint node.

Support for most fields of the Viewpoint node is provided in the Interactive profile. The Immersive profile provides full support for the fieldOfView and description fields, which may be optionally supported under the Interactive profile. The Viewpoint node has the fields defined in Table 4.2. Node syntax is shown in Table 4.3.

The default Viewpoint parameters are designed to provide a satisfactory view of default-size objects at the origin. It is located 10 meters along the $+z$-axis, looking toward the local origin, with the $+y$-axis pointing up and parallel to the view display plane. The default field of view is typically a rectangle, perpendicular to the view direction, with a minimum apex angle of $45°$.

A Viewpoint node's description field is a short string that the browser can use to identify each viewpoint. It is common practice (though not required) for browsers to provide a viewpoint list showing each of these descriptions, allowing easy user navigation to major parts of the scene. The interface works best if each Viewpoint description is a short, clearly worded phrase.

Browsers provide the ability to examine an object by rotating around it, ordinarily using the NavigationInfo EXAMINE mode. The identification of the local rotation center is defined by the field centerOfRotation. This field defines a point in the local coordinate system that is the center of the camera's rotation during EXAMINE mode. This field can be automatically changed when the user is in the NavigationInfo LOOKAT mode and selects geometry of interest.

Type	accessType	Name	Default	Range	Profile
SFVec3f	inputOutput	centerOfRotation	0 0 0	$(-\infty, \infty)$	Interactive
SFString	inputOutput	description	"" (null string)		Immersive
SFFloat	inputOutput	fieldOfView	$\pi/4$	$(0, \pi)$	Immersive
SFBool	inputOutput	jump	true		Interactive
SFRotation	inputOutput	orientation	0 0 1 0	$[-1,1], (-\infty, \infty)$	Interactive
SFVec3f	inputOutput	position	0 0 0	$(-\infty, \infty)$	Interactive
SFBool	inputOnly	set_bind			Interactive
SFBool	outputOnly	isBound			Interactive
SFTime	outputOnly	bindTime			Interactive
SFNode	inputOutput	metadata	NULL	[X3DMetadataObject]	Core

Table 4.2. Field Definitions for Viewpoint Node

Viewpoints can be animated to provide guided tours through a scene. This is accomplished either by run-time modification of the local position and orientation fields, or else by modifying one or more of the parent Transforms. A discussion of the basic animation process is provided in Chapter 7, Event Animation and Interpolation. Additionally, Chapter 8, User Interactivity Nodes, includes more tips and techniques regarding Viewpoint node animation.

Example scene Viewpoint.x3d in Figure 4.2 loads the Kelp Forest exhibit. Multiple viewpoints are provided in this scene. Many of the Viewpoint nodes are peers of animated geometry, allowing the different animated actors to serve as tour guides to the action as it occurs.

XML Syntax (.x3d)	ClassicVRML Syntax (.x3dv)

`<Viewpoint DEF="MyViewpointNode"`
`    description="hello, world!"`
`    position="0 0 0"`
`    orientation="0 0 1 0"`
`    jump="true"`
`    centerOfRotation="0 0 0"/>`
	`DEF MyViewpointNode Viewpoint {`
	`    description "hello, world!"`
	`    position 0 0 0`
	`    orientation 0 0 1 0`
	`    jump TRUE`
	`    centerOfRotation 0 0 0`
	`}`

Table 4.3. Node Syntax for Viewpoint

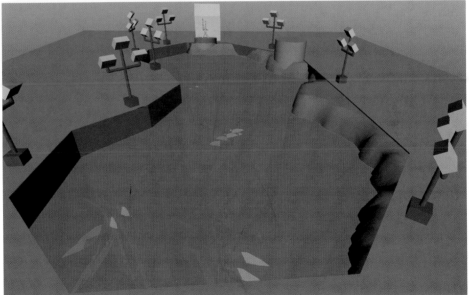

Figure 4.2. A variety of viewpoints are available in the Kelp Forest Exhibit, some of them moving with the tank inhabitants. Locations shown in the figure include the initial view, roof top, Lefty the shark, Nancy the diver, and various animals of interest.

(Continued)

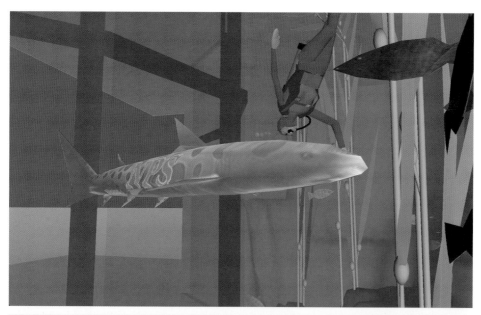

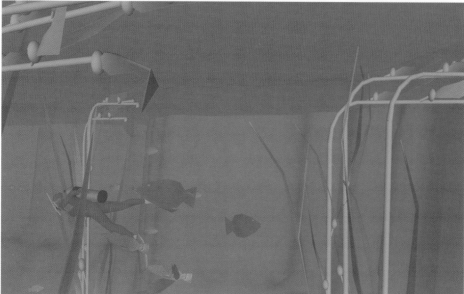

Figure 4.2. (Cont'd.)

3.1.1. description

The description field provides either explanatory text or a navigation hint to be displayed for this Viewpoint node. Descriptions are quite important! Clearly and succinctly describe what each view is showing the user. Viewpoint descriptions are the user's primary way to navigate through big scenes and around unfamiliar objects.

3.1.2. position

The position field describes the initial Viewpoint location (x, y, z in meters) relative to local coordinate system. Upon arriving at this position, the user may navigate farther by using pointer (mouse) or arrow keys to move. Many browsers provide a reset function to restore the initially defined position and orientation after looking around. Default operation of the Home and End Keys on the keyboard shifts to the initial and final Viewpoint nodes, respectively.

3.1.3. orientation

The orientation field describes the viewpoint rotation (three-tuple axis, angle in radians) relative to the default $-z$-axis direction in the local coordinate system. To calculate this properly, first imagine the default Viewpoint looking from `position="0 0 10"` toward the origin, along the direction of the $-z$-axis. Then compute the rotation needed to point the camera's view in the desired direction—that value is the new orientation. Thus the orientation field describes this change as a relative Viewpoint angle, not the absolute rotation angle in the world coordinate system.

3.1.4. fieldOfView

The fieldOfView is the preferred minimum viewing angle as seen from this viewpoint, measured in radians. A small field of view roughly corresponds to a telephoto lens, while a large field of view roughly corresponds to a wide-angle lens. The fieldOfView field defines the shortest of horizontal or vertical height, depending on the current browser aspect ratio.

3.1.5. jump

The jump field controls the change of the user view of the world when this Viewpoint is selected. If `jump="true"` when a new Viewpoint is selected, then the user's view is changed according to the transitionType field of the currently bound NavisationInfo node, moving to the position and orientation specified in the Viewpoint node. The change in the user's view does not cause any collision, proximity, or visibility sensors to activate.

If `jump="false"`, then the user's view does not change. The X3D browser records the offset from current position and orientation, and then converts these values to a corresponding offset from the newly assigned Viewpoint node. The user's view does not move during this reassignment. Subsequent navigation or animation occurs relative to the newly assigned Viewpoint node changes to the user's view or the Viewpoint's position and orientation, or both.

This behavior can be very subtle. A good example of `jump="false"` might be switching viewpoints from a floor to an elevator. Upon entering the elevator, the user or scene might bind a `<Viewpoint DEF="InsideElevatorView" jump="false"/>`. The apparent view to the user does not change, but animating the elevator to shift floors will move this child Viewpoint (and the bound user) along with it.

3.1.6. centerOfRotation

The centerOfRotation point is used by the NavigationInfo node when operating in the EXAMINE mode. The user rotates about this relative location when moving the camera to inspect an object. This location is likely to change if the user first selects LOOKAT mode in the bound NavigationInfo, and then selects different target geometry using the pointing device or keyboard.

3.1.7. Hints and warnings

Modifying the distance between a Viewpoint and an object of interest (by animating Viewpoint position or other Transform nodes) may be the best method for zooming in and out. Interesting effects can also be achieved by animating fieldOfView.

Warning: the fieldOfView value may not be correct for different window sizes and aspect ratios, especially after resizing a window. When using the Interchange profile, this field may be ignored.

Orientation hint: complex rotations and special animations can be accomplished one axis at a time by using parent Transform nodes above the Viewpoint.

There is no such field as depthOfView. Special photographic effects (such as making distant objects out of focus) require special effects that are not directly supported in X3D.

Viewpoint nodes within Inlined scenes are not automatically bound at load time, even if no Viewpoint node appears in the parent scene.

Keyboard navigation defaults use the PageUp and PageDown keys for selecting next and previous viewpoints, respectively. The Home key binds the first viewpoint on the viewpoint list, and the End key binds the last viewpoint on the viewpoint list.

3.2. NavigationInfo node

NavigationInfo indicates how a browser can best support user motion though a 3D scene. This is primarily accomplished through specifying type of navigation. Additional information is defined for visibility distance and the avatar, which is a virtual representation of the user.

The NavigationInfo node is in the Interactive and Immersive profiles. Fields avatarSize, speed, and visibilityLimit are optionally supported in the Interactive profile. NavigationInfo includes the fields defined in Table 4.4. Node syntax is shown in Table 4.5.

An author first decides how to use NavigationInfo by considering the scene it serves and setting the type field. Other fields support a variety of special effects. Field descriptions follow.

3.2.1. type

The type field controls the navigation mode. It is a multivalued string array, meaning that each value must be quoted. The values can be any combination of `"WALK"`,

Type	accessType	Name	Default	Range	Profile
MFString	inputOutput	type	["EXAMINE" "ANY"]	"ANY" "FLY" "EXAMINE" "LOOKAT" "WALK" "NONE" etc.	Interactive only requires support for "ANY" FLY" "EXAMINE" "LOOKAT", otherwise use Immersive
SFFloat	inputOutput	speed	1.0	[0, ∞)	Immersive, under optional Interactive
SFBool	inputOutput	headlight	true		Interactive
MFString	inputOutput	transitionType	["LINEAR"]	["TELEPORT "LINEAR" "ANIMATE"]	Interactive
SFBool	outputOnly	transition Complete			Immersive
MFTime	inputOutput	transition Time	1.0	[0, ∞)	Immersive
SFFloat	inputOutput	visibilityLimit	0.0	[0, ∞)	Immersive, optional under Interactive
MFFloat	inputOutput	avatarSize	[0.25 1.6 0.75]	[0, ∞)	Immersive, optional under Interactive
SFBool	inputOnly	set_bind			Interactive
SFBool	outputOnly	isBound			Interactive
SFTime	outputOnly	bindTime			Interactive
SFNode	inputOutput	metadata	NULL	[X3DMetadataObject]	Core

Table 4.4 Field Definitions for NavigationInfo Node

"FLY","EXAMINE", "LOOKAT", "ANY", and "NONE". Note that the case of each value is important, since only capital letters are used.

Solitary objects that might be rotated or inspected usually have 'EXAMINE" mode set as the default, that is, "EXAMINE" appears as the first value in the array of allowed types. Larger scenes are often better served by "FLY" for free navigation or "WALK" for terrain-following mode.

More than one type value can be provided to allow the user a choice. User selection among different modes of NavigationInfo type is a browser-specific feature. If the author wants to directly control navigation and provide the user with a fixed experience, either a single mode is set or else simply "NONE" is specified.

XML Syntax (.x3d)	Classic VRML Syntax (.x3dv)
```<NavigationInfo DEF="MyNavigationInfoNode" avatarSize="0.25 1.6 0.75" headlight="true" speed="1" type='"EXAMINE" "ANY"' visibilityLimit="0" transitionTime="1" transitionType="LINEAR"/>```	```DEF MyNavigationInfoNode NavigationInfo { avatarSize 0.25 1.6 0.75 headlight true speed 1 type ["EXAMINE" "ANY"] visibilityLimit 0 transitionTime 1 transitionType "Linear" }```

Table 4.5. Node Syntax for NavigationInfo

A summary of various NavigationInfo type modes is provided in Table 4.6.

Additional browser-specific type values may be provided for NavigationInfo (for example, 3D wands or pressure-sensitive haptic devices). If nonstandard type values are used, consider also including some of the previously mentioned standard modes so that the X3D content remains navigable on different systems and in different browsers.

Careful consideration reveals that each navigation mode carefully maps the two degrees of spatial freedom provided by a 2D mouse, namely x–y relative motion, into

NavigationInfo type Value	Description of User-Navigation Modes
"WALK"	Used when exploring a virtual world on the ground. The user's eye level stays above the ground geometry and collision detection prevents the user from falling if underlying geometry is present.
"FLY"	Similar to "WALK", but terrain following and collision detection is ignored. This type of navigation has the fewest constraints.
"EXAMINE"	Used to view individual objects. Scene navigation consists of rotating the user viewpoint about the center of the observed object. The centerOfRotation field of the currently bound Viewpoint node values determines which local point centers the view rotation.
"LOOKAT"	Shifts the current view and related centerOfRotation values to track or zoom toward objects of interest as indicated by the user.
"ANY"	The browser is allowed to provide whichever navigation type seems appropriate for the task at hand, modifying the user interface if necessary.
"NONE"	All navigation interfaces are disabled and hidden. Navigation still remains possible via animation of viewpoint position and orientation or by binding other viewpoints, either via a viewpoint-list selection or using an Anchor node to bind another viewpoint.

Table 4.6 NavigationInfo Types and Modes of User Navigation

precisely constrained set of 3D movements. In this way, the 2D pointing device can change both position and direction for the 3D viewpoint in an intuitive fashion. This approach allows effective 3D-scene navigation even when only 2D interfaces (such as mice or arrow keys) are available.

3.2.2. speed

The speed field determines how quickly a user can navigate through a scene. The default value of 1.0 meter per second is rather slow for many scenes, particularly when flying or walking long distances. Experiment with different speed values to achieve controllable and stimulating mobility. Some browsers provide accelerator keys (such as the Shift key) to apply a speedup factor as a special feature. However, such options are not guaranteed and not defined in the X3D specification.

3.2.3. headlight

The headlight field enables (or disables) a white directional light that always points in the direction the user is looking. Other lights in the scene also contribute, but the headlight tends to dominate because it is always directly aligned with the line of sight.

It is important to note that headlight is not a headlamp as found on a miner helmet. Rather the headlight is a DirectionalLight with intensity that does not fall off with distance from the viewer along the line of sight vector. If a headlamp effect is desired, set `headlight="false"` then create a Spotlight (see Chapter 11) and use a ProximitySensor (see Chapter 12) to keep the position and orientation correct.

3.2.4. transitionType, transitionTime and transitionComplete

The transitionType field determines the type of path followed when transitioning between viewpoints. Allowed choices are `"ANIMATE"`, `"LINEAR"`, and `"TELEPORT"`. Once again, because these are SFString values in an MFString array, each value must be quoted. This field only affects the user's view transition when a viewpoint is bound.

A transitionType value of `"TELEPORT"` causes an immediate change (during the next rendered frame) in camera position. The `"LINEAR"` setting causes a linear interpolation from the current camera position to the new camera position. If transitionType is `"ANIMATE"`, then the browser animates the transition from the current camera position to the new viewpoint's camera position in a browser-specific manner.

A transitionComplete event is sent when a transition completes.

The initial array value of the transitionTime field is the duration of any viewer movement between Viewpoint nodes. Transition is instantaneous if `transitionType = "TELEPORT"`. Browser-unique durations are allowed if `transitionType = "ANIMATE"`.

Be careful when animating to some viewpoints, because the user may be maneuvered through obscuring geometry. Viewpoint transitions through object interiors can be disorienting.

3.2.5. visibilityLimit

The visibilityLimit field allows the author to set the maximum distance expected to the most distant visible object. Geometric objects beyond this range are not rendered. The default value 0.0 means that there are no range limits on visibility.

Objects within the visibility limit are not necessarily guaranteed to be visible, because they might be obscured by closer objects or outside the camera's field of view.

3.2.6. avatarSize

The avatarSize array is a triplet of float values corresponding to (0) collision distance between user and geometry, (1) viewer height above terrain, and (2) tallest height of a step or wall on the terrain that a viewer can WALK over. These measurements are illustrated in Figure 4.3.

The default values for avatarSize are [0.25 1.6 0.5], which provide an eye level of 1.6 meters above the viewpoint, a cylinder radius of 0.25 meters for detecting collisions with scene objects, and allow the user to "step over" objects up to 0.5 meters high when NavigationInfo type is WALK mode.

3.2.7. Hints and warnings

If the headlight is disabled and there are no other light nodes in the scene, everything is black and nothing in the scene is visibly rendered.

A NavigationInfo node with field headlight="true" must be bound for the headlight to be activated.

If scenes are not defined in accordance with the X3D convention that the y-axis is up, then NavigationInfo does not work properly.

It is a good idea to keep the quantity defined by avatarSize.CollisionDistance divided by visibilityLimit less than 10,000 in order to avoid undesirable *aliasing* artifacts (also known as *tearing* of polygons). These terms correspond to the ratio of near-culling distance and far-culling distance of the view frustum. This phenomenon can occur because most floating-point computations on computer-graphics hardware-acceleration

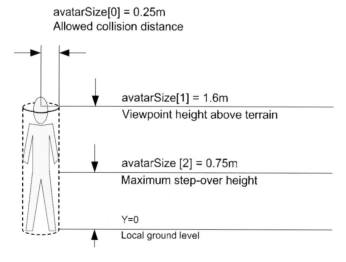

avatarSize[0] = 0.25m
Allowed collision distance

avatarSize[1] = 1.6m
Viewpoint height above terrain

avatarSize [2] = 0.75m
Maximum step-over height

Y=0
Local ground level

Figure 4.3. NavigationInfo avatarSize is a three-element array describing allowed camera-to-object collision distance default, Viewpoint height above ground, and maximum stepover height for colliding geometry when in WALK mode.

cards are performed with single precision (32-bit), rather than double precision (64-bit). Thus ratios higher than 10,000 can cause floating-point roundoff errors. This aliasing of polygons is a symptom that the graphics hardware is unable to consistently distinguish which of two coplanar (or approximately coplanar) polygons is closer.

The first element of the avatarSize field array is not the near culling plane, that is, the closest distance where geometry remains visible. The first element is the distance of a box that is used for determining collision detection, meaning the closest distance that a view can approach a collidable object.

NavigationInfo nodes within Inlined scenes are not automatically bound at load time, even if no NavigationInfo node appears in the parent scene.

Arrow keys can be used for navigation. The usual mappings are the arrow keys to corresponding mouse movement, and the Enter key to make a selection. Actual navigation reactions correspond to the currently bound NavigationInfo type value (such as EXAMINE, WALK, FLY, LOOKAT, and so on).

3.3. Anchor node

Anchor is a Grouping node that can contain most nodes. Clicking anchored geometry either switches to a new Viewpoint or loads content specified by the uniform resource locator (url) field. Loaded content either completely replaces content in the current window or is loaded in a separate window, if so indicated by the parameter field.

The functionality of the Anchor node is therfore similar to the `<a href='someUrl'>` anchor element with hyperlink reference (href) attribute found in the Extensible Hypertext Markup Language (XHTML). This is also the case for HTML. Note that the primary difference between them is that XHTML web pages must be strictly legal Extensible Markup Language (XML).

The Anchor node is in the Interactive profile. Anchor includes the fields defined in Table 4.7. Node syntax is shown in Table 4.8.

Type	accessType	Name	Default	Range	Profile
SFString	inputOutput	description	"" (null string)		Interactive
MFString	inputOutput	url	"" (null string)		Interactive
MFString	inputOutput	parameter	"" (null string)		Interactive
MFNode	inputOutput	children	[ ]	[X3DChildNode]	Interactive
MFNode	inputOnly	addChildren	[ ]	[X3DChildNode]	Interactive
MFNode	inputOnly	removeChildren	[ ]	[X3DChildNode]	Interactive
SFVec3f	initializeOnly	bboxCenter	0 0 0	$(-\infty, \infty)$	Interactive
SFVec3f	initializeOnly	bboxSize	$-1 -1 -1$	$[0, \infty)$ or $-1 -1 -1$	Interactive
SFNode	inputOutput	metadata	NULL	[X3DMetadataObject]	Core

Table 4.7. Field Definitions for Anchor Node

XML Syntax (.x3d)	ClassicVRML Syntax (.x3dv)
```<Anchor DEF="MyAnchorNode"` ` description="click to jump!"` ` url="#LocalViewpointName"` ` bboxCenter="0 0 0"` ` bboxSize="-1 -1 -1">` ` <Group DEF="MySelectableGroup"/>` `</Anchor>```	```DEF MyAnchorNode Anchor {` ` bboxCenter 0 0 0` ` bboxSize -1 -1 -1` ` children [DEF MySelectableGroup` ` Group { }]` `}```

Table 4.8. Node Syntax for Anchor

The Anchor node provides a means to link external content from within X3D worlds. It functions similarly to the HTML anchor tag (<a>). The node identifies a collection of geometry as active. Selection of any part of the geometry with the pointing device causes activation of Anchor node, at which point the resource identified by the specified url is retrieved. If the url is a valid X3D world, it replaces the current world. If it is not a valid X3D world (instead, for example, an HTML page), then the browser determines how the new content is handled.

User selection of geometry activated by the Anchor node is dependent on the pointing device and the particular X3D browser in use. For a typical configuration on a desktop system with a mouse, the Anchor node is activated by moving the cursor over the active geometry and clicking with the left (or only) mouse button. The Enter key is also an allowed means of selection when the cursor is pointing to the anchored geometry. Most browsers helpfully change the cursor presentation and display the description text whenever the pointing device is placed over activated Anchor geometry.

If there are more than one nested Anchor nodes for a particular collection of geometry, the most specific Anchor node is activated. This is the Anchor node lowest and closest in the scene graph to this collection of geometry. If there are multiple Anchor nodes tied for the lowest level, then all those nodes are activated at once (though the result of loading multiple new content files is undefined and may be unpredictable).

The appearance of an object (or even a portion of an object) does not affect whether selection occurs. Thus transparent geometry can be selected.

3.3.1. description

The author uses the description field to provide information regarding the expected action of this node. This hint helps the user decide whether or not to select the geometry.

3.3.2. url

The url field either indicates a bookmark or provides the address of a replacement document. This url can point to any resource: another X3D scene, an XHTML page, a Scalable Vector Graphics (SVG) drawing, a text file, and so on. This action is triggered by selecting the Anchor's child geometry.

Each of the options provided by the Inline node's url field (described in Chapter 3, Grouping Nodes) are identically provided for Anchor. Because many different content types may be selected from the url field, both the Anchor and the Inline nodes are part of the X3D Networking Component.

A bookmark example to select a viewpoint follows.

```
<Viewpoint DEF="SpecialViewpointName"/>
<!-other nodes->
<Anchor url="#SpecialViewpointName" description="select the box to
      see the special viewpoint!">
  <Shape><Box/></Shape>
</Anchor>
```

3.3.3. parameter

The parameter field provides additional information to the browser regarding the redirection of loaded url results. Setting parameter to a value such as "target=_blank" causes a web browser to load the target url into a blank frame, or set parameter="target=frame_name" to load the target url into another frame. (Take care to get the quotation marks correct.)

Note that this approach is similar to that used by XHTML web pages, where an anchor link might look like <a href="website.com" target="frame_name">website</a>. Again, X3D Anchor node functionality is intentionally similar to that provided by the XHTML anchor in order to properly support 3D graphics for the World Wide Web.

Typically the parameter field is ignored if the browser is solely a standalone X3D viewer rather than a fully XHTML-capable Web browser. The parameter field may be ignored if used in a scene under the Interchange profile.

3.3.4. Keyboard emulation of pointing device

Usually motion by the pointing device is the primary means for user navigation. Keyboard navigation is also possible, using the recommended default actions shown in Table 4.9. EXAMINE-mode orbital rotations are performed around the local center of rotation.

Keyboard navigation is usually disabled when a KeySensor or StringSensor is enabled. These nodes discussed in Chapter 8, User Interactivity Nodes.

Key	Emulated Action	WALK **mode**	FLY **mode**	EXAMINE **mode**
Up arrow	Pointer up	forward	forward	orbit up
Down arrow	Pointer down	backward	backward	orbit down
Left arrow	Pointer left	left	left	orbit left
Right arrow	Pointer right	right	right	orbit right

Table 4.9. Recommended Keyboard Navigation Keys and Responses

3.3.5. Hints and warnings

XML encoding for the quotation-mark character is ", which is one of several XML character entity definitions.

Warning: strictly match directory and filename capitalization for http links. Windows systems are deceptively forgiving of such errors, which thus hampers Web interoperability and portability. Unix-based operating systems and http servers have no such tolerance and reject miscapitalized addresses as "not found."

Hint: for strict url conformance, replace any embedded blank (characters) in url queries with %20 for each blank character.

Hint: depending on browser support for Javascript, authors can popup a new window from a web browser with a url value as follows:

```
url="JavaScript:window.open('HelloWorld.x3d','popup','width=240,
    height=240');"
```

Note that popup blockers may prevent such windows from appearing. Browser policies for handling user privacy and preferences vary and are not formally specified. The supported protocols are determined by the browser. At a minimum, http:// and file:// are supported but the browser is not required to support the display or processing of any linked content, unless it is an X3D scene. Most X3D browsers launch an external browser such as Firefox, Internet Explorer, or Opera when encountering non-X3D content. Browsers are not required to support the javascript: protocol.

LoadSensor can detect progress and success when retrieving Anchor resources pointed to by the url. The LoadSensor node is described in Chapter 12, Environment Sensor and Sound Nodes.

3.4. Billboard node

Billboard is an X3DGroupingNode that can contain zero or more X3DChildNodes. Child content within the Billboard node faces the user, rotating about a specified axis. By default this rotation is about the upward y-axis, though any axis may be achieved by applying a parent Transform. The Billboard node can also be aligned to face the user viewpoint at any angle, swiveling about a point without attempting to align with a local axis of rotation.

The Billboard node is in the Interactive and Immersive profiles. The Immersive profile provides full support for the load field. The node has the fields defined in Table 4.10. Node syntax is shown in Table 4.11.

Billboards are a great technique to make scenes more understandable and navigable. Be generous with signs and indicators when authoring larger scenes so that users have a sense of context and can better comprehend what is available to them. Sometimes a series of Billboard nodes with corresponding Viewpoint nodes are constructed to provide an interactive guided path that users can follow through a virtual world.

Billboard nodes usually need to be placed in the scene graph as close to the rotating geometry as possible, usually as the immediate parent. The Billboard node is then nested inside a Transform that properly locates it in the local coordinate system.

Billboard node functionality is always enabled, and cannot be turned off.

Type	accessType	Name	Default	Range	Profile
SFVec3f	inputOutput	axisOfRotation	0 1 0	(−∞, ∞)	Immersive
MFNode	inputOutput	children	[]	[X3DChildNode]	Immersive
MFNode	inputOnly	addChildren	[]	[X3DChildNode]	Interactive
MFNode	inputOnly	removeChildren	[]	[X3DChildNode]	Interactive
SFVec3f	initializeOnly	bboxCenter	0 0 0	(−∞, ∞)	Immersive
SFVec3f	initializeOnly	bboxSize	−1 −1 −1	[0,∞) or −1 −1 −1	Immersive
SFNode	inputOutput	metadata	NULL	[X3DMetadataObject]	Core

Table 4.10. Field Definitions for Billboard Node

XML Syntax (.x3d)	ClassicVRML Syntax (.x3dv)

``
<Billboard DEF="MyBillboardNode"
 axisOfRotation="0 1 0"
  bboxCenter="0 0 0"
  bboxSize="-1 -1 -1">
 <Group DEF="WatchMeRotate"/>
</Billboard>
``
	``
	DEF MyBillboardNode Billboard {
	  axisOfRotation 0 1 0
	  bboxCenter 0 0 0
	  bboxSize -1 -1 -1
	  children [
	     DEF WatchMeRotate Group { }
	  ]
	}
	``

Table 4.11. Node Syntax for Billboard

Individual shapes and larger models can all be placed inside a Billboard node because it is an X3DGroupingNode.

The billboard example (Billboard.x3d) shown in Figure 4.4 provides two viewpoints for looking at the text message above the exhibit. The first view shows both exhibit and text from the front. Moving to a second viewpoint on the side of the tank rotates the Billboard so that the navigation instructions in the text remain visible.

3.4.1. axisOfRotation

The axisOfRotation field controls how the coordinate system of child geometry is rotated toward the camera. The axisOfRotation direction is relative to local coordinate system. Billboard content does not face the user very well if the current viewpoint is set along the rotation axis. Setting `axisOfRotation="0 0 0"` rotates content about all axes to always face the viewer.

3.4.2. Hints and warnings

Note that axisOfRotation is relative to the coordinate system defined by its parents in the scene graph hierarchy. Some care may be needed to get the proper axis of rotation if the local subscene is not aligned with the *y*-axis upward.

Figure 4.4. Two views of the Kelp Forest Exhibit scene demonstrate how Billboard-rotated text remains facing the user.

When DEF and USE nodes are translated to create multiple instances of a Billboard node, each one correctly rotates the local child coordinate system to face the viewer.

Put each Billboard node as close to the geometry as possible, nested inside a Transform for a local coordinate system.

Do not put a Viewpoint node inside a Billboard, because unpredictable behavior may result. This is because each movement of the Billboard node automatically moves the slaved Viewpoint, which again moves the Billboard. Most browsers will likely fail in some fashion when confronted with this inherently unstable construct.

3.5. Collision node

Collision is another grouping node that defines camera-to-object object collision detection properties for each of its children. Collision capabilities can be disabled, allowing the view camera to pass through objects. Proxy geometry can also be subsituted, which does not render visually but can provide more computationally efficient collision-detection performance. This means that faster rendering is more likely than when attempting to compute polygonal intersections among complex shapes in real time.

The Collision node is also an X3DSensorNode and in the Immersive profile. Collision includes the fields defined in Table 4.12. Node syntax is shown in Table 4.13.

Browsers detect geometric collisions between the camera and objects in the scene by using the current Viewpoint position along with NavigationInfo avatarSize.

The enabled and isActive fields are covered by X3DSensorNode. Of historical note is that the enabled field was originally called *collide* in the VRML97 specification.

The Collision node example in Figure 4.5 illustrates how `enabled= "true "` prevents the viewer from passing through the tank glass, while `enabled= "false "` allows the viewer to walk or fly through the geometry of the glass.

Type	accessType	Name	Default	Range	Profile
SFBool	inputOutput	enabled		true	Immersive
SFTime	inputOutput	collideTime			Immersive
SFBool	outputOnly	isActive			Immersive
SFNode	initializeOnly	proxy	NULL	Shape or X3DChildNode	Immersive
MFNode	inputOutput	children	[]	[X3DChildNode]	Immersive
MFNode	inputOnly	addChildren	[]	[X3DChildNode]	Immersive
MFNode	inputOnly	removeChildren	[]	[X3DChildNode]	Immersive
SFVec3f	initializeOnly	bboxCenter	0 0 0	$(-\infty,\infty)$	Immersive
SFVec3f	initializeOnly	bboxSize	$-1\;-1\;-1$	$[0,\infty)$ or $-1\;-1\;-1$	Immersive
SFNode	inputOutput	metadata	NULL	[X3DMetadataObject]	Core

Table 4.12. Field Definitions for Collision Node

XML Syntax (.x3d)	ClassicVRML Syntax (.x3dv)

`<Collision DEF="MyCollisionNode"`
`            enabled="true"`
`  bboxCenter="0 0 0"`
`    <bboxSize="-1 -1 -1">`
`  <Group DEF="MyCollidableGroup"`
`   containerField="children"/>`
`  <Shape DEF="MyHiddenProxy"`
`   containerField="proxy"/>`
`</Collision>`
	`DEF MyCollisionNode Collision {`
	`  enabled TRUE`
	`  bboxCenter 0 0 0`
	`  bboxsize -1 -1 -1`
	`  children [DEF MyCollidableGroup`
	`  Group {}]`
	`  proxy DEF MyHiddenProxy Shape {}`
	`  ()`
	`}`

Table 4.13. Node Syntax for Collision

3.5.1. collideTime

The collideTime field provides an output SFTime event indicating a collision between camera (avatar) and geometry. This value can be connected with a ROUTE to trigger other behaviors.

3.5.2. proxy

Collision can contain a single proxy child node for substitute collision-detection geometry. Proxy geometry is not rendered. Good choices for a Shape node holding proxy geometry are Box, Cylinder, or Sphere, because they are often good approximations for more complicated geometry and are highly optimizable by browsers.

3.5.3. Hints and warnings

NavigationInfo type values WALK and FLY support camera-to-object collision detection. Only geometry nodes can cause a collision, with exceptions for points, lines and text: the PointSet, IndexedLineSet, LineSet, and Text nodes do not trigger collisions.

Text nodes are not normally collidable, but adding a coincident and transparent Rectangle2D (or Box or IndexedFaceSet) under a peer Shape node can achieve the same effect.

4. Summary

4.1. Key ideas

Viewpoint and NavigationInfo nodes allow users to effectively look around and move around. A scene can become more responsive to the presence of the user when nodes such as Billboard and Collision are employed. The Anchor node provides hyperlink capabilities to different viewpoints, different X3D scenes, or even different information

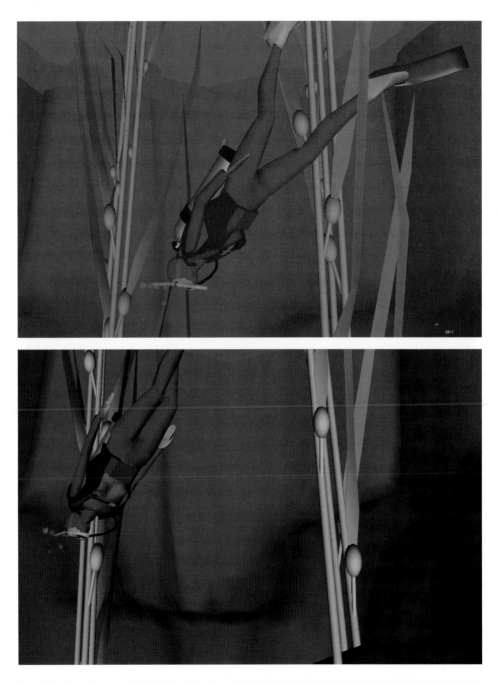

Figure 4.5. Example screen shots first show the viewer being stopped by glass gemetry, then the viewer passing through the tank glass for a closer view. Collision `enabled="true"` or `enabled="false"` result in different navigation responses.

resources (such as XHTML pages). These features truly make X3D a Web-based language for 3D web pages.

4.2. Related nodes and concepts

A heads-up display (HUD) is frequently needed for continually displaying information to the user. A HUD is constructed using several nodes and is described in Chapter 8, User Interactivity Nodes in the section on the ProximitySensor node.

4.3. Next chapter

The next chapter presents Appearance, Material, and Texture. These essential nodes allow authors to apply sophisticated color and imagery to 3D geometry.

5

Appearance, Material, and Textures

Things are not always as they appear.

1. What this chapter covers

Once geometry has been created, appropriate coloring is needed to make things interesting. This chapter covers material coloring, transparency, and texturing.

Materials apply a variety of colors and shading parameters to make the appearance look shiny, dull, transparent, opaque, glowing, and so on. Texture nodes read 2D-image or 2D-movie files and apply them pixel-by-pixel to the polygons of the associated geometry, thereby wrapping a picture around the object. The Texture Transform and TextureCoordinate nodes allow shifting, rotating, shrinking, or enlarging of each texture image.

Materials and textures account for the majority of polygonal coloring used by X3D authors. They are important nodes to master.

X3D provides two other related options for applying color to model geometry. Per-vertex (i.e., once per point) or per-polygon coloring is applied using Color or ColorRGBA nodes as children to X3DGeometryNode types. The Color/ColorRGBA approach is described in Chapter 6, Geometry Nodes, Part 2: Points, Lines, and Polygons.

The nodes discussed in this chapter are Appearance, Material, ImageTexture, PixelTexture, MovieTexture, TextureTransform, TextureCoordinate, and TextureCoordinateGenerator.

2. Concepts

Appearance, materials, and textures are fundamental capabilities that allow authors to make their 3D objects look similar to objects in the real world.

Lighting is also important, because most material values and textures are not visible without it. The X3D lighting nodes are computational and emulate the role of light sources shining on material properties, shaded as appropriate for perspective and distance, resulting in a perceived color. For simple scenes, a basic NavigationInfo headlight can provide necessary light so that geometric objects can be seen. Lights are discussed further in Chapter 11, Lighting and Environment Nodes.

2.1. Purpose and common functionality

The appearance, material, and texture nodes provide realism to geometry that might otherwise look like a pile of grey boxes and triangles. The core functionality of these nodes includes the following capabilities:

- Each Shape node can contain a single Appearance node and a single X3DGeometryNode type. Thus Shape is a container node that associates a given appearance with specific geometry.

- Each Appearance node may contain one Material node, a FillProperties node, a LineProperties node, and one Texture node. Texture nodes in turn may contain a TextureTransform or TextureTransformGenerator node. These allowable parent-child relationships are strictly enforced.

- Material values define transparency and a variety of different color properties.

- FillProperties and LineProperties nodes can apply special patterns for the application of fill and border material colors. This can help to distinguish shapes of particular interest.

- Texture nodes apply 2D-image or 2D-movie files to the corresponding geometry. A TextureTransform or TextureTransformGenerator node can also be used to customize the positioning, rotation, and scaling of the textured image.

- DEF and USE node repetition enables consistent, efficient coloring and texturing among multiple related objects.

Texturing is a sophisticated capability that allows a lot of variation in how texture maps are mapped to 3D objects. Texturing concepts pertain to PixelTexture, ImageTexture, MovieTexture, and MultiTexture nodes.

2.1.1. Texture coordinates

Texture maps are defined in a 2D coordinate system (s,t) with range [0.0, 1.0] in both directions. The bottom edge of the image corresponds to the s-axis of the texture map, and left edge of the image corresponds to the t-axis of the texture map. The lower-left pixel of the image corresponds to $s = 0$, $t = 0$, and the top-right pixel of the image corresponds to $s = 1$, $t = 1$. Texture maps may be viewed as 2D color functions that, given an (s,t) coordinate, return a color value *color(s,t)*.

Figure 5.1 from the X3D Specification shows an example texture. Texture coordinates are used to compute repeating texture patterns, either horizontally or vertically (or both). Texture coordinates are also used to rotate or scale images, as determined by the TextureTransform node.

The primary benefit of the texture coordinate system is that the exact number of row and column pixels in an image no longer matter. Authors can use normalized texture units for images of any size or aspect ratio (width:height ratio).

2.2. Abstract node types

2.2.1. X3DAppearanceNode and X3DAppearanceChildNode types

The X3DAppearanceNode and X3DAppearanceChildNode types implement the X3DNode interface. This means that all such nodes can include DEF or USE identifiers as well as a single metadata node.

Figure 5.1. Example texture image, taken with permission from the X3D Specification.

2.2.2. X3DMaterialNode type

The X3DMaterialNode type implements the X3DAppearanceChildNode interface, meaning that a Material node is normally only found as a child of an Appearance node. Putting a Material node by itself as a child of a grouping node is an error. All X3DMaterialNode nodes implement the fields defined by their interfaces. Thus Material also can include either a DEF or USE identifier, as well as a single metadata node as a child.

2.2.3. X3DTextureNode, X3DTextureCoordinateNode, and X3DTextureTransformNode types

Each of these interfaces is primarily a marker interface that identifies the proper parent-child node content model. Each includes X3DMetadataObject for a metadata node as an allowed child, and no other fields.

The X3DTextureNode type is the base type for all node types that specify sources for texture images. Similarly, X3DTextureTransformNode is the base type for all node types that specify a transformation of texture coordinates. X3DTextureNode and X3DTextureTransformNode each implement the X3DAppearanceChildNode interface, meaning that a Texture node and a TextureTransform node are each an allowed child of an Appearance node. Putting a Texture or a TextureTransform node as an immediate child of a grouping node is an error.

X3DTextureCoordinateNode implements the X3DGeometricPropertyNode interface, and is the base type for all node types that specify texture coordinates. X3DTextureCoordinateNode nodes are only allowed as children of appropriate geometry nodes, so placing them elsewhere in the scene graph is an error. This approach makes sense because isolated texture or texture transformation nodes need corresponding geometry within the same parent Shape in order to apply an effect.

2.2.4. X3DTexture2DNode type

The X3DTexture2DNode type implements the already defined X3DTextureNode interface, and is the base type for all node types that specify 2D file sources (or streaming sources) for texture images. X3DTexture2DNode contains the following fields shown in Table 5.1.

Type	accessType	Name	Default	Range	Profile
SFBool	initializeOnly	repeatS	true		Interchange
SFBool	initializeOnly	repeatT	true		Interchange
SFNode	inputOutput	metadata	NULL	[X3DMetadataObject]	Core

Table 5.1. Field Definitions for X3DTexture2DNode

2.2.4.1. repeatS and repeatT

The field repeatS indicates whether to horizontally repeat texture along the *s* axis, and repeatT indicates whether to vertically repeat texture along the *t* axis.

2.2.5. X3DTextureTransform2DNode type

The X3DTextureTransform2DNode type implements the X3DTextureTransformNode interface defined previously, and is the base type for all node types that specify a 2D transformation of texture coordinates. X3DTextureTransform2DNode fields exactly match those defined for the TextureTransform node.

3. Node descriptions

3.1. Appearance node

Each Shape node defines a single geometric object along with a corresponding Appearance. Several different kinds of material, texture or line and fill properties are possible, with each optionally provided as child nodes within the Appearance node. Material nodes are most commonly used, because Material provides a variety of ways to uniformly color an object and modify its shading.

New since VRML97, the FillProperties and LineProperties nodes can modify the style used to draw simple colors, enabling dotted lines, hatch fills, and so on. A texture node applies a 2D image to the geometry, and a TextureTransform may be added to shift the image positioning. Textures usually override underlying Material colors, although the textured 2D image itself may include transparent pixels that allow the underlying material colors to show through.

Some geometry nodes (such as IndexedFaceSet and the triangle-based nodes) provide an alternative means for defining colors and shading: the Color and Normal nodes. These approaches are covered in Chapter 6, Geometry Nodes, Part 2: Points, Lines, and Polygons. Appearance is more commonly used, and mixing the two techniques is not recommended.

The Appearance node is in the Interactive and Full profiles, which provides full support for LineProperties. Appearance includes the fields defined in Table 5.2. Node syntax is shown in Table 5.3.

Appearance is a frequently used node because it is part of each defined geometric Shape. Essentially Appearance collects one or more of the other visual-property nodes described in this chapter. Appearance node examples are shown as part of the other examples in this chapter.

3.1.1. Hints and warnings

When authoring new content, enter a Shape node before adding an Appearance node and corresponding geometry.

When using Interchange profile for simple content, Material, ImageTexture, Texture Transform, and Texture Coordinate are the only allowed child nodes inside an Appearance node.

Type	accessType	containerField Name	Default	Range	Profile
SFNode	inputOutput	material	NULL	[X3DMaterialNode]	Interchange
SFNode	inputOutput	texture	NULL	[X3DTextureNode]	Interchange
SFNode	inputOutput	textureTransform	NULL	[X3DTexture TransformNode]	optional under Interchange, supported under Immersive
SFNode	inputOutput	fillProperties	NULL	[FillProperties]	Full
SFNode	inputOutput	lineProperties	NULL	[LineProperties]	Immersive
SFNode	inputOutput	metadata	NULL	[X3DMetadataObject]	Core

Table 5.2. Field Definitions for Appearance Node

3.2. Material node

The Material node specifies surface visual properties that are applied equally across all of the polygons in a geometric object. Material defines the parameters that define how light within the scene interacts with the object. Lights are therefore essential for objects and appearance in a scene to be visible to a user.

Various types of lights can be defined and positioned in a scene. Some are directional, and most allow specifying color. The most common form of lighting is provided by a headlight, which follows the user's viewpoint and shines directly ahead. Lights are defined in Chapter 11, Lighting and Environment Nodes.

The exact rendering effects produced by the interaction of Material values, lighting parameters, and viewing perspective are defined by the X3D Lighting Model, which is an optimized set of rules and equations that reasonably approximate the physical behavior of light and vision in the real world. The X3D Specification describes these requirements in complete technical detail so that various X3D browsers can render the appearance of X3D content identically.

Used by itself, the Material node tends to produce a somewhat plastic-like appearance. The surface is smooth with little variation over the surface, except for rendering variations based on user perspective and shininess. Subtle variations in choice of colors and material values can make a scene more realistic and more aesthetically pleasing.

Material implements the X3DMaterialNode interface. The Material node has partial support in the Interchange profile and full support in the Immersive profile. The Interactive profile only supports for the ambientIntensity, shininess, specularColor, and transparency fields. Material has the fields defined in Table 5.4. Node syntax is shown in Table 5.5.

XML Syntax (.x3d)	ClassicVRML Syntax (.x3dv)

``
<Shape>
  <Box/>
  <Appearance DEF="MyAppearance">
    <FillProperties filled="true"
        hatchColor="1 1 1"
        hatchStyle="1"
        hatched="true"/>
    <LineProperties linetype="1"
        linewidthScaleFactor="1.0"/>
    <Material DEF="MyMaterial"
        diffuseColor="0 0.6 0.6"
        shininess="0.2"/>
    <ImageTexture DEF="EarthImage"
        url="earth-topo.png"/>
    <TextureTransform
        rotation="0.78"/>
  </Appearance>
</Shape>
``
	``
	Shape {
	  geometry Box { }
	  appearance DEF MyAppearance
	    Appearance {
	        fillProperties FillProperties {
	            filled TRUE
	            hatchColor 1 1 1
	            hatchStyle 1
	            hatched TRUE
	    }
	
	    lineProperties LineProperties {
	        linetype 1
	        linewidthScaleFactor 1.0
	    }
	    material DEF MyMaterial Material {
	        diffuseColor 0 0.6 0.6
	    }
	    texture DEF EarthImage
	    ImageTexture {
	        url ["earth-topo.png"]
	    }
	    textureTransform
	    TextureTransform {
	        rotation 0.78
	    }
	  }
	}
	``

Table 5.3. Node Syntax for Appearance

A surprisingly large variety of colors and visual properties are possible using the Material field definitions for color and effects. It is a good idea to experiment with different color values to see how the rendered appearance can vary. Web authors should double check their work using the browser plugins that are most likely to be used by their audience.

The Basic X3D examples archive provided on the book's website includes the Universal Media Materials library. Over 450 unique materials are presented, grouped in

Type	accessType	Name	Default	Range	Profile
SFFloat	inputOutput	ambientIntensity	0.2	[0,1]	Optional support in Interchange. Complete support in Immersive.
SFColor	inputOutput	diffuseColor	0.8 0.8 0.8	[0,1]	Interchange
SFColor	inputOutput	emissiveColor	0 0 0	[0,1]	Interchange
SFFloat	inputOutput	shininess	0.2	[0,1]	Optional support in Interchange. Complete support in Immersive.
SFColor	inputOutput	specularColor	0 0 0	[0,1]	Optional support in Interchange. Complete support in Immersive.
SFFloat	inputOutput	transparency	0.0	[0,1]	One-bit support in Interchange profile (transparency >= 0.5 is transparent). Complete support in Immersive profile.
SFNode	inputOutput	metadata	NULL	[X3DMeta dataObject]	Core

Table 5.4. Field Definitions for Material Node

XML Syntax (.x3d)	ClassicVRML Syntax (.x3dv)

```<Material DEF="MyMaterial"```
 ```   ambientIntensity="0.2"```
 ```   diffuseColor="0.8 0.8 0.8"```
 ```   emissiveColor="0 0 0"```
 ```   shininess="0.2"```
 ```   specularColor="0 0 0"```
 ```   transparency="0"```
 ```   containerField="material"/>```
	```DEF MyMaterial Material {```
	 ``` ambientIntensity 0.2```
	 ``` diffuseColor 0.8 0.8 0.8```
	 ``` emissiveColor 0 0 0```
	 ``` shininess 0.2```
	 ``` specularColor 0 0 0```
	 ``` transparency 0```
	 ```}```

Table 5.5. Node Syntax for Material

collections of visually pleasing palettes. Categories include Art Deco, Autumn, Glass, Metals, Neon, Rococo, Santa Fe, Sheen, Silky, Spring, Summer, Tropical, and Winter. Copying and applying these material values can noticeably improve the variety and composition of authored scenes.

3.2.1. ambientIntensity

The ambientIntensity field specifies how much ambient light this surface shall reflect. Ambient light is omnidirectional and depends only on the light sources, not their positions with respect to the surface. Ambient color is calculated as ambientIntensity × diffuseColor.

3.2.2. diffuseColor

The diffuseColor field reflects all X3D light sources depending on the angle of the surface with respect to the light source. The more directly the surface faces the light, the more diffuse light reflects.

The example scene diffuseColor.x3d provides a simple example of how to use the diffuseColor field, shown in Figure 5.2.

3.2.3. emissiveColor

The emissiveColor field models glowing objects. This can be useful for displaying prelit models (for which the light energy is computed explicitly), or for displaying scientific

Figure 5.2. Sphere with `diffuseColor="1 0 0"` and no other colors specified in the sibling Material node.

data. Objects with an emissiveColor component are visible even when no light source is directed at the object.

The example scene emissiveColor.x3d provides a simple example of how to use the emissiveColor field, shown in Figure 5.3.

3.2.4. specularColor and shininess

The specularColor and shininess fields determine the specular highlights (for example, the shiny spots on an apple). Specifically, when the angle from the light to the surface is close to the angle from the surface to the viewer, the specularColor is added to the diffuse and ambient color calculations. Lower shininess values produce soft glows, while higher values result in sharper and smaller highlights.

The example scene specularColor.x3d provides a simple example of how to use the specularColor field, shown in Figure 5.4.

3.2.5. transparency

The transparency field specifies how clear an object is, with 1.0 being completely transparent, and 0.0 completely opaque. Some graphics languages use the corresponding term *alpha*, which describes opaqueness and equals the quantity *1-transparency*. The example scene transparency.x3d in Figure 5.5 provides a simple example of semi-transparent geometry.

Figure 5.3. Sphere with `emissiveColor="0 0 1"` and no other colors specified. Note how emissiveColor flattens the rendering and can hide shading cues.

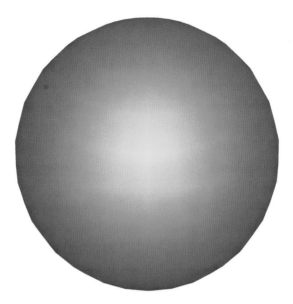

Figure 5.4. Sphere with `specularColor="0 1 0"` and `diffuseColor="1 0 0"` with no other colors specified. Note that the highlighted specular region is colored yellow, which is a combination of the green and red contributions.

3.2.6. Hints and warnings

When first adding Material values to color an object, a parent Appearance node must be a sibling of the corresponding geometry.

Appropriate Material values ought to be defined even if a texture is provided for an object, because these colors are used if any delay occurs when downloading and applying the image file. Thus, adding a material to accompany each texture is a good practice that can sometimes improve initial user recognition and navigation in large scenes.

The Color, ColorRGBA, and Normal nodes can also be used to provide separate color and shading to objects. These nodes are described in Chapter 6, Geometry Nodes, Part 2: Points, Lines, and Polygons.

The Pellucid materials editor is a free Java applet that simulates the VRML/X3D illumination model. It provides a default view of a sphere, a default directional light with direction [−1 −1 −1], and a default material. This is a good way to see how different material values look on a 3D object. It is available at www.acm.org/tog/resources/applets/vrml/pellucid.html.

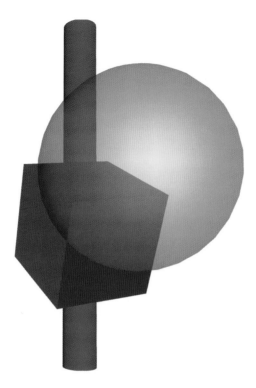

Figure 5.5. Semitransparent sphere in front of an opaque box and an opaque cylinder.

The Universal Media Material library has hundreds of interesting example material values that can save authors a great deal of trial-and-error time. These are in the X3D Basic Examples archive, online at the book's website. Figure 5.7 shows an example of the material combinations available. Looking at the accompanying hypertext markup language (HTML) page shows values that can be copied.

3.3. FillProperties node

A FillProperties node specifies additional properties that are applied to all polygons in the adjacent geometry node, in addition to whatever other material or texture properties are also contained in the parent Appearance node. Hatch patterns are applied on top of the already-rendered appearance of the node. Hatches are not affected by lighting.

The FillProperties node is in the Interactive and Full profiles. The node has the fields defined in Table 5.6. Node syntax is shown in Table 5.7.

3.3.1. filled

The boolean field filled indicates whether the appearance of the associated geometry is filled. The default value is filled="true" so that an object is visible. Turning off appearance fill may sometimes provide a useful contrast when applying hatching.

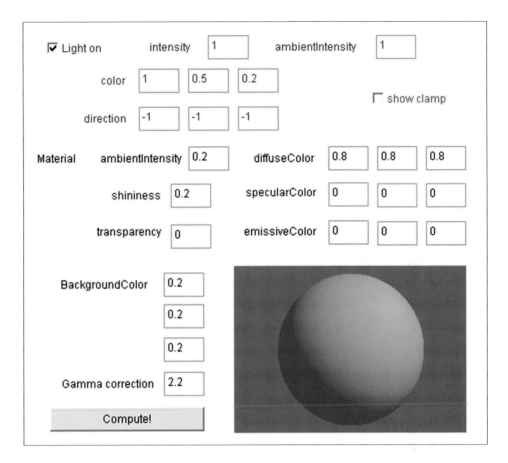

Figure 5.6. The Pellucid tool shows precise coloring for different lighting and material combinations.

3.3.2. hatched

The boolean value hatched can be used to turn hatching on or off. This can be a helpful interactive technique in X3D scenes, either to show selected geometry of interest or to highlight objects with common characteristics.

3.3.3. hatchColor

The hatchColor field is used for hatching patterns overlaid on top of the geometry's appearance. It is a good practice to ensure that hatchColor is different from the underlying appearance so that the hatching is distinguishable.

3.3.4. hatchStyle

The X3D fill patterns for hatchStyle shown in Table 5.8 are defined in the International Register of Graphical Items (see http://jitc.fhu.disa.mil/nitf/graph_reg/graph_reg.html).

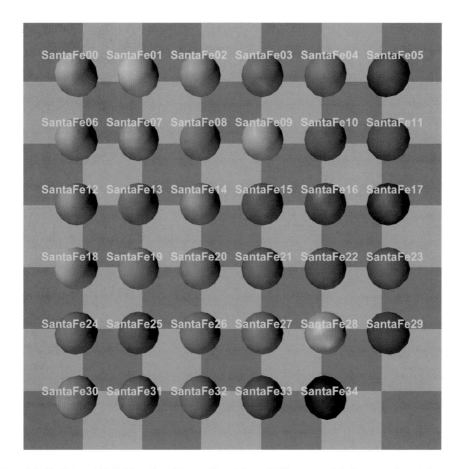

Figure 5.7. The Universal Media Materials archive provides a rich set of different materials that are easily copied into other scenes.

3.3.5. Hints and warnings

FillProperties is part of the X3D Full profile and was not included in the original VRML97 Specification. If application of FillProperties is essential to the 3D user interface, a good authoring practice for backward compatibility is to present FillProperties information redundantly (perhaps using text in the scene or as a TouchSensor description) in case the browser is unable to render it.

3.4. LineProperties node

The LineProperties node specifies additional features that are applied to associated line geometry. The linetype and linewidth are only applied when `applied="true"`. If `applied="false"` then a solid line of nominal width is produced.

Type	accessType	Name	Default	Range	Profile
SFBool	inputOutput	filled	true		Full
SFColor	inputOutput	hatchColor	1 1 1	[0,1]	Full
SFBool	inputOutput	hatched	true		Full
SFInt32	inputOutput	hatchStyle	1	[0,∞)	Full
SFNode	inputOutput	metadata	NULL	[X3DMetadataObject]	Core

Table 5.6. Field Definitions for FillProperties Node

XML Syntax (.x3d)	ClassicVRML Syntax (.x3dv)

`<FillProperties DEF="MyFillProperties"`
`  filled="true"`
`  hatched="true"`
`  hatchColor="1 1 1"`
`  hatchStyle="1"`
`  containerField="fillProperties"/>`
	`DEF MyFillProperties`
	`    FillProperties{`
	`        filled TRUE`
	`        hatchColor 1 1 1`
	`        hatchStyle 1`
	`        hatched TRUE`
	`    }`

Table 5.7. Node Syntax for FillProperties

The color of a line is specified by the emissiveColor value of the associated Material node. When no value is provided, lines are black (`emissiveColor="0 0 0"`) by default.

The LineProperties node is in the Full profile, and has the fields defined in Table 5.9. Node syntax is shown in Table 5.10.

3.4.1. applied

The applied field is a boolean value that can be used to turn line properties on or off. Toggling the applied field can be a helpful interactive technique in X3D scenes, either to show selected geometry of interest or to highlight objects with common characteristics.

3.4.2. linewidthScaleFactor

The linewidthScaleFactor value is multiplicative and scales a browser-dependent nominal linewidth by the linewidth scale factor. This resulting value is then mapped to the nearest available line width. A linewidthScaleFactor value less than or equal to zero refers to the minimum available line width.

Enumeration Code	Hatch Pattern
1	Horizontal equally spaced parallel lines
2	Vertical equally spaced parallel lines
3	Positive slope equally spaced parallel lines
4	Negative slope equally spaced parallel lines
5	Horizontal/vertical crosshatch
6	Positive slope/negative slope crosshatch
7	(cast iron or malleable iron and general use for all materials)
8	(steel)
9	(bronze, brass, copper, and compositions)
10	(white metal, zinc, lead, babbit, and alloys)
11	(magnesium, aluminum, and aluminum alloys)
12	(rubber, plastic, and electrical insulation)
13	(cork, felt, fabric, leather, and fibre)
14	(thermal insulation)
15	(titanium and refractory material)
16	(marble, slate, porcelain, glass, etc.)
17	(earth)
18	(sand)
19	(repeating dot)

Table 5.8. Patterns Corresponding to FillProperties hatchStyle Codes (optional values in parentheses)

Type	accessType	Name	Default	Range	Profile
SFBool	inputOutput	applied	true		Immersive
SFInt32	inputOutput	linetype	1	$[1,\infty)$	Immersive
SFInt32	inputOutput	linewidthScaleFactor	0	$(-\infty,\infty)$	Immersive
SFNode	inputOutput	metadata	NULL	[X3DMetadataObject]	Core

Table 5.9. Field definitions for LineProperties node

XML Syntax (.x3d)	ClassicVRML Syntax (.x3dv)
`<LineProperties DEF="MyLineProperties"` `linetype="1"` `linewidthScaleFactor="0"` `containerField="lineProperties"/>`	`DEF MyLineProperties` `LineProperties {` `linetype 1` `linewidthScaleFactor 0` `}`

Table 5.10. Node Syntax for LineProperties

3.4.3. linetype

The linetype field selects a line pattern as defined in the International Register of Graphical Items. X3D browsers are required to support linetypes 1 through 5, with linetype 1 being the default. X3D browsers may support any of the other registered linetypes. If a linetype that is not supported is requested, linetype 1 is used. Table 5.11 specifies the first sixteen linetypes as defined in the Linetype Section of the International Register of Graphical Items.

3.4.4. Hints and warnings

LineProperties is part of the X3D Full profile and was not included in the original VRML97 Specification. If application of LineProperties is essential to the 3D user interface, a good authoring practice for backwards compatibility is to present LineProperty information redundantly (using text in the scene or as a TouchSensor description) in case the browser is unable to render it.

Pay attention to the proper capitalization of linewidthScaleFactor and linetype.

3.5. ImageTexture node

Texturing describes the 3D graphics technique of applying 2D imagery to 3D shapes, draping a picture around geometry as a way to increase visual fidelity cheaply. ImageTexture is the most commonly used node for applying a 2D texture to geometric objects.

The ImageTexture node refers to an external image file containing the texture. X3D browsers are required to support the Portable Network Graphics (.png) and Joint Photographic Experts Group (.jpg or jpeg) image file formats. Other formats may be supported depending on the X3D browser. Support for the Graphics Interchange Format (.gif) format is recommended. PNG offers the best quality and compression for most images, and JPEG often provides the best color fidelity for photographs.

In comparison to PixelTexture and MovieTexture, ImageTexture is the preferred node for texturing most objects. It leads to more compact X3D files because the images are not specified in the X3D file and the standard formats use sophisticated image compression techniques to reduce file size. Alternatively, PixelTexture can be used when the

Enumeration Code	linetype Pattern
1	Solid
2	Dashed
3	Dotted
4	Dashed-dotted
5	Dash-dot-dot
6	(single)
7	(single dot)
8	(double arrow)
9	(chain line)
10	(center line)
11	(hidden line)
12	(phantom line)
13	(break line 1)
14	(break line 2)
15	User-specified dash pattern

Table 5.11. Patterns Corresponding to LineProperties linetype Codes (optional values in parentheses)

image is simple, when file or network retrieval is not possible (for example as an email attachment), or when the image needs to be modified by the X3D scene at run-time.

ImageTexture implements the X3DTexture2DNode interface. The ImageTexture node is in the Interchange profile, though support may not be guaranteed for images larger than 512 × 512 pixels. ImageTexture has the fields defined in Table 5.12. Node syntax is shown in Table 5.13.

Even when applying a texture that fully covers an object, specifying material properties for each object often improves user interaction and navigation. This is because texture loading may not occur immediately, particularly when the browser is constructing large scenes or has network delays. Having material properties that provide basic coloring for each object helps to keep the scene intelligible. This may turn out to be critical if the texture file is not available as a result of some other external failure, such as a lost network connection.

3.5.1. url

The url field points to the ImageTexture file being loaded. Each of the options provided by the Inline node's url field (described in Chapter 3, Grouping Nodes) are also provided for ImageTexture. The example scenes Garibaldi.x3d and Garibaldi-remote.x3d in Figure 5.8 have identical content but demonstrate the difference between immediate local loading versus delayed network loading of an image texture.

Type	accessType	Name	Default	Range	Profile
MFString	inputOutput	url	[]	[urn]	Interchange
SFBool	initializeOnly	repeatS	true		Interchange
SFBool	initializeOnly	repeatT	true		Interchange
SFNode	inputOutput	metadata	NULL	[X3DMetadataObject]	Core

Table 5.12. Field Definitions for ImageTexture Node

XML Syntax (.x3d)	ClassicVRML Syntax (.x3dv)
```<ImageTexture DEF="MyImageTexture" repeatS="true" repeatT="true" url='"earth-topo.png" "earth-topo.jpg"' containerField="texture"/>```	```DEF MyImageTexture ImageTexture { repeatS TRUE repeatT TRUE url ["earth-topo.png" "earth-topo.jpg"] }```

Table 5.13. Node Syntax for ImageTexture

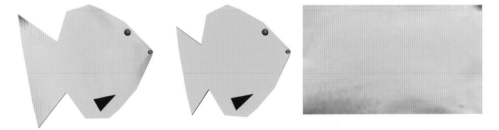

Figure 5.8. Image texturing, using either local or networked retrieval of the image. The first image is the textured geometry, the second image shows the geometry prior to applying the texture, the third image is the texture file itself.

The url field points to the ImageTexture file being loaded. Each of the options defined for the Inline node's url field (described in Chapter 2, Grouping Nodes) are also provided for ImageTexture.

3.5.2. Hints and warnings

Properly designed relative subdirectory links can work both on local systems and on web servers. This helps make large scenes with a lot of content portable so that they work identically on CDs, DVDs, disk drives, or web servers.

It is important to include both relative and persistent (online) url addresses. Use relative links first, because they are the most portable and do not require unnecessary use of the network. One special case is worth noting: list online links before relative links when updated network versions of content are preferred. This will retrieve transient online data first (such as weather information or a traffic report) before falling back to a locally provided version, in case network connectivity is not available.

Authors must strictly match directory and filename capitalization for http links. Mismatched capitalization leads to link failures when retrieving from an http server and on Unix-based systems. This problem is hidden for local links on Windows systems because that operating system ignores capitalization.

Ensure each url link is valid. These can be easily checked manually using X3D-Edit by producing a pretty-print HTML version of the scene and then clicking on each linked address.

If an ImageTexture file is large and used more than once, it is a good idea to DEF a name for the original and then USE that name for all copies, in order to reduce both download delays and system memory requirements.

Periodically run a link checker to verify that url values remain correct. Many such tools are available, including the World Wide Web Consortium (W3C) Link Checker and Xenu's Link Sleuth.

LoadSensor can detect progress and success when retrieving texture-file resources. LoadSensor is described in Chapter 12, Environment Sensor and Sound Nodes.

Example scenes provided for this book follow these conventions.

3.6. MovieTexture node

The MovieTexture node applies animated external movie files as textures on geometry. This technique can provide interesting displays within a scene. Usually MovieTexture is applied sparingly, because video resources in combination with 3D graphics are computationally expensive and may slow down browser responsiveness.

MovieTexture nodes are required to support MPEG1-System (audio and video) and MPEG1-Video (video only) file formats, defined by the Motion Picture Expert Group. Additional file formats (such as QuickTime and .avi) may be supported by various browsers.

MovieTexture nodes are usually referenced as an Appearance node's texture field. MovieTexture can also replace AudioClip as a Sound node's source field (for audio purposes only).

MovieTexture implements the X3DTexture2DNode, X3DSoundSourceNode and X3DUrlObject interfaces. The MovieTexture node is in the Immersive profile. The node has the fields defined in Table 5.14. Node syntax is shown in Table 5.15.

As with the other texture nodes, MovieTexture uses repeatS and repeatT to control the repetition of the texture over the surface of associated geometry.

A movie starts playing when the system time is greater than or equal to the startTime value. If the system time is less than the value of the startTime field and speed is positive, then the first frame of the movie is used for initial texturing. The last frame of the movie is used for initial texturing if speed is negative.

Type	accessType	Name	Default	Range	Profile
SFBool	inputOutput	loop	false		Immersive
SFTime	inputOutput	resumeTime	0	$(-\infty, \infty)$	Immersive
SFTime	inputOutput	pauseTime	0	$(-\infty, \infty)$	Immersive
SFFloat	inputOutput	speed	1.0	$(-\infty, \infty)$	Immersive
SFTime	inputOutput	startTime	0	$(-\infty, \infty)$	Immersive
SFTime	inputOutput	stopTime	0	$(-\infty, \infty)$	Immersive
MFString	inputOutput	url	[]	[urn]	Immersive
SFBool	initializeOnly	repeatS	true		Immersive
SFBool	initializeOnly	repeatT	true		Immersive
SFNode	inputOutput	metadata	NULL	[X3DMetadataObject]	Core

Table 5.14. Field Definitions for MovieTexture Node

XML Syntax (.x3d)	ClassicVRML Syntax (.x3dv)

<pre><MovieTexture DEF="MyMovieTexture"
  url="'MovieName.mpg'"
  loop="false"
  pauseTime="0"
  repeatS="true"
  repeatT="true"
  resumeTime="0"
  speed="1.0"
  startTime="0"
  stopTime="0"
  containerField="texture"/></pre>
	<pre>DEF MyMovieTexture MovieTexture {
	  url ["MovieName.mpg"]
	  loop FALSE
	  pauseTime 0
	  repeatS TRUE
	  repeatT TRUE
	  resumeTime 0
	  speed 1.0
	  startTime 0
	  stopTime 0
	}</pre>

Table 5.15. Node Syntax for MovieTexture

Actual play time for the movie is the original movie duration divided by the absolute value of the speed. A movie plays either until all frames are completed (with loop="false"), or until the current-clock system time exceeds stopTime (usually accomplished by resetting stopTime to equal current time).

The pauseTime and resumeTime events allow for temporary interruptions of normal play. When the system time exceeds pauseTime, all activity in the MovieTexture node stops. The current frame remains displayed as the texture and no new events are generated. When the system time exceeds resumeTime, the MovieTexture node resumes all activity.

If the movie input is a live feed, several image frames may need to be received before playback of complete images can commence. Once stopped or paused, the final displayed movie frame is used as the texture for the object.

3.6.1. loop

The movie repeats indefinitely when `loop="true"`, and repeats playback only once when `loop="false"`.

3.6.2. speed

The speed field is a rate factor to speed up or slow down movie playback. If `speed="1.0"` the movie will run at normal speed. If speed is positive, then the last frame to play is the last frame in the file. Negative values for speed set the last frame to play as the first frame in the file, and the first frame to play as the last frame in the file. Thus, for example, `speed="2"` causes the movie to play forward at twice its normal speed, and `speed="-0.5"` causes the movie to play backward at half its normal speed.

3.6.3. startTime and stopTime

The startTime field begins the MovieTexture playback and this input is usually set by using ROUTE to connect a TimeSensor or TouchSensor output. The stopTime field is only used to stop the clip from playing. All time values are absolute time, that is, the number of seconds since January 1, 1970, 00:00:00 GMT.

3.6.4. pauseTime and resumeTime

The pauseTime field is an input field, usually connected via ROUTE to animation values that provide the current clock time when pausing. When current time is greater than or equal to pauseTime, isPaused becomes true and the MovieTexture becomes paused. When resumeTime becomes less than or equal to current time, isPaused becomes false and the MovieTexture becomes active.

3.6.5. isActive and isPaused

Both isActive and isPaused are output events that can be connected via a ROUTE to synchronize other animation behaviors in a scene. Each sends a true value on commencement or pausing, respectively. Each sends a false value upon completion or resumption, respectively.

3.6.6. duration_changed and elapsedTime

The duration_changed field is the length of time in seconds for one cycle of the movie. The elapsedTime is the current elapsed time since the MovieTexture activated and began running, with SFTime units cumulative in seconds and not counting any paused time.

3.6.7. Hints and warnings

It is usually a good idea to provide a viewpoint that allows a clear and unwarped view of a MovieTexture so that users can easily see all details.

LoadSensor can detect progress and success when retrieving texture-file resources. LoadSensor is described in Chapter 12, Environment Sensor and Sound Nodes.

If a MovieTexture is used more than once in a scene, it is a good idea to DEF a label name for the original node and USE the label name for all copies to reduce download delays and system-resource requirements. Although browsers might automatically cache (save) duplicated movies or use http negotiation to check timestamps, a full download of each file may be required before any such comparison checking for duplication can occur. Node DEF and USE efficiencies eliminate the possibility of repeating such time-consuming delays.

3.7. PixelTexture node

PixelTexture contains the bit pattern of an image as a set of data within an X3D scene, allowing a single file to contain both geometry and texture images. The image data format follows a specially defined X3D field type called SFImage.

PixelTexture implements the X3DTexture2DNode interface. The PixelTexture node is in the Immersive profile. The node has the fields defined in Table 5.16. Node syntax is shown in Table 5.17.

3.7.1. SFImage Type

An SFImage type is defined for the image field that contains the PixelTexture data structure. The first three elements of this data type are the number of width pixels, number of height pixels, and number of components in the image. The special case of no image is

Type	accessType	Name	Default	Range	Profile
SFImage	inputOutput	image	0 0 0		Immersive
SFBool	initializeOnly	repeatS	true		Immersive
SFBool	initializeOnly	repeatT	true		Immersive
SFNode	inputOutput	metadata	NULL	[X3DMetadataObject]	Core

Table 5.16. Field Definitions for PixelTexture Node

XML Syntax (.x3d)	ClassicVRML Syntax (.x3dv)

`<PixelTexture DEF="MyPixelTexture">`
`  image="0 0 0"`
`  repeatS="true"`
`  repeatT="true"`
`  containerField="texture"/>`
	`DEF MyPixelTexture PixelTexture {`
	`  image 0 0 0`
	`  repeatS TRUE`
	`  repeatT TRUE`
	`}`

Table 5.17. Node Syntax for PixelTexture

indicated by zero values for width, height, and number of components (`image="0 0 0"`). After the first three numbers, an array of pixel information contains width × height integer values. Each integer defines red-green-blue (RGB) values for the number of bytes indicated in the number of components. Each byte of pixel data can range from 0 to 255; 0 is full off and 255 is full on.

Pixel values are typically represented in hexadecimal form for readability. Thus 0xFF0000 is red, 0x00FF00 is green, and 0x0000FF is blue for a 3-component value.

Pixel data is uncompressed, and so PixelTexture information can be much larger than a corresponding ImageTexture file. The size increase does not matter much for simple texture patterns. File size for PixelTexture scenes can be reduced in several ways: through gzip compression, extraction of the image as a separate file, or use of the X3D compressed binary encoding.

The X3D specification allows the number of components in an SFImage to range from one to four. If there is one component, then the image pixels simply define intensity from black to white. A two-component SFImage is the intensity in the first (upper) byte and the alpha opacity in the second (lower) byte. An opacity value of 255 is fully opaque (fully obscuring) and a value of 0 is fully transparent (i.e., not visible). Three-component images describe RGB color where the first byte is red, the second byte is green, and the third byte is blue. An SFImage with four components has the upper three bytes for RGB and the lowest byte for alpha opacity. A value of 0x00 is completely transparent, 0xFF is completely opaque. Note that *alpha* equals the quantity *1.0-transparency,* and that actual values for alpha and transparency are each in the range [0.0, 1.0].

The lower-left pixel of the image is the first image datum specified (namely the fourth element of the data structure). Successive data values fill horizontal image pixels until the width of the image has been specified. Once a row has been defined, the next row up is defined. This is repeated until the image is fully defined. Any missing data values are defined to be 0. The last pixel defined (if all elements are present) is the upper-right image pixel.

The fields repeatS and repeatT separately control the repetition of the overall image in the specified dimension. The default value causes the texture to be repeated in that direction. Setting either field to false causes the texture to be stretched to fit the geometry in that direction.

The image field can be modified at run-time using Script techniques, though the repeatS and repeatT controls can only be set during node initialization.

3.7.2. image

The image field contains SFImage data as previously defined. Example values are shown in Table 5.18.

Figures 5.9 through 5.11 illustrate the use of PixelTexture. The first example (PixelTextureBW.x3d) shows a black/white checkerboard using a PixelTexture applied to a cube. The second example (PixelTexture.x3d) shows a colored checkerboard using a PixelTexture applied to the four X3D primitive-geometry Nodes. The last example (PixelTextureGaribaldi.x3d) shows a PixelTexture applied to our favorite fish.

Components	SFImage Value	Description	Image
0	0 0 0	Empty image	
1	1 2 1, 0xFF 0x00	Intensity (black & white) example: checkerboard pattern	
2	2 1 2, 0xCCFF 0x2277	Intensity & transparency example	
3	2 4 3, 0xFF0000 0xFF00 0 0 0 0 0xFFFFFF 0xFFFF00	Red-green-blue (RGB) example	
4	3 2 4, 1 0 0 255, 0 1 0 255, 0 0 1 255, 1 0 0 127, 0 1 0 127, 0 0 1 127	Red-green-blue-alpha (RGBA) example	

Table 5.18. Example SFImage Content with 0, 1, 2, 3, or 4 Components. Each PixelTexture image is shown on a Box in front of a checkerboard background so that partial transparencies of some of the textures are visible.

Figure 5.9. A simple PixelTexture presenting an 8 × 8 image of black and white pixels. With use of the TextureTransform node, this can be reduced to 2 × 2 pixel texture.

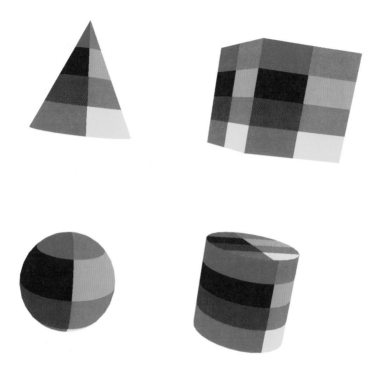

Figure 5.10. PixelTexture producing a color image, shown on the geometric primitive nodes to illustrate mappings on different surfaces.

3.7.3. Hints and warnings

PixelTexture is a good way to package one or more images into a single scene file, avoiding multiple file downloads. This technique is especially helpful when sending a single X3D scene as an email attachment for standalone viewing.

3.8. TextureTransform node

The TextureTransform node defines a 2D transformation for texture coordinates that can better align texture images on top of the geometry. The transformation consists of a 2D translation, rotation, and scaling that effectively moves the texture along the surface of the object to achieve the desired effect.

The TextureTransform node is in the Immersive profile, though browsers can choose to support it as part of the Interactive profile. The TextureTransform node has the fields defined in Table 5.19. Node syntax is shown in Table 5.20.

Transformations are applied to the (s,t) coordinates in the following order: translation, rotation, scale. This is the same order as the Transform node, except that the transformations apply to the coordinate system, not the texture. As a result, that the texture appears to move in the opposite direction for each change in translation, rotation, and scale.

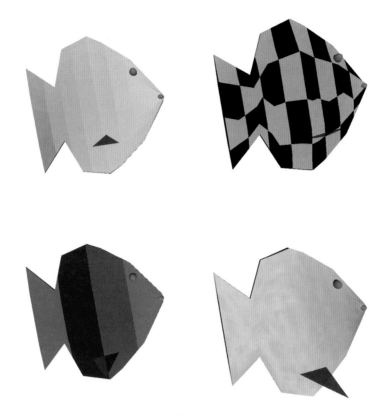

Figure 5.11. Various PixelTexture images applied to the Garibaldi fish model. The first PixelTexture defines 12 × 7 pixels. Note that stripes on the Garibaldi in the top left that has PixelTexture rather than the ImageTexture (bottom right).

Type	accessType	Name	Default	Range	Profile
SFVec2f	inputOutput	center	0 0	(−∞, ∞)	Immersive
SFFloat	inputOutput	rotation	0	(−∞, ∞)	Immersive
SFVec2f	inputOutput	translation	0 0	(−∞, ∞)	Immersive
SFVec2f	inputOutput	scale	1 1	(−∞, ∞)	Immersive
SFNode	inputOutput	metadata	NULL	[X3DMetadataObject]	Core

Table 5.19. Field Definitions for TextureTransform Node

XML Syntax (.x3d)	ClassicVRML Syntax (.x3dv)

`<TextureTransform DEF=`
 `  "MyTextureTransform"`
 `center="0 0"`
 `translation="0 0"`
 `rotation="0"`
 `scale="1 1"`
 `containerField="textureTransform"/>`
	`DEF MyTextureTransform`
	 `  TextureTransform {`
	 `  center 0 0`
	 `  translation 0 0`
	 `  rotation 0`
	 `  scale 1 1`
	 `}`

Table 5.20. Node Syntax for TextureTransform

The TextureTransform fields can also be animated so that the texture moves over the object's surface. Chapter 7, Event Animation and Interpolation includes examples for modifying values in the field types provided by TextureTransform. PositionInterpolator2D can animate the translation field, ScalarInterpolator can animate the rotation field, and PositionInterpolator2D can animate the scale field.

It is possible to achieve the effect of water flowing over a hard surface by creating a texture that has ripples and lots of transparent pixels. A PositionInterpolator2D node driving a TextureTransform node moves the water over the surface.

3.8.1. translation

The translation field controls the placement of the image on the surface. Changing this field changes the position on the object mapped to the lower-left corner of the image. The field provides 2 values in the (s,t) coordinate system as described in the X3DTexture2DNode section earlier in this chapter. The values in the field range from minus one to positive one, inclusive. Values outside the range are mapped back into range by taking the modulus with one (in other words, using only the fractional part). A value of zero does not change the location for that coordinate.

The example in Figure 5.12 (TextureTransformTranslation.x3d) shows how a texture is mapped to a box and the effect of translating the texture. The example shows no translation (top), `translation=".33 .5"` (bottom-left) and `translation=".25 .33"` (bottom-right).

3.8.2. center and rotation

The rotation of the texture is applied about the center, although in a counterintuitive way. The center is specified in (s,t) texture coordinates as an offset from the middle of the texture image. The rotation is applied to the definition of local (s,t) coordinate axes, not the coordinate values themselves. This axes-centric (rather than image-centric) approach means that the direction of rotation is opposite to what might otherwise be expected. The rotation value is specified in radians and follows the right-hand rule, meaning that a positive clockwise rotation value for the (s,t) axes correspondingly rotates the texture coordinates counterclockwise. This relationship is shown in Figure 5.13.

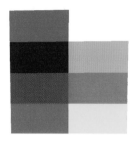

Figure 5.12. TextureTransform can translate a texture image (shown above) to better align with underlying geometry (shown below).

3.8.3. scale

Shrinking or magnifying the texture is controlled by the scale field. This field specifies a two-component scale factor that is applied to the (s,t) coordinates prior to mapping the texture to the object. Nonuniform values are possible, meaning that the scale components along each (s,t) axis can be different. Thus a `scale="3 0.5"` shows one third of the texture along the s-axis and two copies of the texture along the t-axis.

The PositionInterpolator2D node can be used to animate TextureTransform scale. PositionInterpolator2D is presented in Chapter 7, Event Animation and Interpolation.

3.8.4. Hints and warnings

TextureTransform is typically a peer of the corresponding texture node.

Simple transformations can usually be accomplished via trial and error. Any non-trivial translation, rotation, and scaling usually requires a sophisticated 3D authoring tool that permits What You See Is What You Get (WYSIWYG) modification of applied textures.

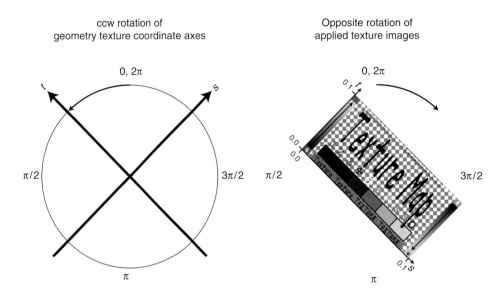

Figure 5.13. Rotation of texture coordinates works in texture coordinate space, changing the alignment of textures on the underlying geometry in the opposite direction.

The primary issue to remember with TextureTransform is that all fields operate on the (s,t) coordinate axes rather than the image itself, so the resulting effects are typically the opposite of what might otherwise be expected.

The final TextureTransform example in Figure 5.15 (TextureTransformFull.x3d) shows different examples of how translation, rotation, and scaling of a texture can be mapped to a cube.

3.9. TextureCoordinate node

The TextureCoordinate node that specifies a set of 2D texture coordinates used by vertex-based geometry nodes. It is a geometry property node, meaning that it can be used as a child in some geometry nodes.

TextureCoordinate implements the X3DTextureCoordinateNode interface. The TextureCoordinate node is in the Interchange profile. The node has the fields defined in Table 5.21. Node syntax is shown in Table 5.22.

IndexedFaceSet and ElevationGrid are example nodes that can contain a TextureCoordinate child to achieve this capability. If no TextureCoordinate node is provided, default texture coordinates are computed ranging from (0,0) at the first vertex to (1,1) at the last vertex.

If the ElevationGrid contains a TextureCoordinate node, the TextureCoordinate node contains at least (xDimension) × (zDimension) texture coordinates. A 2D (s,t) texture coordinate is provided for each ElevationGrid height vertex, ordered as follows:

Figure 5.14. Scaling of texture coordinates can create the appearance of an 8×8 PixelTexture from a 2×2 PixelTexture.

Figure 5.15. TextureTransform can translate, rotate, and scale textures in combination.

Type	accessType	Name	Default	Range	Profile
MFVec2f	inputOutput	point	[ ]	(−∞, ∞)	
SFNode	inputOutput	metadata	NULL	[X3DMetadataObject]	Core

Table 5.21. Field Definitions for TextureCoordinate Node

XML Syntax (.x3d)	ClassicVRML Syntax (.x3dv)

`<TextureCoordinate DEF=`
`  "MyTextureCoordinate"`
`  point="0 0, 0 1, 1 1, 1 0"`
`  containerField="texCoord"/>`
	`DEF My TextureCoordinate`
	`  TextureCoordinate {`
	`    point [ 0 0, 0 1, 1 1, 1 0 ]`
	`}`

Table 5.22. Node Syntax for TextureCoordinate

`VertexTexCoord[i,j]` = `TextureCoordinate[i + j × xDimension]`, where $(0 \leq i <$ xDimension) and $(0 \leq j <$ zDimension), and `VertexTexCoord[i,j]` is the texture coordinate for the vertex defined by `height[i + (j × xDimension)]`.

3.9.1. point

The point array contains a set of MFVec2f (*s*,*t*) floating-point coordinates. Each 2-tuple value provides a proper 2D texture coordinate ranging [0,1] for the corresponding geometry vertex. This enables fine-grained mapping of texture pixels to arbitrarily complex geometry.

3.9.2. Hints and warnings

Because TextureCoordinate is in the Interchange profile, texturing can be a good way to achieve highly detailed shapes even when restricted to fewer X3D nodes. A single texture image may be a composite of multiple adjacent subimages, each of which is sliced out by various TextureCoordinate arrays and then applied to the appropriate piece of geometry. This technique is reminiscent of laying out clothing patterns on a piece of cloth. Usually special authoring-tool support is needed for accomplishing this task with multiple TextureCoordinate nodes.

As with TextureTransform, simple texture mappings may be achievable via trial and error. Any nontrivial mapping of texture coordinates usually requires a sophisticated 3D authoring tool that permits WYSIWYG modification of applied textures.

3.10. TextureCoordinateGenerator node

TextureCoordinateGenerator enables the automatic computation and generation of texture coodinates for geometric shapes. It can be used as a substitute for

TextureCoordinate node, which instead provides explicit (*s*,*t*) mappings for geometry vertices.

TextureCoordinateGenerator implements the X3DTextureCoordinateNode interface. The TextureCoordinateGenerator node is in the Immersive profile. The node has the fields defined in Table 5.23. Node syntax is shown in Table 5.24.

3.10.1. mode and parameter

Eleven procedural modes are provided for computing texture coordinates, each identified by a predefined string. The setup parameter values necessary for each mode are contained in the corresponding MFFloat parameter array.

Table 5.25 is copied from the X3D Specification (with permission) and describes texture coordinate generation nodes.

3.10.2. Hints and warnings

Some texture coordinate generation modes may be hardware accelerated, and some modes are view dependent.

Most models are quite sophisticated and likely require special authoring-tool support.

Type	accessType	Name	Default	Range	Profile
SFString	inputOutput	mode	"SPHERE"	see Table 5.25	Immersive
MFFloat	inputOutput	parameter	[ ]	see Table 5.25	Immersive
SFNode	inputOutput	metadata	NULL	[X3DMetadataObject]	Core

Table 5.23. Field Definitions for TextureCoordinateGenerator Node

XML Syntax (.x3d)	ClassicVRML Syntax (.x3dv)

`<TextureCoordinateGenerator DEF=`
`  "MyTextureCoordinateGenerator"`
`  mode="SPHERE"`
`  parameter="0 0, 0 1, 1 1, 1 0"`
`  containerField="texCoord"/>`
	`DEF MyTextureCoordinateGenerator`
	`  TextureCoordinateGenerator {`
	`  mode "SPHERE"`
	`  parameter [0 0, 0 1, 1 1, 1 0]`
	`}`

Table 5.24. Node Syntax for TextureCoordinateGenerator

Mode	Description
SPHERE	Creates texture coordinates for a spherical environment or "chrome" mapping based on the vertex normals transformed to camera space. $u = N_x/2 + 0.5$ $v = N_y/2 + 0.5$ where u and v are the texture coordinates being computed, and N_x and N_y are the x and y components of the camera-space vertex normal. If the normal has a positive x component, the normal points to the right, and the u coordinate is adjusted to address the texture appropriately. Likewise for the v coordinate: positive y indicates that the normal points up. The opposite is of course true for negative values in each component. If the normal points directly at the camera, the resulting coordinates should receive no distortion. The +0.5 bias to both coordinates places the point of zero-distortion at the center of the sphere map, and a vertex normal of $(0, 0, z)$ addresses this point. Note that this formula doesn't take account for the z component of the normal.
CAMERASPACENORMAL	Use the vertex normal, transformed to camera space, as input texture coordinates, resulting coordinates are in –1 to 1 range.
CAMERASPACE POSITION	Use the vertex position, transformed to camera space, as input texture coordinates
CAMERASPACE REFLECTIONVECTOR	Use the reflection vector, transformed to camera space, as input texture coordinates. The reflection vector is computed from the input vertex position and normal vector. $R = 2 \times DotProd(E,N) \times N - E$; In the preceding formula, R is the reflection vector being computed, E is the normalized position-to-eye vector, and N is the camera-space vertex normal. Resulting coordinates are in –1 to 1 range.
SPHERE-LOCAL	Sphere mapping but in local coordinates
COORD	Use vertex coordinates
COORD-EYE	Use vertex coordinates transformed to camera space
NOISE	Computed by applying Perlin solid noise function on vertex coordinates, parameter contains scale and translation [scale.x scale.y scale.z translation.x translation.y translation.z]
NOISE-EYE	Same as above but transform vertex coordinates to camera space first
SPHERE-REFLECT	Same as above but transform vertex coordinates to camera space first
SPHERE-REFLECT-LOCAL	Similar to "SPHERE-REFLECT", parameter[0] contains index of refraction, parameter[1 to 3] the eye point in local coordinates. By animating parameter [1 to 3] the reflection changes with respect to the point. Resulting coordinates are in –1 to 1 range.

Table 5.25. TextureCoordinateGenerator Mode and Parameter Values

4. Summary

4.1. Key ideas

Appearance is fundamental to all objects in an X3D scene, collecting individual geometry nodes together with material, texture, and line and fill properties. Material colors and transparencies are quite sophisticated, approximating the lighting response of objects in the real world. Textures allow 2D images or movies to be applied to geometric objects, enabling the possibility of photographic realism in certain objects. Fill and line properties provide further ways to highlight 3D shapes so that objects of interest can be identified or selected by a user.

4.2. Related nodes and concepts

Color and ColorRGBA nodes are alternatives to material and texture appearance, and are described in the following chapter. MultiTexture is an advanced appearance technique that is beyond the scope of this book.

The ability to ROUTE events that control movies or change other appearance-related values is described in Chapter 7, Event Animation and Interpolation.

4.3. Next chapter

Many more geometry nodes are described in Chapter 6, Geometry Nodes, Part 2: Points, Lines, and Polygons. These provide a great variety of ways to construct shapes that can be rendered using the appearance techniques described in this chapter.

Geometry Nodes, Part 2: Points, Lines, and Polygons

Drawing is a struggle between nature and the artist, in which the better the artist understands the intentions of nature, the more easily he will triumph over it. For him it is not a question of copying, but of interpreting in a simpler and more luminous language.
—Charles Baudelaire, *On the Ideal and the Model*, 1846.

1. What this chapter covers

Authors have a lot of flexibility when building shapes and creating X3D content because there are many different geometry nodes to choose from. Some nodes are quite detailed, providing direct control over individual coordinates when drawing points, lines, triangles, and polygons. Often these nodes are also used by 3D conversion programs, which export X3D from other file formats.

The geometry nodes are split into three separate chapters. Chapter 2 covers the basic primitive shapes and text. Chapter 6 (this chapter) covers the fundamental building nodes for points, lines, and polygons. Chapter 10, Geometry 2D, presents planar nodes. Chapter 13, Triangles, covers the low-level geometric shapes such as triangle sets. It is interesting that the triangle-based nodes in Chapter 13, although considered advanced topics, actually use low-level detail and simple verbose structures to produce geometry.

This geometry chapter covers the following nodes: Color and ColorRGBA, Coordinate and CoordinateDouble, PointSet, IndexedLineSet and IndexedFaceSet, ElevationGrid, and Extrusion. It provides a good mix of simple high-level expressive power and detailed low-level control over geometric definitions.

2. Concepts

This chapter presents the most commonly used geometry nodes for points, lines, and polygons. First presented are several nodes that are building blocks to construct polygonal geometry: Color and Coordinate, along with their further-detailed counterparts ColorRGBA and CoordinateDouble. The fundamental nodes PointSet, LineSet, IndexedLineSet, and IndexedFaceSet are commonly used for basic geometry definition. ElevationGrid and Extrusion are more powerful and can describe sophisticated shapes using straightforward, concise, high-level definitions.

As with the other geometry nodes, each of these geometry nodes can be paired with a sibling Appearance/Material or Appearance/Texture combination under the shared parent Shape node. However, alternative finer-grained control of coloring for each point, line segment, polygon, or surface in the geometry is also possible by using the Color and Normal nodes instead.

These node descriptions include a lot of detail because the nodes themselves provide low-level control over the geometry being drawn. Fortunately, however, the concepts for these nodes are straightforward and consistent throughout. Once the basics are mastered, most of the effort needed for authoring these nodes has to do with bookkeeping chores: defining points accurately, listing index values in proper order, and so on.

2.1. Purpose and common functionality

Most shapes that are defined and rendered in X3D are polygonal in nature. Their root definitions may be simple, abstract primitive geometry defined from a mathematical perspective (such as Sphere and Cone) but they are constructed and drawn as polygonal surfaces. This means that most X3D geometric objects are usually reduced to triangles and quadrilaterals by the browser prior to rendering.

The polygonal nodes presented in this chapter provide X3D authors with much closer control over the definition of specific geometric shapes. These are often used for the following tasks:

- defining individual or aggregated polygonal surfaces, point by point

- defining individual colors, either for each polygon or for each vertex (i.e., point)

- rapidly defining square height-field surfaces, such as a terrain landscape or the height output of a 2-input function

- simply specifying complex shapes by extruding a cross-sectional surface of revolution along a spine

Common characteristics of geometry nodes are described in the following section.

2.2. Common geometry fields

Because the geometry nodes available in X3D are quite varied, there is only one primary X3DGeometryNode type. Geometry nodes implement the X3DGeometryNode as a marker interface to permit strong type checking during scene graph construction. Because of X3D's strong typing of nodes, geometry is only allowed to be placed inside a Shape node. As a result, geometry always has some kind of default appearance or color, and a wide variety of other potential errors constructing the scene graph are avoided.

The X3DGeometryNode type does not require any specific field definitions because of the diversity found in the geometry nodes. Nevertheless, many common fields can be found. Most of the geometry-primitive nodes included in this chapter have common child nodes: Color, Coordinate, Normal, and TextureCoordinate nodes. Common simple fields such as ccw, colorPerVertex, convex, and creaseAngle describe frequently used functionality and have consistent definitions.

Table 6.1 lists commonly occurring geometry fields. The solid field is described in Chapter 2, Geometry Nodes, Part 1: Primitives. Descriptions of other fields follow.

2.2.1. ccw

The ccw (counterclockwise) field describes the relationship between the ordering of vertex coordinates and the orientation of the normal (perpendicular) vector. A counter-clockwise

Type	accessType	Name	Default	Range	Profile
SFBool	initializeOnly	ccw	true		Interchange
SFBool	initializeOnly	colorPerVertex	true		Interchange
SFBool	initializeOnly	convex	true		Interchange
SFFloat	initializeOnly	creaseAngle	0	$[0,\infty)$	Interchange
SFBool	initializeOnly	normalPerVertex	true		Interchange
SFBool	initializeOnly	solid	true		Interchange
MFInt32	initializeOnly	colorIndex	[]	$[0,\infty)$ or -1	Interchange
MFInt32	initializeOnly	coordIndex	[]	$[0,\infty)$ or -1	Interchange
MFInt32	initializeOnly	normalIndex	[]	$[0,\infty)$ or -1	Interchange

Table 6.1. Common Fields for Geometry Nodes

ordering (ccw="true") means that the perpendicular vector derived from the points follows the right-hand rule, so that the curve of the fingers of the right hand follow the direction of the points, and the right thumb points in the direction of the normal vector. For example, holding your right hand in front of a clock face with the thumb pointing straight out from the center of the clock towards your point of view shows the fingers rotating in a counter-clockwise direction.

Because polygons in 3D graphics have two independent sides, switching the value of ccw on a single-sided polygon (i.e., solid="true") reverses the side on which polygons are visible.

2.2.2. colorPerVertex

The colorPerVertex field describes whether Color node color values are applied per vertex (colorPerVertex="true") or per polygon (colorPerVertex="false").

When colors are appled on a vertex-by-vertex basis, the intermediate colors between points are interpolated linearly. The changing color of pixels across a polygon are computed as a weighted linear average among the red, green, and blue values respectively. This property can also be used for interesting special effects, such as those produced using a ColorInterpolator node (described in Chapter 7, Event Animation and Interpolation).

The Example scene ColorPerVertexExamples.x3d and Figure 6.1 show colorPerVertex effects for IndexedFaceSet and IndexedLineSet, respectively.

2.2.3. convex

The convex field describes whether all polygons in a shape are convex (convex="true"), or whether one or more polygons are possibly concave (convex="false"). A convex polygon is planar, does not intersect itself, and each interior angle is less than 180 degrees. The opposite of convex is concave. One way to remember these terms is that concave polygons have "caves" in them, and convex polygons do not. More precisely, a polygon is only convex if connecting any two of its vertices does not intersect space outside the polygon boundaries.

Freehand drawing can reveal that all triangles are convex. Figure 6.2 illustrates five convex and two concave polygons.

Graphics hardware uses many rendering optimizations to draw triangles as quickly as possible, thereby improving frame rate. Assuming that polygons with 4 or more sides

Figure 6.1. colorPerVertex="true" and colorPerVertex="false" effects for IndexedFaceSet and IndexedLineSet.

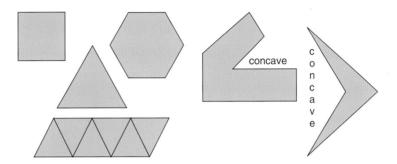

Figure 6.2. Convex and concave shapes.

are convex allows more efficient and faster drawing, because the hardware does not have to check and correct for concave polygons.

2.2.4. creaseAngle

The creaseAngle field defines the angle (in radians) that is used to determe whether adjacent polygons are drawn with sharp edges or smooth shading. If the angle between normals of two adjacent polygons is less than creaseAngle, smooth shading is rendered across the shared line segment.

Experimenting with creaseAngle can lead to interesting effects on complex geometry such as scanned figures. Note however that creaseAngle has no effect on adjacent edges shared with separate geometry nodes, which may occur if the overall geometry is produced as multiple nodes that are collected together.

Direct control of all creases is possible: `creaseAngle="0"` means all edges are rendered sharply, `creaseAngle="3.14159"` ("π radians", which equals 180°) means polygon edges change color gradually and are rendered smoothly.

The creaseAngle field has no effect on the smoothness or roughness of rendered silhouette edges at geometry boundaries.

2.2.5. Index fields: colorIndex, coordIndex, and normalIndex

Each of these three index fields describes the order in which to connect and apply array values in the child Color, Coordinate, and Normal nodes. This allows for a highly compact representation when constructing polygons from points, assigning colors to vertices or polygonal faces, and so on.

The colorIndex values provide the order in which colors are applied, either on a per-vertex or per-polygon basis. The initial color corresponds to colorIndex 0, the second color is colorIndex 1, and so on.

The coordIndex indices provide the order in which Coordinate point values are applied. The order of the contained point array starts at index 0, and commas are optional between each set of defined values. The flag value of −1 indicates that the current line (or polygon) is complete, and that any subsequent points start a new line (or polygon).

Similarly, normalIndex values provide the order in which normal (i.e., perpendicular) vectors are applied, either on a per-vertex or per-polygon basis. Normals are discussed further in Chapter 13, the fourth geometry chapter which covers the triangle nodes.

2.2.6. Hints and warnings

A polyline or polygon can be connected (formally called *closed*) by using the same index as both first and last values. This is especially valuable if you are reusing Color and Coordinate nodes to provide IndexedLineSet outlines of IndexedFaceSet geometry. If the first and last index values are not identical, then lines are not closed but polygons are filled in.

Translated outputs from modeling tools are often inconsistent, so switching ccw from true to false can sometimes reorient geometry properly. This can be especially helpful if only one side of the geometry is to be drawn.

Concave polygons can always be split into convex triangles, either manually or through the use of an authoring tool that splits and fixes concave polygons. Such prior optimization of scene geometry is a good practice that can prevent drawing mishaps on older, less-capable software and hardware.

3. Node descriptions

3.1. Color and ColorRGBA nodes

The colors of individual polygons, line segments, and points can each be defined as 3-tuple RGB or 4-tuple RGBA values. RGB stands for Red Green Blue, with values ranging [0,1] for each color component. The A in RGBA stands for Alpha, meaning the opacity coefficient. Alpha can be thought of as the opposite of transparency (literally alpha=1−transparency). Alpha values range from 0 to 1 for fully transparent to fully opaque, respectively. The definition of specific color values is contained in the single field of this node, named color (in lower case).

The Color and ColorRGBA nodes can appear in the color field of the following nodes: PointSet, IndexedLineSet, IndexedFaceSet, IndexedTriangleFanSet, IndexedTriangleSet, IndexedTriangleStripSet, TriangleFanSet, TriangleSet, and TriangleStripSet. The first four nodes are discussed in this chapter. The remaining Indexed nodes are discussed in Chapter 13, Geometry Nodes, Part 4: Triangles. The field signatures for the Color and ColorRGBA nodes are shown in Table 6.2. Node syntax is shown in Table 6.3.

The example scene Color.x3d in Figure 6.3 provides a simple example of how to use the Color node.

Type	accessType	Name	Default	Range	Profile
MFColor/ MFColorRGBA	inputOutput	color	NULL	[0,1]	Interchange
SFNode	inputOutput	metadata	NULL	[X3DMetadataObject]	Core

Table 6.2. Field Definitions for Color and ColorRGBA Nodes

XML Syntax (.x3d)	ClassicVRML Syntax (.x3dv)

<Color DEF="MyColorNode"
   color="0 0 0, 1 1 1, 1 0 0,
    0 1 0, 0 0 1"/>
or
<ColorRGBA DEF="MyRGBAColorNode"
   color="0 0 0 0.5, 1 1 1 0.5,
    1 0 0 0.5, 0 1 0 0.5,
    0 0 1 0.5"/>
	DEF MyColorNode Color {
	   color [0 0 0, 1 1 1, 1 0 0,
	    0 1 0, 0 0 1]
	}
	or
	DEF MyColorRGBANode ColorRGBA {
	   color [0 0 0 0.5, 1 1 1 0.5,
	    1 0 0 0.5, 0 1 0 0.5, 0 0 1
	    0.5]
	}

Table 6.3. Node Syntax for Color

3.1.1. Hints and warnings

If both a Material node and a ColorRGBA node are specified for a geometric shape, the color values of the Color node supercede the diffuse and transparency components of the Material node.

3.2. Coordinate and CoordinateDouble nodes

The vertices of points, lines, and polygons are each defined as coordinates in 3-space. The Coordinate node defines these points in floating-point coordinates, which has 32-bit precision and is satisfactory for most scenes. The CoordinateDouble node defines these points when double-precision (64-bit) accuracy is needed. The definition is contained in the single field of this node, called point.

The Coordinate and CoordinateDouble nodes can appear in the coord field of the following nodes: PointSet, IndexedLineSet, IndexedFaceSet, IndexedTriangleFanSet, IndexedTriangleSet, IndexedTriangleStripSet, TriangleFanSet, TriangleSet, and TriangleStripSet. The first four nodes are discussed in this chapter. The remaining Indexed nodes are discussed in the fourth geometry chapter (Chapter 13, Geometry

Figure 6.3. Example use of the Color node to provide `colorPerVertex="true"` to the pump house in the Kelp Forest world.

Nodes, Part 4: Triangles). The field signatures for the Coordinate and CoordinateDouble nodes are in Table 6.4. Node syntax is shown in Table 6.5.

Coordinate points may be used in direct sequential order (as with several of the various unindexed triangle nodes described in Chapter 13), or they may be indexed to appear in any order. Indexing is a good way to reduce the size of a large Coordinate node when certain points are referenced and reused many times.

3.2.1. Hints and warnings

Commas are generally treated as whitespace. In the XML-based .x3d encoding, commas can only be placed between point values, not inside the individual $(x\ y\ z)$ 3-tuples. Therefore the use of commas is a personal preference, because commas can sometimes help readability and debugging efforts. Commas usually are not used during large conversions of content, because file size reduction is valuable and multitudinous coordinate points are unlikely to be read by a human anyway.

Type	accessType	Name	Default	Range	Profile
MFVec3f/ MFVec3d	inputOutput	point	NULL	(−∞, +∞)	Interchange
SFNode	inputOutput	metadata	NULL	[X3DMetadataObject]	Core

Table 6.4. Field Definitions for Coordinate and CoordinateDouble Nodes

XML Syntax (.x3d)	ClassicVRML Syntax (.x3dv)

`<Coordinate DEF="MyCoordinateNode"`
`    point="0 0 0, 1 1 1"/>`
	`DEF MyCoordinateNode`
	`        Coordinate {`
	`    point [0 0 0, 1 1 1]`
	`    }`

Table 6.5. Node Syntax for Coordinate

A correct example with acceptable commas between each 3-tuple is `<Coordinate point="1 2 3, 4 5 6"/>`, and an incorrect example with excessive commas is `<Coordinate point="11, 12, 13, 14, 15, 16"/>`.

In general, use a Coordinate node rather than CoordinateDouble for geometry definitions. CoordinateDouble is only needed when the scales in a scene are exceptionally large (such as geographic positioning) or exceptionally small (such as unscaled molecular distances). For such cases it may be more practical to use a local coordinate scale other than meters, restoring metric scale via a Transform at the top level of the scene.

Avoiding double precision saves both memory and processing time. Because most 3D-graphics hardware cards only use single precision for rendering, double-precision inputs usually have no effect on rendering quality.

3.3. PointSet node

The PointSet node creates a series of simple unconnected points. Each separate point is defined by each of the point-array values within a child Coordinate node. Because each contained Coordinate value defines a separate point, no indexing is necessary.

Color can be set uniformly for all points using the emissiveColor field of a sibling Material node. Alternatively, individual colors for each point can be set by the sequentially corresponding color values in a Color (or ColorRGBA) node. The diffuseColor field and other fields of an adjacent Material node are then ignored and have no effect.

The PointSet node is in the Interchange profile. The node has the fields defined in Table 6.6. Node syntax is shown in Table 6.7.

Type	accessType	Name	Default	Range	Profile
SFNode	inputOutput	color	NULL	[X3DColorNode]	Interchange
SFNode	inputOutput	coord	NULL	[X3DCoordinateNode]	Interchange
SFNode	inputOutput	metadata	NULL	[X3DMetadataObject]	Core

Table 6.6. Field Definitions for PointSet Node

XML Syntax (.x3d)	ClassicVRML Syntax (.x3dv)

``
<PointSet DEF="MyPointNode">
    <Color color="1 0 0, 0 1 0, 0 0 1,
        0.8 0.8 0.8"/>
    <Coordinate point="−2 0 0, 0 0 0,
        0 0 2, 0 0 4"/>
</PointSet>
``
	``
	DEF MyPointNode PointSet {
	  color Color {
	    color [1 0 0, 0 1 0, 0 0 1,
	      0.8 0.8 0.8]
	  }
	  coord Coordinate {
	    point [−2 0 0, 0 0 0, 0 0 2,
	      0 0 4]
	  }
	}
	``

Table 6.7. Node Syntax for IndexedPointSet

The browser is free to determine the number of pixels used to draw each point; however, the number is the same for every point. Many browsers choose to draw a point as a single pixel. Browsers driving high-resolution displays may choose to draw each point with more than one pixel.

The term *pixel* is an abbreviation for picture element, that is, the smallest drawable color on a display screen. Because pixel size can vary quite widely depending on screen resolution, authors thus have little control over the actual on-screen size of each point. Different displays and different resolutions can make points look quite different.

The example scene PointSet.x3d in Figure 6.4 shows how a PointSet node is used to make the waypoints of the shark's path through the virtual exhibit.

3.3.1. Hints and warnings

When coloring a PointSet using a Material node, be sure to assign a value to emissiveColor. Other objects are primarily colored by diffuseColor, but color fields other than emissiveColor have no effect on a PointSet.

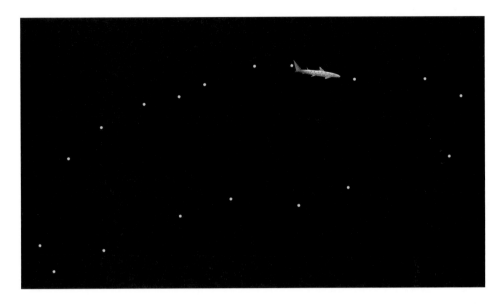

Figure 6.4. Example use of PointSet node highlight the waypoints of the shark's path. The points have been increased in size to better illustrate them.

Be sure to use a different color than the current Background to make points visible. The Background node is described in Chapter 11, Lighting and Environment Nodes.

Points are notoriously difficult to see because they are small. Furthermore, because the size of each point does not vary regardless of distance from the user's current view, they can often be confusing because perspective is not preserved. This rendering approach works against a proper perspective, making it difficult to tell whether points are closer or farther than another object.

Because of these perspective inconsistencies, PointSet is seldom used. Use PointSet sparingly (if at all) and reserve it for special effects. Consider using boxes or billboarded rectangular polygons when displaying numerous small objects at a distance.

3.4. IndexedLineSet node

The IndexedLineSet node creates a set of lines. A single node can create multiple disconnected lines, and each line may have multiple segments. Thus each set of connected line segments is called a *polyline* and is piece-wise linear.

IndexedLineSet is a geometry node that can contain a Color node and a Coordinate node. Either the Color node values (if supplied) or Material emissiveColor values are used to color lines and points. The diffuseColor field and other fields of a Material node are ignored and have no effect.

Lines are not lit, are not texture-mapped, and do not participate in collision detection.

Each line consists of at least two vertices and all points in the virtual space that lie on the straight line connecting these adjacent vertices. The IndexedLineSet node does not define a surface, though authors can construct wireframes that suggest a surface. Lines can be closed (meaning connected) when the end-point is the same as the start-point. Even then it is just a polyline, because the interior is never filled.

The IndexedLineSet node is in the Interchange profile. The node has the fields defined in Table 6.8. Note that the IndexedLineSet fields are a strict subset of the fields for IndexedFaceSet. Node syntax is shown in Table 6.9.

Type	accessType	Name	Default	Range	Profile
MFInt32	initializeOnly	colorIndex	[]	[0,∞) or −1	Interchange
SFBool	initializeOnly	colorPerVertex	true		Interchange
MFInt32	initializeOnly	coordIndex	[]	[0,∞) or −1	Interchange
SFNode	inputOutput	color	NULL	[X3DColorNode]	Interchange
SFNode	inputOutput	coord	NULL	[X3DCoordinateNode]	Interchange
SFNode	inputOutput	metadata	NULL	[X3DMetadataObject]	Core

Table 6.8. Field Definitions for IndexedLineSet Node

XML Syntax (.x3d)	ClassicVRML Syntax (.x3dv)

`<IndexedLineSet DEF=`
`  "DefaultIndexedLineSet"`
`  colordIndex="0 1 2 3 −1"`
`  colorIndex="0 1 2 3 −1"`
`  colorPerVertex="true"`
`  containerField="geometry">`
`<Coordinate point="−2 0 0, 0 0 0,`
`  0 0 2, 0 0 4"/>`
`<Color color="1 0 0, 0 1 0, 0 0 1,`
`  0.8 0.8 0.8"/>`
`</IndexedLineSet>`
	`DEF DefaultIndexedLineSet`
	`  IndexedLineSet {`
	`    colorIndex [ 0 1 2 3 −1 ]`
	`    coordIndex [ 0 1 2 3 −1 ]`
	`    coord Coordinate {`
	`      point [ −2 0 0, 0 0 0,`
	`        0 0 2, 0 0 4 ]`
	`    }`
	`    color Color {`
	`      color [ 1 0 0, 0 1 0, 0 0 1,`
	`        0.8 0.8 0.8 ]`
	`    }`
	`  }`

Table 6.9. Node Syntax for IndexedLineSet

The IndexedLineSet and IndexedFaceSet nodes define geometry vertex by vertex (meaning point by point), using index values to carefully sequence each value from the Coordinate node point array. This approach allows for a highly compact representation of the vertices. A vertex may thus be used many times, but only needs to be listed once in the Coordinate node. Because Coordinate nodes can be shared by DEF and USE naming, this approach can also be an efficient way to save space when repeatedly defining similar geometries.

The order of the vertices in the Coordinate node can be decided at the convenience of the author, because the coordIndex sequence can refer to them in any order needed. Each grouped set of indices is terminated by a −1 sentinel value, creating polyline segments and disconnecting from any further segment definitions. It is not necessary (but a good practice) to also terminate the last set of indices with a −1 value, because the same Coordinate node can then be reused to produce a connected IndexedLineSet outline of an IndexedFaceSet.

The appearance of lines is noticably different from surfaces. Lines are not affected by lights and cannot be texture-mapped. Because emissiveColor is applied, they tend to glow and may be the only objects visible if all lights are turned off.

When a child Color node is provided, the colorPerVertex field controls how colors are applied to the polyline segments. If `colorPerVertex="true"` then colors are applied point by point and blended (interpolated) in between. If `colorPerVertex="false"` then a single color is applied to each polyline segment.

The color values are applied to each line segment in the order determined by the colorIndex field. If no colorIndex values are provided, then each of the colors is applied in order: the first-defined line segment receives the first color, the second-defined line segment has the second color applied, and so on. In this case, there must be at least as many colors in the Color node as there are line segments. If the colorIndex field is used, then there must be at least as many values in the colorIndex field as there are line segments, and the index values (counting from zero) must not be greater than the maximum index of the defined color values.

Lines have several properties that are different from polygonal surfaces, summarized as follows:

- Lines do not participate in collision detection.

- Lines are solid and drawn with 1–pixel thickness by default.

- The LineProperties node can specify lineType and width properties applicable to line geometry.

The example scene IndexedLineSet.x3d in Figure 6.5 shows the shark's path moving through the virtual exhibit. The line width has been thickened so that it is more easily visible in this book, and might not appear so large on a computer monitor.

3.4.1. Hints and warnings

When coloring an IndexedLineSet node with a Material node, be sure to assign a value to emissiveColor. Other objects are primarily colored by diffuseColor, but that field has no effect on an IndexedLineSet.

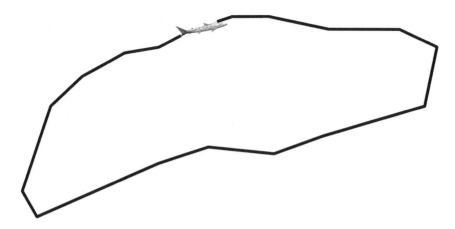

Figure 6.5. Shark waypoints connected as an IndexedLineSet show the path travelled.

If lines need to be collidable with the viewer, add transparent polygonal geometry at the same location as each line. A Box or a simple rectangular IndexFacedSet can work well because it has few faces, which keeps the computational cost of collision low. Nonrendered Collision proxy geometry (described in Chapter 12, Environment Sensors and Sound Nodes) needs to be as minimalist as possible in order to achieve the desired effect.

Try to use a different color than the current Background to make isolated lines easily visible. The Background node is described in Chapter 11, Lighting and Environment Nodes.

Consider using long narrow boxes or billboarded rectangular polygons when displaying numerous lines at a distance and when true perspective is needed.

Step-wise colors or linear interpolation of colors can be used as good scientific visualization techniques to map arbitrary function values to a color map.

3.5. LineSet node

The LineSet node also creates a set of lines. Rendering of colors and interaction behavior are similar in most respects to IndexedLineSet, except for defining which Coordinate points to use.

Rather than use coordIndex and colorIndex fields to define polyline segments, the LineSet node uses Coordinate and Color values directly in the order they are defined. The field vertexCount is an array of integers that defines how many sequential point values are used for each polyline.

The LineSet node is in the Interchange profile. The node has the fields defined in Table 6.10. Node syntax is shown in Table 6.11.

Type	accessType	Name	Default	Range	Profile
MFInt32	initializeOnly	vertexCount	[]	[0, ∞) or −1	Interchange
SFNode	inputOutput	color	NULL	[X3DColorNode]	Interchange
SFNode	inputOutput	coord	NULL	[X3DCoordinateNode]	Interchange
SFNode	inputOutput	metadata	NULL	[X3DMetadataObject]	Core

Table 6.10. Field Definitions for LineSet Node

XML Syntax (.x3d)	ClassicVRML Syntax (.x3dv)
```<LineSet DEF="MyLineSet"` ` containerField="geometry"` ` vertexCount="2 2">` ` <Coordinate point="−2 0 0, 0 0 0,` ` 0 0 2, 0 0 4"/>` ` <Color color="1 0 0, 0 1 0, 0 0 1,` ` 0.8 0.8 0.8"/>` `</LineSet>```	```DEF MyLineSet LineSet {` ` vertexCount [2 2]` ` coord Coordinate {` ` point [−2 0 0, 0 0 0,` ` 0 0 2, 0 0 4]` ` }` ` color Color {` ` color [1 0 0, 0 1 0, 0 0 1,` ` 0.8 0.8 0.8]` ` }` `}```

Table 6.11. Node Syntax for LineSet

The LineSet nodes define geometry vertex by vertex from the point array in the contained Coordinate or CoordinateDouble node. This approach provides a reasonably compact representation of the vertices in polylines. Because the points must be provided in order, any specific point location that is used more than once must be repeated.

If a Color or ColorRGBA node is also contained, then color values are applied in order, one at a time for each vertex. Colors between each vertex vary according to the weighted linear average, providing a smooth transition of colors.

As with IndexedLineSet, LineSet lines are not lit, are not texture-mapped, and do not participate in collision detection.

The example scene LineSet.x3d in Figure 6.6 is the same example as IndexedLineSet.x3d in Figure 6.5, except that it uses the LineSet node rather than the IndexedLineSet node, and waypoints are also displayed. As before, line widths and point sizes have been enhanced for better visibility.

3.5.1. Hints and warnings

The same hints and warnings provided for IndexedLineSet are applicable to LineSet.

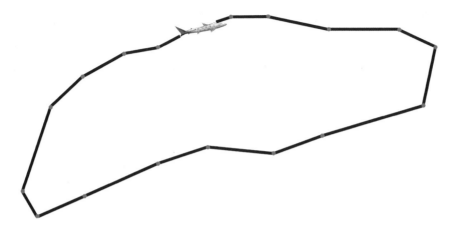

Figure 6.6. Shark waypoints connected with a LineSet show the path travelled. The lines have been made thicker to better illustrate them.

3.6. IndexedFaceSet node

The IndexedFaceSet node creates a set of polygons, sometimes refered to as faces. Each polygon face is defined vertex by vertex, meaning point by point. Each point value is defined in a contained Coordinate or CoordinateDouble node.

IndexedFaceSet has many features. It is the most commonly used node for creation of shapes polygon by polygon. Although there are a lot of details to learn, it is an important node to master. Understanding how IndexedFaceSet works makes it easier to understand many other geometry nodes.

The IndexedFaceSet node is in the Interchange profile. The node has the fields defined in Table 6.12. Node syntax is shown in Table 6.13.

The IndexedLineSet and IndexedFaceSet nodes define geometry vertex by vertex, using index values to sequence each value from the Coordinate node point array. This approach allows for a highly compact representation of the vertices. Thus a vertex may be reused many times, but only needs to be listed once in the Coordinate node. This is an efficient way to save space when approximating a curved surface with a tightly connected mesh of polygons.

Both IndexedFaceSet and IndexedLineSet nodes define their geometry using an index into the vertex array (which is contained in the child Coordinate node). This allows for a highly compact representation of the vertices. A vertex may be used many times, but only needs to be listed once. The order of the vertices in the Coordinate node can thus be sequenced however the author wants, as long as the ordered array of coordIndex values correspond to point values correctly.

The coordIndex field provides the indices of the vertices needed to produce properly connected polygons, each sequenced in the order needed. Each set of vertex indices corresponding to a single polygon is terminated by a −1 sentinel value. It is not necessary (but

Type	accessType	Name	Default	Range	Profile
SFBool	initializeOnly	ccw	true		Interchange
SFBool	initializeOnly	convex	true		Interchange
SFBool	initializeOnly	solid	true		Interchange
SFFloatl	initializeOnly	creaseAngle	0	[0,∞)	Interchange
SFBool	initializeOnly	colorPerVertex	true		Interchange
SFBool	initializeOnly	normalPerVertex	true		Interchange
MFInt32	initializeOnly	colorIndex	[]	[0,∞) or −1	Interchange
MFInt32	initializeOnly	coordIndex	[]	[0,∞) or −1	Interchange
MFInt32	initializeOnly	normalIndex	[]	[0,∞) or −1	Interchange
MFInt32	initializeOnly	texCoordIndex	[]	[0,∞)	Interchange
SFNode	inputOutput	color	NULL	[X3DColorNode]	Interchange
SFNode	inputOutput	coord	NULL	[X3DCoordinateNode]	Interchange
SFNode	inputOutput	normal	NULL	[X3DNormalNode]	Interchange
SFNode	inputOutput	texCoord	NULL	[X3DTexture CoordinateNode]	Interchange
SFNode	inputOutput	metadata	NULL	[X3DMetadataObject]	Core

Table 6.12. Field Definitions for IndexedFaceSet Node

remains a good authoring practice) to also terminate the final set of polygon indices with a −1 value.

When a contained Color node is provided (meaning the color field is non-NULL), the colorPerVertex field controls the interpretation and application of color values. If `colorPerVertex="false"` then a single color is applied to each polygon and no blending of colors takes place within the polygons. The specific choice of color applied to each polygon is then determined by the colorIndex field. If no colorIndex array is provided, then the colors from the Color node are applied in order. The first-defined polygon receives the first color, the second-defined polygon gets the second color, and so on. Thus, there must be at least as many colors in the Color node as there are polygons. If the colorIndex field is not empty, then the colorIndex field array is used to index the values in the Color node to determine which color is applied to each polygon. In this case, there must be at least as many color indices in the colorIndex field as there are polygons defined by the coordIndex array. As with coordIndex, the order of the indices is critical for determining which value goes where.

If per-vertex coloring has been specified (`colorPerVertex="true"`), then a separate color value is applied to each point defining the geometry. The color is blended within

XML Syntax (.x3d)	ClassicVRML Syntax (.x3dv)
```<IndexedFaceSet DEF= "MyIndexedFaceSet" containerField="geometry" ccw="true" colorPerVertex="true" convex="true" creaseAngle="0" normalPerVertex="true" solid="true"> <Coordinate DEF="DefaultCoordinate" containerField="coord"/> <Color DEF="DefaultColor" containerField="color"/> </IndexedFaceSet>```	```geometry DEF MyIndexedFaceSet IndexedFaceSet { ccw TRUE colorPerVertex TRUE convex TRUE creaseAngle 0 normalPerVertex TRUE solid TRUE coord DEF DefaultCoordinate Coordinate { } color DEF DefaultColor Color { } }```

Table 6.13. Node Syntax for IndexedFaceSet

the borders of the polygon, meaning across each polygon face. The specific choice of color applied to each vertex is determined by the colorIndex field. If the field holds an empty array, then the specified colors from the Color node are applied in order: the first-defined vertex receives the first color, the second-defined vertex gets the second color, and so on. In this case, the number of colors in the Color node must be at least equal to the number of vertices. If the colorIndex field is not empty, then the colorIndex field value is used to index the values in the Color node to determine the color of the line segment. There must be at least as many color indices in the colorIndex field as there are coordinate vertices defined.

The example scene IndexedFaceSet.x3d in Figure 6.7 provides a simple example illustrating the use of the IndexedFaceSet node.

3.6.1. Hints and warnings

IndexedFaceSet nodes are quite powerful and are often supported by various conversion programs that output VRML97 or X3D. Given the complexity of some geometric shapes, an authoring tool may be needed to take full advantage of its capabilities.

3.7. ElevationGrid node

The ElevationGrid node takes a rectangular array of floating-point values and creates a corresponding quadrilateral-based surface above (or below) the baseline $y=0$ rectangular plane.

Figure 6.7. The pump house is built using IndexedFaceSet. The rocker arm and piston are built using X3D primitives.

The ElevationGrid node is in the Interactive profile. Support for the ccw field is optional under the Interactive profile and fully supported under the Immersive profile. The node has the fields defined in Table 6.14. Node syntax is shown in Table 6.15.

ElevationGrid is a fundamental geometric shape that can create a variety of results. Because it takes a rectangular 2D array of values as an input, it can directly map a surface function of two sampled input values. ElevationGrid is often used for laying out terrain landscapes, and can also build the squared-off walls and floors of a house or village.

The ElevationGrid is sized by the xDimension and zDimension fields, so the height field must always contain an array of (xDimension × zDimension) values. If either dimension is less than 2, then no quadrilaterals are produced. The xSpacing and zSpacing fields are positive values that determine how many meters apart each point is placed. Thus, the overall footprint of an ElevationGrid node is (xDimension × xSpacing) by (zDimension × zSpacing) meters squared. Figure 6.8 (adapted with permission from the

Type	accessType	Name	Default	Range	Profile
SFBool	initializeOnly	ccw	true		Interchange
SFBool	initializeOnly	colorPerVertex	true		Interchange
SFBool	initializeOnly	normalPerVertex	true		Interchange
SFBool	initializeOnly	solid	true		Interchange
MFFloat	initializeOnly	height	[]	$(-\infty, \infty)$	Interchange
MFFloat	inputOnly	set_height	[]	$(-\infty, \infty]$	Interchange
SFFloatl	initializeOnly	creaseAngle	0	$[0, \infty)$	Interchange
MFInt32	initializeOnly	xDimension	0	$[0, \infty)$	Interchange
MFInt32	initializeOnly	xSpacing	1.0	$(0, \infty)$	Interchange
MFInt32	initializeOnly	zDimension	0	$[0, \infty)$	Interchange
MFInt32	initializeOnly	zSpacing	1.0	$(0, \infty)$	Interchange
SFNode	inputOutput	color	NULL	[X3DColorNode]	Interchange
SFNode	inputOutput	normal	NULL	[X3DNormalNode]	Interchange
SFNode	inputOutput	texCoord	NULL	[X3DTexture CoordinateNode]	Interchange Interchange
SFNode	inputOutput	metadata	NULL	[X3DMetadataObject]	Core

Table 6.14. Field Definitions for ElevationGrid Node

XML Syntax (.x3d)	ClassicVRML Syntax (.x3dv)
```<ElevationGrid DEF= "MyElevationGridNode" ccw="true" colorPerVertex="true" containerField="geometry" creaseAngle="0" normalPerVertex="true" solid="true" xDimension="0" xSpacing="1.0" zDimension="0" zSpacing="1.0"/>```	```DEF MyElevationGridNode ElevationGrid { ccw TRUE colorPerVertex TRUE creaseAngle 0 normalPerVertex TRUE solid TRUE xDimension 0 xSpacing 1.0 zDimension 0 zSpacing 1.0 }```

Table 6.15. Node Syntax for ElevationGrid

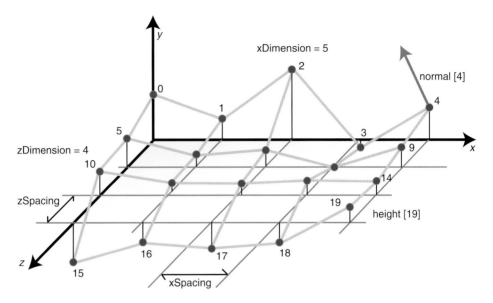

Figure 6.8. Indexing scheme for the ElevationGrid height array.

X3D Specification) shows the numbering order for individual points taken from the height field.

The colorPerVertex and normalPerVertex nodes control the application of sequential values from child Color node or Normal node, as available. When no Color (or ColorRGBA node) is provided, any accompanying Appearance, Material or texture nodes are used. Because there are no colorIndex or normalVertex fields, color or normal values that are used more than once must be repeated for each polygon (or vertex). Thus Color and Normal nodes inside an ElevationGrid can be quite verbose.

Normal vectors provide special effects or more efficient rendering computations, and are covered in Chapter 13.

If no Normal node is provided, normal values are automatically calculated by the browser and so provide proper shading. As a result, normals are not usually provided except for special effects. Tiled terrain landscapes built from multiple ElevationGrid nodes often merit special attention, however. In these scenes the Normal values are usually precalculated as a whole, so that the normals for coincident border segments of adjacent tiles are computed identically and seam artifacts due to mismatched normal values are avoided along the boundaries.

Perhaps surprisingly, it is quite easy to create nonplanar polygons through this approach. The example scene ElevationGridNonPlanarQuadrilaterals.x3d shown in Figure 6.9 demonstrates the different ways that a single quadrilateral made up of 3 planar points and 1 out-of-plane point can be tesselated in two different directions. The two

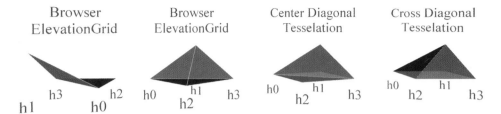

Figure 6.9. Alternate forms of tesselation are possible for nonplanar ElevationGrid quadrilaterals.

left-most views show the back and front of a simple 4-point ElevationGrid with `height="0 0 0 1"`.

The third view shows an alternate tesselation, where the nonplanar quadrilateral is divided via the center diagonal (from height[0] to height[3]). The fourth view shows the tesselation when the cross-diagonal (from height[1] to height[2]) is used instead.

The ccw, creaseAngle, and solid fields (described at the beginning of this chapter) operate as they do for other geometry nodes.

3.7.1. Hints and warnings

ElevationGrid artifacts resulting from nonplanar quadrilaterals are often minimized by setting creaseAngle suffiently high that tessellation differences are smoothly colored.

The height field is of accessType inputOnly as a performance optimization, so that browsers do not have to maintain this large float array in memory after tesselating an ElevationGrid into triangles. If the original values in the the height field are needed for other special computations, advanced techniques such as Scripting (Chapter 9) or Prototype declarations (Chapter 14) are necessary.

3.8. Extrusion node

The Extrusion node starts with a planar cross-section outline, and stretches it out around a series of line segments called a spine. The spine is a list of 3D points for a piecewise-linear curve that form a series of connected vertices. The spine can be open or closed (i.e., disconnected or connected start and end points). This approach can create shapes that are much like what happens when molten plastic is extruded through a hole pattern. Bending and twisting of the cross-section pattern is also possible at each defined spine point.

The Extrusion node is in the Immersive profile. The node has the fields defined in Table 6.16. Node syntax is shown in Table 6.17.

Extrusion is definitely one of the most flexible nodes available because so many different shapes can be constructed using it. It is also quite concise: just a few numbers can generate a complicated geometry. A crossSection can approximate many outlines, and

Type	accessType	Name	Default	Range	Profile
SFBool	initializeOnly	ccw	true		Immersive
SFBool	initializeOnly	convex	true		Immersive
SFBool	initializeOnly	beginCap	true		Immersive
SFBool	initializeOnly	endCap	true		Immersive
SFBool	initializeOnly	solid	true		Immersive
SFFloat	initializeOnly	creaseAngle	0	$[0,\infty)$	Immersive
MFVec2f	initializeOnly	crossSection	[1 1,1 −1,−1 −1, −1 1,1 1]	$(-\infty,\infty)$	Immersive
MFVec3f	initializeOnly	spine	[0 0 0,0 1 0]	$(-\infty,\infty)$	Immersive
MFVec2f	initializeOnly	scale	[1 1]	$(0,\infty)$	Immersive
MFRotation	initializeOnly	orientation	[0 0 1 0]	$[-1,1]$ $(-\infty,\infty)$	Immersive
SFNode	inputOutput	metadata	NULL	[X3DMetadataObject]	Core

Table 6.16. Field Definitions for Extrusion Node

XML Syntax (.x3d)	ClassicVRML Syntax (.x3dv)

`<Extrusion DEF="MyExtrusionNode"`
`    containerField="geometry"`
`    beginCap="true"`
`    ccw="true"`
`    convex="true"`
`    creaseAngle="0.0"`
`    crossSection="1 1, 1 −1, −1 −1,`
`      −1 1, 1 1"`
`    endCap="true"`
`    orientation="0 0 1 0"`
`    scale="1 1"`
`    solid="true"`
`    spine="0 0 0, 0 1 0"/>`
	`DEF MyExtrusionNode Extrusion {`
	`    beginCap TRUE`
	`    ccw TRUE`
	`    convex TRUE`
	`    creaseAngle 0.0`
	`    crossSection [1 1, 1 −1, −1 −1,`
	`      −1 1, 1 1]`
	`    endCap TRUE`
	`    orientation [0 0 1 0]`
	`    scale [1 1]`
	`    solid TRUE`
	`    spine [0 0 0, 0 1 0]`
	`}`

Table 6.17. Node Syntax for Extrusion

the spine is the path along which the crossSection is extruded. Nevertheless the Extrusion node can be difficult to handle, and can even define impossible or self-intersecting shapes, so take care when assembling one. It is definitely worth your time to understand the concepts involved because trial-and-error modifications can produce confusing results.

Follow these steps to build an extrusion:

- Define a 2D cross-section of connected line-segment coordinates, typically centered about the origin. Conceptually these are in the *x-z* plane. Repeat the first coordinate as the last coordinate if a closed cross-section is desired.

- Define a spine vector of 3D coordinates. Each spine point is the center about which a cross-sectional outline is placed.

- Optionally define an array of 2D scaling values that shrinks or expands the cross-section appearing at each spine point. A scaling value of "1 1" is uniform, a scaling value of "1 2" will nonuniformly double the *z* coordinates of the cross-section, and so on. If used, there must be one 2D scaling value for each spine point.

- Optionally define an array of orientation values that rotate each cross-section. Again, if used, there must be one 4-tuple rotation value for each spine point.

The Extrusion generator in the X3D browser uses each of these definitions first to construct the points for the outer hull of the extruded geometry, and then "connects the dots" to draw only the polygons that make up the outer shape.

Figure 6.10, adapted from the X3D Specification, shows how each spine point defines a *Spine-aligned Cross-section Plane (SCP)* where the cross-sections are each repeated. The SCP is also the reference plane for scaling and orientation changes at each point.

Most of the polygonal fields described at the beginning of this chapter are part of an Extrusion definition. Two additional fields are also provided, described in the following section.

3.8.1. beginCap and endCap

The beginCap and endCap fields are boolean values that determine whether the cross-sectional areas are drawn at the beginning and end of the Extrusion.

3.8.2. Extrusion examples

The first example presented here (ExtrusionPentagon.x3d) in Figure 6.11 is a regular pentagon at the cross section, centered about the origin, then extruded vertically along the *y*-axis at *y*-values of 0, 1, and 1.5 meters. The left-hand images show the final result, while the right-hand images reveal the cross-section areas and spine (which are not actually drawn).

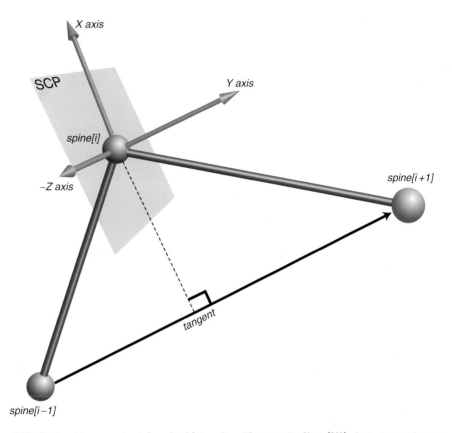

Figure 6.10. Points making up a spine define a local Spine-aligned Cross-section Plane (SCP) where cross-sections are repeated.

```
<Extrusion
    crossSection="-3.5 -1, -2.1 2.9, 2.2 2.9, 3.6 -1, 0 -3.5, -3.5 -1"
    spine="0 0 0, 0 1 0, 0 1.6 0"
    scale="1 1, 1 1, 0.2 0.2"
    solid="true"/>
```

The second example presented here (ExtrusionRoomWalls.x3d) in Figure 6.12 is a wall definition for a room laid out as the cross section, not centered about the origin, and extruded vertically along the y-axis at y-values of 0 and 2.5 meters.

```
<Extrusion
    crossSection="0 0, 0 6, 3 6, 3 5, 1 5, 1 1, 9 1, 9 5, 5 5, 5 6, 10 6, 10 0"
    solid="true" spine="0 0 0, 0 2.50"/>
```

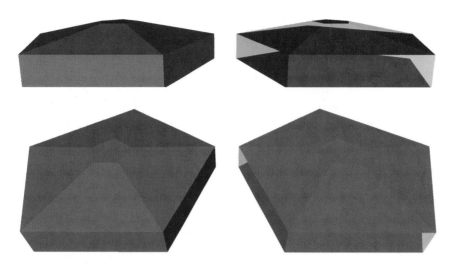

Figure 6.11. Example pentagon extrusion views showing default rendering on left and SCP on right.

The third example (ExtrusionCrossSectionExampleShip.x3d) in Figure 6.13 provides four different Extrusion nodes, each illustrated via an ExtrusionCrossSection prototype (included on the website in the examples for Chapter 14). The Extrusion for the ship's hull shows the use of the orientation array to tilt the endCap bow forward. Also note how `creaseAngle="3.14"` can smooth out the shading of hull polygons, eliminating blockiness that otherwise might distract by revealing the underlying cross-sectional shape.

```
<Extrusion DEF="Hull" creaseAngle="3.14"
    crossSection="0 1, 0.38 0.92, 0.71 0.71, 0.92 0.38, 1 0, 0.92
    −0.38, 0.71 −0.71, 0.38 −0.92, 0 −1"
    orientation="1 0 0 0, 1 0 0 0, 1 0 0 0, 0 1 0 0, 0 0 1 −0.5"
    scale="3 4, 4 4, 4 4, 4 4, 5.1" solid="false"
    spine="−20 0 0, −17 0 0, 0 0 0, 10 0 0, 22 1 0"/>
```

3.8.3. Hints and warnings

Setting `solid="false"` ensures that both sides of all polygons are drawn. This can help a great deal when trying to make sense of work in progress, when some Extrusion polygons may be flipped around and invisible when viewing the opposite side.

Figure 6.12. Extrusion example constructing the walls of a building.

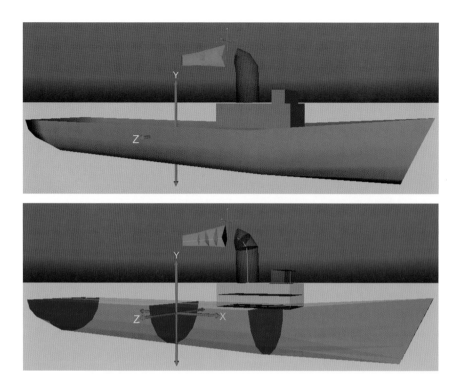

Figure 6.13. Extrusion example constructing the hull, superstructure, and smoke trail of a ship.

It is usually best to order the *x-z* cross-section points in accordance with the right-hand rule so that the normal vector is pointing upward along the *y* axis. Alternatively, change the counterclockwise parameter `ccw="false"` after to reverse the computation of normal direction.

4. Summary

This chapter presents the key geometry nodes: Color and ColorRGBA, Coordinate and CoordinateDouble, PointSet, IndexedLineSet, LineSet, IndexedFaceSet, ElevationGrid, and Extrusion.

4.1. Key ideas

Polygonal geometry is the essence of X3D graphics. Almost everything rendered is based on the tesselation of various geometry shapes into triangles. Working with examples is the best way to learn.

Be patient, remembering that the principles are consistent throughout each of these nodes. There is a lot of detail involved, but it becomes familiar with practice.

4.2. Related nodes and concepts

The primary related geometry chapters are Chapter 2, Geometry Nodes, Part 1: Primitives; and Chapter 13, Geometry Nodes, Part 4: Triangles. Chapter 5, Appearance, Material, and Textures describes how to modify the colors and shading used across entire shapes (as opposed to use of Color node for individual vertices and polygons). Chapter 3, Grouping Nodes describes how to modify the position, orientation, and size of shapes.

4.3. Next chapter

Chapter 7, Event Animation and Interpolation shows how to modify many aspects of shapes and shading at run time, bringing scenes to life.

Event Animation and Interpolation

If it ain't moving, it ain't 3D.
—Andy van Dam, SIGGRAPH pioneer, Brown University, Providence Rhode Island

1. What this chapter covers

High-quality 2D pictures can show perspective and depth, but they do not allow a viewer to look around or move objects in the image. As a result, spatial relationships can be unclear or confusing. However, when objects in an image can move in response to a user's interaction, the sense of depth and perspective immediately becomes evident. Therefore, motion and animation are fundamentally important to real-time 3D graphics. Scenes without changing perspective or object motion do not seem like 3D graphics to most users.

Many different kinds of animation are available in X3D. Fortunately for authors, a consistent event model makes the creation of scene animation fairly easy. The same pattern is used over and over again with only slight variations.

After describing general interpolation and animation concepts, this chapter covers the basic animation nodes available: TimeSensor, ScalarInterpolator, ColorInterpolator, PositionInterpolator, OrientationInterpolator, NormalInterpolator, CoordinateInterpolator, PositionInterpolator2D, and CoordinateInterpolator2D.

Interesting kinds of animation are possible by sensing user inputs and responding to scene activity. Sensor nodes are covered in Chapter 8, User Interactivity Nodes. Sequencers are discrete-value event producers that are similar to continuous-value interpolators. These nodes are covered in Chapter 9, Event Utilities and Scripting.

2. Concepts

2.1. Animation as scene-graph modification

The basic animation principle in X3D is simple: most field values can be modified at run time. Changes to field values are called *events*, each consisting of a timestamp and the update value. Some nodes have field sources that produce events, and then are connected via a ROUTE to fields in target nodes. Therefore, a *behavior* can be defined as the act of changing one or more values within an X3D scene graph to animate 3D content.

In the earliest days of VRML (VRML1, circa 1995), objects did not change shape or color, move, or otherwise modify any of their properties. Worlds were static and perfectly preserved, with the only animation in the scene caused by changing viewpoint. This is often referred to as *Museum VRML* because many scenes simply arranged various objects for a viewer to walk around and visit. Increased CPU computation power on personal computers opened up real-time 3D graphics to a much larger range and rate of change. Second-generation VRML97 allows the content creator to change everything in the world—objects can move, change shape, and vary appearance, with texture images emulating other effects. Third-generation X3D continues to extend the animation capabilities set by VRML97 by making all aspects of the scene graph directly and easily animatable.

From a browser perspective, the process of animation is accomplished by repeatedly recomputing the scene graph and then drawing a new view frame (or snapshot) in the output window. Changing views are achieved by modifying the position and orientation of objects in the scene. As one might expect, the faster an object moves in 3D coordinates relative to the camera viewpoint, the faster the motion is perceived by the user. Such animation of positions and orientations is common and works well. The same event-routing principles apply to animating any other aspect of the 3D scene: scale, color, applying texture images, and even changing the active viewpoint.

The figures in this chapter show only one or two frames of each example animation. Be sure to run each example so that the animation results are fully understood.

2.2. Purpose and common functionality

Most X3D animations follow a consistent pattern, making them easy to build and understand. The basic idea is that a sensor or trigger first activates a clock node, usually a TimeSensor. The TimeSensor then sends fraction values to an interpolator, which in turn computes output values that are sent to modify the desired parameter. At each step an event is passed from one node's output field to another node's input field via a ROUTE. This process is straightforward.

Figure 7.1 shows the basic animation sequence. This is a common design pattern and is applicable to the majority of event-generation tasks using interpolator and sequencer nodes. The initializing TouchSensor (or similar node) that triggers the animation is optional if the TimeSensor is in loop mode.

This pattern can be repeated and connected many times. Thus sophisticated behavior responses are usually a combination of simple interpolation chains, creating a chain of activity and response. For Figure 7.1, each arrow represents a strictly typed event, passed by a ROUTE connection, each defining output-to-input relationships between pairs of nodes.

There are several details that deserve attention. The next section explains how Interpolator nodes generate a continuous stream of floating-point animation values, and then describes how to build an animation chain which connects events from animation producers to animation consumers via pair-wise ROUTE definitions.

2.3. ROUTE connections

A ROUTE connects the output field of one node to the input field of another node. Ordinarily, nodes in a scene graph have any number of possible outputs. A ROUTE passes events of interest. The type of the output field must exactly match the type of the corresponding input field. This requirement is called *strict typing*. It ensures that the value of an event being delivered to the destination node is properly usable.

This approach allows authors to set up the cause-and-effect relationships which are essential to declarative programming. No imperative "do this, then do that" programming is required. Established relationships are allowed to proceed in parallel.

As the simulation clock proceeds and users interact with a scene, values are generated by some nodes and sent via ROUTE connections as time-stamped events to other nodes. This chain of events continues until no new events are generated. The full process is called an *event cascade*, commencing and completing within a single time step. A rendering update of the user's view is performed after the event cascade is complete.

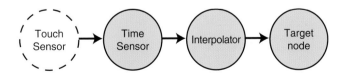

Figure 7.1. Event-animation chain connecting trigger, clock, event-producer node, and event-consumer node. Depending on an author's design, trigger nodes (such as TouchSensor) are not always needed.

Because events are not generally passed unless a ROUTE connects two nodes, this approach is computationally efficient. That is important because such quick calculations permit high frame rate and a more interactive response to users.

More than one ROUTE may connect a single output field to other nodes. This technique is called *multiple fan out*.

More than one ROUTE may also expose a single input field to the output of more than one event-producing node. This technique is called *multiple fan in*. This approach is error prone and often nondeterministic, however, because one of the input events may override another if they both occur during the same timestamp. Such overloading is usually noticed as flip-flopping or unpredictable rendering in the scene.

Table 7.1 shows the proper syntax for creating a ROUTE.

2.3.1. Hints and warnings

A ROUTE is not an X3D node, although it is expressed as an XML element in the .x3d encoding.

ROUTE declarations must always occur after the DEF naming of the source and destination nodes. A ROUTE that refers to a previously undeclared DEF name is erroneous.

It is a good authoring practice to place ROUTE statements immediately after declaration of the second of the two nodes.

Duplicate ROUTEs are ignored. Nevertheless it is better to avoid duplicating identical ROUTEs since this might lead to trouble if the event logic is later changed.

Avoid multiple fan-in ROUTE connections because they can cause unexpected and nondeterministic behavior. Such authoring challenges are best avoided by restructuring the event logic of a scene.

ROUTE connections must refer to DEF-named nodes and to legal field names in each node.

2.4. Interpolation

Interpolation to create animation values is an interesting concept. The X3D computational model simply assumes that any arbitrary function of output values over time can be approximated by piecewise-linear line segments. This capability allows the author to approximate both continuous and discontinuous functions to whatever degree of fidelity or precision is needed.

Figure 7.2 shows a piecewise approximation of a single continuous curve. Note how each key and key Value pair of coordinates defines a point on the graph. Six points

```
<ROUTE fromNode="OrbitalTimeInterval" fromField="fraction_changed"
    toNode="SpinThoseThings" toField="set_fraction"/>

ROUTE OrbitalTimeInterval.fraction_changed TO
    SpinThoseThings.set_fraction
```

Table 7.1. ROUTE Syntax Comparison for XML (.x3d) and ClassicVRML (.x3dv) Encodings

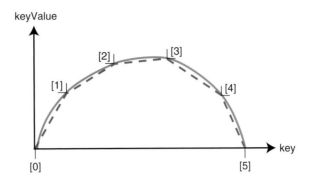

Figure 7.2. A piecewise-linear approximation (dotted line) of a smooth curve (solid line).

(indices [0] through [5] respectively) provide an approximation that is sufficiently accurate for most visual animations. This approach requires much less computation at run time than a sine curve or high-order polynomial function might require.

Figure 7.2 represents `<ScalarInterpolator key="0 0.2 0.4 0.6 0.8 1" keyValue="0 5 8 9 4 0"/>`.

Step-wise functions can also be created by repeating a key when a discontinuity is desired.

Figure 7.3 represents `<ScalarInterpolator key="0 0.25, 0.25 0.5, 0.5 1" keyValue="1 1, 2 2, 3 4"/>`. Interestingly, the first two constant-value step-function outputs are similar to discrete-valued sequencer outputs. Unlike sequencer nodes, however, interpolator outputs are floating point and are continuously generated.

Figure 7.4 shows simultaneous modification of red-green-blue (RGB) color values. The combination of the RGB components equals the final hue, as demonstrated in the ColorInterpolator example.

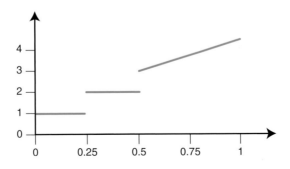

Figure 7.3. A step-wise discrete function, showing step values and discontinuities in the output.

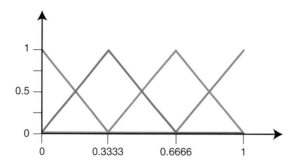

Figure 7.4. Respective RGB values produced as output from an example ColorInterpolator node.

Figure 7.4 represents `<ColorInterpolator key="0, 0.3333, 0.6666, 1" keyValue="1 0 0, 0 1 0, 0 0 1, 1 0 0"/>`.

Note that commas can be inserted for clarity, as long as they only appear between atomic-type values. Thus, inserting comments within RGB values is an error, but inserting commas between RGB-triplet values is allowed. An erroneous example is as follows:

```
<ColorInterpolator DEF="keyValueCommaError" key="0 0.3333 0.6666 1"
                   keyValue="1, 0, 0, 0, 1, 0, 0, 0, 1, 1, 0, 0"/>
```

2.5. Constructing animation chains: 10 steps

Because nearly any field in the scene graph can be changed, any aspect of a scene can be animated. That is a powerful capability! Mastering the details of animation is important so that you can innovate imaginatively and effectively.

The basic set of steps for designing an animation event chain are listed as follows.

1. *Pick target.* Pick the node and target field to animate (i.e., the field that receives the changing animation values).

2. *Name target.* Provide a DEF label for the node of interest, giving it a name.

3. *Check animation type.* Determine if the target field is a floating-point type: SFFloat, SFVec3f, MFVec3f, SFColor, and so on. The target field will either be a singleton SF type or an array MF type. In the X3D type-naming convention, SF means Single Field, and MF means Multiple Field.

4. *Determine whether Sequencer or Script.* If the target type is an SFBool or SFInt32, use a sequencer node as the event source. If the target type is an SFNode or MFNode, use a Script node as the event source.

5. *Determine if Interpolator.* If you are not using a sequencer or Script node, determine the corresponding Interpolator which produces that type of

value_changed output. For example, a PositionInterpolator produces SFVec3f value_changed events.

6. *Triggering sensor*. If desired, add a sensor node at the beginning of the chain to provide the appropriate SFTime or SFBool triggering input to start the animation. Sometimes the triggering event is an output from another animation chain.

7. *TimeSensor clock*. Add a TimeSensor as the animation clock, then set its cycleInterval field to the desired duration interval of animation. Set `loop="false"` if an animation only runs once at certain specific times. Set `loop="true"` if it loops repeatedly.

8. *Connect trigger*. ROUTE the sensor or trigger node's output field to the TimeSensor input in order to start the animation chain.

9. *Connect clock*. ROUTE the TimeSensor fraction_changed field to the interpolator (or sequencer) node's set_fraction field in order to drive the animation chain.

10. *Connect animation output*. ROUTE the interpolator, sequencer, or Script node's value_changed field to the target node and field of interest in order to complete the animation chain.

This approach works for any of the basic field types (see Chapter 1). As shown in Figure 7.1, the goal is to create sets of (field output, ROUTE, field input) relationships that each connect trigger, clock, event-generator, and event-consumer nodes.

Most input fields begin with the `"set_"` prefix and most output fields end with the `"_changed"` suffix. These can be omitted in ROUTE definitions. Usually it is a good authoring practice to include them for clarity.

Note that initializeOnly fields cannot be connected via ROUTE statements because they neither produce nor consume events.

Also note that inputOutput field names generally do not start with a "set_" prefix or end with a "_changed" suffix. As with inputOnly and outputOnly fields, it is a good authoring practice to include them for clarity.

Figure 7.5 shows an example scene graph demonstrating this basic animation chain: TouchSensor, TimeSensor, OrientationInterpolator and target Transform.

Figure 7.6 shows a snapshot of the 3D output from the scene graph in Figure 7.5. The values of the TimeSensor clock are sent to drive an OrientationInterpolator, which in turn computes an incremental rotation update, and then sends the new value to the parent Transform above our world of interest. This screen snapshot was taken as the animated text orbited past the viewer.

The following steps document the details of the 10-step animation process for this example, with each numbered step indicated in Figure 7.5.

1. *Pick target*. The target node is a Transform, and the target field is set_rotation.

2. *Name target*. The Transform is named `DEF="EarthCoordinateSystem"`.

3. *Check animation type*. As shown by the Transform node field-definition table in Chapter 3 and the X3D-Edit tooltip, the set_rotation field has type SFOrientation.

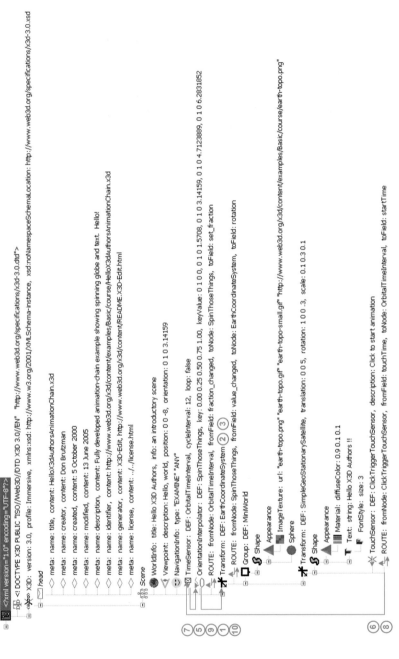

Figure 7.5. Example animation scene graph providing continuous rotation values for the Hello World example, built using the 10-step animation-chain construction process.

Figure 7.6. Snapshot view of rotating Hello X3D Authors example.

4. *Determine whether sequencer or Script.* These special node types are not applicable to this example.

5. *Determine if interpolator.* The animating OrientationInterpolator is named `DEF="SpinThoseThings"` and placed just before the Transform.

6. *Triggering sensor.* A triggering TouchSensor is added next to the geometry to be clicked, and then named `DEF="ClickTriggerTouchSensor"`.

7. *TimeSensor clock.* The TimeSensor is added at the beginning of the chain, named `DEF="OrbitalTimeInterval"` and has both the cycleInterval and loop fields set.

8. *Connect trigger.* Add ROUTE to connect the triggering TouchSensor node's touchTime output field to the clock node's startTime input field.

9. *Connect clock.* Add ROUTE to connect the clock node's fraction_changed output field to the interpolator node's set_fraction input field.

10. *Connect animation output.* Add ROUTE to connect the interpolator node's value_changed output field to the original target input field, set_rotation.

Note that the animation technique for replacing nodes is different than changing field values, although the design pattern is similar. See Chapter 9 for scripting techniques that replace full nodes. This is an advanced technique that is not often needed because modifying simple-type field values can handle most needs.

Table 7.2 lists several common example animation chains, each following the common pattern described in Section 7.2.5 and shown in Figure 7.1. The right-most column lists nodes commonly targeted for animation that in turn produce a visible effect in the scene graph. Note that a ROUTE statement must connect each node with the next node on the right in order to pass events.

Once the basic 10-step design pattern of trigger-clock-generator-consumer nodes is familiar, the primary emphasis for authors constructing animation chains is to ensure that input and output field types are matched exactly. Practice makes perfect.

The rest of this chapter looks at the details of the pertinent node types and nodes used in event animation.

Triggering Nodes (Optional)	Clock Nodes	Value-Producing Nodes	Value-Consuming Nodes, Fields
TouchSensor	TimeSensor	ScalarInterpolator	Material (transparency)
VisibilitySensor	TimeSensor	ColorInterpolator	Material (color field)
	TimeSensor	PositionInterpolator	Transform (translation, scale)
PrimarySensor	TimeSensor	OrientationInterpolator	Transform (rotation)
TouchSensor		MovieTexture	
MovieTexture (loop complete)	TimeSensor	PositionInterpolator2D	Rectangle2D

Table 7.2. Example Animation Chains: Each Row Shows a Commonly Authored Sequence of Nodes

2.6. Abstract node types

2.6.1. X3DTimeDependentNode type

The X3DTimeDependentNode type matches the template for the TimeSensor node (discussed later in this chapter). It is identified as a separate node type in anticipation of future nodes (or prototype definitions) that might compatibly extend the functionality of the TimeSensor node. Defining X3DTimeDependentNode as an abstract node type formalizes that possibility, allowing both *backwards compatibility,* that is, consistent with historic usage, and *forward compatibility,* that is, consistent with future extensibility.

The X3DTimeDependentNode signature matches the TimeSensor node signature, which is described later in the chapter.

2.6.2. X3DSensorNode type

Sensor nodes generate events based on external inputs to the rendered scene. Example sensor inputs include user interaction, browser changes, receipt of network data, or the passage of time. TheX3DSensorNode type is implemented by the TimeSensor node in this chapter, and also by each of the Sensor nodes in Chapter 8, User Interactivity Nodes. Field definitions for the X3DSensorNode types are shown in Table 7.3.

2.6.3. X3DInterpolatorNode type

The X3DInterpolatorNode type produces continuous outputs of type-specific floating-point values. It implements the X3DChildNode interface. All nodes of type X3DInterpolatorNode include all of the fields in Table 7.4 and usually no others.

Type	accessType	Name	Default	Range	Profile
SFBool	inputOutput	enabled	true		Interactive
SFBool	inputOutput	isActive	true		Interactive
SFNode	inputOutput	metadata	NULL	[X3DMetadataObject]	Core

Table 7.3. Field Definitions for X3DSensorNode

Type	accessType	Name	Default	Range	Profile
MFFloat	inputOutput	key	[]	$(-\infty, \infty)$	Interchange
MF<type>	inputOutput	keyValue	[]	(type dependent)	Interchange
SFFloat	inputOnly	set_fraction			Interchange
[SFL; MF]<type>	outputOnly	value_changed			Interchange
SFNode	inputOutput	metadata	NULL	[X3DMetadataObject]	Core

Table 7.4. Field Definitions for X3DInterpolatorNode

The type of the key array is always MFFloat. The types of the keyValue arrays and value_changed output events strictly match the type of the named node. Thus, ScalarInterpolator uses MFFloat and SFFloat for keyValue and value, respectively. Similarly ColorInterpolator uses MFColor and SFColor for keyValue definitions and value outputs, respectively.

Interpolated values are simply a time-weighted average between consecutive outputs in the keyValue array. Figure 7.7 presents a pseudocode algorithm that computes the precise mathematical relationships between fractional timestep t, index i, key array, keyValue array, and the computed output value_changed. After checking boundary-condition results, the algorithm first computes the relative fraction of time that has occurred during the current time interval between *key [i]* and key *[i + 1]*. The resulting output value is then computed by applying that fraction to the difference between the corresponding *keyValue [i]* and *keyValue [i + 1]*. This interpolated result matches whatever type is provided for the keyValue array. This is a typical linear-interpolation algorithm.

```
// Key array is sequenced in numerically nondecreasing order
// n is number of key, keyValue pairs
// index i constrained 0<i<n-1
// a fractional timestep is usually (but not necessarily)
// within range [0, 1]
// type-aware linear interpolation algorithm follows
if (t<key[0]) result = keyValue[0];
else if (t>key[n-1]) result = keyValue [n-1];
else find largest index i such that key[i] < t;

part = (t-key [i])/(key[i+1]-key[i]);
result = keyValue[i] + part * (keyValue[i+1]-keyValue[i]);
value_changed = result; // send output value for field
```

Figure 7.7. Piecewise-linear interpolation algorithm for X3DInterpolatorNode computations, expressed in pseudocode.

Thus, interpolation of output values is accomplished through two sets of weighted averaging. First the fraction is computed between appropriate values in the key array. Then a weighted-average output is computed between corresponding values in the keyValue array. This process is illustrated in Figure 7.8.

If the keyValue array has a base type of 2-tuple, 3-tuple, or higher-tuple keyValues, the same piecewise linear interpolation between successive keyValues is performed for each set of corresponding terms. Thus weighted averaging can be used to smoothly transition between successive values for each of the basic types: 2-tuple MFVec2f size values, 3-tuple MFVec3f position values, 3-tuple RGB MFColor color values, 4-tuple MFRotation axis-angle rotation values, and so on.

Once again, X3D animation provides a consistent animation model for fields of any numeric type in the scene graph. This approach is also robust, because the types of all calculated values are required to exactly match the ROUTE destination. Thus the translation field of a Transform node is always animated via a PositionInterpolator, the diffuseColor field of a Material node is always animated by a ColorInterpolator, and so on.

2.6.3.1. key and keyValue

The key and keyValue arrays together define a linear-interpolation function. The key array lists relative-time intervals, usually in range [0,1] and provided in nondecreasing order and corresponding to keyValues. The keyValue array lists the corresponding output values for linear interpolation.

2.6.3.2. set_fraction and value_changed

The set_fraction field is the floating-point input value to the interpolator function, usually in the range [0,1]. This fraction is compared to the key array using linear interpolation.

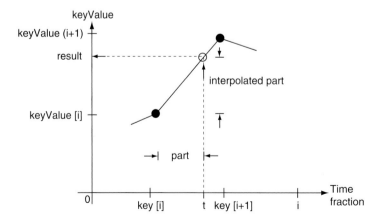

Figure 7.8. Two-way weighted averaging is used to compute interpolation-output results from matched key and keyValue arrays.

A corresponding value is computed from the corresponding keyValue array values, and that averaged value is then sent as value_changed.

2.6.3.3. Similar functionality: sequencer nodes

Sequencers are similar to interpolator nodes, but instead of continuously computing intermediate floating-point values they episodically produce discrete values, such as booleans or integers. Sequences outputs are impulse functions that only issue an event when each indexed key is triggered (rather than continuously sending the same value throughout). Sequencer nodes are discussed in Chapter 9, Event Utilities and Scripting.

Table 7.5 lists each of the basic X3D types, along with the corresponding type-matched interpolator or sequencer node that produces appropriate animation values suitable for ROUTE connections.

Note that no interpolators are currently provided in X3D that can animate ColorRGBA, MFFloat, most MF types, or double-precision field values. If needed, such values can be computed and provided by a Script node. The process of creating a Script node for such tasks is described in Chapter 9, Event Utilities and Scripting.

2.6.3.4. Hints and warnings

Note that set_fraction and the key array are always floating point, allowing precise comparison of timing values.

Also note that the keyValue field is an array of values corresponding to the type of the value_changed array. If the single value_changed output of the interpolator is itself a multi-field (MF) array, then keyValue is an MF array of arrays.

Field type	Description	Interpolator/Sequencer animation nodes
SFBool	Single-field boolean value	BooleanSequencer
SFColor	Single-field Color value, red-green-blue	ColorInterpolator
SFInt32	Single-field 32-bit Integer value	IntegerSequencer
SFFloat	Single-field single-precision floating-point value	ScalarInterpolator
SFRotation	Single-field Rotation value using 3-tuple axis, radian angle form	ColorInterpolator
SFTime	Single-field Time value	TimeSensor
SFVec2f	Single-field 2-float vector value	PositionInterpolator2D
MFVec2f	Multiple-field 2-float vector array	CoordinateInterpolator2D
SFVec3f	Single-field vector value of 3-float values	PositionInterpolator
MFVec3f	Multiple-field vector array of 3-float values	CoordinateInterpolator

Table 7.5. X3D Field Types and Corresponding Animation Nodes

For any interpolator, the number of float values in the key array must exactly match the number of *n*-tuple values in the keyValue array.

Counting is important when constructing an interpolator or a sequencer node. The size of the key array multiplied by the size of the value_changed field must match the size of the keyValue array. Thus if a key array provides 5 input color values, a corresponding keyValue array of type MFcolor has $3 \times 5 = 15$ floating-point elements.

The value_changed field is usually one of the SF-(single field) types, and the key and keyValue fields have the corresponding MF (multiple field) type.

When the input to an interpolator is driven by a TimeSensor fraction_changed event, float values in the interpolator's key array usually correspond and cover the range [0,1].

Despite the common [0,1] range constraint applied to the key array, advanced techniques are possible. Authors can put a full range of key and keyValue pairs across the key range $(-\infty, +\infty)$ if they want to use the interpolator as a open-ended piecewise-linear function. Such full-range interpolators essentially define arbitrary functions, and can either be driven by a ScalarInterpolator or used as a data field by Script nodes.

Defining a sufficient number of key and keyValue pairs allows authors to efficiently define and compute a close approximation to any function of interest.

3. Node descriptions

3.1. TimeSensor node

The TimeSensor node is the heartbeat of an animation. It provides the pulse that triggers the event cascade and computations for the next displayed frame. Figure 7.9 shows the basic output response of a TimeSensor fraction, varying from 0 to 1 as time (*t*) in seconds loops every cycleInterval seconds.

It is important to remember that the TimeSensor node tracks along with the computer clock and updates following each screen redraw, rather than ensuring a uniform-timestep frame rate. Avoiding a fixed frame rate allows the scene update to render as quickly as possible, slowing down or speeding up slightly as needed for each frame. Animations are defined in terms of the number of real-time seconds needed to complete them, not the number of frames rendered. It is the content creator's responsibility to ensure that the computations can be completed quickly enough to achieve the desired frame rate. Because these calculations are quite efficient, interpolator performance is rarely an issue.

The TimeSensor node implements the X3DTimeDependentNode and X3DSensorNode interfaces. The TimeSensor node is in the Core profile. X3D has extended the original TimeSensor of VRML97 to provide full support for pause and resume features. The node has the fields defined in Table 7.6. Node syntax is shown in Table 7.7.

The TimeSensor fraction output produces a sawtooth function depending on time. Figure 7.10 presents a pseudocode algorithm expressing the precise mathematical relationships among current time, startTime, cycleInterval duration, loop indicator, and the computed fraction output.

TimeSensor has many fields, described in the following sections.

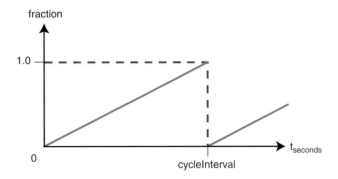

Figure 7.9. TimeSensor fraction_changed varies over the range [0,1] for each cycleInterval repetition.

3.1.1. enabled

Inherited from X3DSensorNode, the enabled field simply enables or disables node operation. Because enabled has accessType inputOutput, it can be changed dynamically at run time.

Type	accessType	Name	Default	Range	Profile
SFTime	inputOutput	cycleInterval	1	$(0,\infty)$	Interchange
SFTime	inputOutput	startTime	0	$(-\infty,\infty)$	Interchange
SFTime	inputOutput	stopTime	0	$(-\infty,\infty)$	Interchange
SFTime	inputOutput	pauseTime	0	$(-\infty,\infty)$	Full
SFTime	inputOutput	resumeTime	0	$(-\infty,\infty)$	Full
SFBool	inputOutput	enabled	true		Interchange
SFBool	inputOutput	loop	false		Interchange
SFTime	outputOnly	fraction_changed			Interchange
SFTime	outputOnly	time			Interchange
SFTime	outputOnly	cycleTime			Interchange
SFTime	outputOnly	elapsedTime			Interchange
SFBool	outputOnly	isActive			Interchange
SFBool	outputOnly	isPaused			Full
SFNode	inputOutput	metadata	NULL	[X3DMetadataObject]	Core

Table 7.6. TimeSensor Fields

XML Syntax (.x3d)	ClassicVRML Syntax (.x3dv)

``
<TimeSensor DEF="MyTimeSensorNode"
    cycleInterval="1"
    startTime="0"
    stopTime="0"
    enabled="true"
    loop="false"
    pauseTime="0"
    resumeTime="0"
/>
``
	``
	DEF=MyTimeSensorNode TimeSensor{
	    cycleInterval 1
	    startTime 0
	    stopTime 0
	    enabled TRUE
	    loop FALSE
	    pauseTime 0
	    resumeTime 0
	}
	``

Table 7.7. Node Syntax for TimeSensor

```
time=now; // output field value
numberOfLoops=(now−startTime) / cycleInterval; // floating-point calculation
f = fractionalPart (numberOfLoops);

if (now == startTime)
    fraction_changed = 0.0; // output field value
else if ((loop=="false") && (now == (startTime + cycleInterval)))
    fraction_changed = 1.0; // output field value
else fraction_changed = f; // output field value
```

Figure 7.10 TimeSensor fraction_changed output algorithm, expressed in pseudocode.

3.1.2. startTime

The startTime field is the time when the Time Sensor can become active, which occurs when the TimeSensor is enabled and current time is greater than or equal to startTime. A ROUTE connection from a TouchSensor touchTime to this field is a good way to start a TimeSensor.

3.1.3. stopTime

An active TimeSensor becomes inactive when stopTime is reached and stopTime is greater than startTime. The stopTime field has no effect if stopTime is less than or equal to startTime.

A set_stopTime event (where startTime < stopTime ≤ now) sent to an active TimeSensor results in events being generated as if stopTime had just been reached. Such a technique might be used as part of a Script controlling timing events.

3.1.4. cycleInterval

The cycleInterval field defines the loop duration in seconds, either for single or looped repetition.

3.1.5. loop

The TimeSensor repeats indefinitely when `loop="true"`, otherwise the TimeSensor output cycle occurs only once when `loop="false"`.

3.1.6. cycleTime

The cycleTime field sends an SFTime output event at the initial startTime, and again at the beginning of each new cycle if looping. This behavior is useful for synchronization with other time-based objects.

3.1.7. isActive

The isActive field sends SFBool true and false events when the TimeSensor starts and stops running, respectively.

3.1.8. isPaused

The isPaused field sends SFBool true and false events when the TimeSensor is paused and resumed, respectively.

3.1.9. pauseTime

When an input SFTime event is sent to this field, and when current time equals (or is greater than) pauseTime, an isPaused true event is sent and the TimeSensor becomes paused.

3.1.10. resumeTime

When an input SFTime event is sent to this field, and when current time equals (or is greater than) resumeTime, an isPaused false event is sent and the TimeSensor becomes active.

3.1.11. elapsedTime

The elapsedTime field is the cumulative number of seconds elapsed since the TimeSensor was activated and began running, without counting any paused time.

3.1.12. Hints and warnings

The two most common ways to initiate a TimeSensor are either to send an input SFTime event to startTime or have the TimeSensor continuously repeat using `loop="true"`. Other techniques might not properly start the TimeSensor. Don't use them!

It is generally best to not explicitly set_stopTime, so that a nonlooping TimeSensor can start and run on a startTime event.

One animation sequence can track the completion of another animation sequence by receiving an isActive field and checking if it is false (by using a Boolean filter node or a Script node). Another means of tracking completion is receiving a TimeSensor cycleTime event as a time trigger.

Because SFTime values are double-precision floating-point numbers and are calculated as an absolute time value (i.e., number of seconds since January 1, 1970, 00:00:00 GMT), simple integer or float values cannot be connected with ROUTE to the startTime field. Always provide SFTime values to SFTime fields.

3.2. ScalarInterpolator Node

The ScalarInterpolator node generates a scalar (single field) SFFloat value, varying over time. ScalarInterpolator is typically driven using a TimeSensor's fraction_changed output sent as a set_fraction input event and then computed from the piecewise-linear key/keyValue function. The generated output value is linearly interpolated by the node, first by determining the fractional difference between the nearest elements of the key array, and then approximating the same amount between the corresponding elements of the keyValue array.

The ScalarInterpolator node is in the Interchange profile. The node has the fields defined in Table 7.8. Node syntax is shown in Table 7.9.

The keyValue field for ScalarInterpolator is an array of scalar float values. It is of type MFFloat. There are exactly as many elements in the keyValue array as there are elements in the key array.

The example scene ScalarInterpolator.x3d shows how a ScalarInterpolator node can be used to change the transparency field in the Material node. Figure 7.11 first shows the fish fully opaque and then shows the same fish in a partially transparent state.

3.2.1. key and keyValue

The key field is an MFFloat array of input bounds. The keyValue field is a corresponding MFFloat array of 1-tuple output values.

Type	accessType	Name	Default	Range	Profile
MFFloat	inputOutput	key	[]	$(-\infty, \infty)$	Interchange
MFFloat	inputOutput	keyValue	[]	$(-\infty, \infty)$	Interchange
SFFloat	inputOnly	set_fraction		$(-\infty, \infty)$	Interactive
SFFloat	outputOnly	value_changed			Interchange
SFNode	inputOutput	metadata	NULL	[X3DMetadataObject]	Core

Table 7.8. Field Definitions for ScalarInterpolator Node

XML Syntax (.x3d)	ClassicVRML Syntax (.x3dv)

`<ScalarInterpolator`
`  key="0 0.5 1"`
`  keyValue="2 4 8"`
`/>`
	`ScalarInterpolator {`
	`  key [ 0 0.5 1 ]`
	`  keyValue [ 2 4 8 ]`
	`}`

Table 7.9. Node Syntax for ScalarInterpolator

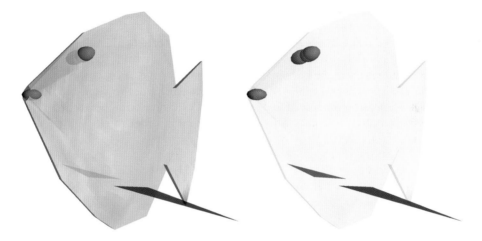

Figure 7.11. ScalarInterpolator is used to modify the transparency of the Garibaldi. This shows the fish at two different times. The left image is nearly fully opaque, and the right one is partially transparent.

3.2.2. Hints and warnings

X3D is strongly typed. Ensure that value_changed is connected via a ROUTE to a target field of type SFFloat.

3.3. ColorInterpolator node

The ColorInterpolator node generates a color value of type SFColor over time. ColorInterpolator is typically driven using a TimeSensor's fraction output sent as a set_fraction input event and then computed from the piecewise-linear key and keyValue function. The generated output value is linearly interpolated by the node, first by determining the fractional difference between the nearest elements of the key array and then calculating the same amount between the corresponding elements of the keyValue array.

The ColorInterpolator node is in the Interactive profile. The node has the fields defined in Table 7.10 Node syntax is shown in Table 7.11.

3.3.1. Example

The following ColorInterpolatorExample.x3d scene in Figure 7.12 illustrates in detail the basic design pattern for animating a field of interest. Note the logically connected flow of events, with multiple ROUTE connections starting from triggering TouchSensor to a clock-ticking TimeSensor, then to color-producing ColorInterpolator, and finally to target field Material diffuseColor.

The same design pattern holds true for all basic animation chains that might be constructed. The primary variation is to substitute a different Interpolator node to match the type of the target field. Often different triggering conditions are used, or else simply omitted when a TouchSensor is not needed. Figure 7.13 shows the specific event chain for this example.

Be sure to note that placing ROUTE statements immediately after the connected nodes is a good authoring practice that improves the readability of a scene. Putting all of the ROUTE statements at the bottom of the scene is legal, and often a common practice, but ROUTE statements at the end are usually much harder to read and debug. Placing a ROUTE before a referenced node produces a load-time error, because the X3D parser expects to learn DEF names before they are used in order to efficiently read a scene in a single pass.

Type	accessType	Name	Default	Range	Profile
MFFloat	inputOutput	key	[]	$(-\infty, \infty)$	Interchange
MFVec3f	inputOutput	keyValue	[]	$(-\infty, \infty)$	Interchange
SFFloat	inputOnly	set_fraction		$(-\infty, \infty)$	Interchange
SFColor	outputOnly	fraction_changed			Interchange
SFNode	inputOutput	metadata	NULL	[X3DMetadataObject]	Core

Table 7.10. Field Definitions for ColorInterpolator Node

XML Syntax (.x3d)	Classic VRML Syntax (.x3dv)

`<ColorInterpolator DEF=`
`    "MyColorInterpolatorNode"`
`key="0 0.5 1"`
`keyValue="0 0 0, 0.2 0.2 0.5,`
`    0.4 0.4 1"/>`
	`DEF MyColorInterpolatorNode`
	`ColorInterpolator {`
	`  key [ 0 0.5 1 ]`
	`  keyValue [ 0 0 0, 0.2 0.2 0.5, 0.4`
	`            0.4 1 ]`
	`}`

Table 7.11. Node syntax for ColorInterpolator

Figure 7.12. ColorInterpolatorExample scene graph displayed by X3D-Edit and annotated with overlaid ROUTE connections.

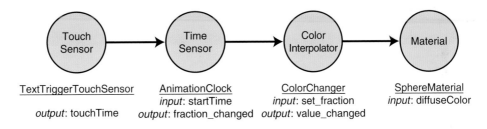

Figure 7.13. Event chain for ColorInterpolator example found in Figure 7.12.

Figure 7.14 shows the initial grey Sphere that is first loaded, then three intermediate snapshots as the color of the Sphere is varied from red to green to blue (and then back to red).

3.3.2. key and keyValue

The key field is an MFFloat array of input bounds, and the keyValue field is a corresponding MFColor array of 3-tuple output values.

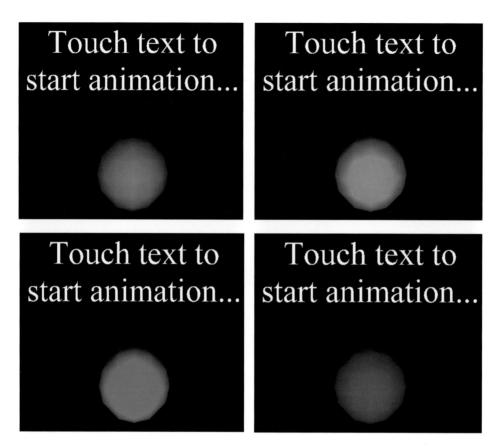

Figure 7.14. Successive views of ColorInterpolator example.

3.3.3. Hints and warnings

Ensure that value_changed is only connected with a ROUTE statement to a target field having type SFColor.

According to the X3D Abstract Specification, computation of ColorInterpolator interpolation values is nominally performed in Hue Saturation Value (HSV) color space. However, many browsers reportedly use Red-Green-Blue (RGB) space instead. If strict control of color is desired, use a detailed set of key and keyValue pairs to increment color changes in small amounts.

Place ROUTE statements immediately after the last-defined node for readability. Note that the X3dToXhtml stylesheet pretty-print capability in X3D-Edit not only links bookmarks to DEF nodes but also inserts a reference comment before each node connected by a ROUTE, showing each input and output event being routed. Warnings and hints are also provided when the inputs or outputs of TimeSensor, interpolator, or sequencer nodes are mismatched or not connected with ROUTE statements. This documentation is a big help when diagnosing and debugging scene animation problems.

Learn more about color spaces and display from Maureen Stone's excellent book, *A Field Guide to Digital Color*, A.K. Peters, August 2003.

As just described, X3D-Edit can generate pretty-print HTML versions displaying a scene graph. The HTML pages themselves are produced by the X3dToXhtml.xslt stylesheet. Figure 7.15 shows an excerpted example. Note that comments are automatically inserted before each node that has a ROUTE connection for events in or out. Also note how any DEF names include hyperlink bookmarks that jump to the identified node.

One more hint: a good way to identify or troubleshoot ROUTE statements is to pretty-print a scene graph, print it out on a color printer in landscape mode, and then draw ROUTE statements of interest on the printout.

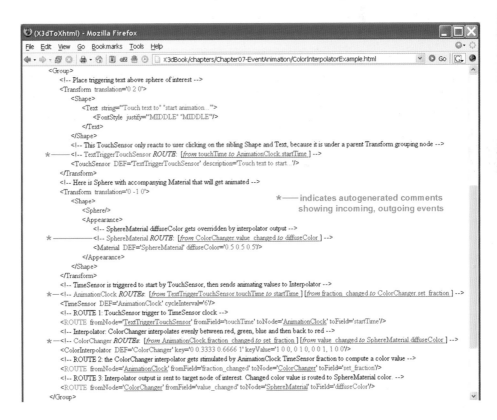

Figure 7.15. Pretty-print HTML page showing ColorInterpolator example, launched via X3D-Edit. Autogenerated comments are inserted that document ROUTE connections for events. DEF and USE names are linked by bookmarks to referenced nodes of interest.

3.4. PositionInterpolator node

The PositionInterpolator node generates a 3-vector value (SFVec3f) over time. PositionInterpolator is typically driven using a TimeSensor's fraction output sent as a set_fration input event, and then computing output fraction-changed events from the piecewise-linear key and keyValue function. The generated output value is linearly interpolated by the node, first by determining the fractional difference between the nearest elements in the key array and then calculating the same amount between the corresponding elements in the keyValue array.

The full functionality of the PositionInterpolator node is in the Interchange profile. The node has the fields defined in Table 7.12. Node syntax is shown in Table 7.13.

The keyValue field for the PositionInterpolator node is an array of 3-vector values. It is of type MFVec3f. There are exactly as many 3-tuple values in the keyValue array as there are scalar values in the key array.

3.4.1. key and keyValue

The keyField is an MFFloat array of input bounds. The keyValue field is a corresponding MFVec3f array of 3-tuple output values.

Type	accessType	Name	Default	Range	Profile
MFFloat	inputOutput	key	[ ]	$(-\infty, \infty)$	Interchange
MFVec3f	inputOutput	keyValue	[ ]	$(-\infty, \infty)$	Interchange
SFFloat	inputOnly	set_fraction		$(-\infty, \infty)$	Interchange
SFVec3f	outputOnly	value_changed			Interchange
SFNode	inputOutput	metadata	NULL	[X3DMetadataObject]	Core

Table 7.12. Field Definitions for PositionInterpolator Node

XML Syntax (.x3d)	ClassicVRML Syntax (.x3dv)

`<PositionInterpolator`
`        DEF="MyPositionInterpolator"`
`  key="0 0.5 1"`
`  keyValue="-3 0 2, 0 0 2, 3 0 2"`
`/>`
	`DEF MyPositionInterpolator`
	`PositionInterpolator {`
	`  key [ 0 0.5 1 ]`
	`  keyValue [ -3 0 2, 0 0 2, 3 0 2 ]`
	`}`

Table 7.13. Node Syntax for PositionInterpolator

3.4.2. Hints and warnings

Ensure that value_changed is only connected via a ROUTE statement to a target field of type SFVec3f.

PositonInterpolator output events are typically passed to the translation field of a Transform node or the position field of a Viewpoint. These values can also be connected via a ROUTE statement to other nonpositional SFVec3f fields if desired.

The example scene PositionInterpolator.x3d in Figure 7.16 shows how our favorite fish is moved along its path in the Kelp Forest Virtual Exhibit.

Figure 7.17 shows example diagrams that can be produced when using graph paper to construct linear approximations of a bouncing behavior to animate a ball.

3.5. OrientationInterpolator node

The OrientationInterpolator node generates a rotation value (SFRotation) over time. OrientationInterpolator is typically driven using a TimeSensor's fraction output sent as a set_fraction input event and then computed from the piecewise-linear key and keyValue function. The generated output value is linearly interpolated by the node, first by determining the fractional difference between the nearest elements of the key array and then by approximating the same amount between the corresponding elements of the keyValue array.

The full functionality of the OrientationInterpolator node is available in the Interchange profile. The node has the fields defined in Table 7.14. Node syntax follows in Table 7.15.

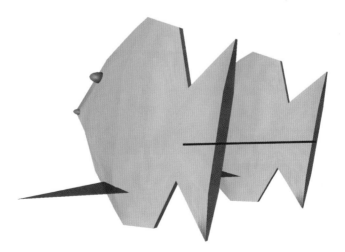

Figure 7.16. PositionInterpolator moves the fish's tail along a the blue straight line (enhanced for printing). The right fish is at the starting position. The left fish is shown a little time later.

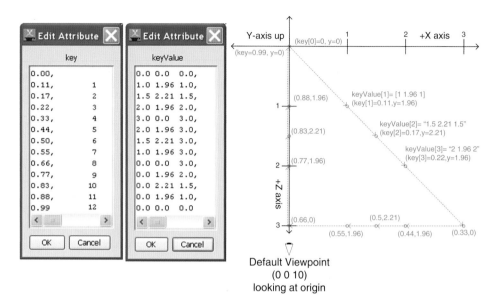

Figure 7.17. Using graphs to plan out and compute values for a PositionInterpolator approximation for a bouncing Box.

Type	accessType	Name	Default	Range	Profile
MFFloat	inputOutput	key	[]	$(-\infty, \infty)$	Interchange
MFRotation	inputOutput	keyValue	[]	$[-1, 1]$ $(-\infty, \infty)$	Interchange
SFFloat	inputOnly	set_fraction			Interchange
SFRotation	outputOnly	value_changed			Interchange
SFNode	inputOutput	metadata	NULL	[X3DMetadataObject]	Core

Table 7.14. Field Definitions for OrientationInterpolator Node

XML Syntax (.x3d)	ClassicVRML Syntax (.x3dv)

`<OrientationInterpolator`
`  DEF="MyOrientationInterpolator"`
`  key="0 0.25 0.5 0.75 1"`
`  keyValue="0 1 0 0, 0 1 0 0.78,`
`  0 1 0 1.57, 0 1 0 2.35, 0 1 0`
`  3.141592653"`
`/>`
	`DEF MyOrientationInterpolator`
	`OrientationInterpolator {`
	`  key [ 0 0.25 0.5 0.75 1 ]`
	`  keyValue [ 0 1 0 0, 0 1 0 0.78, 0`
	`  1 0 1.57, 0 1 0 2.35, 0 1 0`
	`  3.141592653 ]`
	`}`

Table 7.15. Node Syntax for OrientationInterpolator

The keyValue field for OrientationInterpolator is an array of rotation values. It is of type MFRotation. There are exactly as many elements in the keyValue array as there are elements in the key array.

OrientationInterpolator value_changed output events are usually passed to the set_rotation field of a Transform node, although they can be used anywhere that an SFRotation event is accepted. An OrientationInterpolator combined with an offset value in the Transform node's center field can be used to rotate an object about an axis that does not go through the local origin. This is useful for creating doors or hanging signs, which rotate about their edge axis (rather than their center axis).

A single-step rotation of exactly π radians (180°) is not well defined, because it is ambiguous regarding whether the object rotates to the right or to the left. If the animation needs to rotate through an angle, π, then subdivide the key and keyValue pairs into at least two steps per π radians (or at least three steps per 2π radians). This is because the initial turn direction using a two-step interpolator for a full rotation is ambiguously defined, and can legitimately produce unpredictable or undesirable results (even to the point of reversing direction midway through the animation). If the interpolator instead uses three steps for a 2π radians (360°) revolution, then the rotation direction is smooth and predictable.

The example scene OrientationInterpolator.x3d in Figure 7.18 shows the animation of the fish's orientation during its movement path. This interpolation makes the fish motion more realistic.

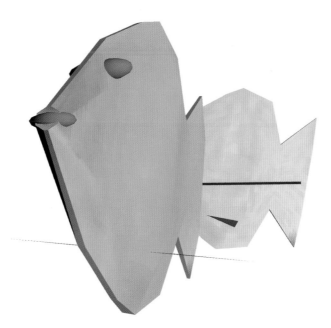

Figure 7.18. OrientationInterpolator combined with the previous PositionInterpolator moves the Garibaldi. The forward-facing fish is at a later animation time than the fish on the right. The straight blue line indicates the nonrotated path of the tail.

3.5.1. key and keyValue

The key field is an MFFloat array of input bounds; and the keyValue field is a corresponding MFRotation array of 4-tuple output values.

3.5.2. Hints and warnings

Ensure that value_changed output event is only connected via a ROUTE to a target field of type SFRotation.

3.6. NormalInterpolator node

Normals are the perpendiculars for each polygon or vertex in a geometry node. These values are used when calculating how light rays are reflected from the surface of a shape. Normals usually are not included with X3D coordinate geometry, instead being calculated by the browser when a scene is first loaded. Nevertheless normals can be pre-calculated and included in the scene, either for faster loading or for more precise shading.

NormalInterpolator is similar to CoordinateInterpolator in that it includes multiple copies of a full set of normal vectors. With each fractional step, the node computes a pairwise interpolation between each corresponding normal pair in the keyValue array. This technique is sometimes used to produce special shading effects.

The NormalInterpolator node is in the Interactive profile. The node has the fields defined in Table 7.16. Node syntax is shown in Table 7.17. The Normal node is described in Chapter 13, Geometry Nodes, Part 4.

Type	accessType	Name	Default	Range	Profile
MFFloat	inputOutput	key	[]	$(-\infty, \infty)$	Interchange
MFVec3f	inputOutput	keyValue	[]	$(-\infty, \infty)$	Interchange
SFFloat	inputOnly	set_fraction		$(-\infty, \infty)$	Interchange
SFVec3f	outputOnly	value_changed			Interchange
SFNode	inputOutput	metadata	NULL	[X3DMetadataObject]	Core

Table 7.16. Field Definitions for NormalInterpolator Node

XML Syntax (.x3d)	ClassicVRML Syntax (.x3dv)

`<NormalInterpolator DEF=`
`  "MyNormalInterpolatorNode"`
`  key="0 0.5 1"`
`  keyValue="0 0 0, 0 1 0, 0 0 0"/>`
	`DEF MyNormalInterpolatorNode`
	`    NormalInterpolator {`
	`      key [0 0.5 1]`
	`      keyValue [0 0 0, 0 1 0, 0 0 0]`
	`  }`

Table 7.17. Node Syntax for NormalInterpolator

3.6.1. key and keyValue

The key field is an MFFloat array of input bounds. The keyValue field is a corresponding MFVec3f array of output 3-tuple values.

3.6.2. Hints and warnings

Ensure that the value_changed output event is only connected via a ROUTE to a target field of type SFVec3f, which is typically the vector field of a Normal node.

Only use NormalInterpolator for calculation of polygon normals, because the interpolation algorithms are performed in polar coordinates and are different than the calculations used for positions. Instead use PositionInterpolator for interpolating between SFVec3f locations (e.g., Transform node translation field, Viewpoint node position field, etc.).

3.7. CoordinateInterpolator node

The CoordinateInterpolator node generates a series of Coordinate values that can be ROUTEd to a `<Coordinate>` node's point field or another MFVec3f attribute. The keyValue is an array of arrays of SFVec3f values, in which the interior array matches the size of the the target Coordinate node point field, and the number of these interior arrays equals the number of key definitions.

The CoordinateInterpolator node is in the Interactive profile. The node has the fields defined in Table 7.18. Node syntax is shown in Table 7.19.

3.7.1. key and keyValue

The key field is an MFFloat array of input bounds; and the keyValue field is a corresponding MFVec3f array of output n-tuple values.

The example scene CoordinateInterpolator.x3d in Figure 7.19 shows the combined effect of the PositionInterpolator, OrientationInterpolator, and CoordinateInterpolator nodes. The CoordinateInterpolator node provides the fish's "wiggle" as it moves.

3.7.2. Hints and warnings

Ensure that the value_changed output event is only connected via a ROUTE to a target field of type MFVec3f.

Type	accessType	Name	Default	Range	Profile
MFFloat	inputOutput	key	[]	$(-\infty, \infty)$	Interchange
MFVec3f	inputOutput	keyValue	[]	$(-\infty, \infty)$	Interchange
SFFloat	inputOnly	set_fraction		$(-\infty, \infty)$	Interchange
MFVec3f	outputOnly	value_changed			Interchange
SFNode	inputOutput	metadata	NULL	[X3DMetadataObject]	Core

Table 7.18. Field Definitions for CoordinateInterpolator Node

XML Syntax (.x3d)	ClassicVRML Syntax (.x3dv)

`<!--Shrink/expand a single triangle -->`
`<CoordinateInterpolator DEF=`
`  "MyCoordinateInterpolatorNode"`
`  key="0 0.5 1"`
`  keyValue="0 0 0, 1 0 0, 0 1 0, 0 0 0,`
`  0.5 0 0, 0 0.5 0, 0 0 0, 1 0 0,`
`  0 1 0"/>`
	`#Shrink/expand a single triangle`
	`DEF MyCoordinateInterpolatorNode`
	`  CoordinateInterpolator {`
	`    key [0 0.5 1]`
	`    keyValue [0 0 0, 1 0 0, 0 1 0,`
	`      0 0 0, 0.5 0 0, 0 0.5 0,`
	`      0 0 0, 1 0 0, 0 1 0]`
	`  }`

Table 7.19. Node Syntax for CoordinateInterpolator

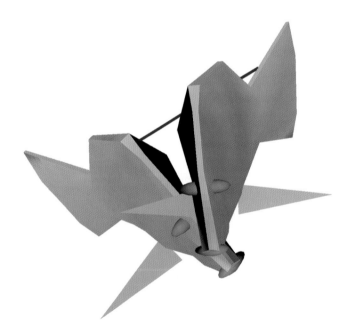

Figure 7.19. The fish's wiggle is added into the animation. The superimposed image shows the fish at two different times with different shapes to its tail. The enhanced blue straight line is the path of the fish's tail.

Also ensure that the total number of keyValue floats equals the quantity (key size) × (length of array in target field).

3.8. PositionInterpolator2D node

The PositionInterpolator2D node generates a 2-vector value (SFVec2f) over time. PositionInterpolator2D is typically driven using a TimeSensor's fraction output sent as a set_fraction input event and then computing output fraction_changed events from the piecewise-linear key and keyValue function. The generated output value is linearly interpolated by the node, first by determining the fractional difference between the nearest elements of the key array and then computing the same amount between the corresponding elements of the keyValue array.

The full functionality of the PositionInterpolator2D node is available in the Full profile. The node has the fields defined in Table 7.20. Node syntax is shown in Table 7.21.

The keyValue field for PositionInterpolator2D is a 2-tuple vector array of type MFVec2f. There are exactly as many 2-tuple elements in the keyValue array as there are elements in the key array.

PositionInterpolator2D events are typically passed to the translation field of a TextureTransform node (described in Chapter 5), although they can be connected via a ROUTE statement to wherever an SFVec2f value is accepted.

3.8.1. key and keyValue

The key field is an MFFloat array of input bounds, and the keyValue field is a corresponding MFVec2f array of output 2-tuple values.

3.8.2. Hints and warnings

Ensure that value_changed is only connected via a ROUTE to a target field of type SFVec2f.

Type	accessType	Name	Default	Range	Profile
MFFloat	inputOutput	key	[]	$(-\infty, \infty)$	Full
MFVec2f	inputOutput	keyValue	[]	$(-\infty, \infty)$	Full
SFFloat	inputOnly	set_fraction		$(-\infty, \infty)$	Full
SFVec2f	outputOnly	value_changed			Full
SFNode	inputOutput	metadata	NULL	[X3DMetadataObject]	Core

Table 7.20. PositionInterpolator Fields

XML Syntax (.x3d)	ClassicVRML Syntax (.x3dv)

`<PositionInterpolator2D DEF=`
`  "MyPositionInterpolator2DNode"`
`  key="0 0.5 1"`
`  keyValue="1 1, 2 2, 3 3"/>`
	`DEF MyPositionInterpolator2DNode`
	`    PositionInterpolator2D {`
	`    key [0 0.5 1]`
	`    keyValue [ 1 1, 2 2, 3 3 ]`
	`  }`

Table 7.21. Node syntax for PositionInterpolator2D

3.9. CoordinateInterpolator2D node

The CoordinateInterpolator2D node generates multiple 2-vector values (MFVec2f) over time. CoordinateInterpolator2D is typically driven using a TimeSensor's fraction output sent as an input-time event and then computed from the piecewise-linear key and keyValue function. The generated output value is linearly interpolated by the node, first by determining the fractional difference between the nearest elements of the key array and then approximating the same amount between the corresponding elements of the keyValue array.

The CoordinateInterpolator2D node is in the Full profile. The node has the fields defined in Table 7.22. Node syntax is shown in Table 7.23.

3.9.1. key and keyValue

The key field is an MFFloat array of input bounds, and the keyValue field is a corresponding MFVec2f array of output 2-tuple values.

3.9.2. Hints and warnings

Ensure that value_changed is connected via a ROUTE to a target field of type MFVec2f.

Ensure that the total number of keyValue floats equals the quantity (key size) × (length of array in target field).

Type	accessType	Name	Default	Range	Profile
MFFloat	inputOutput	key	[]	$(-\infty, \infty)$	Full
MFVec2f	inputOutput	keyValue	[]	$(-\infty, \infty)$	Full
SFFloat	inputOnly	set_fraction		$(-\infty, \infty)$	Full
MFVec2f	outputOnly	value_changed			Full
SFNode	inputOutput	metadata	NULL	[X3DMetadataObject]	Core

Table 7.22. Field Definitions for CoordinateInterpolator2D Node

XML Syntax (.x3d)	ClassicVRML Syntax (.x3dv)

`<CoordinateInterpolator2D DEF=`
`  "MyCoordinateInterpolator2DNode"`
`  key="0 0.5 1"`
`  keyValue="1 1, 1 1, 2 2, 2 2,`
`    3 3, 3 3"/>`
	`DEF MyCoordinateInterpolator2DNode`
	`  CoordinateInterpolator2D {`
	`    key [ 0 0.5 1 ]`
	`    keyValue [ 1 1, 1 1, 2 2, 2 2, 3 3,`
	`      3 3 ]`
	`}`

Table 7.23. Node Syntax for CoordinateInterpolator2D

The final example in this chapter, Interpolator.x3d in Figure 7.20, is a combination of all of the example scenes. It shows the use of all of the Interpolation nodes. This screen shot captures the fish as it cycles through the various colors and transparencies. The Garibaldi's texture has been turned off so that the changes to the color and transparency are visible.

4. Summary

4.1. Key ideas

Animation is crucial for X3D scenes to be interesting and interactive. Fortunately the steps needed to construct animation sequences follow a consistent design pattern for all the many diverse X3D nodes that might be animated. Learning this pattern once essentially unlocks all X3D animation techniques for a diligent author.

Again note that the X3dToXhtml.xslt pretty-print stylesheet produces color-coded documentation versions of X3D scenes that insert bookmark links for all node DEF labels. It further annotates a scene by inserting linked comments noting ROUTE connections prior to each connected node in an animation sequence. This documentation can be a big help in debugging and diagnosing ROUTE problems to achieve desired animation behaviors.

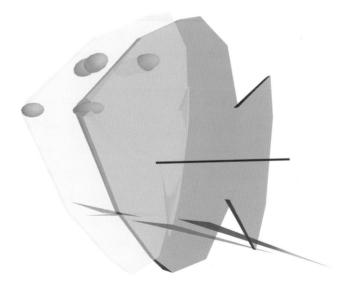

Figure 7.20. Combination animation showing ScalarInterpolator, ColorInterpolator, PositionInterpolator, OrientationInterpolator, and CoordinateInterpolator in a superimposed image. The transparent blue fish is closer to the viewer and occurs at a different time than the opaque reddish fish.

Animation of 3D objects and the user's camera view is exciting and fundamentally important. Animation and interaction are what make 3D graphics a new media type. 3D graphics can be even richer than 2D images and video, which are usually slaved to a fixed viewpoint.

It may be interesting to know that students at the Naval Postgraduate School (NPS) in Monterey, California USA do not take written exams on X3D. Instead they must pass the *quantitatively cool* test. They build X3D scenes and create projects that interact with users in interesting ways. At the end of the course, each student gives a live X3D demonstration (also known as a *demo*) of their final project.

In the 3D graphics community, running a demo is how people show great results to each other. In some ways, it is like running an experiment, that is, proving that a concept actually works. NPS students know when their demo project is worth an A grade— when the audience says "Cool!" That is a measurable result, and that is what *quantitatively cool* means.

Try out your X3D demos on your friends and colleagues, too. It's fun, everyone learns something each time, and good demos are cool.

4.2. Related nodes and concepts

Sequencers produce discrete-value outputs that function similarly to the continuous-value interpolators presented here. Scripts can also be constructed to perform custom animation techniques. Sequencers and Script nodes are discussed in Chapter 9, Event Utilities and Scripting.

4.3. Next chapter

Chapter 8, User Interactivity Nodes is closely related to event animation. A wide variety of nodes respond to different user inputs, providing triggers to TimeSensor clocks, interpolators, and sequencers. This combination enables animation to be interactive and responsive to user commands.

User Interactivity Nodes

Nobody knows the kind of trouble we're in. Nobody seems to think it all might happen again.
—Gram Parson, *One Hundred Years from Now*

1. What this chapter covers

Animated scenes are interesting. Dynamic scenes that offer user interaction and respond to user choices can be compelling. Users not only control the action but can become immersed in experiencing a scene.

This chapter covers the primary sensor nodes that support user interactivity. These nodes are TouchSensor, PlaneSensor, CylinderSensor, SphereSensor, KeySensor, and StringSensor.

The Anchor node can also be considered a type of pointing-device sensor because it detects user picking, binding to another viewpoint or loading another url when selected. Anchor is covered in Chapter 3, Grouping Nodes. Other nodes for user interactivity are LoadSensor, Collision, ProximitySensor and VisibilitySensor. These are covered in Chapter 11, Lighting and Environment Nodes.

2. Concepts

X3D uses sensor nodes to detect various sources of interactive information. Results are converted into events that can be connected to other parts of the scene via ROUTE statements. This makes X3D authoring straightforward, because sensor nodes are handled in the same way that interpolators provide events.

Pointing devices are the primary means of interacting with scenes. Because X3D is an international standard for Web-based 3D graphics, great care is taken to only define functionality for pointing-device hardware in a system-neutral way, so that any programming language or operating system might support X3D functionality equivalently.

Pointing devices available to an X3D viewer might include a mouse, a touchpad, a touchscreen, keyboard arrow keys, tracked wand, a trackball, a game controller, or a data glove. X3D scenes can work compatibly with any of these devices, because device definitions are sensitive to which scene object is being pointed at or selected. This approach is more general than which signals are generated or which buttons are pushed. Thus X3D scenes are portable and usable across a wide range of interaction and display devices.

The computer keyboard is another X3D input device, providing the ability to sense character keypresses and string entry. Special checks are also provided for function keys as well as the shift, alternate, and control key modifiers. Default behaviors are also provided for scene navigation using arrow keys, PageUp, and PageDown keys, and so on.

2.1. Purpose and common functionality

These nodes provide the following capabilities:

- Pointing-device sensors detect user motion of a cursor by using a mouse, wand, touchpad, touchscreen, keyboard arrow keys, or some other device. Viewer applications usually move a 2D cursor icon in front of the rendering 3D scene to show current screen position of the pointing device.

- Geometric shapes with a sibling or parent pointing-device sensor node can be selected using the pointing device. Ordinarily this is done by moving a pointer icon on the display to a screen location over a geometry shape, and then pressing the primary selection button (such as the left button on a 3-button mouse). Events can then be connected by ROUTE statements to trigger interaction.

- Sensor descriptions alert users both to the presence and the purpose of individual sensor nodes. With proper scene setup, the pointing device can also be used to click and drag selected shapes.

- Individual keystroke characters or collected single-line strings can be provided as input from the computer keyboard.

- Keyboard events corresponding to modifier keys (shift/control/alternate), function keys and navigation keys can also be captured and connected with ROUTE statements.

Abstract node type definitions are described in the following sections.

2.2. X3DSensorNode type

X3DSensorNode is the abstract base type for all sensor interfaces. Thus, all Sensor nodes include the fields and functionality described in Table 8.1.

2.2.1. enabled

This field turns a sensor on or off, using the values `enabled="true"` or `enabled="false"` respectively. Disabled sensors are not activated when the cursor passes over the associated geometry. Enabled sensors can produce events when active.

2.2.2. isActive

When all preconditions for a given sensor are met, the isActive field outputs an event with the value true. For example, when a mouse is sensed over TouchSensor-enabled geometry and the action button is pressed, then an isActive true event is sent. When the pointer is moved off of the object, or if the action button is deselected, then an isActive false event is sent.

Keeping track of these events allows a carefully constructed scene to invite user interaction and respond properly.

2.2.3. Hints and warnings

Sometimes it is necessary to distinguish between isActive true and isActive false events. The BooleanFilter, BooleanToggle, and BooleanTrigger nodes can help with that task, and are described in Chapter 9, Event Utilities and Scripting.

If multiple sensors affect a single piece of geometry, then only the sensor closest in the scene graph hierarchy is utilized.

2.3. X3DPointingDeviceSensorNode type

A pointing-device sensor implements this abstract node type. Such sensors are activated when the mouse (or wand, or other pointing device) is located above corresponding peer

Type	accessType	Name	Default	Range	Profile
SFBool	inputOutput	enabled	true		Interactive
SFBool	outputOnly	isActive			Interactive
SFNode	inputOutput	metadata	NULL	[X3DMetadataObject]	Interactive

Table 8.1. Field Definitions for X3DSensorNode Type

or child geometry. A mouse is a form of 2D input device, while wands, joysticks, and other specialty equipment are considered 3D input devices. The sensor model provided by X3D lets an author create a single scene that can operate consistently over a wide range of input devices, avoiding portablity problems and the need for special hardware customizations.

A pointing device has an associated bearing value indicating the direction of the pointer in 3D space. For 2D sensors, this bearing usually is defined by the vector connecting the viewer's position through the pointer's position. The pointer's position is conceptually located on a plane perpendicular to the line of sight. For 3D sensors, the bearing vector is simply the direction of the pointer extended from its center location in 3D space.

X3DPointingDeviceSensorNode implements the X3DSensorNode interface and thus includes the enabled, isActive, and metadata fields. Additional fields are listed in Table 8.2.

2.3.1. description

The description field allows an author to communicate information about the sensor to the user. Typically a browser displays this text next to the pointing-device icon and above the sensor-enabled geometry. A good description indicates the purpose of the sensed geometry, tells the user how to activate it, and indicates the expected action. For example, "clicking the door lets you go inside" describes all three pieces of information. Specifically, the geometric object is a door, pointing-device activation opens it, and user exploration can follow.

2.3.2. isOver

The isActive and isOver fields have closely related functionality. For example, when the pointing device is moved above some geometry with a corresponding peer or parent pointing-device sensor, an isOver true event is sent. Similarly, when the pointing moves off the active geometry, an isOver false event is sent. The isOver field remains unaffected by isActive sensor activation, and isOver events do not occur when a sensor is disabled.

2.3.3. Hints and warnings

It is a good authoring practice to always include a description with each sensor. Although there are no limits on length, keep the description short so that it is readable and does not interfere with viewing the world.

Type	accessType	Name	Default	Range	Profile
SFString	inputOutput	description	""		Interactive
SFBool	outputOnly	isOver			Interactive

Table 8.2. Additional Field Definitions for X3DPointingDeviceSensorNode Type

2.4. X3DTouchSensorNode type

The X3DTouchSensorNode type implements the X3DPointingDeviceSensorNode and X3DSensorNode interfaces, and thus includes the enabled, description, isActive, isOver, and metadata fields. One additional field is added: touchTime, which is described in the TouchSensor section. The additional field for X3DTouchSensorNode is shown in Table 8.3.

2.5. X3DDragSensorNode type

Dragging means to select and activate an object, then move the pointing-device icon while the geometry is still activated. This action causes output events to be continuously generated during the motion. There are three drag-sensor nodes: CylinderSensor, PlaneSensor, and SphereSensor. Each has similar functionality that makes them suitable for detecting translation or rotation actions.

The drag-sensor nodes share additional common fields: offset and [someValue]_changed events. The type and name of these events differ for each node, with each corresponding to the proper output type of the given sensor.

The basic notion of dragging in 3D space is an interesting concept, and more sophisticated than clicking and dragging in 2D interfaces. Pointer devices typically only have 2 degrees of freedom (DOF), namely left-right motion and up-down motion. Meanwhile objects in a 3D scene have 6 degrees of freedom, namely (x y z) and corresponding rotations around each axis. Thus, it is not possible to have a 2-DOF device like a mouse convert the user's intentions into simultaneous changes in position and orientation all at one time, because two unconstrained inputs by themselves are simply insufficient to produce six (or even three) independent outputs. The nodes implementing the X3DDragSensorNode interface constrain that 2-DOF input into a 2-DOF output: PlaneSensor converts pointer changes into *x-y* plane motion, CylinderSensor converts pointer changes into a planar rotation about a fixed cylindrical axis, and SphereSensor converts pointer changes into a fixed-radius 3D rotation about the center of a sphere.

The X3DDragSensorNode type implements X3DPointingDeviceSensorNode and parent interfaces, and so includes all of their required fields: enabled, description, isActive, isOver, and metadata. It also adds the fields shown in Table 8.4.

CylinderSensor and SphereSensor each produce an output SFRotation rotation_changed event, and PlaneSensor outputs an SFVec3f translation_changed event.

Type	accessType	Name	Default	Range	Profile
SFTime	outputOnly	touchTime			Interactive

Table 8.3. Additional Field Definition for X3DTouchSensorNode Type

Type	accessType	Name	Default	Range	Profile
SFBool	inputOutput	autoOffset	true		Interactive
SFVec3f	outputOnly	trackPoint_changed			Interactive
(node dependent)	inputOutput	offset		(node dependent)	Interactive
(node dependent)	outputOnly	[someValue]_changed		(node dependent)	Interactive

Table 8.4. Additional Field Definition for X3DDragSensorNode Type

2.5.1. offset and autoOffset

The offset field provides an additional value applied to whatever amount a sensor has changed while dragging from its original activation position. For example, when a drag motion is completed, an offset_changed event is generated.

When `autoOffset="true"` then the value of the offset field is retained after X3DDragSensorNode deactivation, ready for use in the next reactivation. This means that any drag changes are accumulated and saved so that the sensor does not snap back to the original setting on deactivation. If `autoOffset="false"` then the offset changes are lost on sensor deactivation, starting again at the original value the next time that the drag sensor is activated.

The type of the offset field varies depending on the output type of the implementing X3DDragSensorNode's [value]_changed field. For the CylinderSensor and SphereSensor nodes, the offset field has type SFRotation and matches the output field rotation_changed. For the PlaneSensor node, the offset field has type SFVec3f and matches the output field translation_changed.

2.5.2. trackPoint_changed

The trackPoint_changed field provides a steady stream of output events as a user drags on sensed geometry. The trackpoint value is computed as the intersection of pointing-device bearing and the affected geometry, referenced to the local coordinate system containing the geometry. No drag events are generated except when the selected pointer is moved.

2.5.3. Hints and warnings

DragSensor behavior may vary for different browsers when a drag motion continues past the boundaries of the selected geometric object.

2.6. X3DKeyDeviceSensorNode type

The X3DKeyDeviceSensorNode type implements and exactly matches the X3DSensorNode interface. This abstract node type is used for nodes that sense the keyboard to produce output events, namely KeySensor and StringSensor.

2.6.1. Hints and warnings

X3DKeyDeviceSensorNode is new to X3D. The KeySensor and StringSensor nodes are not supported as a part of VRML97 browsers.

3. Node descriptions

3.1 TouchSensor node

The TouchSensor node provides basic pointing-device contact interaction with various objects in the environment. By keeping track of pointing-device direction, TouchSensor sends an isOver true event when geometry is first pointed at, and an isOver false event when geometry is no longer pointed at, as well as isActive true and false events when the geometry is selected or deselected.

A TouchSensor node can be activated by pointing at any of its peer and child geometry in the scene graph. Thus, the structure of collecting and separating geometric Shape nodes with Group, Transform, and other grouping nodes has a big effect on the interaction provided to the user. For example, if a single TouchSensor is provided at the top level of a scene, then everything is activated equally, which does not provide the user much selection choice. For another example, if a set of buttons trigger separate tasks, each of the button shapes is likely to be positioned with their own Transform node. In turn, these transform nodes can also hold and separate the corresponding TouchSensor nodes.

The TouchSensor node is fully supported in the Interactive profile, implements the X3DTouchSensorNode interface, and has the fields defined in Table 8.5. Node syntax follows in Table 8.6.

All geometry nodes that are peers (or children of peers) of a TouchSensor node are sensed when enabled="true" and the the pointing device is aimed at them. The sensor reports isOver and isActive status via a single true or false event on each transition. Position of the cursor on the geometry (hitPoint_changed), the local normal vector (hitNormal_changed), and (u,v) texture coordinate of the intersection (hitTexCoord_changed) are reported continuously when changing.

A TouchSensor is associated with all of its sibling geometry nodes. It is usually wrapped up with the specific geometry as a child of a grouping node (for example, Group, Transform, or Switch). There is no way to disable TouchSensor activation on a portion of the grouped geometry, though a single TouchSensor can be copied with DEF and USE to handle more than one group of geometry. Separate activation functionality needs to be provided by separate, individually grouped TouchSensor nodes.

If more than one TouchSensor is in the scene graph at the same level or above the affected geometry, then only the TouchSensor that is nearest in the scene-graph hierarchy is activated. If there is a tie for multiple TouchSensors at the same distance in the hierarchy, then each of the nearest peer (or parent) TouchSensors is enabled.

Type	accessType	Name	Default	Range	Profile
SFBool	inputOutput	enabled	true		Interactive
SFString	inputOutput	description	""		Interactive
SFBool	outputOnly	isOver			Interactive
SFBool	outputOnly	isActive			Interactive
SFTime	outputOnly	touchTime			Interactive
SFVec3f	outputOnly	hitNormal_changed			Interactive
SFVec3f	outputOnly	hitPoint_changed			Interactive
SFVec2f	outputOnly	hitTexCoord_changed			Interactive
SFNode	inputOutput	metadata	NULL	[X3DMetadataObject]	Core

Table 8.5. Field Definitions for TouchSensor Node

XML Syntax (.x3d)	ClassicVRML Syntax (.x3dv)

`<TouchSensor DEF="MyTouchSensor" description="Click to activate"/>`	`DEF MyTouchSensor TouchSensor {`
	 `  description "Click to activate"`
	 `}`

Table 8.6. Node Syntax for TouchSensor

If the current position of the cursor indicates that multiple enabled TouchSensor-associated geometries might be activated, then only the TouchSensor geometry closest to the current viewpoint is activated. If activated geometry is obscured by other non-sensed geometry, no sensing occurs.

A change in pointer position is needed to activate a TouchSensor. Animated geometry that happens to move under the cursor does not automatically generate an isOver event. However, if geometry is moved under the pointer and then the pointer is moved, an isOver event is generated when the cursor is first moved over the geometry.

A common use for a TouchSensor is button activation to trigger some animation in the world, for example, opening a door. Generally users do not want a door to open if the cursor happens to pass over the door's geometry. Controlling the interaction by selecting (i.e., clicking) the doorknob is much more deliberate. Capturing a click on the door often means using the event isActive. The isActive field generates a true event on mouse button selection, which can be sent to a TimeTrigger node (see Chapter 9, Event Utilities and Scripting) to generate a startTime for a TimeSensor (see Chapter 7, Event Animation and Interpolation) to run an animation of the door opening. Alternatively, the touchTime event might be used to indicate Touchsensor deselection. Figure 8.1 shows both approaches in action.

If the door needs to open automatically when approached, then a ProximitySensor can be used instead Figure 8.2 shows the example TouchSensor.X3d where the piston is activated by depressing the pointer button over the sensed geometry (see Chapter 12, Environment Sensor and Sound Nodes).

3.1.1. touchTime

A touchTime event is generated whenever an isActive true, isActive false, or isOver true event is generated. Thus, the touchTime event indicates that the primary button was selected or released while the cursor remained over the associated geometry.

Figure 8.1. This example shows two TouchSensors, the door on the left is activated on a button-down (isActive true) event. The door on the right is opened on a button-up (touchTime) event.

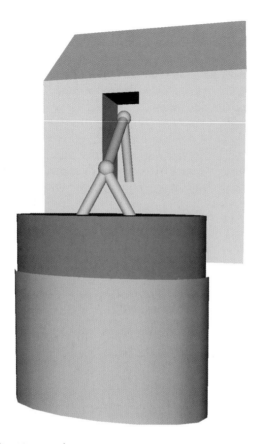

Figure 8.2. This example (TouchSensor.x3d) shows the pump house, which is activated when the button is pressed down while the cursor is over the pump house.

The following list describes the three requirements for user interaction to produce a touchTime event.

- The pointing device begins pointing at the geometry (an isOver true event is generated).

- The pointing device was pointing towards the geometry when initially activated (an isActive true event is generated).

- The pointing device is deactivated (an isActive false event is generated).

No touchTime event is generated if the pointer no longer points at the geometry during deselection, although an isOver false event is generated.

The current-clock value of touchTime has the same value as the time of the isActive false event. The touchTime event can be connected with a ROUTE statement directly to the startTime field of a TimeSensor to commence animation, or via a TimeTrigger (see

Chapter 9, Event Utilities and Scripting) to convert this SFTime event into an SFBool boolean event. Example doors.x3d in Figure 8.1 shows these two conditions in action.

3.1.2. Hints and warnings

There are times when the desired action needs to occur on a button-up event. This is the case of many control-panel type buttons. The pointer must still point to the geometry when deselected in order to create an isActive false event and a corresponding touchTime event. Deselection after moving the pointer off the geometry bypasses the isActive false event generation.

A double-click can be determined by using a Script node (see Chapter 9, Event Utilities and Scripting), and determining if the difference in subsequent button-up times is within the desired threshold. An example implementation is provided in the Savage X3D examples archive under Tools, Animation: DoubleClickTouchSensorPrototype and DoubleClickTouchSensorExample. Links to the Savage X3D examples archive are provided in Appendix B, Help: X3D Examples, and the book's website.

3.2. PlaneSensor node

The PlaneSensor node converts select-and-drag pointer motion into 2D translation parallel to the local $z=0$ plane. When connected to the translation field of a Transform node, output values allow the user to drag geometric objects and reposition them anywhere along a flat surface. Boundary limits can constrain motion within a preset rectangular area.

Similar to TouchSensor, a PlaneSensor node can be activated at run time by pointing at any of its peer and child geometry in the scene graph. The PlaneSensor node also provides basic contact interaction capabilities by providing output from isOver and isActive events.

The PlaneSensor node is in the Interactive profile. The node has the fields defined in Table 8.7. Node syntax is shown in Table 8.8.

The PlaneSensor node detects cursor motion over the associated geometry, and translates it into scene-graph output motion in the local plane. The motion plane is parallel to the $z=0$ plane of the local coordinate system and intersects the geometry at the initial point of the primary button–down event. Motion is tracked in this plane as long as the primary button is down, meaning as long as the user continues to drag the object.

Careful application of parent Transform rotation values can reorient a PlaneSensor into the desired plane of action. Ordinarily this orientation matches the same plane as the object(s) being animated.

As long as the cursor is moving over the associated geometry and the PlaneSensor is active, the node generates trackPoint_changed and translation_changed events. The trackPoint_changed field provides the local coordinates of the intersection with the associated geometry. The translation_changed event has the value of the total translation in the motion plane, relative to the initial offset when the primary button was depressed, plus the initial offset value. The initial offset value is stored in the offset field.

PlaneSensor translation motion can be clamped to not exceed minimum or maximum values in either the x or y direction (for both directions). This feature simplifies construction of a slider sensor. The clamping of the translation only effects the

Type	accessType	Name	Default	Range	Profile
SFBool	inputOutput	enabled	true		Interactive
SFString	inputOutput	description	""		Interactive
SFVec2f	inputOutput	minPosition	0 0	$(-\infty, \infty)$	Interactive
SFVec2f	inputOutput	maxPosition	−1 −1	$(-\infty, \infty)$	Interactive
SFVec3f	inputOutput	offset	0 0 0	$(-\infty, \infty)$	Interactive
SFBool	inputOutput	autoOffset	true		Interactive
SFBool	outputOnly	isOver			Interactive
SFBool	outputOnly	isActive			Interactive
SFVec3f	outputOnly	trackPoint_changed			Interactive
SFVec3f	outputOnly	translation_changed			Interactive
SFNode	inputOutput	metadata	NULL	[X3DMetadataObject]	Core

Table 8.7. Field Definitions for PlaneSensor Node

XML Syntax (.x3d)	ClassicVRML Syntax (.x3dv)
```<PlaneSensor DEF="MyPlaneSensor" description="Adjust Intensity" maxPosition="1 0" minPosition="−1 0" offset="0 0 0"/>```	```DEF MyPlaneSensor PlaneSensor { description "Adjust Intensity" maxPosition 1 0 minPosition −1 0 offset 0 0 0 }```

Table 8.8. Node Syntax for PlaneSensor

translation_changed values, not the trackPoint_changed values. The clamping is achieved by use of the fields minPosition and maxPosition. Setting the x or y components to the same values in these two fields indicates that the coordinate is constrained to only take on that value.

Some user perspectives may make it difficult to activate the sensed geometry. It is important to carefully position the local coordinate system so that the desired active plane is parallel to the local $z=0$ plane (meaning the x–y plane at the origin). It is usually important to give the user a viewpoint that simplifies positioning for smooth PlaneSensor operation. For example, if the local coordinate system is rotated so that the z-axis is in the plane of the display, then it may be difficult to get the full response range from the sensor unless viewer position is changed.

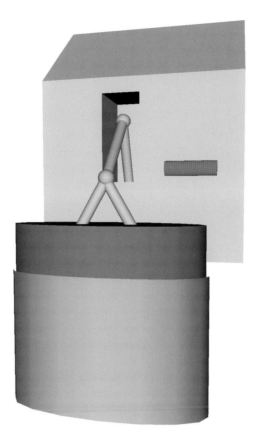

Figure 8.3. A PlaneSensor is indicated by the red bar. The sensor output controls the amplitude of the pump.

A plane sensor is frequently used as a 1-dimensional (1D) or slider control. In the example PlaneSensor.x3d in Figure 8.3, a red bar is used to indicate the value of the PlaneSensor. Changes in the position of the red bar change the pertinent output value of the PlaneSensor and the corresponding amplitude of the piston stroke.

3.2.1. minPosition and maxPosition

The minPosition and maxPosition fields set the minimum and maximum translation values allowed for the sensor. The individually generated x and y values cannot be less than the minPosition values nor can they exceed the maxPosition values. If either maxPosition x or y components are less than the corresponding minPosition x or y components, then positive and negative sensed values along that direction are not clamped. If either of the minimum components is equal to the corresponding maximum component, then the value of that component direction is fixed to that single value.

The default values `minPosition="0 0"` and `maxPosition="-1 -1"`, which provide minimum values greater than the maximum values, meaning that no constraints are applied to the x and y values generated by the PlaneSensor. Thus, such a PlaneSensor is unconstrained laterally and can extend out to any x-y value in the plane.

3.2.2. offset

The offset field is the initial SFVec3f value applied to the translation once the drag motion is initiated. If `autoOffset="true"`, then the last value of translation_changed is stored in the offset field, and an offset_changed event is generated when the PlaneSensor is deactivated. This lets the PlaneSensor effectively "remember" prior drag motions and not snap back to the default initial position after each use.

3.2.3. trackPoint_changed

The trackPoint_changed field is an output event that provides the local coordinate position of the cursor on the associated geometry. This field is not limited or clamped by minPosition or maxPosition, and the z-coordinate is not constrained to remain in the $z=0$ motion plane. This event is sent continuously while dragging.

3.2.4. translation_changed

The translation_changed field is usually the primary sensor output of interest, providing the translation value of the dragged geometry along the motion plane. The motion plane is parallel to the local-coordinate $z=0$ plane and intersects the associated geometry at the point where the PlaneSensor was activated. If appropriate, the values of this event are clamped to not exceed minPosition and maxPosition. This event is sent continuously while dragging.

3.2.5. Hints and warnings

Adding a semitransparent Rectangle2D or flat Box for the plane that cuts through the affected geometry shows the area of intended effect for the PlaneSensor.

Authoring may require some trial-and-error testing. It is important to first align the PlaneSensor with the desired plane of motion. This may require first rotating the PlaneSensor in one direction, and then rotating the child geometry of interest back in the opposite direction, so that the viewed shapes remain properly oriented.

Mouse motion of PlaneSensor geometry can be difficult unless the user has an unobstructed perspective of both the affected geometry and the underlying x-y translation plane. Adding a Viewpoint to facilitate user interaction may help.

3.3. CylinderSensor node

The CylinderSensor node converts select-and-drag pointer motion into a 3D rotation around the local y-axis. When connected to the rotation field of a Transform node, output values allow the user to rotate a geometric object around an axis. Boundary limits can constrain the rotation angle within a specific range of minimum-maximum radians.

Similar to TouchSensor, a CylinderSensor node can be activated by pointing the mouse (or other pointing device) at any of the rendered peer and child geometry. The

CylinderSensor node also provides basic contact-interaction capabilities via output from isOver and isActive events.

The CylinderSensor node is in the Interactive profile. The node has the fields defined in Table 8.9. Node syntax is shown in Table 8.10.

The CylinderSensor node defines user interactivity for single-angle rotations. As with the other user-interactivity sensors, the sensor defines an invisible geometry that is used for modeling the interaction. For this node, a cylinder is the nonrendered geomet-

Type	accessType	Name	Default	Range	Profile
SFBool	inputOutput	enabled	true		Interactive
SFString	inputOutput	description	""		Interactive
SFVec2f	inputOutput	minAngle	0	$(-2\pi, 2\pi)$	Interactive
SFVec2f	inputOutput	maxAngle	−1	$(-2\pi, 2\pi)$	Interactive
SFFloat	inputOutput	diskAngle	$\pi/12$	$[0, \pi/2]$	Interactive
SFFloat	inputOutput	offset	0	$(-\infty, \infty)$	Interactive
SFBool	inputOutput	autoOffset	true		Interactive
SFBool	outputOnly	isOver			Interactive
SFBool	outputOnly	isActive			Interactive
SFVec3f	outputOnly	trackPoint_changed			Interactive
SFRotation	outputOnly	rotation_changed			Interactive
SFNode	inputOutput	metadata	NULL	[X3DMetadataObject]	Core

Table 8.9. Field Definitions for CylinderSensor Node

XML Syntax (.x3d)	ClassicVRML Syntax (.x3dv)
```<CylinderSensor DEF= "MyCylinderSensor" diskAngle="0" enabled="true" maxAngle="1.57" minAngle="-1.57" description="Click and drag to rotate view"/>```	```DEF MyCylinderSensor CylinderSensor { diskAngle 0 enabled TRUE maxAngle 1.57 minAngle -1.57 description "Click and drag to rotate view" }```

Table 8.10. Node Syntax for CylinderSensor

ric shape that is used. The sensor can measure rotation on its side (like a thumbwheel) or its end caps (like a knob).

When the sensor is enabled and the cursor is over any child geometry of the sensor's parent node, the CylinderSensor can be activated by pressing down on the pointing device's primary button. The sensor then grabs all cursor motion events, maps them into a cylindrical rotation change, and generates corresponding rotation events while dragging until the primary button is released. When the button is released, the sensor stops grabbing all cursor-motion events and no further rotation events are produced.

The diskAngle field and the initial geometry-intersection point control the mode of the CylinderSensor. The vector from the local coordinate's origin to the cursor's intersection point is called the *bearing vector*. The acute angle between the local *y*-axis and the bearing vector is called the *bearing angle*. If the bearing angle is greater than or equal to the value of diskAngle, then the rotation control is treated as if along the sides of the unrendered sensing cylinder. If the bearing angle is less than the value of diskAngle, then the rotation is considered to be in disk mode and tracked as if around the nearest end cap of the unrendered sensing cylinder. These relationships are illustrated in Figure 8.4.

When the sensor is in disk mode, the perpendicular vector from the *y*-axis to the initial cursor position defines the zero-rotation axis. Dragging motion of the cursor is mapped to a rotation about the positive *y*-axis and generates a rotation_changed event. A CylinderSensor can be forced to always operate in disk mode by setting diskAngle="1.5707" ($\pi/2$ radians). This mode is useful to simulate the turning of knobs.

When the sensor is operating in cylinder-rotation mode, the zero-angle position is determined by the initial intersection point. The perpendicular distance from the intersection point to the local *y*-axis determines the radius of the cylinder. As the cursor is dragged, rotation events are generated based on the cumulative rotation from the initial

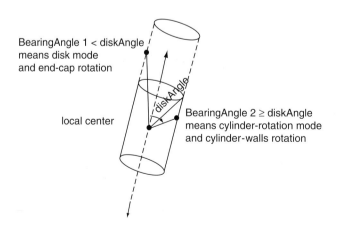

Figure 8.4. Shows how the diskAngle field determines whether a user's drag motion produces a rotation that is either in end-cap disk mode or cylinder-walls rotation mode.

point, plus any offset value if autoOffset is enabled. A CylinderSensor node can be forced to always operate in cylinder mode by setting `diskAngle="0"`.

Note that, although the cylindrical bearing-angle relationships are SFFloat values, the sensor's rotation_changed output event is an SFRotation suitable for object transformations.

The example (CylinderSensor.x3d) in Figure 8.5 emulates the functionality of a knob. Rotating the knob changes the viewing angle to the pump house.

Figure 8.6 shows the scene-graph design pattern needed to rotate the axis of a CylinderSensor's rotation at an angle different than the sensed geometry.

3.3.1. minAngle

The minAngle field sets the minimum rotation angle value, preventing any rotation less than this value. If maxAngle is less than minAngle, then the output rotation value is not clamped. This scalar value equals rotation angle in radians about the local y-axis, not a 4-tuple SFRotation axis-angle value.

Figure 8.5. The position of the CylinderSensor is indicated by the red knob and pointer. Rotating the knob changes the user's viewing angle.

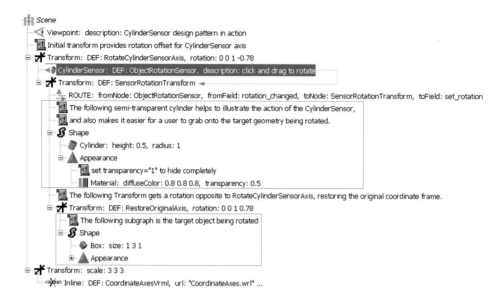

Figure 8.6. Setting a CylinderSensor's axis of rotation to be different from sensed geometry is best accomplished by using the design pattern shown in this scene graph.

3.3.2. maxAngle

The maxAngle field sets the maximum rotation angle value, preventing any rotation greater than this value. If maxAngle is less than minAngle, then the output rotation value is not clamped.

3.3.3. diskAngle

The diskAngle field determines how the CylinderSensor treats rotation motions at various points on the associated geometry. Two modes are specified: cylinder mode (when dragging the sides of the transparent-cylinder sensor) and disk mode (when dragging the end caps of the transparent-cylinder sensor). The default value of $\pi/12$ (0.262 radians or 15°) usually provides a good compromise value for most sensed geometry.

Upon selecting geometry that is activated by a CylinderSensor, the bearing angle is computed and compared to the diskAngle value. If the bearing angle value is greater than or equal to the diskAngle value, then the CylinderSensor operates in cylinder mode. If the bearing angle value is less than the diskAngle value, then the CylinderSensor operates in disk mode. A diskAngle value of zero forces the sensor to always operate in cylinder mode, and a diskAngle value of $\pi/2$ radians (1.57 radians or 90°) forces the CylinderSensor to always operate in disk mode. The net result for users is more-intuitive manipulation when rotating cylindrically sensed objects.

3.3.4. offset

The offset field is the initial SFFloat value applied to the axial rotation once the drag motion is initiated. If autoOffset="true", then the last value of rotation_changed is stored in the offset field and an offset_changed event is generated when the CylinderSensor is deactivated. This lets the CylinderSensor effectively "remember" prior drag motions and not snap back to the default initial rotation after each use.

3.3.5. trackPoint_changed

The trackPoint_changed field is the local coordinate position on the projected rotation cylinder under the cursor. This field is not limited or clamped by minAngle or maxAngle. This event is sent continuously while dragging.

3.3.6. rotation_changed

The rotation_changed field is the user-controlled 3D-output rotation in the reference frame of the CylinderSensor. This SFRotation event is generated whenever the cursor is moved and the sensor is activated. If appropriate, event values are clamped to not exceed minAngle and maxAngle. This event is sent continuously while dragging.

3.3.7. Hints and warnings

Adding a semi-transparent cylinder around the affected geometry helps to show the effect of the CylinderSensor to a user. This is a useful debugging technique that can later be retained without visual effect by setting the corresponding `transparency="0"`. This may also help to expose small geometry and make it more accessible to users. Take care to not obscure other sensed geometry.

It is crucial to first align the CylinderSensor with the desired axis of motion. This may require first rotating the CylinderSensor in one direction and then rotating the child geometry of interest back in the opposite direction so that the viewed shapes remain oriented properly.

Pointer manipulation of CylinderSensor geometry can be difficult unless the user's view has an unobstructed perspective view of the affected geometry. Consider adding a special viewpoint to facilitate sensor operation.

3.4. SphereSensor node

The SphereSensor node converts select-and-drag pointer motion into a 3D rotation around the local origin. When connected to the rotation field of a Transform node, output values allow the user to arbitrarily rotate any geometric object. No boundary limits are provided that might constrain rotation within a specific range.

Similar to TouchSensor, a SphereSensor node can be activated by pointing at any of its peer or child geometry in the scene graph. The SphereSensor node also provides basic contact interaction capabilities by producing isOver and isActive output events.

The SphereSensor node is in the Interactive profile. The node has the fields defined in Table 8.11. Node syntax is shown in Table 8.12.

The SphereSensor node defines user interactivity for full 3D rotations. When the cursor is over the associated geometry, the sensor can be activated by selecting the object (as also occurs with TouchSensor selection). Once the sensor is activated, the SphereSensor grabs all cursor motion until the selection button is released. All cursor motions are mapped into a 3D rotation and generate a corresponding rotation_changed event.

Type	accessType	Name	Default	Range	Profile
SFBool	inputOutput	enabled	true		Interactive
SFString	inputOutput	description	""		Interactive
SFBool	inputOutput	autoOffset	true		Interactive
SFRotation	inputOutput	offset	0 1 0 0	[−1, 1], (−∞, ∞)	Interactive
SFBool	outputOnly	isOver			Interactive
SFBool	outputOnly	isActive			Interactive
SFVec3f	outputOnly	trackPoint_changed			Interactive
SFRotation	outputOnly	rotation_changed			Interactive
SFNode	inputOutput	metadata	NULL	[X3DMetadataObject]	Core

Table 8.11. Field Definitions for SphereSensor Node

XML Syntax (.x3d)	ClassicVRML Syntax (.x3dv)

`<SphereSensor DEF=`
`    "MySphereSensor"`
`  description=`
`    "Click and drag to view"/>`
	`DEF MySphereSensor SphereSensor {`
	`    description "Click and drag to`
	`    view"`
	`}`

Table 8.12. Node Syntax for SphereSensor

When the geometry is selected, the distance from the local origin to the intersection of the cursor position on the associated geometry determines the radius of the sensed rotation sphere. This nonrendered rotation sphere is centered at the origin of the local coordinate system. The initial intersection point defines the zero-rotation point. When the sensor becomes activated, all drag motions rotate the rotation sphere away from the zero-rotation point based on the distance dragged and the radius of the sphere.

Example SphereSensor.x3d in Figure 8.7 allows the user to manipulate the orientation of the NPS shark relative to the current viewpoint. The SphereSensor is attached to the blue sphere.

3.4.1. offset

The offset field is the SFRotation value applied to the rotation once the drag motion is initiated. If `autoOffset="true"`, then the last value of rotation_changed is stored in the offset field, and an offset_changed event is generated when the SphereSensor is deactivated. This lets the SphereSensor effectively "remember" prior drag motions and not snap back to the default initial rotation after each use.

Figure 8.7. The orientation NPS shark is manipulated with a SphereSensor on the blue sphere.

3.4.2. trackPoint_changed

The trackPoint_changed field is the local coordinate position on the projected rotation sphere under the cursor. This event is sent continuously while dragging.

3.4.3. rotation_changed

The rotation_changed field is the user-controlled 3D output rotation of the SphereSensor. This SFRotation event is generated whenever the cursor is moved and the sensor is activated. If appropriate, event values are clamped to not exceed minAngle and maxAngle. This event is sent continuously while dragging.

3.4.4. Hints and warnings

Adding a semitransparent Sphere around the affected geometry helps to show the effect of the SphereSensor.

See related hints and warnings for CylinderSensor in section 8.3.3.7, which also pertain to SphereSensor.

3.5. KeySensor node

The KeySensor node provides a character-by-character interface to the keyboard. KeySensor returns a single event consisting of a single-character SFString for each keyboard press and release. The Control, Alternate, and Shift modifier keys can also be pressed or released, providing corresponding true and false values for the controlKey, altKey, and shiftKey output events, respectively. Special-function keys (called *actionKeys*) are also reported as output events.

The KeySensor node is in the Interactive profile, and has the fields defined in Table 8.13. Node syntax is shown in Table 8.14.

The KeySensor node generates an event whenever the state of the keyboard changes. Each keypress or key release, including Shift, Control, and Alternate, generates an event. An isActive true event is sent when a key is pressed, followed by an isActive false event when the key is released.

The KeySensor is not dependent on the relative location of any geometry or its position in the scene graph.

The user's viewpoint is controlled with a KeySensor in the example (KeySensor.x3d) in Figure 8.8. Pressing on the "n" key advances the user to the next viewpoint. Pressing on the "p" key returns the user to the previous viewpoint in the stack. The shark's orientation can still be manipulated with the blue sphere.

Processing of the events from a KeySensor requires a Script node. Script nodes are discussed in Chapter 9, Event Utilities and Scripting. The Script node in example KeySensor.x3d treats upper and lower case letters as lower case letters.

3.5.1. actionKeyPress and actionKeyRelease

The actionKeyPress and actionKeyRelease are SFInt32 output values that respectively indicate the pressing or releasing of an action key. Action key values are listed in Table 8.15.

3.5.2. altKey, controlKey, and shiftKey

The altKey, controlKey, and shiftKey events are SFBool output events that respectively indicate pressing or releasing the Alternate, Control, or Shift keys. A value of true indi-

Type	accessType	Name	Default	Range	Profile
SFBool	inputOutput	enabled	true		Interactive
SFInt32	outputOnly	actionKeyPress			Interactive
SFInt32	outputOnly	actionKeyRelease			Interactive
SFString	outputOnly	keyPress			Interactive
SFString	outputOnly	keyRelease			Interactive
SFBool	outputOnly	shiftKey			Interactive
SFBool	outputOnly	controlKey			Interactive
SFBool	outputOnly	altKey			Interactive
SFBool	outputOnly	isActive			Interactive
SFNode	inputOutput	metadata	NULL	[X3DMetadataObject]	Core

Table 8.13. Field Definitions for KeySensor Node

XML Syntax (.x3d)	ClassicVRML Syntax (.x3dv)

`<KeySensor DEF="MyKeySensor"`
`    enabled="false"/>`
	`DEF MyKeySensor KeySensor {`
	`    enabled FALSE`
	`}`

Table 8.14. Node Syntax for KeySensor

cates that the special key has been pressed, and a false event indicates that the special key has been released.

3.5.3. keyPress and keyRelease

The keyPress and keyRelease events contain a single-character, Universal Text Format (UTF-8) encoded SFString value for the specific key that was pressed. Different keyboards and implementations may produce different sets of characters. These events are only generated when a key that generates a character is pressed and released.

3.5.4. isActive

When a key is pressed, an isActive true event is sent. When that key is released, an isActive false event is sent.

3.5.5. Hints and warnings

The various action keys (other than the special function keys) also have default mappings for navigation and pointer interaction. The arrow up, down, left, and right keys can also be interpreted as moving the pointer interpreted as cursor up, down, left, and

Key	Value	Interaction Default
F1–F12	1–12	
Home	13	First viewpoint
End	14	Last viewpoint
PageUp	15	Prior viewpoint
PageDown	16	Next viewpoint
Arrow up	17	Cursor up
Arrow down	18	Cursor down
Arrow left	19	Cursor left
Arrow right	20	Cursor right

Table 8.15. Default Values and Responses for actionKeyPress

Figure 8.8. The KeySensor example allows the user to change the viewpoint.

right respectively. The Enter key can be interpreted as a pointer selection. Home and End respectively bind the first and last viewpoints available. PageUp and PageDown shift to the next or preceding viewpoints (if one exists). Normally these interpretations are active unless an enabled KeySensor or StringSensor is intercepting keyboard activity.

The X3D specification recommends that browsers provide a means of disabling the keyboard. No single mechanism is defined for achieving this functionality because browser interfaces vary widely.

3.6. StringSensor node

The StringSensor node provides a string-based interface to the keyboard. Each character keypress is collected until the user presses the Enter key, terminating the string and initiating the output events.

The StringSensor node is in the Interactive profile and has the fields defined in Table 8.16. Node syntax is shown in Table 8.17.

StringSensor node defines user interactivity for character strings. The node accepts characters until a string termination character is received. On receiving the termination character, it generates a finalText event and clears the node's internal storage for the next string. StringSensor is not dependent on any geometry or its position in the scene graph.

A StringSensor allows the entry of a sequence of characters into the X3D world. The string is terminated by the local system's string-termination character. This is usually the Enter key. The example StringSensor.x3d shown in Figure 8.9 accepts text from the keyboard and displays it as it is typed on the yellow rectangle. An Enter key (for most systems) terminates the entry of the string. The next character clears the existing string and starts a new string.

3.6.1. deletionAllowed

When `deletionAllowed="true"` a previously entered character can be deleted when the user presses the delete key. If `deletionAllowed="false"` then no characters are removed and the key code for the delete key is added to the string buffer. This may be helpful when authors want to parse the original unmodified set of key strokes.

3.6.2. enteredText

An enteredText event is generated for each character-generating keypress. The value of the event is the string of UTF-8 characters that comprise the current character string, including the most recently pressed key. This may be helpful for scene scripts that want to monitor user progress.

Type	accessType	Name	Default	Range	Profile
SFBool	inputOutput	deletionAllowed	true		Interactive
SFString	outputOnly	enteredText			Interactive
SFString	outputOnly	finalText			Interactive
SFNode	inputOutput	metadata	NULL	[X3DMetadataObject]	Core

Table 8.16. Field Definitions for StringSensor Node

XML Syntax (.x3d)	ClassicVRML Syntax (.x3dv)

`<StringSensor DEF="MyStringSensor"`
`    deletionAllowed="true"/>`
	`DEF MyStringSensor StringSensor {`
	`    deletionAllowed TRUE`
	`}`

Table 8.17. Node Syntax for StringSensor

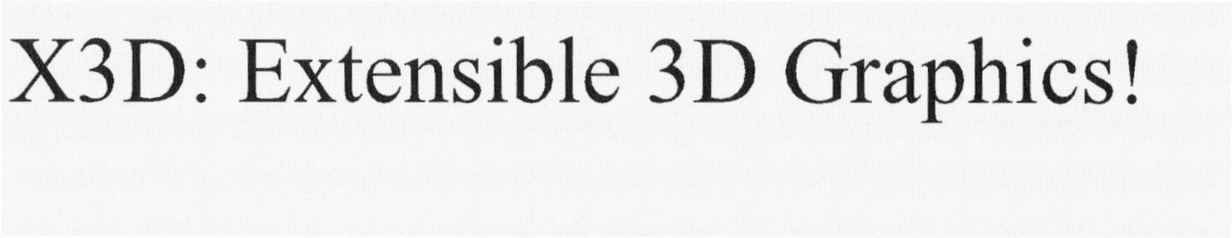

X3D: Extensible 3D Graphics!

Figure 8.9. A StringSensor allows the entry of the string "X3D: Extensible 3D Graphics!" into this X3D world.

3.6.3. finalText

The finalText event is generated when the user enters the character that the browser recognizes as terminating the string (usually the Enter key). The value of the finalText string is the same as the final enteredText value. After enteredText and finalText events are generated, enteredText is cleared (set to the empty string) in preparation for the next string entry.

3.6.4. isActive

An isActive true event is sent by the StringSensor when the user starts entering text. When the user finishes entering a text string (typically by pressing the Enter key), an isActive false event is sent.

3.6.5. Hints and warnings

When designing scene interaction, think carefully about whether single-character interaction is sufficient, or if longer text entry is needed. Often single-character keypresses are sufficient if hints are provided to the user. Such an approach allows immediate interaction. It also avoids the possibility that the user has forgotten (or doesn't realize) that pressing the Enter key is needed. This approach can be achieved by monitoring the enteredText field, or by substituting a KeySensor instead.

Deliberately enabling and disabling a KeySensor or StringSensor node as needed can prevent mutual interference.

4. Summary

4.1. Key ideas

User interaction can bring people's attention deep into a scene. Starting and stopping animations, moving and rotating objects, intuitively traveling and navigating through a scene, and even keyboard typing helps provide a sense of immersion. Adding interactivity to animation makes 3D graphics a more sophisticated medium than 2D animation or fixed-viewpoint video.

Think about scene design and the user experience when putting together animation and interaction capabilities. The "Kiss" principle can help: keep it simple, smartypants! Often a straightforward logical progression is more effective than many simultaneous choices.

4.2. Related nodes and concepts

TouchSensor is a common way to initiate animation chains, described in Chapter 7, Event Animation Interpolation.

Viewpoint, NavigationInfo, and Sensor nodes utilize certain keyboard events if KeySensor and StringSensor are either disabled or both absent from a scene.

4.3. Next chapter

Chapter 9 presents event utilities and scripting. The event utilities open up scene-graph capabilities to allow connection of nearly any input or any output as desired. Programming script code using ECMAScript or Java enables customized computation for any animation purpose. These combined capabilities make X3D a rich media for authoring interactive 3D scenes.

Event Utilities and Scripting

Action is eloquence.
—William Shakespeare, Coriolanus, Act III, Scene II

1. What this chapter covers

The event utility nodes are used to convert events from one type to another, often improving animation capabilities by converting the typed output of one source node to match the typed input of another target node. Together with the other animation nodes, authors can usually find a built-in combination of one or more event-utility nodes to natively handle common animation tasks without needing the capabilities of the Script node.

Script nodes are used to create special-purpose capabilities. An author defines whatever initialization and input and output fields are needed, and then either wraps ECMAScript source or points to external ECMAScript or Java code to compute whatever functionality is needed. Scripts allow authors to extend the capabilities of a scene beyond those already provided by X3D.

Scripts have many powerful capabilities and their construction can be quite complex. Simple Script nodes are straightforward, but sophisticated Script authoring is definitely an advanced topic. This chapter assumes that authors have a good understanding of event routing from Chapter 7, Event Animation and Interpolation; and Chapter 8, User Interactivity Nodes. The various field types (SFBool, MFFloat, etc.) from Chapter 1, Technical Introduction are also worth reviewing.

2. Concepts

X3D scenes mostly contain geometry and appearance definitions. What makes a 3D environment interesting is the behaviors associated with geometries and the resulting interactions with users. Basic behaviors and interactions can be implemented with environmental sensors and interpolation nodes, but complex behaviors and interactions may require special handling or even programming.

There are many different nodes that can produce output events in the scene graph. Furthermore, nearly every node has fields that can be modified by receiving events. ROUTE statements can usually be used to directly connect events originating from output fields to the target input fields. However, direct connections are not always possible because the types must match: for example, a singleton float from a ScalarInterpolator cannot modify an integer LOD level, a timestamp cannot replace a boolean input, and so on.

Because all event passing is strongly typed, each event getting passed by a ROUTE must match the type of the destination field exactly or else a run-time error results. Event utility nodes are provided to simplify type conversions and handle common authoring tasks, making it easier to connect nodes together as an event-animation chain in a way that achieves the intended action.

The Script node provides a more general way to create functions as desired, enabling authors to include special-purpose code for any type of scene animation.

2.1. Purpose and common functionality

The primary routing and animation capabilities provided by X3D are reasonably thorough. However, some authoring tasks go beyond the palette of capabilities already available to an author. How can a boolean output set the time for a TimeSensor to start? How can a single-digit floating point value modify a 3-tuple *x-y-z* scale value? Event utility nodes and Script nodes can provide the glue needed to properly connect inputs to outputs, especially whenever the event type produced as an output does not conveniently match the event type needed by an input.

The event utility nodes have been added to X3D to provide frequently needed authoring functions. They include BooleanFilter, BooleanSequencer, BooleanToggle, BooleanTrigger, IntegerSequencer, IntegerTrigger, and TimeTrigger. The Script node provides a general way to create functions as desired, defining input and output parameters as appropriate. A summary of node functionality follows.

- BooleanFilter and BooleanToggle simplify the negation and combination of boolean true/false logic, making it easier to set up the appropriate response to a given input.

- BooleanSequencer and IntegerSequencer are similar to Interpolator nodes, producing streams of values. Sequencers provide single discrete values one at a time, rather than a continuous stream of floating-point values.

- BooleanTrigger, IntegerTrigger, and TimeTrigger can each produce a predetermined output value when triggered by an input of a different type.

- Script nodes define a set of interfaces and encapsulate arbitrary functionality in small ECMAScript or Java programs.

- Scripting mechanisms and interfaces for ECMAScript and Java are designed to work equivalently, either when embedded within a Script node or else contained externally in an HTML page.

Each of these nodes can appear anywhere in the scene graph where children nodes are allowed. The position of these nodes in the scene graph does not change their functionality or operation in any way, though they must precede any ROUTE statements that connect them.

Abstract node types are defined in the following sections.

2.2. X3DScriptNode type

The X3DScriptNode type implements the X3DChildNode and X3DUrlObject interfaces. Field definitions are shown in Table 9.1.

Taken at face value, this default node interface is quite simple. Of course, the nature of a Script node is that authors create definitions for further fields.

Any node having X3DScriptNode type may contain a metadata node.

Full details for the Script node are presented later in this chapter.

2.3. X3DSequencerNode type

The X3DSequencerNode type implements the X3DChildNode interface, meaning that it can be placed in the scene graph anywhere other children nodes are allowed. Implemented fields and defaults are shown in Table 9.2. Each occurrence of [type] must be identical for a given X3DSequencerNode implementation.

Note that, unlike interpolators, each discrete value_changed output event is only sent once during each *key[i]* interval. That is because there is no point in repeatedly sending an identical boolean or integer value until the next *key[i+1]* timestep is reached.

Type	accessType	Name	Default	Range	Profile
SFNode	inputOutput	metadata	NULL	[X3DMetadataObject]	Core

Table 9.1. Field Definition for X3DScriptNode Type

Type	accessType	Name	Default	Range	Profile
SFBool	inputOnly	next			Interactive
SFBool	inputOnly	previous			Interactive
SFFloat	inputOnly	set_fraction		$(-\infty, \infty)$	Interactive
MFFloat	inputOutput	key		$(-\infty, \infty)$	Interactive
MF[type]	inputOutput	keyValue		$(-\infty, \infty)$	Interactive
SF[type] or MF[type]	outputOnly	value_changed			Interactive
SFNode	inputOutput	metadata	NULL	[X3DMetadataObject]	Core

Table 9.2. Field Definition for X3DSequencerNode Type

Once sent, the action of this event is complete until a different keyValue is matched and sent as the value_changed event.

2.3.1. next and previous

The next and previous fields provide simplified ways to increment the input and output of a sequencer. Sending a true event to the next field advances the node state to the following key and keyValue pair. If already at the last key index, the next event wraps around to the beginning of the arrays and then produces a corresponding value_changed output event. Similarly, sending a true event to the previous field advances the node state to the preceding key and keyValue pair. If already at the initial key index, the previous event wraps around to the end of the arrays, and then produces a corresponding value_changed output event.

2.3.2. key and keyValue

The key and keyValue arrays together define a sequencer input-output function. The key array lists relative-time intervals, usually in the range of [0,1], provided in nondecreasing order and corresponding to keyValues. The keyValue array lists the corresponding output values, and each element of the array has the same type associated with the specific value-changed output field of the node. Conceptually this is nearly identical to interpolar node operations, except that no interpolation is computed between key intervals.

2.3.3. set_fraction and value_changed

The set_fraction event is the floating-point input value to the sequencer function, usually in the range of [0,1]. This SFFloat value is compared to the key array. When a given input set_fraction value first becomes equal to or greater than one of the element values in the key array, the corresponding value is found in the keyValue array. That value is then sent as value_changed, again using the specific type associated with the output of the node.

Note that the value_changed output is only sent when set_fraction first exceeds a particular key element. No interpolation occurs, and subsequent arrivals of set_fraction events whose values remain between the current array element *key[i]* and the subsequent array element *key[i+1]* have no effect. It is only when set_fraction

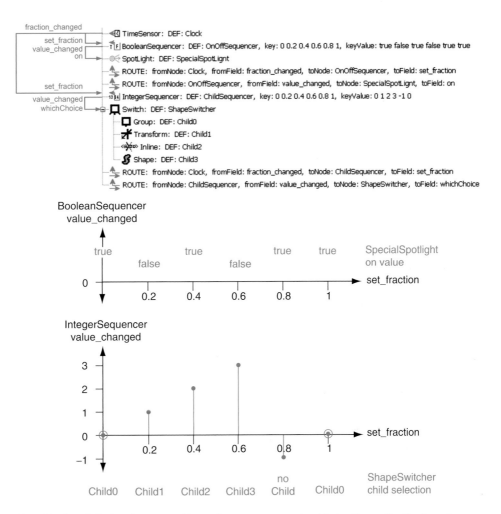

Figure 9.1. Example Boolean Sequencer and IntegerSequencer scene graph and timing diagram. Together these show enabling and disabling a Spotlight, synchronized with choosing different children of a Switch.

finally is equal to or greater than *key[i+1]* that the next output result *keyValue[i+1]* is finally sent (for a single time) as value_changed. The process then repeats.

2.3.4. Hints and warnings

Note that key array and set_fraction values are always floating point, allowing precise measurement of animation timing.

Also note that the keyValue field is an array of values corresponding to the type of the value_changed array.

Counting is important when constructing a sequencer node. The size of the key array must exactly match the size of the keyValue array, because each corresponding pair of values defines the functional characteristic of the sequencer.

2.4. X3DTriggerNode type

The X3DTriggerNode type also implements the X3DChildNode interface. The field signature for X3DTriggerNode is shown in Table 9.3.

This interface is the simplest default node interface possible. Any node having X3DTriggerNode type may contain a metadata node.

2.4.1. Hints and warnings

Note that the value of set_boolean is ignored, but it is a good practice to only send true events, because false events seem logically inconsistent. Such filtering can be accomplished using a BooleanFilter node.

3. Node Descriptions

3.1. BooleanFilter node

BooleanFilter is used in a ROUTE chain to filter boolean events, allowing for selective routing of true or false values. BooleanFilter can also be used to negate inputs. This functionality is particularly helpful because many sensors send pairs of true and false events in series as the sensor is activated and subsequently deactivated.

The BooleanFilter node is in the Interactive profile and has the fields defined in Table 9.4. Node syntax is shown in Table 9.5.

BooleanFilter is commonly used to screen or negate boolean events in order to modify the default logic that is provided by X3D nodes and thereby match the logical values that are needed in an authored scene. The example BooleanFilter.x3d in Figure 9.2 shows how a BooleanFilter is used to start one animation and turn off another. The animation is started on a mouse-down isActive true event from the TouchSensor (see Chapter 8) on the pump house. The pump animation is stopped on a mouse-up isActive false event from the same TouchSensor.

Type	accessType	Name	Default	Range	Profile
SFNode	inputOutput	metadata	NULL	[X3DMetadataObject]	Core

Table 9.3. Field Definitions for X3DTriggerNode Type

Type	accessType	Name	Default	Range	Profile
SFBool	inputOnly	set_boolean			Interactive
SFBool	outputOnly	inputTrue			Interactive
SFBool	outputOnly	inputFalse			Interactive
SFBool	outputOnly	inputNegate			Interactive
SFNode	inputOutput	metadata	NULL	[X3DMetadataObject]	Core

Table 9.4. Field Definitions for BooleanFilter Node

XML Syntax (.x3d)	ClassicVRML Syntax (.x3dv)
`<BooleanFilter DEF=` `        "MyBooleanFilter"/>`	`DEF My BooleanFilter BooleanFilter {` `}`

Table 9.5. Node Syntax for BooleanFilter

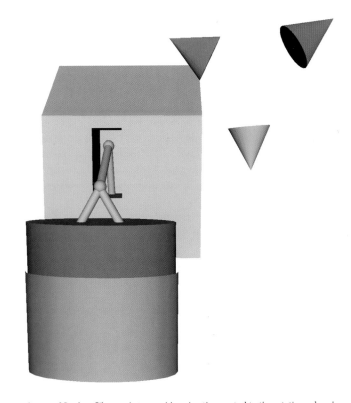

Figure 9.2. An example use of BooleanFilter node to provide animation control to the rotating colored cones.

3.1.1. set_boolean

The set_boolean event is the sole input to the BooleanFilter node. It may be provided from a sensor, Script, or another event-utility node.

3.1.2. inputTrue and inputFalse

Upon receipt of a set_boolean input event, either an inputTrue event or else an inputFalse event is generated. Each of these output events only has value true.

3.1.3. inputNegate

Upon receipt of a set_boolean input event, an inputNegate output event is also produced that has the opposite value of the set_boolean input.

3.1.4. Hints and warnings

Arbitrarily complex behavior logic can be constructed using BooleanFilter in combination with other event utility and Script nodes.

Two-input boolean functions such as AND, OR, XOR, and so on are not provided in X3D. Nevertheless, such functions can be written using a Script node.

3.2. BooleanSequencer node

The BooleanSequencer node has a keyValue array of boolean values that can each be sequentially sent at appropriate time intervals, in order to sequentially enable or disable another behavior.

The BooleanSequencer node implements the X3DSequencerNode type. It is in the Interactive profile and has the fields defined in Table 9.6. Node syntax is shown in Table 9.7.

A possible use of BooleanSequencer is to open and shut a door or window, depending on the progress of a TimeSensor clock. This technique is particularly helpful for

Type	accessType	Name	Default	Range	Profile
SFBool	inputOnly	next			Interactive
SFBool	inputOnly	previous			Interactive
SFFloat	inputOnly	set_fraction		$(-\infty, \infty)$	Interactive
MFFloat	inputOutput	key	[]	$(-\infty, \infty)$	Interactive
MFBool	inputOutput	keyValue	[]		Interactive
SFBool	outputOnly	value_changed			Interactive
SFNode	inputOutput	metadata	NULL	[X3DMetadataObject]	Core

Table 9.6. Field Definitions for BooleanSequencer Node

XML Syntax (.x3d)	ClassicVRML Syntax (.x3dv)
`<BooleanSequencer DEF=` `   "MyBooleanSequencer"/>`	`DEF My BooleanSequencer BooleanSequencer {` `}`

Table 9.7. Node Syntax for BooleanSequencer

creating extended animation sequences, and can also be used to choreograph the play-back of a long-running standalone simulation.

BooleanSequencer fields are defined by the X3DSequencerNode abstract node type. The defining keyValue array and output value_changed fields each use boolean values.

The BooleanSequencer example (BooleanSequencer.x3d) in Figure 9.3 turns the pump house animation on and off. While the animation is turned off, the animation clock continues to advance, leading to intermittent motion of the pump.

3.2.1. Hints and warnings

Other possible uses of BooleanSequencer include turning lights on and off, as well as binding or unbinding Viewpoint nodes. Viewpoint and other X3DBindableNodes (such as Fog, NavigationInfo, and lights) can be activated or deactivated with a ROUTE statement from the BooleanSequencer to the appropriate set_bind input field.

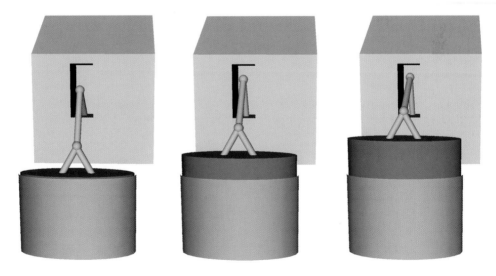

Figure 9.3. Example use of BooleanSequencer that turns the pump animation on and off. The piston jumps among the pictured positions through its animation cycle. The figure shows three successive views of the piston animation cycle.

3.3. BooleanToggle node

The BooleanToggle node saves a boolean value and negates the toggle field on receipt of a set_boolean true input event. Thus the output toggle field alternates between true and false.

The BooleanToggle node is in the Interactive profile and has the fields defined in Table 9.8. Node syntax is shown in Table 9.9.

Upon receipt of a `set_boolean="true"` event, the toggle field is negated, sent as an output value, and retained for further use. Conversely `set_boolean="false"` events are ignored, because the semantic meaning of such an event indicates that toggle operation is not performed. Honoring true events while ignoring false events is an especially helpful feature when connecting a TouchSensor as the input to a BooleanToggle node, because each `isActive true` (or `isOver true`) event is automatically followed by a corresponding `isActive false` (or `isOver false`) event when the pointing device is no longer selected (or over) the sensed shape of interest.

A BooleanToggle node is used in the example BooleanToggle.x3d in Figure 9.4 to pause and resume the pump house animation. The animation state is changed by manipulating the `pauseTime` and `resumeTime` fields of the TimeSensor node that controls the animation. It is necessary to use a BooleanToggle to toggle the pause-on to pause-off state. A BooleanFilter node is used to separate the events with value `true` from those with value `false`. Finally two TimeTrigger nodes are used to convert each SFBool event to an SFTime event that is sent to the TimeSensor node that controls the animation. See Chapter 7 for details on TimeSensor operation.

Type	accessType	Name	Default	Range	Profile
SFBool	inputOnly	set_boolean			Interactive
SFBool	inputOutput	toggle	false		Interactive
SFNode	inputOutput	metadata	NULL	[X3DMetadataObject]	Core

Table 9.8. Field Definitions for BooleanToggle Node

XML Syntax (.x3d)	ClassicVRML Syntax (.x3dv)
`<BooleanToggle DEF=` `    "MyBooleanToggle"/>`	`DEF MyBooleanToggle BooleanToggle {` `}`

Table 9.9. Node Syntax for BooleanToggle

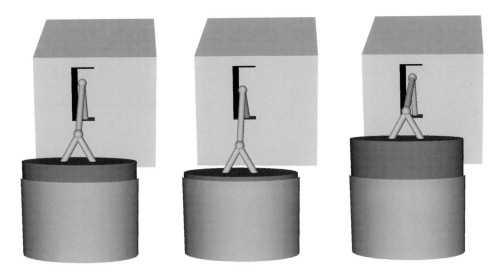

Figure 9.4. Clicking on the pump house starts or stops the movement of the piston. The animation clock continues to run so the piston jumps when an "on" click occurs.

3.4. BooleanTrigger node

The BooleanTrigger node converts input time events to output boolean true events.

The BooleanTrigger node implements the X3DTriggerNode type. It is in the Interactive profile and has the fields defined in Table 9.10. Node syntax is shown in Table 9.11.

On receipt of a set_trigger SFTime event, BooleanTrigger sends an output event via field triggerTrue. The triggerTrue output value is always true.

A BooleanTrigger node is especially helpful for connecting timing events (such as TimeSensor cycleTime or TouchSensor touchTime) to SFBool boolean inputs (such as another node's enabled field). If a false value is needed instead, connect a BooleanFilter node into the event-animation chain in order to negate the triggerTrue output event.

The example BooleanTrigger.x3d in Figure 9.5 uses a mouse-down event to start the animation of the pump house. In this example, once the animation has started, it cannot be stopped.

3.5. IntegerSequencer node

The IntegerSequencer node accepts either a float set_fraction or boolean next/previous events as input, and then produces an output integer value corresponding to the predefined key and keyValue impulse function.

The IntegerSequencer node implements the X3DSequencerNode type. It is in the Interactive profile and has the fields defined in Table 9.12. Node syntax is shown in Table 9.13.

Type	accessType	Name	Default	Range	Profile
SFTime	inputOnly	set_trigger			Interactive
SFBool	outputOnly	triggerTrue			Interactive
SFNode	inputOutput	metadata	NULL	[X3DMetadataObject]	Core

Table 9.10. Field Definitions for BooleanTrigger Node

XML Syntax (.x3d)	ClassicVRML Syntax (.x3dv)
`<BooleanTrigger DEF=` `    "MyBooleanTrigger"/>`	`DEF MyBooleanTrigger BooleanTrigger {` `}`

Table 9.11. Node Syntax for BooleanTrigger

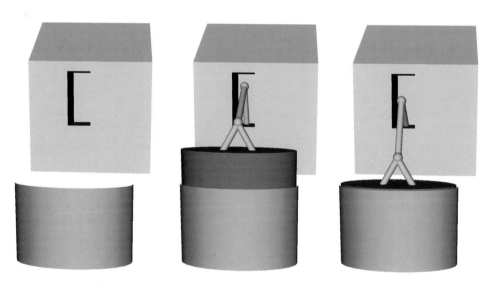

Figure 9.5. Example use of BooleanTrigger node to start animation in scene BooleanTrigger.x3d. The images show the initial state (left), shortly after the animation starts (middle), and nearing the end of the first animation cycle (right).

IntegerSequencer is a discrete-valued step-function version of the ScalarInterpolator node. On first receipt of a set_fraction value that is equal to or greater than one of the values in the key array, the corresponding value in the keyValue array is assigned to output event value_changed. The IntegerSequencer example (IntegerSequencer.x3d) is in Figure 9.6. Successive clicks on the pump house cycle through the colored cones. This is done through the next field. The example does not show the use of the set_fraction field.

Type	accessType	Name	Default	Range	Profile
SFBool	inputOnly	next			Interactive
SFBool	inputOnly	previous			Interactive
SFFloat	inputOnly	set_fraction		$(-\infty, \infty)$	Interactive
MFFloat	inputOutput	key	[]	$(-\infty, \infty)$	Interactive
MFInt32	inputOutput	keyValue	[]	$(-\infty, \infty)$	Interactive
SFInt32	outputOnly	value_changed			Interactive
SFNode	inputOutput	metadata	NULL	[X3DMetadataObject]	Core

Table 9.12. Field Definitions for IntegerSequencer Node

XML Syntax (.x3d)	ClassicVRML Syntax (.x3dv)
`<IntegerSequencer DEF=` `    "MyIntegerSequencer"/>`	`DEF MyIntegerSequencer IntegerSequencer {` `}`

Table 9.13. Node Syntax for IntegerSequencer

Note that no output *keyValue[i+1]* results are sent except upon set_fraction first exceeding *key[i+1]*, thus making the sequences an impulse function rather than a continuous-output function.

If only a single output value is ever needed, an IntegerTrigger node can be used instead.

3.6. IntegerTrigger node

The IntegerTrigger node converts input boolean events to output single-valued integer trigger events.

The IntegerTrigger node implements the X3DTriggerNode type. It is in the Interactive profile and has the fields defined in Table 9.14. Node syntax is shown in Table 9.15.

On receiving a set_boolean input event, an IntegerTrigger node produces a triggerValue output event with the current value of integerKey. Note that integerKey only holds one value at a time.

If a variety of different output values are desired, an IntegerSequencer node can be used instead. If the IntegerTrigger is used frequently but the output value only needs to change occasionally, then the integerKey value may be modified (because it has accessType inputOutput).

A collection of three IntegerTrigger nodes are used for the example IntegerTrigger.x3d in Figure 9.7. Clicking on a colored cone causes that cone to disappear and the next one to appear. The switching between the cones is accomplished with a Switch node. When running this example, it is usually easiest to leave the cursor in a single spot and quickly click when the cone passes underneath the cursor.

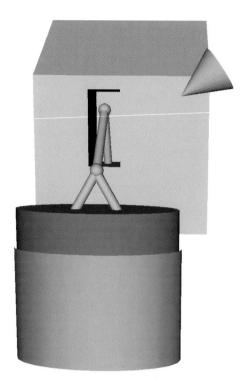

Figure 9.6. The IntegerSequencer node is used to sequentially display the colored cones in example IntegerSequencer.x3d.

Type	accessType	Name	Default	Range	Profile
SFBool	inputOnly	set_boolean			Interactive
SFInt32	inputOutput	integerKey	−1	(−∞, ∞)	Interactive
SFInt32	outputOnly	triggerValue			Interactive
SFNode	inputOutput	metadata	NULL	[X3DMetadataObject]	Core

Table 9.14. Field Definitions for IntegerTrigger Node

XML Syntax (.x3d)	ClassicVRML Syntax (.x3dv)
```<IntegerTrigger DEF=``` ``` "MyIntegerTrigger"/>```	```DEF MyIntegerTrigger IntegerTrigger {``` ```}```

Table 9.15. Node Syntax for IntegerTrigger

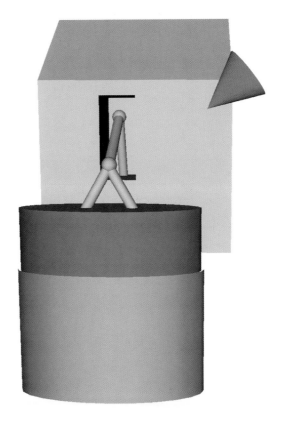

Figure 9.7. Three IntegerTrigger nodes are used to switch between the three colored cones in example IntegerTrigger.x3d.

3.7. TimeTrigger node

The TimeTrigger node converts input boolean events to output SFTime-valued trigger events.

The TimeTrigger node implements the X3DTriggerNode type. It is in the Interactive profile and has the fields defined in Table 9.16. Node syntax is shown in Table 9.17.

On receiving a set_boolean event, a TimeTrigger node produces a triggerTime event. The value of triggerTime matches the time at which the set_boolean value is received.

Whether the value of set_boolean might be true or false is ignored. If you want the TimeTrigger to only activate on set_boolean true events, precede it with a BooleanFilter node.

Example TimeTrigger.x3d in Figure 9.8 shows how the TimeTrigger node is used to activate a single animation cycle of the pump. The animation stops after each cycle. The TouchSensor on the house starts a new cycle.

Type	accessType	Name	Default	Range	Profile
SFBool	inputOnly	set_boolean			Interactive
SFTime	outputOnly	triggerTime			Interactive
SFNode	inputOutput	metadata	NULL	[X3DMetadataObject]	Core

Table 9.16. Field Definitions for TimeTrigger Node

XML Syntax (.x3d)	ClassicVRML Syntax (.x3dv)
`<TimeTrigger DEF="MyTimeTrigger"/>`	`DEF MyTimeTrigger TimeTrigger {` `}`

Table 9.17. Node Syntax for TimeTrigger

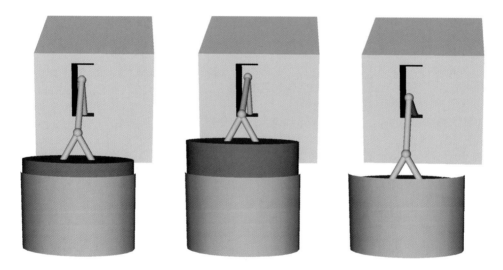

Figure 9.8. Three images from an animation cycle in example TimeTrigger.x3d. The animation is triggered by a click on the pump house. The animation stops after a cycle is complete. Subsequent clicks cause the animation cycle to restart.

3.8. Script node

The Script node allows authors to embed program code into an X3D scene. The code can be written in a variety of programming languages, and different Script nodes can use different languages within the same scene. Language bindings are defined for the ECMAScript (also known as JavaScript) and Java programming languages. For browsers that conform to the Immersive profile or better, support for ECMAScript is required.

The Script node interacts with the X3D scene graph through the standard event-passing mechanism. Each Script defines a set of fields that can be used to send and receive events via ROUTE statements. Ordinarily a Script node sits passively in the scene graph without doing anything. Once an event is delivered to a Script field, a corresponding method is invoked in the script code to handle the arriving value. The Script may then compute a new result and, when appropriate, respond with one or more output events that are sent via a ROUTE back to the scene. Scripts that need to originate output values frequently may be triggered by similarly frequent timing events from a TimeSensor.

The full details of programming X3D at this level are defined by the Scene Authoring Interface (SAI), which is the application programming interface (API) defined for X3D that provides consistent bindings for each programming language. A full description of the SAI is beyond the scope of this book. Nevertheless programming in ECMAScript is quite straightforward, and examples show how to accomplish many tasks using a Script node.

The Script node is in the Immersive profile. The node has the required fields defined in Table 9.18. Additional fields can be defined by the author, as described in Table 9.19. Allowed field types are found in Chapter 1, Table 1.4, X3D Field Types. Field type default values can be found in Chapter 14, Table 14.3. Node syntax is shown in Table 9.20.

Type	accessType	Name	Default	Range	Profile
MFString	inputOutput	url	[]		Immersive
SFBool	initializeOnly	directOutput	false		Immersive
SFBool	initializeOnly	mustEvaluate	false		Immersive
SFNode	inputOutput	metadata	NULL	[X3DMetadataObject]	Core

Table 9.18. Field Definitions for Script Node

Type	accessType	Name	Default	Range	Profile
[fieldType]	initializeOnly	[fieldName]	[author specified]	[datatype defaults]	Immersive
[fieldType]	inputOutput	[fieldName]	[author specified]	[datatype defaults]	Immersive
[fieldType]	inputOnly	[fieldName]			Immersive
[fieldType]	outputOnly	[fieldName]	[default for field type]		Immersive

Table 9.19. Additional Author-Specified Field Definitions for Script Node

XML Syntax (.x3d)	ClassicVRML Syntax (.x3dv)
```<Script DEF="MyScript" directOutput="false" mustEvaluate="false" url=' "externalFile.js", "ecmascript:..." '> <field name="field1" type="SFString" accessType=initializeOnly" value="test string"/> <field name="field2" type="MFFloat" accessType="inputOutput" value="3.14159, 2.718, .43"/> <field name="field3" type="SFTime" accessType="inputOnly"/> <field name="field4" type="SFInt32" accessType="outputOnly"/> </Script>```	```DEF MyScript Script { directOutput FALSE mustEvaluate FALSE url ["externalFile.js", "ecmascript:...."] initializeOnly SFString field1 "test string" inputOutput MFFloat field2 [3.14159, 2.718, .43] inputOnly SFTime field3 outputOnly SFInt32 field4 }```

Table 9.20. Node Syntax for Script

Each Script node has only one active set of scripting code. This code is either retrieved from the source-code excerpt that is contained inside the Script, or else retrieved from the first working address in the url field. Each set of Script code provided usually has functional methods defined with the same name as each field having `accessType="inputOnly"`, and may also have source-code methods defined for fields having `accessType="inputOutput"`.

ECMAScript support is required for all X3D browsers that include scripting capabilities, so it is a good choice for authoring most programming tasks within a Script node.

ECMAScript source code begins with the `ecmascript:` keyword, immediately followed by a colon, and then followed by the embedded source code. Be sure that function (i.e., method) definitions are preceded by the `function` keyword.

For X3D's XML encoding, the preferred way to embed ECMAScript code is to use a child CDATA text block instead of using the url field. CDATA sections are character data sections that are exempt from the usual processing rules of XML. Thus, any source code in the CDATA block is not subject to interpretation of < and > characters as XML element angle brackets. Whitespace is also preserved, because otherwise linefeeds might be ignored, and then any inline comment (beginning with //) would make further source code irrelevant. CDATA blocks are the preferred mechanism for embedding ECMAScript source code inside Script nodes when using the XML encoding (.x3d file extension).

```
<Script DEF="Control">
  <field accessType="inputOnly" name="angle" type="SFFloat"/>
  <field accessType="outputOnly" name="posRed" type="SFVec3f"/>
  <field accessType="outputOnly" name="posGrn" type="SFVec3f"/>
  <field accessType="outputOnly" name="posTuq" type="SFVec3f"/>
  <field accessType="outputOnly" name="orRed" type="SFRotation"/>
  <field accessType="outputOnly" name="orGrn" type="SFRotation"/>
  <field accessType="outputOnly" name="orTuq" type="SFRotation"/>
<![CDATA[
      ecmascript:

//  The function 'angle' computes the position
//  and orientation of each of the cones. The
//  values 2.094 and 4.189 are 1/3 and 2/3 of 2*pi
//  radians.

//  The path followed by each cone is an ellipse
//  50% higher than its width. Each cone makes two
//  complete revolutions while traveling along the path.

function angle (value) {
  posRed = new SFVec3f (Math.cos (value), 1.5 * Math.sin(value), .5);
  posGrn = new SFVec3f (Math.cos (value+2.094), 1.5 * Math.sin(value+2.094),   0)
  posTuq = new SFVec3f (Math.cos (value+4.189), 1.5 * Math.sin(value+4.189), -.5)

  orRed = new SFRotation (0, 0, 1, -2*value);
  orGrn = new SFRotation (0, 0, 1, -2*(value+2.094));
  orTuq = new SFRotation (0, 0, 1, -2*(value+4.189));

}
]]>
  </Script>
```

Figure 9.9. The preferred form to embed ECMAscript code within a Script node using the XML encoding (.x3d files) is to contain a CDATA section within the Script elements.

There are a number of examples provided for the Script node. The examples range from the simple processing of events to complex scripts with incoming, outgoing, and looping events. Some of the examples are listed in the following sections.

The first example (ScriptEvents.x3d) in Figure 9.10 shows how to process an event within the event cascade. The Script provides the animated position and orientation of the colored cones used earlier in this chapter. The cones follow an elliptical path and spin while traveling on the path. A single event goes in and six events (position and orientation for each cone) come out. Each outgoing event is calculated during every event cascade, and no values are retained between cascades. The animation is started by clicking on the pump house.

Functional descriptions of common fields, default methods, and author-defined methods for the Script node follow.

3.8.1. url

The url field has multiple purposes: it can either point to an external script file or else contain ECMAScript source code.

When the url points to an external file, multiple addresses can be included. This allows authors to first refer to a copy of the script code using a relative address, and then refer to a copy of the script code using an absolute address. In this manner a script can be part of an archive that works efficiently when installed either on a server or on a client machine. Each address is delimited by quotation marks because the url field is of type MFString.

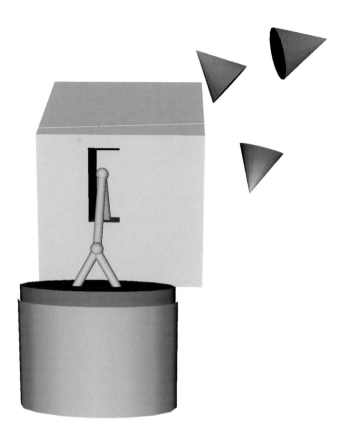

Figure 9.10. An example use of a Script node to quickly process incoming events and generate outgoing events to procedurally animate the cones.

A common use of the Script node's url field is to contain ECMAScript source. This approach is usually used in the ClassicVRML encoding because it guarantees that the code is always available with the scene, avoiding potential network or file-system access problems when trying to deliver multiple files. Embedding the source also makes a script easy to scrutinize and debug, because the code of interest is immediately adjacent to the field definitions. Embedded script code must begin with the `ecmascript` keyword followed by a colon.

When referring to an external ECMAScript file, the filename usually ends in the extension `.js` which stands for JavaScript, the original name of the ECMAScript language. When referring to a Java class, the url needs to point to the already-compiled bytecode file (with file extension `.class`) rather than the Java source file (with file extension `.java`). Some Java-capable browsers may support referencing a `.class` file within a Java Archive (`.jar`) file, but this capability is not yet an X3D requirement.

Further information on MFString can be found in Chapter 1, Technical Introduction in the section discussing field types. For more details on the construction of url addresses, see the Anchor node section in Chapter 3, Grouping Nodes.

3.8.2. directOutput

In general most X3D browsers avoid unnecessary work in order to maximize rendering performance. Once various portions of the scene graph are initialized, they are usually not recomputed unless there is a specific reason to do so. If a value is connected with ROUTE within the scene, that usually triggers recomputation of the affected geometry.

Script nodes typically use ROUTE statements to send values in and out of their fields, allowing their operations to be similarly efficient. However, Script nodes have the added capability of directly referring to other nodes in the scene graph, and a Script node may even modify such field nodes directly without a ROUTE value.

The directOutput field provides an authoring hint to the browser regarding whether the Script node might change other nodes in the scene graph without ROUTE connections.

Set `directOutput="true"` if the Script references one or more fields of type SFNode or MFNode, and if the script uses direct access to modify the attributes of a referenced node in the scene. This tells the browser to take extra care whenever the Script node is invoked so that any direct animations of SFNode or MFNode fields are properly handled and not erroneously ignored.

3.8.3. mustEvaluate

The mustEvaluate field provides an authoring hint to the browser regarding the timing sensitivity of the Script code. A potential X3D browser optimization is to bundle input events until they might be needed. If `mustEvaluate="false"` (which is the default), then the browser may delay sending input events to the Script until outputs are needed. This permits browsers to avoid interrupting the rendering process unnecessarily, waiting until deferrable computations by a Script node are less likely to cause a delay in rendering speed or user interactivity.

If `mustEvaluate="true"`, then Script must receive input events immediately without browser delays. Set `mustEvaluate="true"` when sending or receiving values through the network or when other ongoing computations need to be frequently performed rather than deferred.

3.8.4. initialize() and shutdown() methods

The script may optionally define initialize() and shutdown() methods. The initialize() method is automatically invoked on first loading the Script, and can include any necessary setup code such as the initialization of variables or printing a diagnostic message. When present, initialization code often uses the default setup values provided by initializeOnly or inputOutput fields. The initialize() method is especially important when a Script Node must first establish network connections.

Similarly, the shutdown() method is automatically invoked when the scene is being shut down, or when the Script node itself is unloaded or replaced. No other script methods may be invoked by the scene once shutdown() is called, though the shutdown()

method itself may generate events or call other local functions as part of its operation. This allows graceful completion of Script functionality, such as providing a final result or closing a network connection.

3.8.5. prepareEvents() method

The optional author-defined prepareEvents() method is called before any ROUTE processing occurs. Typical prepareEvents() functionality includes reading network buffers and checking on external listeners, allowing asynchronously generated data to be updated in a timely manner. The prepareEvents() method might also generate events to be handled by the browser's normal event-processing sequence as if it were a built-in sensor node. If defined, prepareEvents() is called only once at the beginning of each event loop.

3.8.6. eventsProcessed() method

The optional author-defined eventsProcessed() method is called after the Script node handles all of its input events. Because more than one event may arrive during a given timestamp, the eventsProcessed() method can sometimes make overall response more efficient. For example, a Script node might recompute a piece of geometry based on three input parameters. It is better to handle all of the inputs first and then recompute geometry a single time, as part of the eventsProcessed() method, rather than unnecessarily recomputing multiple times when multiple changes arrive at once.

For a single event cascade, the eventsProcessed() method is invoked only once. Events generated from an eventsProcessed() method are given the timestamp of the last event processed.

3.8.7. Browser functions

The Browser class includes many helpful utility functions. These functions are available to ECMAScript and Java implementations, and are required for other programming-language bindings. A partial list of available Browser functions appears in Table 9.21. Authors can utilize these functions in their Script code.

Foremost among these services is the Browser.print() function, which lets the script write output text to the browser's console window. Generous use of Browser.print functions is often essential for debugging script operation. Rather than delete print statements when debugging is successful, it is often better to simply comment these lines out so that future development efforts can take advantage of them, if needed.

3.8.8. Script control: event passing, directOutput, and SAI

Events are used to update the state of the scene graph state. Events can be produced by interpolators, sequencers, sensors, and Script nodes. Fields with accessType inputOnly are event consumers, and fields with accessType outputOnly are event producers. Fields with accessType inputOutput can produce or consume events. Fields with accessType inputOutput can produce or consume events. It is interesting to note that, although fields having accessType initializeOnly are not allowed to produce or consume events, they can nevertheless be modified by the Script itself during run time, usually in order to maintain local state.

Function Name	Returns
Browser.getName	Name of the X3D browser.
Browser.getVersion	Provides the version identifier of the X3D browser.
Browser.getCurrentSpeed	Provides the navigation speed of the current world, obtained from currently bound NavigationInfo node, in meters/second for the coordinate system of the currently bound Viewpoint.
Browser.getCurrentFrameRate	Provides the current display update rate in frames/second.
Browser.getSupportedProfiles	Lists all profile names supported by the browser, for example "Interactive" "Immersive" "Full"
Browser.getSupportedComponents	Lists all supported component names.
Browser.createScene	Creates a new, empty scene that conforms to the provided profile and component declarations.
Browser.replaceWorld	Replaces the current world with the world provided as a parameter.
Browser.importDocument	Imports a W3C Document Object Model (DOM) document, or document fragment, and converts it to an X3D scene.
Browser.loadURL	Inserts the content identified by the url value into the current world.
Browser.setDescription	Sets the description title in the browser title bar, if available.
Browser.createX3DFromString	Creates X3D nodes from a string input.
Browser.createX3DFromStream	Creates X3D nodes from a network stream input.
Browser.createX3DFromURL	Creates X3D nodes from a file referred to by an url.
Browser.getRenderingProperties	Provides a list of the current hardware-rendering capabilities available to the browser.
Browser.getBrowserProperties	Provides a list of the current functional capabilities provided by the browser.
Browser.changeViewpoint	Changes the currently bound viewpoint based on input value Next, Previous, First, or Last.
Browser.print	Prints a string message to the browser's console.
Browser.dispose	Indicates that the client is about to exit, and the browser can dispose any consumed resources.

Table 9.21. Functions Supported by the Browser Interface for Use in Script Source Code.

Script nodes are quite special in that author-defined fields can be created having any combination of type and accessType. The fields of a Script node define the desired interfaces and the fundamental functionality that is provided. ROUTE statements and event passing thus provide the primary mechanism whereby a Script node interacts with a scene.

When provided with other nodes from the scene graph via fields of type SFNode, Script nodes can also modify the contents of other nodes directly. This is done by setting the field values of the passed-by-reference nodes. Also, set `directOutput="true"` for those cases because the execution engine may need to determine whether to recalculate portions of the scene graph that might be affected.

One other means exists for a Script node to control other objects. The Scene Access Interface (SAI) provides a way to interact with an external Extensible Hypertext Markup Language (XHTML) browser or an external application. This provides a powerful technique for connecting executable code in web pages or other applications within the X3D scene. The SAI definitions are consistently specified for internal (X3D browser) and external (XHTML browser) use. Of historical note is that this unification of scripting techniques is an improvement over the VRML97 External Authoring Interface (EAI), which provided different mechanisms than those used within an X3D scene.

The SAI is thorough, well defined, functionally stable, and implemented by several X3D browsers. Unfortunately, SAI details are beyond the scope of this book.

Figure 9.11 shows all three of the basic means by which a Script node is able to exert control: event passing, directOutput manipulation of other nodes, and SAI interactions with an external application or web browser. These control mechanisms must be equivalently supported by all conformant X3D browsers in order to ensure that the behavior of scripting code is consistent regardless of platform.

3.8.9. Execution model and event cascade

Although the passage of simulation time appears to be continuous while rendering, in fact each render cycle that refreshes the pixels seen in the 3D browser is paused after each full

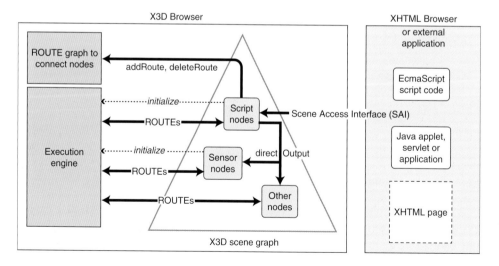

Figure 9.11. Events are connected with ROUTE statements between nodes for most animation. Scripts may also bypass the event model, either through directOutput control of other nodes or else SAI access of an external application (such as a web browser).

redraw. Events are passed at this point. This approach allows state updates to be completed consistently, and also ensures that the drawn image does not change at some intermediate step during a redraw.

The X3D execution model governs the precise sequence of operations for event processing and scene-graph rendering. The following steps are repeatedly performed in strict order while an X3D scene is being animated.

1. Update camera based on currently bound Viewpoint position and orientation.

2. Evaluate input from sensors and other event producers, and then place events on queue for delivery.

3. ROUTE events to their defined destinations, updating scene graph field values.

4. If any events were generated and routed in steps 2 and 3, go to step 2 and repeat until there are no more pending events.

The repetition of event reading and routing is called an event cascade, allowing input events to trigger output events for continued processing within a single timestamp. Event cascades persist no longer than a single timestamp interval.

On completing processing of all events in an event cascade, several more steps occur as part of each frame's rendering cycle.

5. The next screen update is rendered (meaning drawn, pixel by pixel) and buffered for display until complete.

6. Double-buffered display systems swap the newly created screen update for the previous one.

7. The browser's simulation clock is updated to match the system clock. This is sometimes described as advancing one clock tick.

8. The browser animation process is repeated by returning to step 1, continuing indefinitely until halted.

It is important to ensure that an event cascade cannot loop indefinitely, or else the displayed scene cannot redraw. A browser guarantees this condition by following the *loop-breaking rule*, which only allows one event to pass along a ROUTE for a given timestamp. This not only prevents a node from generating a repeated event to itself, but also prevents cyclic dependencies among two or more nodes that might mutually trigger each other. In any case, infinite loops of event generation are prevented for a single timestamp.

The exact order of events generated within a single timestamp cannot be guaranteed, and indeed may vary among browsers for a given script. Authors creating complex scripts with extensive event cascades need to ensure that their animation logic is written in a deterministic way, operating independently of the particular order of events that may be triggered. The flexibility of this event model in the X3D specification allows a variety of programming languages and approaches to optimize animation and rendering as well as possible. This partial relaxation of timing constraints within a single event cascade is provided primarily to benefit browser builders. It also puts Script authors on notice that the logic of their script code ought not to depend on the side effects of event timing within a single event loop. Therefore, script logic needs to depend on deliberate causes and directly intended effects for reliable operation.

The lifecycle of Script node invocation, the execution model, event-cascade timing, and looping logic are illustrated in Figure 9.12.

3.8.10. Additional Script node execution semantics

After initialization, code in the Script node resumes execution whenever one or more new events are received. Script execution may also be triggered by the prepareEvents() method, if provided by the author. The Script node executes the appropriate method corresponding by name to each inputOnly or inputOutput event received. Depending on

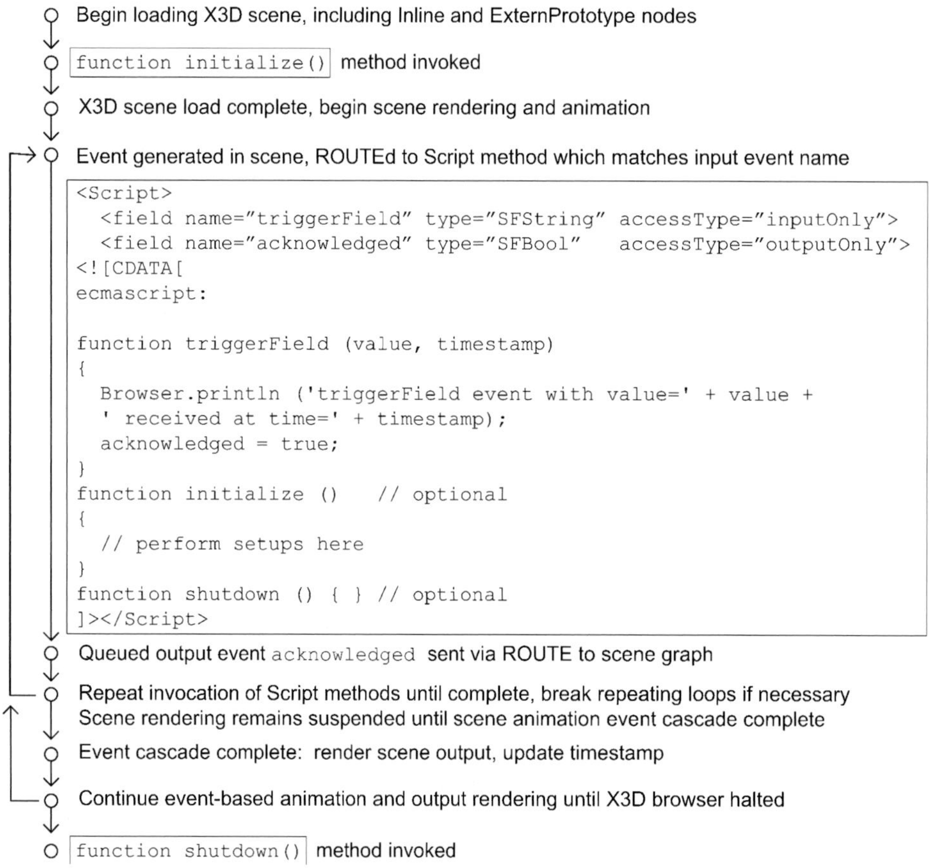

Begin loading X3D scene, including Inline and ExternPrototype nodes

`function initialize()` method invoked

X3D scene load complete, begin scene rendering and animation

Event generated in scene, ROUTEd to Script method which matches input event name

```
<Script>
  <field name="triggerField" type="SFString" accessType="inputOnly">
  <field name="acknowledged" type="SFBool"  accessType="outputOnly">
<![CDATA[
ecmascript:

function triggerField (value, timestamp)
{
  Browser.println ('triggerField event with value=' + value +
  ' received at time=' + timestamp);
  acknowledged = true;
}
function initialize ()    // optional
{
  // perform setups here
}
function shutdown () { } // optional
]></Script>
```

Queued output event `acknowledged` sent via ROUTE to scene graph

Repeat invocation of Script methods until complete, break repeating loops if necessary
Scene rendering remains suspended until scene animation event cascade complete

Event cascade complete: render scene output, update timestamp

Continue event-based animation and output rendering until X3D browser halted

`function shutdown()` method invoked

Figure 9.12. The Script node lifecycle begins with the initialize() method, is triggered when an event arrives, continues through an event cascade, repeats for each animation loop, and finally ends with the shutdown() method.

the source code functionality, an invoked method usually performs calculations and generates an output event. If a Script node generates multiple output events from multiple inputs, the eventsProcessed() method can be used for any necessary finishing actions after all events in the Script node are processed for a given timestamp and event cascade.

A Script node may receive multiple incoming events. It is possible that more than one event is delivered to the node with the same timestamp. It is up to the author-written script code to process the events properly. The events may be processed in any order, or even in a time-sharing manner. All events with the same timestamp must be processed before any events received with a later timestamp. All output events have the same timestamp as the input events. It is even possible to use a ROUTE statement to send an output event from a Script node back into a different input event of the same Script node, thus triggering additional operations during the same timestamp.

All events with the same timestamp are processed at the same X3D environment time. The events usually are processed sequentially, but the order of processing different events within a given timestamp cannot be strictly determined prior to the event occurring. Multiprocessor systems may actually process the events in parallel. Any events sent as output from the Script (or any other) node are processed prior to the current timestamp completion as part of the current event cascade. This means that a Script node can send output events, another node can accept them as inputs, and processing continues until complete. This approach ensures that simulation actions are logically updated and complete before rendering the next frame. For example, updating position without updating a corresponding orientation can produce incorrect results, so this type of partial (and logically inconsistent) behavior is prevented.

Routing an output event back into the same input event that generated it causes a circular loop. All browsers have a loop-breaking mechanism built in, and so these conditions do not cause an infinite loop. Once an event loop is detected, no more incoming events in that loop are delivered until the next event cascade. Perhaps of note is that circular loops are based solely on the data path, not the actual data being sent. A circular loop is broken even if the data is different between two events, ensuring that infinite loops cannot be caused by the events themselves. This safeguard does not protect against infinite loops occurring within the embedded program source code, however.

Each incoming event has an associated function to process the event. The function accepts two arguments. The first argument is the incoming event value, and the second optional argument is the timestamp of the event. The function activates when the event is received. The function may call any other function defined in the Script node. During the execution of the function, the function may set one or more output events by assigning a value to a previously defined outputOnly or inputOutput field name. Such output events are marked with the same timestamp as the input event and delivered within the current event cycle.

The individual elements of vector events (for example, SFVec3f) can be accessed using subscripts. The indices are zero-based. If a *value* parameter is of SFVec3f datatype, then *value*[0] refers to the *x*-component, *value*[1] refers to the *y*-component, and *value*[2] refers to the *z*-component. Array events (for example MFRotation) use double indexing to reference individual elements. If a *values* parameter is of MFRotation type, then *values*[0][3] refers to the rotation angle [3] of the first rotation [0].

Fields with accessType initializeOnly or inputOutput can be used to save state, allowing a Script node to remember values between invocations and also share data between different functions. For example, saving state is needed when two separate actions can affect a single object, such as a 3-way light switch. The current state of the light needs to be maintained internally so that the controls correctly change the light state.

This property is illustrated in the example ScriptComplexStateEvents.x3d in Figure 9.13. This example uses the same virtual world as the previous examples with a switch box and a light bulb. In this example, each push on the button causes the light to step to the next brightness level. At the end of the sequence, the light goes off. The current light state is maintained in the initializeOnly field buttonDown. Note that initializeOnly does not refer to the Script code's internal ability to modify the field, just the ability of external events in the X3D environment to modify, set, or read the value of that field.

3.8.11. Hints and warnings

Processing Script code temporarily stops the graphics-rendering cycle until invocation of all methods during the current time-step event cascade is complete. Avoid long looping computations to prevent undesirable halting of visual scene updates.

The ECMAScript language does not include capabilities for reading and writing via network sockets. Thus author-defined network communications ordinarily use Java. Sometimes effective network communication can be performed via url fields using http connections. Although beyond the scope of this book, X3D nodes are defined that implement the Distributed Interactive Simulation (DIS) protocol for shared networked state among moving entities. Achieving effective network streaming remains a busy area for ongoing research and development.

Java source code cannot be placed in the url field, it must be separately compiled and saved in a .class file that is referenced by the addresses in the url field.

Some browsers support collecting multiple .class files in a .jar archive, but this capability is not yet required by the X3D specification and so cannot be guaranteed.

It is possible to have a Script node with no fields. Usually the only reason to define such a node is to take advantage of the initialize() or shutdown() methods, providing source code that is solely executed during scene startup or shutdown.

If script code takes a long time to execute, then the event cascade and scene rendering may slow or stall while the code executes. Such calculations may be better run outside of the context of the Script node, either as a distributed process providing occasional updates or else as a separate application producing X3D code.

Sometimes precomputation and storage of results helps to reduce computational delays at runtime. Updates can be retrieved via the Inline or Anchor node, and distributed computing can be accomplished (with some effort) by using Java networking or the DIS-based EspduTransform node. These are considered advanced capabilities and are hopefully subjects for future books.

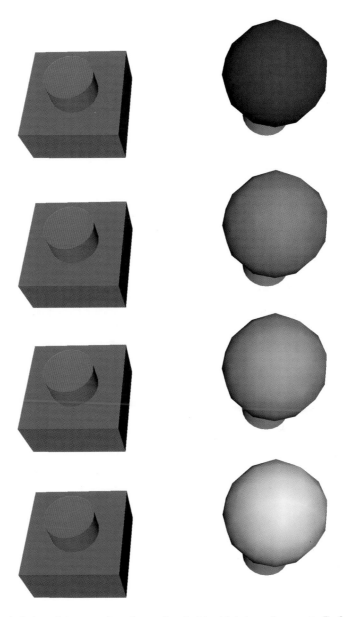

Figure 9.13. Use of a Script node to process incoming events and retain state between those events. The Script remembers the state of the 3-way bulb as shown in these four images. Sequential clicks on the red button cycle the light through various stages of brightness.

4. Summary

4.1. Key ideas

X3D animation is based on event passing. Because events are strongly typed (e.g., SFBool, MFFloat, etc.) the types of events generated by a producer node and then connected with a ROUTE statement to another target node in the scene graph must exactly match the type of the destination field.

The utility nodes simplify the generation and type conversion of events, particularly for boolean, time and integer (SFBool, SFTime and SFInt32) values. Utility nodes are often inserted into an animation chain to help achieve an author's intended animation logic. These nodes are simple and effective.

Script nodes are sophisticated but flexible wrappers around source code that allow an author to define programmatic processing for input and output events. Scripts provide a good way to match up the declarative logic of X3D scenes with the imperative step-by-step logic of programming procedures. Script source code can encapsulate any kind of black-box input-output functionality needed. Thus Script nodes provide powerful authoring flexibility and extension capabilities for X3D scenes.

Scripts can be written in ECMAScript or Java, which are each written with different syntax but provide equivalent capabilities as defined in the X3D Abstract Specification. Future versions of X3D may support additional programming languages.

4.2. Related nodes and concepts

Chapter 7, Event Animation and Interpolation describes TimeSensor and the animation process, including the typical design pattern for building an animation chain. Chapter 8, User Interactivity Nodes describes sensors and event generation from user actions. Each set of nodes is often augmented by the event utilities presented in this chapter in order to match up desired event types.

4.3. Next chapter

The Geometry 2D nodes provide simple ways to define planar geometry. This can be helpful when constructing elementary signs or user-interface widgets.

Geometry Nodes, Part 3: Geometry2D Nodes

Theorem. For a triangle with a right-angle between sides a *and* b, *with hypotenuse* c, $a^2 + b^2 = c^2$
—Pythagoras

1. What this chapter covers

Although the purpose of X3D is to define 3D scenes, occasionally authors need flat two-dimensional (2D) shapes. Advanced authors often want to create simple layouts as part of an overlay or a user interface. The Geometry2D nodes provide simple, commonly used geometries for creating 2D objects.

The nodes covered in this chapter are Arc2D, ArcClose2D, Circle2D, Disk2D, Polyline2D, Polypoint2D, Rectangle2D, and TriangleSet2D.

2. Concepts

2.1. Purpose and common functionality

The 2D geometry nodes include basic arcs, line segments, points, circles, rectangles, and triangles. These can be considered convenience nodes, because each of the geometry results might instead be constructed using 3D nodes for points, lines, and planar polygons.

The 2D nodes are not intended to support full-scale production of images or diagrams. Rather, a simply designed set of nodes has been chosen that provides a good selection of functionality. Nevertheless it is possible to construct 3D shapes using 2D nodes. For example, an author might create separate Rectangle2D nodes with independent ImageTexture images to construct the walls of a building.

The primary precaution to take when authoring 2D nodes is to avoid viewing them from the side. Because they are perfectly flat, these nodes are not visible when the user's viewpoint is in the same plane. This means that effort must be made to ensure that 2D geometry is either carefully oriented to face well-defined viewpoints, or else rotated to be vertical and then placed inside a Billboard node.

The Geometry2D nodes are particularly useful for creating heads-up displays (HUDs) that always keep the geometry directly in front of the user's views. An example HUD is presented in Chapter 12, Environment Sensor and Sound Nodes. Note that the nodes in the Geometry 2D component are ordinarily considered part of the full profile. An alternative way to specify support for these 2D nodes in a scene is to use the Immersive profile with component Geometry 2D level 2. Example syntax follows in Table 10.1.

Common characteristics of geometry nodes are described in section 2.2.

```
XML Syntax(.x3d)

<X3D version ="3.0" profile = "Immersive">
  <head>
    <component name = "Geometry2D" level = "2"/>
  </head>
<Scene/>
</X3D>
```

```
Classic VRML Syntax(.x3dv)

#X3D V3.0 vtf8
PROFILE Immersive
COMPONENT Geometry2D:2
```

Table 10.1. X3D Header Syntax for Geometry2D Component Support

2.2. Common geometry fields

There are no special geometry fields that are common to all of the Geometry2D nodes. The fields provided for each node are minimalist, defining just enough information to produce simple points, lines, and polygons. Because rendering is uncomplicated for these geometries, common 3D geometry fields (e.g., ccw, convex, colorPerVertex, creaseAngle, etc.) aren't necessary.

As with other 3D geometry, the solid field describes whether geometry is viewable from one or both sides of the polygons. For the polygonal Geometry2D nodes, setting `solid="false"` allows the geometry to be seen from both sides (i.e., turning backface culling off). The default value of `solid="true"` means that the geometry is only viewable from the front (and is transparent when viewed from behind). Further description of the solid field appears in Chapter 2, Geometry Nodes, Part 1: Primitives.

LineProperties and FillProperties in a sibling Appearance node can also be applied to corresponding 2D geometry nodes. LineProperties is appropriate for line-drawing nodes, while FillProperties is appropriate for polygonal nodes. These nodes are described in Chapter 5, Appearance, Material, and Textures.

Textures in a sibling Appearance node can be applied to the polygonal 2D nodes when `solid="true"` and both sides when `solid="false"`. Textures are applied to the front-facing (+z-axis) side, and oriented appropriately if a TextureTransform node is present. Texture and TextureTransform nodes are also covered in Chapter 5.

3. Node descriptions

3.1. Arc2D node

As with the other 2D nodes, Arc2D is a geometry node. Arc2D is line based, specifying a linear circular arc with the center at local origin (0,0). The startAngle and endAngle fields are measured in a counterclockwise direction, starting at the positive x-axis and sweeping toward the positive y-axis. Figure 10.1 illustrates an Arc2D node. This matches right-hand rule conventions.

The Arc2D node implements the X3DGeometryNode type and is in the Full profile. It has the field definitions shown in Table 10.2. Node syntax is shown in Table 10.3.

3.1.1. Example

The Arc2D example (Arc2D.x3d) in Figure 10.2 shows two arcs. Note that the use of the scale field in the Transform node changes one arc to a portion of an ellipse.

3.1.2. Hints and warnings

The radius field must be greater than zero.

Using the same value for startAngle and endAngle produces a complete circular line.

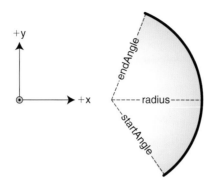

Figure 10.1. Example Arc2D node. The startAngle and endAngle fields are measured counterclockwise from the positive x-axis to the positive y-axis.

Type	accessType	Name	Default	Range	Profile
SFFloat	initializeOnly	startAngle	0	$[-2\pi, +2\pi]$	Immersive + Geometry2D:2 component, or full profile
SFFloat	initializeOnly	endAngle	$\pi/2$	$[-2\pi, +2\pi]$	Immersive + Geometry2D:2 component, or full profile
SFFloat	initializeOnly	radius 1		$(0, \infty)$	Immersive + Geometry2D:2 component, or full profile
SFNode	inputOutput	metadata	NULL	[X3DMetadataObject]	Core

Table 10.2. Field Definitions for Arc2D Node

3.2. ArcClose2D node

Similar to the Arc2D node, ArcClose2D is a geometry node that specifies the area of a arc with center (0,0) that ranges between startAngle and endAngle. ArcClose2D defines an enclosed area, not simply lines. The ArcClose2D adds either one or two line segments to the circular perimeter: a closing chord, or 2 lines connecting the arc endpoints to the center. The closureType field determines which type of 2D geometry is drawn, illustrated in Figure 10.3.

XML Syntax (.x3d)	ClassicVRML Syntax (.x3dv)
```<Arc2D DEF="MyArc2DNode" startAngle="-.5" endAngle="1.5" radius=".75"/>```	```DEF MyArc2DNode Arc2D { startAngle -.5 endAngle 1.5 radius .75 }```

Table 10.3. Node Syntax for Arc2D

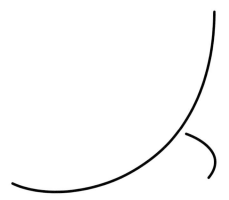

Figure 10.2. Arc2D example display. The lines have been thickened to make them more visible.

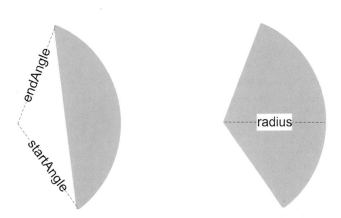

Figure 10.3. Example ArcClose2D nodes, first with `closureType="CHORD"` and then with `closureType="PIE"`.

The ArcClose2D node implements the X3DGeometryNode type, is in the Full profile, and has the field definitions shown in Table 10.4. Node syntax is shown in Table 10.5.

3.2.1. Example

The ArcClose2D example (ArcClose2D.x3d) in Figure 10.4 expands on the Arc2D example. Each arc is shown closed in a different manner: one is closed as a pie wedge, and one is closed using a chord.

3.2.2. Hints and warnings

The radius field must be greater than zero.

If the absolute difference between startAngle and wdAngle is greater than or equal to 2π, then a complete circle is produced with no radial line drawn from the center.

Type	accessType	Name	Default	Range	Profile
SFFloat	initializeOnly	startAngle	0	$[-2\pi, 2\pi]$	Immersive + Geometry2D:2 component, or Full profile
SFFloat	initializeOnly	endAngle	$\pi/2$	$[-2\pi, 2\pi]$	Immersive + Geometry2D:2 component, or Full profile
SFFloat	initializeOnly	radius	1	$(0, \infty)$	Immersive + Geometry2D:2 component, or Full profile
SFBool	initializeOnly	solid	false		Immersive + Geometry2D:2 component, or Full profile
SFString	initializeOnly	closureType	"PIE"	["PIE" | "CHORD"]	Immersive + Geometry2D:2 component, or Full profile
SFNode	inputOutput	metadata	NULL	[X3DMetadata Object]	Core

Table 10.4. Field Definitions for ArcClose2D Node

XML Syntax (.x3d)	ClassicVRML Syntax (.x3dv)

`<ArcClose2D DEF="MyArcClose2DNode"`
  `startAngle="-.5"`
  `endAngle="1.5"`
  `radius=".75"`
  `solid="true"/>`
	`DEF MyArcClose2DNode ArcClose2D {`
	  `startAngle -.5`
	  `endAngle 1.5`
	  `radius .75`
	  `solid TRUE`
	`}`

Table 10.5. Node Syntax for ArcClose2D

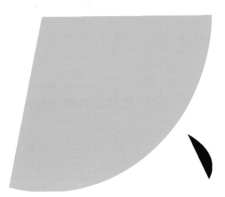

Figure 10.4. An ArcClose2D example display. The blue shape is closed with `closureType="CHORD"`, and the pink shape uses `closureType="PIE"`.

3.3. Circle2D node

Similar to the Arc2D node, the Circle2D node is line-based.

Circle2D specifies a planar circle with center (0,0) and a positive-valued radius, illustrated in Figure 10.5.

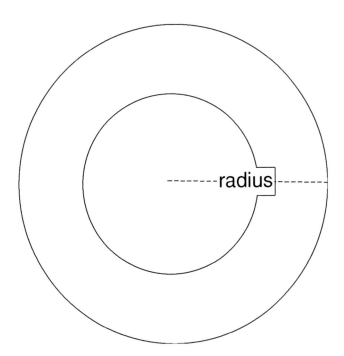

Figure 10.5. An example Circle2D node.

The Circle2D node implements the X3DGeometryNode type, is in the Full profile, and has the field definitions shown in Table 10.6. Node syntax is shown in Table 10.7.

3.3.1. Example

The Circle2D example (Circle2D.x3d) in Figure 10.6 shows two circles. One of the circles has a non-uniform scale field applied through a parent Transform node.

Type	accessType	Name	Default	Range	Profile
SFFloat	initializeOnly	radius	1	(0, ∞)	Immersive + Geometry2D:2 component, or Full profile
SFNode	inputOutput	metadata	NULL	[X3DMetadata Object]	Core

Table 10.6. Field Definitions for Circle2D Node

XML Syntax (.x3d)	ClassicVRML Syntax (.x3dv)
Circle2D DEF="MyCircle2DNode" radius=".75"/>	DEF MyCircle2DNode Circle2D { radius .75 }

Table 10.7. Node Syntax for Circle2D

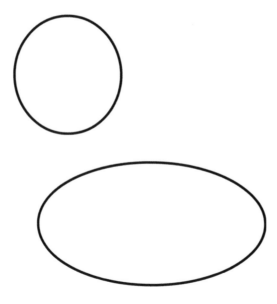

Figure 10.6. A Circle2D example display. The lines have been thickened to make them more visible.

3.3.2. Hints and warnings

The radius field must be greater than zero.

3.4. Disk2D node

Disk2D defines a circular disk centered at (0, 0) in the local coordinate system, with the outside perimeter defined by the outerRadius field. The innerRadius field defines a hole in the middle of the circle, producing a result similar to a washer for a bolt. Figure 10.7 illustrates the definition of the Disk2D node.

The Disk2D node implements the X3DGeometryNode type, is in the Full profile, and has the field definitions shown in Table 10.8. Node syntax is shown in Table 10.9.

3.4.1. Example

The example (Disk2D.x3d) in Figure 10.8 is similar to the Circle2D example. One of the disks has a center hole, and the other does not.

3.4.2. Hints and warnings

One endcap of a Cylinder node can be used as an alternative to a Disk2D node with an inner radius of zero.

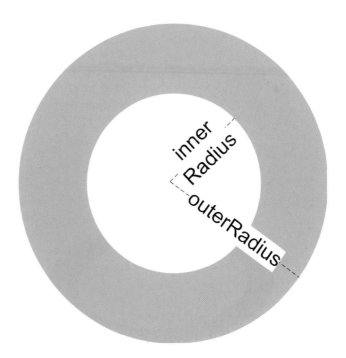

Figure 10.7. An example of a Disk2D node.

Type	accessType	Name	Default	Range	Profile
SFFloat	initializeOnly	innerRadius	0	[0, ∞)	Immersive + Geometry2D:2 component, or Full profile
SFFloat	initializeOnly	outerRadius	1	(0, ∞)	Immersive + Geometry2D:2 component, or Full profile
SFBool	initializeOnly	solid	false		Immersive
SFNode	inputOutput	metadata	NULL	[X3DMetadata Object]	Core

Table 10.8. Field Definitions for Disk2D Node

XML Syntax (.x3d)	ClassicVRML Syntax (.x3dv)

`<Disk2D DEF="MyDisk2DNode"`
`  innerRadius=".75"`
`  outerRadius="2.1"/>`
	`DEF MyDisk2DNode Disk2D {`
	`  innerRadius .75`
	`  outerRadius 2.1`
	`}`

Table 10.9. Node Syntax for Disk2D

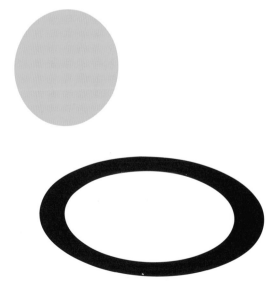

Figure 10.8. A Disk2D example display. The blue disk has a nonzero innerRadius.

The outerRadius field must be greater than zero, though the innerRadius field may equal zero.

The innerRadius field must be less than or equal to outerRadius. If innerRadius equals outerRadius, Disk2D produces a circular line with no interior geometry (similar to a Circle2D node).

3.5. Polyline2D node

Polyline2D specifies a connected set of 2D vertices in a contiguous set of line segments. Disconnected lines must be constructed using separate Polyline2D nodes. Point values are contained in the lineSegments field. Figure 10.9 shows an example Polyline2D node.

The Polyline2D node implements the X3DGeometryNode type, is in the Full profile, and has the field definitions shown in Table 10.10. Node syntax is shown in Table 10.11.

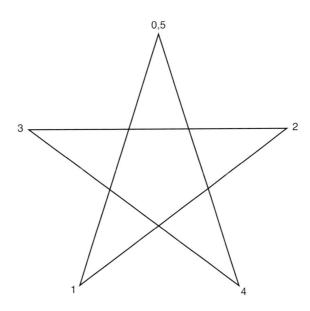

Figure 10.9. An example Polyline2D node; a set of six 2D coordinates defining five contiguous line segments.

Type	accessType	Name	Default	Range	Profile
MFVec2f	initializeOnly	lineSegments	[]	$(-\infty, \infty)$	Immersive + Geometry2D:2 components, or Full profile
SFNode	inputOutput	metadata	NULL	[X3DMetadata Object]	Core

Table 10.10. Field Definitions for Polyline2D Node

XML Syntax (.x3d)	ClassicVRML Syntax (.x3dv)

`<Polyline2D DEF="MyPolyline2DNode"`
`   lineSegments="0 0, 1 2, 2, 8, 5 3, 4 0"/>`
	`DEF MyPolyline2DNode`
	`   Polyline2D {`
	`      lineSegments [0 0, 1 2,`
	`      2, 8, 5 3, 4 0]`
	`   }`

Table 10.11. Node Syntax for Polyline2D

3.5.1. Example

The example for Polyline2D (Polyline2D.x3d) in Figure 10.10 shows a closed, continuous, piecewise-linear curve. In fact the node can only generate a continuous, piecewise-linear curve. If multiple curves are needed, then multiple Polyline2D nodes must be used.

3.5.2. Hints and warnings

Polyline2D rendering is identical to other line nodes (LineSet and IndexedLineSet) defined in Chapter 6, Geometry Nodes Part 2: Points Lines and polygons. The same hints and warnings apply. In particular, only the emissiveColor field of the accompanying Material node has any effect on Polyline2D rendering.

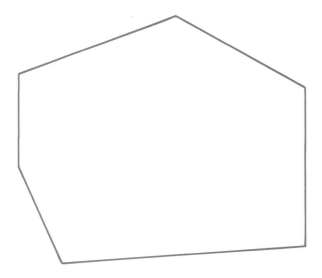

Figure 10.10. A Polyline2D example. The lines have been thickened to make them more visible.

3.6. Polypoint2D node

Polypoint2D specifies a set of 2D points. Figure 10.11 illustrates a single example Polypoint2D node.

The Polypoint2D node implements the X3DGeometryNode type, is in the Full profile, and has the field definitions shown in Table 10.12. Node syntax is shown in Table 10.13.

Figure 10.11. An example Polypoint2D node containing 22 2D point values. Point size is exaggerated for visibility, because each point is actually drawn as a single pixel.

Type	accessType	Name	Default	Range	Profile
MFVec2f	inputOutput	point	[ ]	(−∞,∞)	Immersive + Geometry2D:2 component, or Full profile
SFNode	inputOutput	metadata	NULL	[X3DMetadata Object]	Core

Table 10.12. Field Definitions for Polypoint2D Node

XML Syntax (.x3d)	ClassicVRML Syntax (.x3dv)
`<Polypoint2D DEF="MyPolypoint2DNode point="0 0, 1 2, 2, 8, 5 3, 4 0"/>`	`DEF MyPolypoint2DNode Polypoint2D {` `point [0 0, 1 2, 2, 8, 5 3, 4 0]` `}`

Table 10.13. Node Syntax for Polypoint2D

Figure 10.12. A Polypoint2D example display. The points have been thickened to make them more visible.

3.6.1. Example

The example (Polypoint2D.x3d) in Figure 10.12 has points at each of the vertices of the Polyline2D example. The points displayed by this node are related only as a collection.

3.6.2. Hints and warnings

Polypoint2D rendering is identical to PointSet, which also is defined in Chapter 6. The same hints and warnings apply. In particular, only the emissiveColor field of the accompanying Material node has any effect on Polypoint2D rendering.

3.7. Rectangle2D node

Rectangle2D defines a rectangular quadrangle, again centered at (0,0) in the local coordinate system and aligned with the local x-y coordinate axes. The size field defines x and y dimensions, each greater than zero, as illustrated in Figure 10.13

The Rectangle2D node implements the X3DGeometryNode type, is in the Full profile, and has the field definitions shown in Table 10.14. Node syntax is shown in Table 10.15.

3.7.1. Example

The Rectangle2D example (Rectangle2D.x3d) in Figure 10.14 shows two rectangles. One is a square and the other is not.

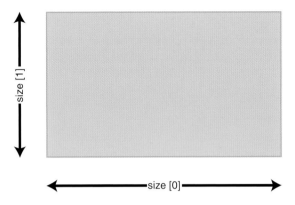

Figure 10.13. An example Rectangle2D node showing 2D size components in *x* and *y* directions respectively. Local origin is at the center.

Type	accessType	Name	Default	Range	Profile
MFVec2f	initializeOnly	size	2 2	(0, ∞)	Immersive + Geometry2D:2 component, or Full profile
SFBool	initializeOnly	solid	false		Immersive
SFNode	inputOutput	metadata	NULL	[X3DMetadata Object]	Core

Table 10.14. Field Definitions for Rectangle2D Node

XML Syntax (.x3d)	ClassicVRML Syntax (.x3dv)
```<Rectangle2D DEF="MyRectangle2DNode" size="1 3" Solid="false"/>```	```DEF MyRectangle2DNode Rectangle2D { size [1 3] solid FALSE }```

Table 10.15. Node Syntax for Rectangle2D

3.8. TriangleSet2D node

TriangleSet2D defines a set of triangles, each created by three 2D vertex points. These points are listed individually as part of a 2D array in the vertices field. Figure 10.15 illustrates a single example TriangleSet2D node.

Figure 10.14. A Rectangle2D example display.

Figure 10.15. An example TriangleSet2D node, containing a set of 15 2D vertices that create 5 2D triangles. Coincident coordinates are listed multiple times.

The TriangleSet2D node implements the X3DGeometryNode type, is in the Full profile, and has the field definitions shown in Table 10.16. Node syntax is shown in Table 10.17.

3.8.1. Example

The TriangleSet2D example (TriangleSet2D.x3d) in Figure 10.16 shows two triangles.

Type	accessType	Name	Default	Range	Profile
MFVec2f	inputOutput	vertices	[]	$(-\infty, \infty)$	Immersive + Geometry 2D:2 component, or Full profile
SFBool	initializeOnly	solid	false		Immersive
SFNode	inputOutput	metadata	NULL	[X3DMetadata Object]	Core

Table 10.16. Field Definitions for TriangleSet2D Node

XML Syntax (.x3d)	ClassicVRML Syntax (.x3dv)

`<TriangleSet2D DEF="MyTriangleSet2DNode"`
`  vertices="0 0 1 1 2 0, -1 1 -4`
`   2 -2 0"`
`solid="true"/>`
	`DEF MyTriangleSet2DNode`
	`   TriangleSet2D {`
	`   vertices [0 0 1 1 2 0,`
	`    -1 1 -4 2 -2 0]`
	`   solid TRUE`
	`}`

Table 10.17. Node Syntax for TriangleSet2D

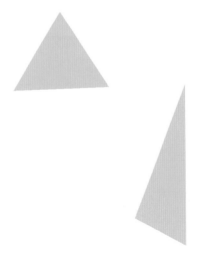

Figure 10.16. A TriangleSet2D example display. A single TriangleSet2D can generate multiple triangles.

3.8.2. Hints and warnings

The total number of TriangleSet2D vertices valves must be evenly divisible by three. One or two excess points are insufficient to draw a triangle and are ignored.

4. Summary

4.1. Key ideas

The Geometry2D nodes provide simple ways of defining planar geometry. These nodes can be more convenient than using other 3D geometry nodes when putting together simple flat images. It is worth remembering that flat polygons are not visible when viewed from the side. Because 2D geometry is defined in the local x-z coordinate plane passing through the origin, care must be taken to align results so that they are visible to the viewer.

Most geometry fields are accessType inputOnly, meaning that they cannot be changed once defined. This prerequisite allows renderers to operate faster and more efficiently. Simple translation, rotation, and scaling with a Transform node can produce excellent animation for most 2D shapes.

Example summary2D.x3d in Figures 10.17 and 10.18 shows all of the nodes in this section. Rotating the example shows how each piece of 2D geometry disappears when viewed edge-on.

4.2. Related nodes and concepts

Related point, line, and polygon nodes are presented in Chapter 6. Other geometry nodes are covered in Chapters 2 and 13. Appearance, Material, FillProperties, LineProperties, TextureCoordinate, and TextureCoordinateGenerator are covered in Chapter 5.

4.3. Next chapter

The next chapter shows how to properly define and place lights in a scene to improve rendering and visibility. Environmental effects are also presented using the Background, TextureBackground, and Fog nodes.

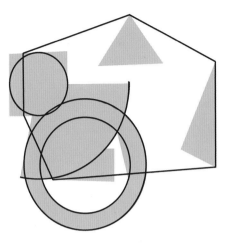

Figure 10.17. The front view of the collection of Geometry2D nodes.

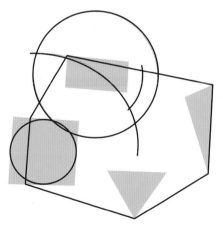

Figure 10.18. The underside view of the same collection of Geometry2D nodes, which is different because some geometry has `solid="true"` which results in backface culling when rendered.

Lighting and Environment Nodes

Daylight encourages good behavior.
—Don Brutzman

1. What this chapter covers

Perhaps surprisingly, creating 3D shapes and lining up a Viewpoint to look at them are only two of three requirements for visualizing a 3D object. Just like in the real world, one or more light sources are needed to illuminate each object and make it visible. Several different kinds of lights are provided in X3D to accomplish this task. These computational lights in 3D graphics emulate many of the characteristics of real lights, allowing a variety of interesting and realistic effects to be rendered as real-time images.

Previous chapters have described the creation of geometry (Chapters 2, 6, and 10) and appearance (Chapters 5 and 6). These techniques are sufficient to create individual 3D objects, but a larger virtual world may not look very realistic or immersive. It is usually necessary to add environment factors to complete a scene: lighting, background, fog, and sound. X3D provides environmental nodes to accomplish these tasks.

The nodes covered in this chapter are DirectionalLight, PointLight, SpotLight, Background, TextureBackground, and Fog.

2. Concepts

The basic notion of lighting in X3D is that virtual lights act as sources of light rays that reflect off a geometric surface to reach the user's current viewpoint. The virtual light rays follow directed paths that may radiate out from a single point source, radiate in parallel as if from a distant source (such as the sun), or radiate in an ambient (omnidirectional) fashion, such as the reflected light in a room that does not appear to originate directly from any specific location.

Similar to actual light rays, the virtual rays provided by light sources illuminate geometric objects by reflecting off of their surfaces. The nature of the reflected illumination depends on the characteristics of the light source as well as the appearance and material properties of the reflecting geometry. Some reflections travel to the viewpoint, where they are rendered as a square array of pixels to produce a frame that is viewed by the user. Thus, there are many contributions that must be calculated and accumulated by the rendering engine of the browser software to create each frame image.

True optics are quite complex. The X3D rendering approach is common for interactive 3D computer graphics and provides a good approximation of actual lighting effects. These techniques are implemented both in software and hardware, using well-defined lighting equations that define view-geometry relationships and interactions between illumination and attenuation. Because using the lighting equations to rapidly repeat the rendering of viewpoint images for a complex scene is computationally intensive, a great deal of optimization is performed by the X3D browser in order to achieve fast rendering and maintain interactive frame rates.

Figure 11.1 shows the basic relationships between light sources, virtual shapes, and the view frame presented to the user.

Because similar approaches are the basis of rendering in most 3D graphics environments, X3D maps well to other common computer-graphics approaches, such as OpenGL, DirectX, Java3D, and others. In fact, specialty techniques in these widely implemented application programming interfaces (APIs) are not adopted in X3D unless equivalent rendering mechanisms can be found across each of the major programming APIs. Thus, the declarative scene-graph approach of X3D tends to fit on top of these other lower-level graphics programming APIs, allowing each of them to be used to implement individual X3D browsers.

Other 3D graphics rendering techniques are possible, including ray tracing, volumetric rendering, light fields, and so on. These technically advanced methodologies usually

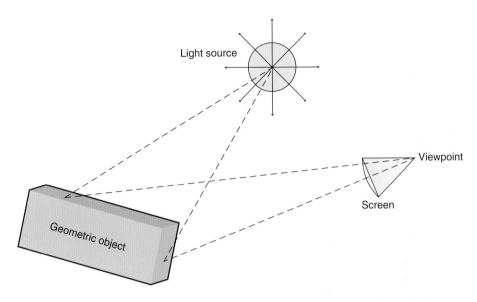

Figure 11.1. X3D lighting and rendering is made up of a light source, rays, geometric object surfaces, reflection, and the screen rendering that displays a user's point of view (POV).

employ fundamentally different rendering algorithms in order to produce 3D scene visualizations, and often are too complex for current computer hardware to maintain interactive display rates. Sometimes laboratories and studios build and maintain rendering farms of networked clusters to conduct parallelized high-performance rendering so that reasonable production rates can be achieved for these advanced techniques. Nevertheless a variety of different computer-graphics approaches can be mapped to X3D constructs, most often through translation programs that permit importing and exporting other formats to and from X3D.

Computer-graphics research continues to progress steadily, and each year brings new capabilities within reach. X3D's extensibility mechanisms and annual standardization updates allow new technical approaches to be harmonized and integrated within the classic scene-graph rendering approach.

Regarding the environment nodes, Background and Fog effects are two additional concepts closely related to lighting and each other. The Background and TextureBackground nodes let the author construct alternative horizons, either using pure color or by stitching together carefully constructed images. The Fog node emulates actual fog by washing out colors as an object's distance from the user's point of view increases. Interestingly, a Fog node can specify any color (not just white or grey), even including black. Because Fog only operates on the pixels presented by viewed objects, both the Fog and Background nodes must specify exactly the same color or else fog-colored objects appear as silhouettes against the Background.

2.1. Purpose and common functionality

2.1.1. Lighting

Lighting in 3D graphics is the mathematical process of emulating how the actual lights, surface reflections, and the basic optics of vision occur in the real world. Virtual lights emit rays that reflect off visible surfaces towards the user's field of view. Rendering is the process that combines color contributions from all light sources, shapes, and effects, computing the total viewed image pixel by pixel. Each completely rendered image is called a *frame*. The number of *frames per second (fps)* must be greater than 10 in order to show smooth motion.

A well-lit scene can be a piece of art. This does not mean that the scene is too dark to see objects, or lit to the point of washing out all surfaces, but that the right amount of light and dark has been achieved. The light is usually supplied by in-scene lights or by integrating lighting effects into texture images that are applied to various surfaces. X3D supports both approaches, the first with the various light nodes, and the second with textures and materials.

Lighting can be directional or ambient. Directional lighting is only visible when directly provided by the light source, reflected off of a visible surface, and then toward the viewer. Ambient lighting is omnidirectional, simulating the background light that is reflected by objects toward each other in the real world.

Many scenes only use one or two lights. X3D requires browser support for at least eight active light sources. These can be any mix of the light nodes supported for that X3D profile. More than eight lights may occur in a scene as long as only eight are active (or in scope) at a given time.

X3D browsers may restrict the number of active lights to eight by arbitrarily disabling some of the lights. The actual result is probably not what the author intended, and gaps in the lighting may prevent some objects from being rendered. Generally speaking, the lighting calculation is not ray tracing but an approximation of the physical interaction of a light source with objects in the scene. The approximation does not allow for shadows or direct reflections; however, diffuse reflected lighting is included. The lack of shadows gives the scene the interesting (or perhaps distressing) property that all surfaces facing the light source are lit, even if obscured by another shape.

If global scope is turned off, illumination is only applied to geometry that is a sibling (or child of a sibling) of the light node. This feature allows content creators to more tightly control the effect of their lights. By properly designing the structure of the scene graph, lights can be used to illuminate the inside of rooms without those same lights illuminating the surrounding objects. This feature was specified in X3D V3.1, making it easier to construct large scenes with many lights dispersed throughout (while avoiding computational overload from too many active lights at one time).

Detailed knowledge of the full lighting equations is rarely needed when authoring X3D scenes, because this functionality is controlled by the browser and is not something that must be directly considered. If fact, avoiding this kind of low-level computation detail is one of the most appealing aspects of X3D's scene-graph approach in comparison to other programming-based APIs.

If needed, definitions for the lighting equations can be found in the X3D abstract specification under the lighting component. The basic lighting equations are described in numerous references, most notably in *Computer Graphics Principles and Practice*, by Foley, van Dam, Feiner, and Hughes.

2.1.2. Background and fog effects

Background simulates both ground and sky, using vertical arrays of gradually varying color values that encircle the scene. These bands of color can emulate both sky above the horizon and land (or ocean) below the horizon. It is also possible to have no horizon, where the sky provides the entire background. Background can also provide a box of image textures that surround the scene on all six sides. With precision preparation, photographs can be warped to provide realistic 360° backdrops from a single point of view.

Fog is another important environmental effect, one that is easy to define and add. Fog can be any color, not just grey. The color of the Fog node gradually replaces the color in geometric objects according to their distance from the viewer. Coefficients for constant, linearly increasing and exponentially increasing fog algorithms are provided. Fog color must match Background color in order to merge smoothly.

If used, the color in Background and Fog node definitions must match each other and must be consistent with lights defined in the scene. Experiment to ensure that results are acceptable.

Abstract node types are defined in the following sections.

2.2. X3DLightNode type

The X3DLightNode abstract type implements the X3DChildNode interface, meaning that an X3DLightNode can appear anywhere in the scene graph where other children nodes are allowed to appear. Implemented fields and defaults are shown in Table 11.1.

Type	accessType	Name	Default	Range	Profile
SFFloat	inputOutput	ambientIntensity	0	[0,1]	Interchange
SFColor	inputOutput	color	1 1 1	[0,1]	Interchange
SFVec3f	inputOutput	direction	0 0 −1	(−∞, ∞)	Interchange
SFFloat	inputOutput	intensity	1	[0,1]	Interchange
SFBool	inputOutput	on	true		Interchange
SFBool	inputOutput	global	false		
SFNode	inputOutput	metadata	NULL	[X3DMetadataObject]	Core

Table 11.1. Field Definitions for X3DLightNode Type

2.2.1. ambientIntensity and intensity

The ambientIntensity field determines the brightness of the environmental contribution of light, meaning the amount of light presumed to come from all directions as part of the basic world-reflected illumination in a scene. Ambient light does not have any associated direction and illuminates all surfaces equally. The effects of ambient light in the real world can be seen inside a room during daylight hours, where everything appears to be well lit even when the sun isn't directly visible.

Similar to ambientIntensity, the intensity field determines the brightness of the primary light rays that emanate directly from a light toward lit objects, shining in straight lines according to the direction of that light. Each of these values can range from 0 (no emission of light) to 1 (full intensity). Values outside the range [0,1] are erroneous.

In common authoring practice, most lights provide only direct illumination using an intensity value, and differences in intensity account for different relative strengths among multiple lights. Nevertheless, providing a nonzero ambientIntensity value is usually a good idea because it ensures that objects are always illuminated and visible. Having ambient lighting available by default in a scene is especially important if the user's headlight might be turned off.

2.2.2. color

The color field specifies the red-green-blue (RGB) spectral components. Thus, `color="1 0 0"` is pure full-intensity red, `color="0 0 1"` is pure full-intensity blue, and so on. When computing the amount of light provided to a point on a geometric surface, this value is multiplied by intensity (or ambientIntensity, as appropriate). Table 11.2 provides a list of typical color values.

Colors can be lightened by proportionately increasing all three components, in effect adding a degree of white light. Colors can be darkened by proportionately decreasing all three components, in effect adding "black light" (conceptually at least).

2.2.3. global

The global field indicates whether a light is global (`global="true"`) or scoped (`global="false"`). Scoped lights only illuminate geometry within the same scene subgraph, meaning all children of the light's parent grouping node. Scoping is often an important performance consideration because there is rarely a need for special lights to illuminate distant objects. Avoiding such situations greatly reduces computational requirements. Added as a part of X3D V3.1, the default value `global="false"` maintains backwards compatibility and minimizes rendering complexity for the best framerate.

Scoped lights are an excellent way to provide special lighting effects, such as shining a spotlight on a single object or illuminating a room differently from the rest of a large scene.

2.2.4. on

The on field determines whether a light is enabled. Setting `on="true"` or `on="false"` is a good way to animate a light, perhaps by letting a user enable or disable the light with

Color	RGB Value	HTML Value
Black	0 0 0	#000000
Green	0 0.5 0	#008000
Silver	0.75 0.75 0.75	#C0C0C0
Lime	0 1 0	#00FF00
Gray	0.5 0.5 0.5	#808080
Olive	0.5 0.5 0	#808000
White	1 1 1	#FFFFFF
Yellow	1 1 0	#FFFF00
Maroon	0.5 0 0	#800000
Navy	0 0 0.5	#000080
Red	1 0 0	#FF0000
Blue	0 0 1	#0000FF
Purple	0.5 0 0.5	#800080
Teal	0 0.5 0.5	#008080
Fuchsia	1 0 1	#FF00FF
Aqua	0 1 1	#00FFFF

Table 11.2. Common Colors and Corresponding RGB and HTML Values

a ROUTE connection from an isActive (or isOver) event produced by a TouchSensor node that is a peer to light-switch geometry.

2.2.5. Hints and warnings

Use lights sparingly because global lights are computationally expensive, requiring an entire rendering pass to calculate each light's contribution. Do not set `global="true"` unless a light is intended to illuminate the entire scene, which includes Inline scenes and any parent scenes.

It is a good authoring practice to put global lights at or near the top of a scene graph, so that their presence and impact is obvious to an author.

Because a light is not rendered as geometry itself, authors frequently place a Cone or Sphere node with a corresponding emissiveColor component at the same location. Although it may be somewhat unrealistic, this trick does let users see where the virtual light source is. Such a shape remains a good candidate for a sibling TouchSensor to turn the light node on or off.

2.3. X3DBackgroundNode type

Nodes implementing the X3DBackgroundNode interface are bindable background nodes, implementing the X3DBindableNode interface. As with other bindable nodes, only one node of each type can be activated at a time. Binding concepts are explained in Chapter 4, Viewing and Navigation.

Common field definitions for the X3DBackgroundNode type are listed in Table 11.3.

Background and TextureBackground are the only nodes that implement the X3DBackgroundNode type. Both can appear on the background node stack, which is used to select which background node is active. Only one Background or TextureBackground node can be active at a given time.

Background nodes can either provide images that are stretched to form a panorama around the horizon, a backdrop of colors that represent earth and sky, or both. The functionality of how a background is constructed and viewed is illustrated in Figure 11.2, showing both side and top perspectives (adapted from the X3D Specification, used with permission).

The centers of the subdiagrams in Figure 11.2 represent the user viewpoint. Objects in the scene are not shown, but all are drawn closer to the point of view than either background images or background colors.

If provided, texture images override background colors. If any of the image pixels in the texture are transparent, then the color mapping underneath becomes visible.

Color transitions are smoothly interpolated in RGB space, allowing natural effects to be created.

All background nodes share the common fields defined in the following sections, each of which are used to construct color maps above and below the horizon.

Type	accessType	Name	Default	Range	Profile
MFFloat	inputOutput	groundAngle	[]	$[0,\pi/2]$	Interactive
MFColor	inputOutput	groundColor	[]	[0,1]	Interactive
MFColor	inputOutput	skyAngle	[]	$[0,\pi]$	Interactive
MFFloat	inputOutput	skyColor	0 0 0	[0,1]	Interactive
SFBool	inputOnly	set_bind			Interactive
SFBool	outputOnly	isBound			Interactive
SFTime	outputOnly	bindTime			Interactive
SFNode	inputOutput	metadata	NULL	[X3DMetadataObject]	Core

Table 11.3. Field Definitions for X3DBackgroundNode

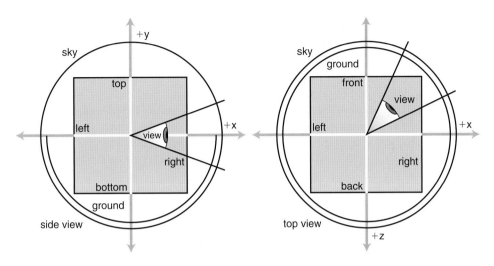

Figure 11.2. Placement of background colors and images relative to the user's viewpoint.

2.3.1. groundAngle and skyAngle

The groundAngle values monotonically increase from 0.0 (nadir, or straight down) to $\pi/2=1.5708$ (horizon), thus proceeding in an upward direction. It is allowed to specify no groundAngle values, in which case the ground hemisphere is colored by the final SkyColor value. Note that, if specified, there must be one more groundColor value than there are groundAngle values.

The skyAngle values monotonically increase from 0.0 zenith (straight up) to $\pi/2=1.5708$ (horizon) to $\pi=3.14159$ (nadir), thus proceeding in a downward direction. Note that, if specified, there must be one more skyColor value than there are skyAngle values. This is because the angle values specify the transition boundary between each color.

2.3.2. groundColor and skyColor

The groundColor array provides the colors below the horizon at various nondecreasing angles, moving upward along the ground's hemisphere. The first value of groundColor begins at an implicit groundAngle of 0.0 radians, representing the nadir (straight down). Subsequent groundColor values approach the horizon at corresponding groundAngle intervals.

The skyColor array provides the color of the sky at various nondecreasing angles moving downward along the sky sphere. The first value of skyColor begins at an implicit skyAngle of 0.0 radians, representing the zenith (straight up). The skyAngle values may continue beneath the horizon, but will be obscured by corresponding groundColor and groundAngle values, if specified.

If no groundColor values are provided, the final skyColor value is clamped and mapped all the way to the nadir so that a complete Background is drawn.

2.3.3. Hints and warnings

It is a good authoring practice to provide appropriate groundColor and skyColor values even when background images are defined. In this way, if image loading suffers from missing files or delayed loading over the network, then a satisfactory substitute is already provided and a less jarring scene is presented to the user.

There must be one more groundColor value than there are groundAngle values, and there must be one more skyColor value than there are skyAngle values.

If used, the initial angle values in the groundAngle and skyAngle arrays are usually greater than 0, because the zeroth color value already corresponds to an angle value of 0 radians.

Values in the groundAngle and skyAngle arrays must increase monotonically.

Nodes implementing the X3DBackgroundNode interface are affected by any rotations that occur in their parent scene-graph hierarchy. Parent translations have no effect because the background is always positioned at the scene's horizon.

With precision preparation, photographs can be warped to provide realistic 360° backdrops from a single point of view. This is an advanced technique that ordinarily requires the use of special image-manipulation software in order to produce seamless boundaries.

3. Node descriptions

3.1. DirectionalLight node

The DirectionalLight node provides light that uniformly illuminates the environment in a single direction. All light rays are defined in parallel from a particular direction. Every surface that faces the light (even from an oblique angle) is illuminated to some degree. This lighting occurs regardless of whether another object is located in between the viewed object and the light source, because intervening geometry does not block virtual light. Neither backfaces nor any surfaces parallel to the light rays are illuminated by direct light contributions. Ambient contributions from a nonzero ambientIntensity field are similarly ignored for those polygons.

The DirectionalLight node is in the Interchange profile. The node has the fields defined in Table 11.4. Node syntax is shown in Table 11.5.

The intensity of light from a DirectionalLight does not diminish with distance. Objects far away are illuminated just as brightly as nearby objects, similar to the effects of sunlight. However, a Fog node does attenuate the light contribution that is reflected back to the viewer from illuminated objects.

Figure 11.3 illustrates the illumination pattern provided by a DirectionalLight source.

The example DirectionalLight.x3d in Figure 11.4 shows the lack of shadows cast by objects lit by a DirectionalLight. The light is illuminating the objects in the direction of the arrows on the left. The objects are positioned inline with the light source.

Type	accessType	Name	Default	Range	Profile
SFFloat	inputOutput	ambient Intensity	0	[0,1]	Interchange
SFColor	inputOutput	color	1 1 1	[0,1]	Interchange
SFVec3f	inputOutput	direction	0 0 −1	(−∞ , ∞)	Interchange
SFFloat	inputOutput	intensity	1	[0,1]	Interchange
SFBool	inputOutput	on	true		Interchange
SFBool	inputOutput	global	false		Interchange
SFNode	inputOutput	metadata	NULL	[X3DMetadataObject]	Core

Table 11.4. Field Definitions for DirectionalLight Node

XML Syntax (.x3d)	ClassicVRML Syntax (.x3dv)
```<DirectionalLight DEF="My DirectionalLight" ambientIntensity=".2" color="1 .5 0" direction="−1 0 0" intensity=".7" on="true" />```	```DEF MyDirectionalLight DirectionalLight { ambientIntensity .2 color 1 .5 0 direction −1 0 0 intensity .7 on TRUE }```

Table 11.5. Node Syntax for DirectionalLight

3.1.1. direction

The direction field provides an *x-y-z* vector value indicating the direction in which the virtual light rays are emanating. Note that this direction is within the local coordinate frame specified by any parent Transform nodes.

3.1.2. Hints and warnings

It can be difficult to debug "missing" directional lights if they are pointing in the wrong direction. Temporarily substituting a PointLight node (which is omnidirectional) can help to determine if a DirectionalLight node is in the right location but simply misaligned.

3.2. Headlight

The headlight is a special light that is not specifically defined as an X3DLightNode type. Rather it is built into the browser as a default DirectionalLight that is fixed at the location and direction of the current user viewpoint. Normally the headlight is turned

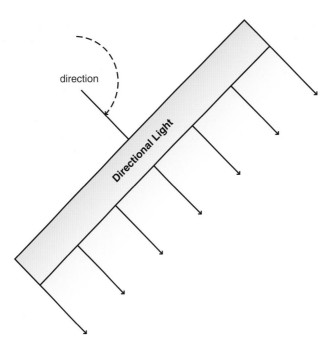

Figure 11.3. DirectionalLight provides a virtual light source where all rays are parallel.

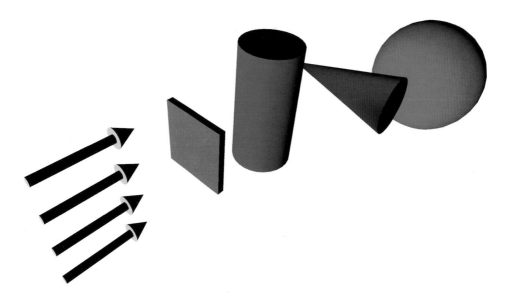

Figure 11.4. DirectionalLight nodes do not interact with objects to cast shadows, and distance does not decrease their intensity.

on by default, and is controlled by the boolean headlight field of the currently bound NavigationInfo node (described in Chapter 4). The headlight is automatically positioned and oriented to match the current user view.

The headlight always has the characteristics `intensity="1"`, `color="1 1 1"`, `ambientIntensity="0.0"`, and `direction="0 0 −1"` within the local-coordinate frame of the current view.

Most browsers provide special user-interface mechanisms to override whether the bound NavigationInfo node is enabling or disabling the headlight, typically with a menu choice or a special hotkey combination. No common approach has been defined for this (and several other) browser-specific capabilities because display screens and browser user interfaces vary so widely.

Scenes that already have multiple lights or utilize special precomputed lighting techniques (such as radiosity approaches) may intentionally turn the headlight off. This is accomplished by setting `enabled="false"` in all of the contained NavigationInfo nodes.

3.3 PointLight node

The PointLight node emulates a single light source that radiates evenly in all directions. A common analogy for a PointLight is a small (but possibly quite bright) light bulb. As with the other X3D nodes implementing the X3DLightNode type, PointLight does not cast a shadow, and its light rays can travel through geometric objects to illuminate other shapes that are otherwise observed.

The PointLight node is in the Interactive profile. The node has the fields defined in Table 11.6. Node syntax is shown in Table 11.7.

The intensity of a PointLight node is dependent on the distance from the light source to the object. The further away the object, the less it is illuminated.

Type	accessType	Name	Default	Range	Profile
SFFloat	inputOutput	ambientIntensity	0	[0,1]	Interactive
SFVec3f	inputOutput	attenuation	1 0 0	[0,∞)	Interactive
SFColor	inputOutput	color	1 1 1	[0,1]	Interactive
SFBool	inputOutput	global	false		Interactive
SFFloat	inputOutput	intensity	1	[0,1]	Interactive
SFVec3f	inputOutput	location	0 0 −1	(−∞, ∞)	Interactive
SFBool	inputOutput	on	true		Interactive
SFFloat	inputOutput	radius	100	[0,∞)	Interactive
SFNode	inputOutput	metadata	NULL	[X3DMetadataObject]	Core

Table 11.6. Field Definitions for PointLight Node

XML Syntax (.x3d)	ClassicVRML Syntax (.x3dv)

``
<PointLight DEF="MyPointLight"
  ambientIntensity=".3"
  attenuation="1 1 1"
  color=".5 1 0"
  intensity=".9"
  location="0 2.3 .1"
  on="true"
  radius="100"
</PointLight>
``
	``
	DEF MyPointLight PointLight {
	  ambientIntensity .3
	  attenuation 1 1 1
	  color .5 1 0
	  intensity .9
	  location 0 2.3 .1
	  on TRUE
	  radius 100
	}
	``

Table 11.7. Node Syntax for PointLight

Attenuation effects due to distance are in addition to the obliqueness of the surface relative to the illuminating rays. The illumination pattern of a PointLight is spherically symmetric, so rotation of the source node or its parent transform has no effect on light characteristics. Figure 11.5 illustrates the illumination pattern provided by a PointLight source.

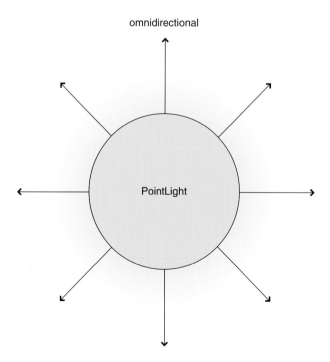

Figure 11.5. PointLight provides a virtual light source such that rays emanate radially in all directions from a single location.

If coloring of polygons in a piece of geometry is uniform, such as when a Material node is used, then the illumination of a surface is computed at the center of each polygon and is constant over the polygon. A large planar (flat) polygon is displayed as if there is uniform lighting across the polygon. The same polygon can be subdivided into smaller regions to make the difference in PointLight incident-angle effects more prominent.

As with the other lights, a PointLight node does not create any geometry or visual representation that is directly visible in the scene. Looking directly at the location of the node does not reveal anything, regardless of whether the node is on or off. If the PointLight node represents an actual light in the world that is ordinarily visible, then the author must create appropriate geometry and apply the proper appearance to portray it.

The PointLight.x3d example in Figure 11.6 shows the effect of distance on the light intensity. The rectangle geometry is white and illuminated with a yellow

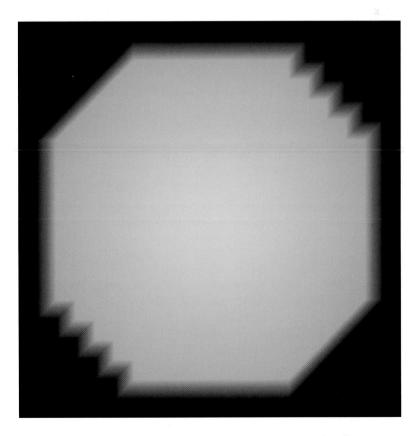

Figure 11.6. The PointLight example shows a 10×10 planar grid and includes unlit geometry (black) that is too far away from the light source to be illuminated. The sawtooth edges are an artifact of the triangulation of the illuminated planar grid.

PointLight. When the geometry is too far away from the light source, there is no illumination. The illumination also shows a slight drop in intensity with increasing distance from the center.

3.3.1. attenuation

The illumination level of a PointLight decreases inversely with distance. Three coefficients are provided as an SFVec3f array for constant, linear, and quadratic attenuation, respectively. The following equation governs the net attenuation effect, where r is the distance from the PointLight position to the geometry being lit. Note that this attenuation factor is clamped to a maximum of 1 so that close-range effects do not inadvertantly increase intensity past its defined value.

$$factor = 1/max(attenuation[0] + attenuation[1] \times r + attenuation[2] \times r^2, 1)$$

Often constant-coefficient or linear-coefficient attenuation is sufficient for a desired effect. Take care before specifying linear or quadratic values, because the attenuation factor must be calculated for every pixel and every frame, making range-dependent effects computationally expensive.

3.3.2. location

The location field provides the offset position of the PointLight within the current coordinate system. This simplifies the respositioning of a light so that it can illuminate nearby geometry. Note that a PointLight placed within geometry usually does not illuminate the outside of the shape, because interior reflections are only properly visible when viewed from within the interior rather than from the outside.

3.3.3. radius

The radius field specifies the maximum effective distance of the light relative to local light position. This distance is affected by any scaling effects in parent transformations, which may be an unexpected side effect that needs to be accounted for, or (better yet) avoided.

3.3.4. Hints and warnings

Lighting an object from inside the geometric shape is problematic. Because only reflected surfaces are visible to the viewer, exterior (normally illuminated) surfaces are not visible. Further confounding this situation is the fact that light passes through polygonal surfaces. Thus, if two-sided polygons are enabled for the interior-lit geometry, the user only sees the interiors. When viewed from outside the geometry itself, this "inside out" rendering can be confusing and disorienting for the user. This problem can be even worse if the geometry is partially transparent. Thus, lights ordinarily are placed outside the geometry they are intended to illuminate.

Avoid the use of quadratic (r^2) attenuation unless it is specifically needed for a special effect, because it is computationally expensive and may significantly slow down the rendering frame rate for lit objects.

3.4. SpotLight node

SpotLight is a light source that illuminates geometry within a conical beam. Light illuminates all geometry and is scoped by the scene-graph hierarchy unless `global="true"`. Lights have no visible shape themselves and shine through occluding geometry.

The SpotLight node is in the Interactive profile. The node has the fields defined in Table 11.8. Node syntax is shown in Table 11.9.

The Spotlight node is a light source that illuminates any geometry appearing within a conical beam. Full intensity occurs across the central cutoffAngle, then reduces to zero at the conical boundary specified by beamWidth as illustrated in Figure 11.7. This intensity dropoff can provide soft edges to spotlit objects.

The central beam of the SpotLight node is clearly visible in the example SpotLight.x3d. Figure 11.8 shows the fall-off in intensity from the central beam region. The geometry is a 10×10 array of rectangles positioned at the edge of the beam distance.

Type	accessType	Name	Default	Range	Profile
SFFloat	inputOutput	ambientIntensity	0	[0,1]	Interactive
SFVec3f	inputOutput	attenuation	1 0 0	[0,∞)	Interactive
SFFloat	inputOutput	beamWidth	$\pi/2$	[0,$\pi/2$]	Interactive (optional), Immersive (guaranteed)
SFColor	inputOutput	color	1 1 1	[0,1]	Interactive
SFFloat	inputOutput	cutOffAngle	$\pi/4$	[0,$\pi/2$]	Interactive
SFVec3f	inputOutput	direction	0 0 −1	[−∞,∞]	Interactive
SFBool	inputOutput	global	false		Interactive
SFFloat	inputOutput	intensity	1	[0,1]	Interactive
SFVec3f	inputOutput	location	0 0 −1	(−∞, ∞)	Interactive
SFBool	inputOutput	on	true		Interactive
SFFloat	inputOutput	radius	100	[0,∞)	Interactive (optional), Immersive (guaranteed)
SFNode	inputOutput	metadata	NULL	[X3DMetadata-Object]	Core

Table 11.8. Field Definitions for SpotLight Node

XML Syntax (.x3d)	ClassicVRML Syntax (.x3dv)
```<SpotLight DEF="MySpotLightNode" ambientIntensity="0" attenuation="1 0 0" beamWidth="1.57" color="1 1 1" cutOffAngle="0.78" direction="0 0 -1" global="true" intensity="1" location="0 0 0" on="true" radius="100"/>```	```DEF MySpotLightNode SpotLight { ambientIntensity 0 attenuation 1 0 0 beamWidth 1.57 color 1 1 1 cutOffAngle 0.78 direction 0 0 -1 global TRUE intensity 1 location 0 0 0 on TRUE radius 100 }```

Table 11.9. Node Syntax for SpotLight

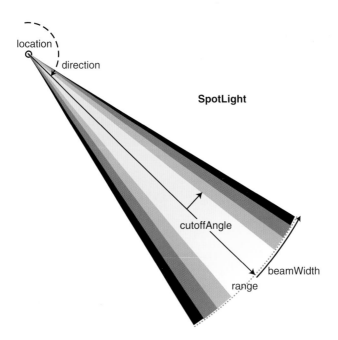

Figure 11.7. SpotLight provides a virtual light source such that rays emanate radially with a conical outline from a single location.

Figure 11.8. Central beam intensity and fall-off are visible in this SpotLight example.

3.4.1. attenuation

SpotLight node illumination intensity decreases in proportion to range from the light's location according to three constant, linear, and quadratic attenuation coefficients. The attenuation factor is described in detail under PointLight node, and the same considerations apply for the SpotLight node.

3.4.2. beamWidth and cutOffAngle

The beamWidth field specifies the half-angle in radians about the Spotlight direction that corresponds to maximum uniform intensity. The cutOffAngle field specifies the half-angle in radians about the SpotLight direction that corresponds to the outer bound of the Spotlight node's effect. Outside of this solid angle, the SpotLight node provides no light.

Between the inner beamWidth angle and outer cutOffAngle, intensity diminishes linearly as described by the following algorithm.

```
//angle = The angle between (SpotLight node's direction vector) and
          (vector from SpotLight location to the point to be illuminated)

//if (angle ≥ cutOffAngle) multiplier = 0
    else if (angle ≤ beamWidth) multiplier = 1
    else multiplier = (angle - cutOffAngle) / (beamWidth - cutOffAngle)
    intensity(angle) = SpotLight.intensity × multiplier
```

If beamWidth is defined to be greater than cutOffAngle (which is likely an authoring mistake) then cutOffAngle still determines the maximum outer bounds and intensity is uniformly set to maximum within this solid angle.

3.4.3. direction

The direction field provides an *x-y-z* vector value indicating the direction in which virtual light rays are emanating. Note that this direction is within the local coordinate frame specified by the aggregate effects of any parent Transform nodes.

3.4.4. location

Similar to PointLight, the location field provides the offset position of the SpotLight node within the current coordinate system. This simplifies the repositioning of a light so that it can illuminate nearby geometry. Again note that a light placed within geometry usually does not illuminate its external surfaces, because interior reflections are only properly visible from within the interior rather than from the outside.

The location field is affected by the accumulated offset, rotation, and scaling of any parent Transform nodes, and may need to be adjusted correspondingly.

3.4.5. radius

The radius field determines the maximum range at which a SpotLight node has an effect. This is an important feature that allows SpotLight nodes to have limited local scope, rather than requiring computational overhead regardless of where geometry is viewed in the scene.

The radius field is also affected by scaling of any parent Transform nodes, and may need to be adjusted to account for different (non-meter) scale units in effect.

3.4.6. Hints and warnings

As with other lights, the SpotLight node has no visible shape itself. Take care to get the settings correct through experimentation if necessary. Shining a SpotLight node against a flat ElevationGrid that is oriented perpendicularly can reveal the effects of beamWidth and cutOffAngle.

Again as with other lights, the SpotLight node simply shines through any occluding geometry to illuminate other objects that are in scope. Because each active light can greatly increase the rendering cost of a scene, it is important to limit their use. Carefully scope lights to only affect objects of interest through separation by grouping nodes and keeping global="false" whenever possible.

3.5. Background node

As discussed in the X3DBackgroundNode section, Background can provide smoothly colored bands for both ground and sky. Background can also provide a box of image textures that surround the scene on all six sides, defined by the MFString url field, which can list separate values for each of the image files.

The Background node implements the X3DBackgroundNode and the X3DBindableNode types. It is in the Interactive profile, though some fields are not guaranteed unless using the Immersive profile. The node has the fields defined in Table 11.10. Node syntax is shown in Table 11.11.

Only one Background node can be active at a given time. Background and TextureBackground nodes share a dedicated binding stack. Activating and deactivating bound nodes is described in Chapter 4, Viewing and Navigation.

Background nodes are used to provide a setting for the X3D world. Figure 11.9 (Background.x3d) demonstrates an ocean background from the Universal Media Panoramas directory in the X3D Basic Examples archive.

3.5.1. backUrl, frontUrl, leftUrl, rightUrl, bottomUrl, topUrl

These url fields refer to each of the six images that provide background textures. Note that since each of these fields has accessType inputOutput, they can be modified at run-time to permit progressive streaming of different background images over time.

Type	accessType	Name	Default	Range	Profile
MFFloat	inputOutput	groundAngle	[]	$(0,\pi/2]$	Interactive (optional)
MFColor	inputOutput	groundColor	[]	[0,1]	Interactive (optional)
MFFloat	inputOutput	skyAngle	[]	$(0,\pi]$	Interactive
MFColor	inputOutput	skyColor	0 0 0	[0,1]	Interactive
MFString	inputOutput	leftUrl		[urn]	Interactive (optional)
MFString	inputOutput	rightUrl		[urn]	Interactive (optional)
MFString	inputOutput	frontUrl		[urn]	Interactive (optional)
MFString	inputOutput	backUrl		[urn]	Interactive (optional)
MFString	inputOutput	topUrl		[urn]	Interactive (optional)
MFString	inputOutput	bottomUrl		[urn]	Interactive (optional)
SFBool	inputOnly	set_bind			Interactive
SFBool	outputOnly	isBound			Interactive
SFTime	outputOnly	bindTime			Interactive
SFNode	inputOutput	metadata	NULL	[X3DMetadata-Object]	Core

Table 11.10. Field Definitions for Background Node

XML Syntax (.x3d)	ClassicVRML Syntax (.x3dv)

`<Background DEF="MyBackgroundNode"`
`    groundAngle="1.55"`
`    groundColor="0 1 0, 0.1 1 0.3"`
`    skyAngle="1.45"`
`    skyColor="0.7 1 0.7, 0.9 1 0.9"`
`    leftUrl="leftImage.png"`
`    rightUrl="rightImage.png"`
`    frontUrl="frontImage.png"`
`    backUrl="backImage.png"`
`    topUrl="topImage.png"`
`    bottomUrl="bottomImage.png" />`
	`DEF MyBackgroundNode Background {`
	`    groundAngle 1.55`
	`    groundColor 0 1 0, 0.1 1 0.3`
	`    skyAngle 1.45`
	`    skyColor 0.7 1 0.7, 0.9 1 0.9`
	`    leftUrl "leftImage.png"`
	`    rightUrl "rightImage.png"`
	`    frontUrl "frontImage.png"`
	`    backUrl "backImage.png"`
	`    topUrl "topImage.png"`
	`    bottomUrl "bottomImage.png"`
	`}`

Table 11.11. Node Syntax for Background

Figure 11.9. This Background example provides a seamless panorama of an ocean environment.

3.5.2. Hints and warnings

Browsers are required to support the JPEG and PNG image file format supports. GIF support is also recommended for browsers (but not required, due to patent encumbrances). Thus GIF support is not guaranteed for authors. Any other 2D image format may also be used, if provided with the scene and supported by the browser.

Background and TextureBackground nodes within Inline-referenced scenes are not automatically bound at load time, even if no Background node appears in the parent scene.

More than two dozen helpful example Background nodes can be found in the Universal Media Panoramas section of the X3D Basic Examples archive, available via the book's website.

Browsers might (or might not) cache images, reducing bandwidth requirements if certain images are used more than once in a scene. Better global control of these images is possible using the TextureBackground node.

When a nonstandard specialty 2D image format is employed, it is best to list it among the first string values in the url array. In that way, other supported formats can be retrieved as a backup solution if the primary specialty-format image fails to load properly.

LoadSensor can detect progress and success when retrieving image resource files pointed to by all the url fields. LoadSensor is described in Chapter 12, Environment Sensor and Sound Nodes.

3.6. TextureBackground node

The TextureBackground is almost identical to the Background node. Instead of using six url fields to refer to the textured images pasted to the background, it uses up to six ImageTexture nodes instead. This means that such ImageTexture nodes might be defined elsewhere in the scene, or used separately by a LoadSensor to determine when loading is complete.

TextureBackground rendering is nearly identical to Background. TextureBackground identically supports the groundColor, skyColor, groundAngle, and skyAngle arrays. As before, these are only visible when ImageTextures are either missing or contain transparent pixels.

TextureBackground also adds support for overall transparency, allowing an X3D scene to have transparent portions that view images or windows behind the current scene. This is a significant new capability first introduced in X3D version 3.1 that was not available in VRML97 or X3D V3.0.

The TextureBackground node implements the X3DBackgroundNode and X3DBindableNode types. It is in the Full profile. The node has the fields defined in Table 11.12. Node syntax is shown in Table 11.13.

The browser handles a TextureBackground just like a Background node, utilizing the same binding stack. Any Background or TextureBackground node can become active by receiving a set_bind true event. See Chapter 4, Viewing and Navigation for further details on binding.

3.6.1. backTexture, frontTexture, leftTexture, rightTexture, bottomTexture, and topTexture

These fields refer to each of the six children nodes that may appear inside a TextureBackground node. See the preceding syntax tables for the proper way to identify the necessary containerField names for each of the child nodes.

Type	accessType	Name	Default	Range	Profile
SFFloat	inputOutput	transparency	0	[0,1]	Full
MFFloat	inputOutput	groundAngle	[]	(0,π/2)	Full
MFColor	inputOutput	groundColor	[]	[0,1]	Full
MFFloat	inputOutput	skyAngle	[]	(0,π]	Full
MFColor	inputOutput	skyColor	0 0 0	[0,1]	Full
SFNode	inputOutput	leftTexture	NULL	[X3DTextureNode]	Full
SFNode	inputOutput	rightTexture	NULL	[X3DTextureNode]	Full
SFNode	inputOutput	frontTexture	NULL	[X3DTextureNode]	Full
SFNode	inputOutput	backTexture	NULL	[X3DTextureNode]	Full
SFNode	inputOutput	topTexture	NULL	[X3DTextureNode]	Full
SFNode	inputOutput	bottomTexture	NULL	[X3DTextureNode]	Full
SFBool	inputOnly	set_bind			Full
SFBool	outputOnly	isBound			Full
SFTime	outputOnly	bindTime			Full
SFNode	inputOutput	metadata	NULL	[X3DMetadataObject]	Core

Table 11.12. Field Definitions for TextureBackground Node

Note that images themselves may also include transparency, though that technique only allows the underlying groundColor and skyColor to show through.

3.6.2. transparency

The transparency field allows an X3D scene to be visibly overlaid on top of other windows or components. A nonzero transparency value allows the underlying application to be seen through the scene, if the running application (or web browser plus plugin combination) supports such compositing.

3.6.3. Hints and warnings

Pay close attention to the syntax differences for SFNode children and containerField naming syntax, comparing the ClassicVRML (.x3dv) and XML (.x3d) encodings.

Background and TextureBackground nodes within Inline-retrieved scenes are not automatically bound at load time, even if no background node appears in the parent scene.

LoadSensor can detect progress and successful loading for contained texture nodes (such as ImageTexture) that refer to external files. LoadSensor is described in Chapter 12, Environment Sensor and Sound Nodes.

3.7. Fog node

The Fog node provides an important environmental effect, though it is only occasionally used. White or gray fog can emulate fog found in the real world. Black-colored fog

XML Syntax (.x3d)	ClassicVRML Syntax (.x3dv)
```<TextureBackground DEF="MyTextureBackgroundNode" transparency="0" groundAngle="1.55" groundColor="0 1 0, 0.1 1 0.3" skyAngle="1.45" skyColor="0.7 1 0.7, 0.9 1 0.9"> <ImageTexture containerField= "leftTexture" url='"leftImage.png"'/> <ImageTexture containerField= "rightTexture" url='"rightImage png"'/> <ImageTexture containerField= "frontTexture" url='"frontImage.png"'/> <ImageTexture containerField= "backTexture" url='"backImage.png"'/> <ImageTexture containerField= "topTexture" url='"topImage.png"'/> <ImageTexture containerField= "bottomTexture" url='"bottomImage.png"'/> </TextureBackground>```	```DEF MyTextureBackgroundNode TextureBackground { transparency 0 groundAngle [1.55] groundColor [0 1 0, 0.1 1 0.3] skyAngle [1.45] skyColor [0.7 1 0.7, 0.9 1 0.9] leftTexture ImageTexture { url "leftImage.png"} rightTexture ImageTexture { url "rightImage.png"} frontTexture ImageTexture { url "frontImage.png"} backTexture ImageTexture { url "backImage.png"} topTexture ImageTexture { url "topImage.png"} bottomTexture ImageTexture { url "bottomImage.png"} }```

Table 11.13. Node Syntax for TextureBackground

can provide a night-time effect in which geometric objects disappear as they get darker and farther away. Because a Fog node gradually replaces the color reflected by objects according to distance from the viewer, Fog color must match Background color to work properly.

The Fog node implements the X3DBindableNode type and is in the Immersive profile. The node has the fields defined in Table 11.14. Node syntax is shown in Table 11.15.

Fog is an important environmental effect that can significantly change the ambience of a scene. Use it sparingly for best impact.

As with many special effects, experimentation with fog is a good idea. Navigate through the scene and look at different objects from various locations to ensure that a good user experience is achieved.

The example Fog.x3d in Figure 11.10 shows the visual attenuation from an active Fog node. The farther an object is from the viewer, the more the geometry colors and textures blend into the fog color.

Type	accessType	Name	Default	Range	Profile
SFColor	inputOutput	color	1 1 1		Immersive
SFString	inputOutput	fogType	"LINEAR"	["LINEAR" | "EXPONENTIAL"]	Immersive
SFFloat	inputOutput	visibilityRange	0	[0, ∞)	Immersive
SFBool	inputOnly	set_bind			Immersive
SFBool	outputOnly	isBound			Immersive
SFTime	outputOnly	bindTime			Immersive
SFNode	inputOutput	metadata	NULL	[X3DMetadataObject]	Core

Table 11.14. Field Definitions for Fog Node

XML Syntax (.x3d)	ClassicVRML Syntax (.x3dv)

`<Fog DEF="MyFogNode"`
`    color="1 1 1"`
`    fogType="LINEAR"`
`    visibilityRange="0" />`
	`DEF MyFogNode Fog {`
	`    color 1 1 1`
	`    fogType "LINEAR"`
	`    visibilityRange 0`
	`}`

Table 11.15. Node Syntax for Fog

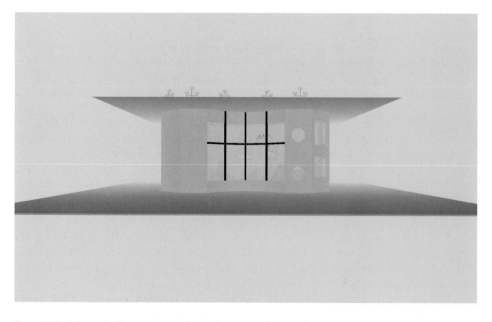

Figure 11.10. A Fog node blends geometry colors and textures to the fog color.

3.7.1. color

The color field is a simple SFColor value with RGB components only. No transparency factor is provided, because a Fog node obscures objects completely.

3.7.2. fogType

The fogType field specifies the algorithm used to blend fog color as object distance from the user's viewpoint increases. "LINEAR" indicates that the proportional reduction in colors drops off linearly between point of view and the visibilityRange. "EXPONENTIAL" indicates that the browser may substitute a nonlinear dropoff function, usually allowing better visibility of nearby objects but still achieving full obscuration at the maximum distance.

3.7.3. visibilityRange

The visibilityRange field indicates the distance from the camera (in meters) where objects are totally obscured by the fog. Note that this range is based on the local coordinate system, so avoid (or account for) any transformation scaling.

3.7.4. Hints and warnings

Fog color must match background color exactly, or else objects fade into fog-colored silhouettes rather than disappearing completely.

Conversely, fog has no effect on the background. Thus a Fog node is best used with a Background node containing a single color value for skyColor and groundColor, and no image textures.

Fog nodes within Inlined scenes are not automatically bound at load time, even if no Fog node appears in the parent scene.

4. Summary

4.1. Key ideas

Lighting makes the difference between scenes that look plastic and toylike, and scenes that approach realism. Different types of lights can provide the proper distribution of color, direction, and intensity depending on the type of objects that appear in the scene. Care must be taken whenever adding lights, because the overall complexity of rendering is directly proportional to the number of lights that are active in a given location. Careful scoping of lights can help to keep overall frame rate high.

The Background and Fog nodes provide important environmental effects that can add overall realism to top-level scenes. A Background can be drawn using either image textures or simply an array of colors. Fog effects can help keep user attention focused on nearby objects and can help scenes emulate night-time effects.

The use of lights is essential in all nontrivial scenes. The Background and Fog nodes, if used, must be carefully coordinated to work properly with defined lights.

4.2. Related nodes and concepts

Materials specify how surfaces react to ambient and diffuse light. Textures are also lit. Appearance, materials, and textures are described in Chapter 5.

Background and TextureBackground share a dedicated binding stack. Fog also has a separate dedicated binding stack. The process of activating and deactivating bindable nodes is described in Chapter 4, Viewing and Navigation.

4.3. Next chapter

The following chapter looks at environment sensor nodes: LoadSensor for detecting when file loading is complete, ProximitySensor for detecting user location, and VisibilitySensor to determine whether the current camera viewpoint can see a location.

Environment Sensor and Sound Nodes

Hereafter, when they come to model heav'n
And calculate the stars, how they will wield
The mighty frame, how build, unbuild, contrive
To save appearances, how gird the sphere
With centric and eccentric scribbled o'er,
Cycle and epicycle, orb in orb.
—John Milton, Paradise Lost, 1667.

1. What this chapter covers

The event-generating and sound-generating nodes covered in this chapter help authors to create scenes that can passively sense and respond to user presence without requiring direct user interaction. The LoadSensor node monitors whether a scene has completed loading external resources. Environment sensors are nodes that generate events based on a user's movement through a scene, detecting either the user's proximity or ability to see a region of interest. Sound nodes are used to place audio sources in a scene and spatially present those sounds based on a user's relative location.

The nodes presented in this chapter are LoadSensor, ProximitySensor, VisibilitySensor, Sound, and AudioClip.

This chapter assumes that you are familiar with the X3D event model, covered in Chapter 7, Event Animation and Interpolation. A related node is Collision, which detects when a user collides with objects in the virtual world. Collision is covered in Chapter 4, Viewing and Navigation.

2. Concepts

The nodes presented in this chapter can be used in subtle ways and are mostly reactive. LoadSensor, ProximitySensor, and VisibilitySensor can each be used to sense whether the scene is ready to respond to a user. Output from sound nodes is spatialized, and these nodes also respond according to user proximity and direction.

The Sound and AudioClip nodes are especially important. Background sounds can add a great deal to the responsiveness in a scene, providing a sense of immersion and helping to establish a suspension of disbelief so that users engage fully in the 3D experience being presented. Adding sound cues can further improve user interactivity and interaction. The X3D specification allows multiple sounds to play at once, which can enhance situational awareness for objects outside the current field of view. Well-chosen sound cues can enhance a user's sense of immersion, because each audio output channel is adjusted by the browser to indicate both strength and direction of an audio clip.

Abstract node types are defined in the following sections.

2.1. X3DEnvironmentSensorNode type

The X3DEnvironmentSensorNode type implements the X3DSensorNode interface. It is the base type for the ProximitySensor and VisibilitySensor nodes, meaning that both nodes implement this interface and support the functionality of the fields in Table 12.1.

2.1.1. center and size

The center and size fields are each SFVec3f values that indicate both the center and the extent of the 3D box corresponding to the sensed volume for the node. These values are relative to the parent transformations that establish the current local coordinate system.

2.1.2. isActive and enabled

The isActive and enabled fields are inherited from the X3DSensorNode type, which is explained in Chapter 8, User Interactivity. An isActive true event or isActive false event

Type	accessType	Name	Default	Range	Profile
SFVec3f	inputOutput	center	0 0 0	$(-\infty, \infty)$	Interactive
SFVec3f	inputOutput	size	0 0 0	$[0, \infty)$	Interactive
SFBool	inputOutput	enabled	true		Interactive
SFBool	outputOnly	isActive			Interactive
SFTime	outputOnly	enterTime			Interactive
SFTime	outputOnly	exitTime			Interactive
SFNode	inputOutput	metadata	NULL	[X3DMetadataObject]	Core

Table 12.1. Field Definitions for X3DEnvironmentSensorNode Type

is sent when the node is activated or deactivated, respectively. Activation conditions vary depending on the intended functionality of the particular sensor node.

The enabled field is used to turn a sensor on or off, which allows simple or sophisticated chains of interaction to be properly sequenced for the user. For example, if the user is searching a series of rooms, a corresponding series of ProximitySensor nodes might detect when each room is successfully reached and then enable or disable sensors controlling animation activity as appropriate.

2.1.3. enterTime and exitTime

Event values for enterTime and exitTime are sent whenever corresponding isActive true or false events are triggered and sent by the parent node. Values for these events are the same as the timestamp of the corresponding isActive event.

2.1.4. Hints and warnings

A Transform node can be used to reposition or reorient sensor nodes that implement the X3DEnvironmentSensorNode interface. This can be useful when DEF and USE copies of a single node create multiple instances of a sensor, each having identical functionality in multiple locations. Nevertheless, avoid overlapping the boundary boxes for the copied USE nodes, or unpredictable results may occur.

Setting any of the three size component values equal to zero indicates a region of zero volume that cannot be entered. This situation is equivalent to setting enabled="false".

2.2. X3DNetworkSensorNode type

The X3DNetworkSensorNode type is the base for any sensors that depend on network activity. X3DNetworkSensorNode in turn implements the X3DSensorNode type, and includes the fields shown in Table 12.2.

The enabled and isActive fields have consistent behavior for all sensor nodes.

Type	accessType	Name	Default	Range	Profile
SFBool	inputOutput	enabled	true		Interactive
SFBool	outputOnly	isActive			Interactive
SFNode	inputOutput	metadata	NULL	[X3DMetadataObject]	Core

Table 12.2. Field Definitions for X3DNetworkSensorNode Type

2.3. X3DSoundNode type

X3DSoundNode is the base type for the Sound node and any related extensions. It is minimalist, mainly supporting the marker design pattern that designates specific unique types. This abstract node type has the interface definition shown in Table 12.3.

Type	accessType	Name	Default	Range	Profile
SFNode	inputOutput	metadata	NULL	[X3DMetadataObject]	Core

Table 12.3. Field Definition for X3DSoundNode Type

2.4. X3DSoundSourceNode type

X3DSoundSourceNode is the base type for the AudioClip and MovieTexture nodes, as well as any related extensions. This abstract node type has the interface definitions shown in Table 12.4.

X3DSoundSourceNode fields are described in the AudioClip node section.

3. Node descriptions

3.1. LoadSensor node

LoadSensor keeps track of progress and completion when downloading external file resources. Thus it is often used as a triggering node in event-animation chains. This capability lets authors carefully delay the commencement of scene animations by waiting until relevant image textures, sounds, and X3D files are properly loaded before commencing an animation sequence.

Type	accessType	Name	Default	Range	Profile
SFString	inputOutput	description	""		Immersive
SFBool	inputOutput	loop	false		Immersive
SFTime	inputOutput	pitch	1.0	[0,∞)	Immersive
SFTime	inputOutput	pauseTime	0	(−∞, ∞)	Immersive
SFTime	inputOutput	resumeTime	0	(−∞, ∞)	Immersive
SFTime	inputOutput	startTime	0	(−∞, ∞)	Immersive
SFTime	inputOutput	stopTime	0	(−∞, ∞)	Immersive
MFString	inputOutput	url	""	[urn]	Immersive
SFTime	outputOnly	duration_changed			Immersive
SFTime	outputOnly	elapsedTime			Immersive
SFBool	outputOnly	isActive			Immersive
SFBool	outputOnly	isPaused			Immersive
SFNode	inputOutput	metadata	NULL	[X3DMetadataObject]	Core

Table 12.4. Field Definitions for X3DSoundSourceNode Type

The LoadSensor node is in the Immersive profile. LoadSensor implements the X3DNetworkSensorNode and X3DSensorNode abstract node types. The node has the fields defined in Table 12.5. Node syntax is shown in Table 12.6.

Type	accessType	Name	Default	Range	Profile
SFBool	inputOutput	enabled	true		Immersive
SFTime	inputOutput	timeOut	0	[0, ∞)	Immersive
MFNode	inputOutput	watchList	[ ]	[X3DUrlObject]	Immersive
SFBool	outputOnly	isActive			Immersive
SFBool	outputOnly	isLoaded			Immersive
SFTime	outputOnly	loadTime			Immersive
SFFloat	outputOnly	progress		[0,1]	Immersive
SFNode	inputOutput	metadata	NULL	[X3DMetadataObject]	Core

Table 12.5. Field Definitions for LoadSensor Node

XML Syntax (.x3d)	ClassicVRML Syntax (.x3dv)

``
<LoadSensor DEF="MyLoadSensor"
   enabled="true"
   timeOut="100">
   <Image Texture   USE="TextureNode1"
                  containerField="watchList"/>
   <AudioClip   USE="AudioNode2"
                  containerField="watchList"/>
   <Inline   USE="InlineScene3"
                  containerField="watchList"/>
</LoadSensor>
``
	``
	DEF MyLoadSensor
	   LoadSensor {
	    enabled TRUE
	    timeOut 100
	    watchList [USE
	    TextureNode1,
	    USE AudioNode2,
	    USE
	    InlineScene3]
	}
	``

Table 12.6. Node Syntax for LoadSensor

The LoadSensor node allows an author to monitor the downloading of images, sounds, or scenes that are referenced by url values within the X3D world. Any node with a url field implements the X3DUrlObject interface and can thus be monitored. One or more nodes may be monitored by each LoadSensor. LoadSensor treats all of the specified watchList nodes as a single group when computing progress and completion. Therefore, a successful load means that all of the listed nodes had a successful url download within the timeout period. If any url resource fails to load within the timeout period, then the overall result is an unsuccessful load.

Note that ExternProtoDeclare statements contain a url field but they cannot be monitored by LoadSensor.

3.1.1. isActive

This field is only true while the LoadSensor is actively monitoring downloads. An isActive true event is sent when the first download starts (which is not necessarily the first node listed in watchList). Eventually an isActive false event is sent when all of the downloads succeed, a url resource fails to successfully download, or the timeout period expires without all url resources successfully completing.

3.1.2. timeOut

The timeOut field defines the maximum number of seconds that a LoadSensor waits for all url resources to load. The default value of 0 seconds means that there is no time limit for waiting, and the LoadSensor continues to be active until all loading has succeeded or failed. Be aware that the network resource might report failure rather than a timeOut condition, however. For example, an http resource may be unavailable or the local file system may report that a file is not found.

All of the child watchList nodes must successfully load within the timeOut period for the LoadSensor to report a successful load.

3.1.3. watchList

The watchList field typically contains USE references for the X3D nodes to monitor, with each listed as a separate node in the MFNode array. It is also possible to load nodes that are being initially defined in the watchList, though such nodes are not rendered and likely need DEF names so that they are actually usable later in the scene. Each node that is listed must implement X3DUrlObject, which simply means that the watched node must have a url field.

Note that independently defined nodes are independently downloaded. Because retrieved resources might change over time, each unique node of interest must have a separate LoadSensor watchList entry. Also note that url values are not listed in USE copies of nodes.

3.1.4. isLoaded and loadTime

When all of the watchList nodes have successfully loaded, then an isLoaded true event is sent. Otherwise an isLoaded false event is sent when the corresponding isActive false event is sent.

The loadTime event is only generated when all the watchList nodes are successfully loaded. As with other SFTime events, the timestamp and value of the event are simply the time when it is issued. When successful, the loadTime event has the same timestamp as the corresponding isLoaded true event.

3.1.5. progress

The status of loading external resources can be monitored through the progress field. Allowed values for the outputOnly progress event are between 0 and 1, inclusive. The specification only requires that the value of 1 be issued when all of the load resources are successfully downloaded. Values less than 1 indicate that some portion of the load resources being watched have not yet downloaded. Individual browsers are allowed to determine how often events are issued, as well as the precise meaning of values less than 1. Possible measures of progress include percentage of bytes loaded, percentage of files loaded, percentage of estimated time to finish, and so on.

3.1.6. Hints and warnings

It is a good practice to use LoadSensor as a starting trigger whenever an animation might otherwise proceed mysteriously or improperly because of a missing resource.

Use multiple LoadSensor nodes for monitoring and responding to progress among different, unrelated network-resource nodes.

Because an ExternProtoDeclare statement is not a node and does not implement the X3DUrlObject interface, it cannot be monitored by the LoadSensor watchlist even though it contains a url field definition. Using a Script initialize () method within the prototype declaration may be a useful way to signal when a ProtoInstance node is loaded, sending an appropriate output event.

Although it is a good practice to provide alternative addresses for url resources, it is not possible for LoadSensor to report which of several alternative url addresses actually succeeded. If such a degree of control is needed, a Script node might be used to sequentially provide individual-address MFString array values to a url field until the LoadSensor reports success.

3.2. ProximitySensor node

The ProximitySensor node detects changes in viewer position and orientation relative to a author-defined box deliminating the active volume of the sensor. Events are sent whenever the viewer enters or exits the box. This box is not visibly rendered but can nevertheless be adjusted by parent transformations. The sensor also reports changes in viewer position, orientation and centerOfRotation when the user is within the sensed box. Sensing and sending this information to other animation nodes via ROUTE statements allows a scene to detect (and react to) user exploration within a scene.

ProximitySensor is in the Interactive profile. The field definitions for ProximitySensor are shown in Table 12.7. Node syntax is shown in Table 12.8.

Type	accessType	Name	Default	Range	Profile
SFVec3f	inputOutput	center	0 0 0	$(-\infty, \infty)$	Interactive
SFVec3f	inputOutput	size	0 0 0	$[0, \infty)$	Interactive
SFBool	inputOutput	enabled	true		Interactive
SFBool	outputOnly	isActive			Interactive
SFTime	outputOnly	enterTime			Interactive
SFTime	outputOnly	exitTime			Interactive
SFVec3f	outputOnly	centerOfRotation_changed			Immersive
SFRotation	outputOnly	orientation_changed			Immersive
SFVec3f	outputOnly	position_changed			Immersive
SFNode	inputOutput	metadata	NULL		Core

Table 12.7. Field Definitions for ProximitySensor

XML Syntax (.x3d)	ClassicVRML Syntax (.x3dv)

`<ProximitySensor DEF="MyProximitySensor"`
`   center="10 20 30"`
`   size="40 40 40"/>`
	`DEF MyProximitySensor`
	`    ProximitySensor {`
	`    center 10 20 30`
	`    size 40 40 40`
	
	`}`

Table 12.8. Node Syntax for ProximitySensor

ProximitySensor implements the fields defined for the X3DEnvironmentSensorNode abstract node type. Descriptions for center, size, enabled, isActive, enterTime, and exitTime are described in section 2.1.

The ProximitySensor defines a 3D rectangular volume in the world and monitors the user's viewing activity within that volume. Any changes are detected and reported through various events. For example, a single enterTime event is sent when a user enters the defined volume, and a single exitTime event is sent when the user leaves the defined volume. While the user's view position is located inside the monitored region, all changes to position and orientation are reported as they occur.

Changes in the user view can occur either by binding a new Viewpoint node or by navigating within the scene. Such camera navigation may itself be animated, for example by using ROUTE statements to send the outputs of a PositionInterpolator and OrientationInterpolator directly to a Viewpoint node's position and orientation fields.

The monitored region's location and size are adjustable during run-time. If the view is outside the monitoring region, or if this sensor node is disabled (`enabled="false"`), then no changes are reported.

If a single ProximitySensor has multiple instances that are translated and rotated to different locations, then the boundary used for isActive, enterTime, and exitTime events matches the union of all of the boxes defined by the various instances. If all of the boxes are non-overlapping, then the position and orientation output events are also generated corresponding to the center of the activated region. If any of the boxes overlap, then the event outputs position_changed, orientation_changed, and centerOfRotation_changed are undefined and cannot be expected to work properly.

3.2.1. center and size

The center and size fields define the monitored region. Each can be changed during run time, by sending an SFVec3f value for *x-y-z* position via a ROUTE statement to the node's center (or set_center) field, or by using a ROUTE statement to send an SFVec3f value to the size (or set_size) field. See section 2.1.1 for a basic description of center and size field functionality.

Note that any change to the center or size fields might change the proximity relationship of the current view and can cause the appropriate sensor output events to be generated. For example, if the value of the center field is shifted so that the current user view falls within the monitored region, the ProximitySensor produces isActive true, position_changed, orientation_changed, and enterTime events. Similarly, changing the value of the center field so that the current view changes from inside to outside the monitored region causes the ProximitySensor to emit isActive false, exitTime, position_changed, and orientation_changed events. In this second case, the final values of position_changed and orientation_changed indicate where the user left the region of interest.

3.2.2. centerOfRotation_changed

This field monitors the centerOfRotation value provided during `<NavigationInfo type="LOOKAT">` navigation mode. When the viewer's LOOKAT point changes, an event is emitted by this field specifying the new point. Changes to the LOOKAT point can be instituted by changes to the ProximityNode's parent coordinate system, changing the bound Viewpoint node, changing the centerOfRotation field in the currently bound Viewpoint node, or changing the Viewpoint node's parent Transform. These changes are only reported if the currently bound NavigationInfo type values include "LOOKAT" as an allowed navigation mode.

3.2.3. orientation_changed

The output value of orientation_changed changes whenever the current view is rotated within the monitored region or whenever its orientation relative to the ProximitySensor's coordinate system changes. This can happen if either the current view or else the orientation of the ProximitySensor itself rotates. Note that a simple rotation does not necessarily generate position_changed events.

3.2.4. position_changed

The position_changed field reports changes in current view location relative to the center of the ProximitySensor node's coordinate system.

3.2.5. Examples

The following figures show different configurations of various ProximitySensor nodes. Note that in all of the images, the outlined orange translucent box is the boundary of the sensor. This semitransparent box is meant for illustrative purposes only, because the ProximitySensor node does not present any geometry on its own. Navigating through any of these worlds results in local position and orientation being sensed by the ProximitySensor and then being printed on the browser console.

At the top of Figure 12.1 is a single ProximitySensor in the scene graph (ProximitySensorSingle.x3d). The middle section (ProximitySensorMultiple.x3d) contains three different ProximitySensors. Each sensor operates independently of the others when generating events. The bottom of the figure (ProximitySensorNoOverlap.x3d) contains a single ProximitySensor that has been multiply instanced by DEF and USE copies. Each sensor is non-overlapping, so events are generated within any of the sensor regions.

Note that although more examples might be produced showing DEF and USE ProximitySensor copies that overlap, such usage is problematic and needs to be avoided because results are undefined.

Figure 12.2 (ProximitySensor.x3d) shows a single ProximitySensor being used to track viewer position and orientation to control a heads-up display (HUD). The viewer's location is obtained from the ProximitySensor and sent through a Script node for datatype conversion. The output of the Script node is then sent via a ROUTE statement to translate the HUD panel to follow the current view location. The net effect is that the HUD panel stays in the same screen location regardless of any user navigation.

Note that it is important to set the relative z-coordinate to be negative. A positive value places contained geometry behind the viewpoint, where it is not visible. Usually, a

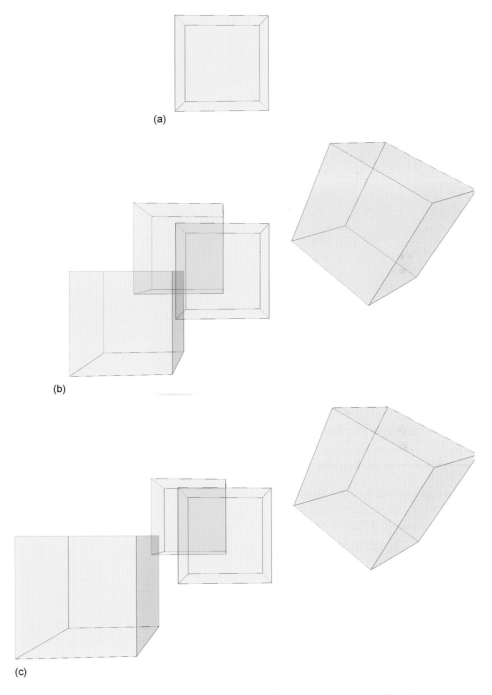

Figure 12.1. Example configurations and uses of ProximitySensor: (a) a single ProximitySensor, (b) multiple independent ProximitySensors, and (c) a single ProximitySensor with multiple instances.

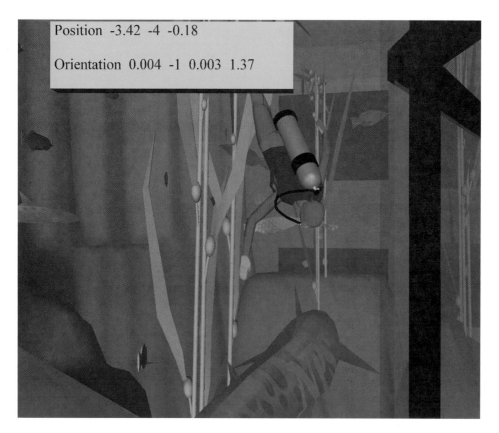

Figure 12.2. ProximitySensor reporting position and orientation in a Heads-Up Display (HUD), stabilizing HUD screen location.

HUD is positioned near the viewer, always staying visible and obscuring other geometry in the scene. Some viewpoints in this example show geometry that gets between the viewpoint and the HUD.

3.2.6. Hints and warnings

Positioning a ProximitySensor at the origin with an extremely large size, for example `<ProximitySensor center="0 0 0" size="1000000 1000000 1000000"/>` at the root of a scene, provides absolute viewer position and orientation anywhere in a world.

Take care to account for any parent transformation above the ProximitySensor, either within the same scene or when the ProximitySensor is inlined as part of another scene.

Multiple separate ProximitySensor nodes may intersect and cover the same volume of space. Each node reacts to user proximity independently, and each node sends its own events in response.

3.3. VisibilitySensor node

The VisibilitySensor node detects whether a specified volume of space is visible from the current user view. It is similar to ProximitySensor but does not detect whether the current user's view is within a predefined region. Rather it merely detects whether the specified boxlike volume of space is visible to the user. Such visibility depends on the direction as well as the position of the current user view.

In general, this capability allows scenes to respond in a timely manner when certain regions become visible, regardless of which direction a user uses to approach (or leave) the region of interest. Intermediate occluding geometry between the current viewpoint and the sensed volume has no effect on the behavior of the VisibilitySensor.

VisibilitySensor is ordinarily used to attract a viewer's interest by switching new geometry into view or activating relevant animation behaviors. Sometimes it is used to carefully build in performance improvements, such as switching out large blocks of unseen shapes or deactivating irrelevant behaviors when they are no longer visible.

VisibilitySensor is in the Interactive profile. The fields for VisibilitySensor are shown in Table 12.9. Node syntax is shown in Table 12.10.

Type	accessType	Name	Default	Range	Profile
SFVec3f	inputOutput	center	0 0 0	$(-\infty, \infty)$	Immersive
SFVec3f	inputOutput	size	0 0 0	$[0, \infty)$	Immersive
SFBool	inputOutput	enabled	true		Immersive
SFBool	outputOnly	isActive			Immersive
SFTime	outputOnly	enterTime			Immersive
SFTime	outputOnly	exitTime			Immersive
SFNode	inputOutput	metadata	NULL	[X3DMetadataObject]	Core

Table 12.9. Field Definitions for VisibilitySensor

XML Syntax (.x3d)	ClassicVRML Syntax (.x3dv)

`<VisibilitySensor DEF="MyVisibilitySensor"`
`  center="10 20 30"`
`  size="10 8 4"/>`
	`DEF MyVisibilitySensor`
	`    VisibilitySensor {`
	`      center 10 20 30`
	`      size 10 8 4`
	`    }`

Table 12.10. Node Syntax for VisibilitySensor

VisibilitySensor implements all of the fields defined for X3DEnvironmentSensorNode (and no others). Descriptions for center, size, enabled, isActive, enterTime, and exitTime are explained in section 2.1.

The VisibilitySensor node is sometimes used to control animations in a specified region of space. A "welcome" animation might try to flag a user's interest. Similarly, when an animation is no longer visible, it can be turned off without affecting the user's view of the world.

VisibilitySensor can also be connected via two IntegerTrigger nodes and ROUTE statements to a Switch node to remove large scene subgraphs from active rendering. For large animations, this approach can reduce the computational load on the processor, reduce requirements for texture memory on the graphics card, and generally speed up browser responsiveness. Such improvements in rendering time are especially important when managing performance in large scenes.

3.3.1. Hints and warnings

Take care to account for any parent transformations above the VisibilitySensor, either within the same scene or when included within another scene via an Inline node.

It is usually a good authoring practice to make the overall volume of a VisibilitySensor fairly large. This can ensure that moving geometry remains within the visibility region throughout the entire animation cycle.

3.4. Sound node

The Sound node identifies the source, location, intensity, direction, and spatial characteristics for a sound source in the scene. The source audio is provided by a child AudioClip node, which retrieves and controls the appropriate audio source. Multiple stationary and moving sounds can be defined within a scene, providing the potential to greatly improve model realism and user engagement.

The Sound node is in the Immersive profile and implements the X3DSoundNode abstract type. Sound includes the fields defined in Table 12.11. Node syntax is shown in Table 12.12.

Including an AudioClip child node as the source field is integral to the proper construction of a Sound node in a scene. These two nodes work together, but have been designed for separate definitions in order to decouple audio file loading (or streaming) from sound spatialization in the scene.

The Sound node has an interesting set of underlying concepts and fields. These fields are described in the following sections.

3.4.1. Sound attenuation and 3D spatialization

If all sounds were equally loud in a 3D scene, scene navigation would be confusing and contradictory, because no sense of location or distance would be communicated to the user. Instead, sound must properly and intuitively support the overall experience when the user is exploring and interacting with 3D geometry. This design requirement

Type	accessType	Name	Default	Range	Profile
SFVec3f	inputOutput	location	0 0 0	$(-\infty,\infty)$	Immersive
SFVec3f	inputOutput	direction	0 0 1	$(-\infty,\infty)$	Immersive
SFFloat	inputOutput	intensity	1	[0,1]	Immersive
SFFloat	inputOutput	priority	0	[0,1]	Immersive
SFBool	inputOutput	spatialize	true		Immersive
SFFloat	inputOutput	minFront	1	$[0,\infty)$	Immersive
SFFloat	inputOutput	minBack	1	$[0,\infty)$	Immersive
SFFloat	inputOutput	maxFront	10	$[0,\infty)$	Immersive
SFFloat	inputOutput	maxBack	10	$[0,\infty)$	Immersive
SFNode	inputOutput	source	NULL	[X3DSoundSourceNode]	Immersive
SFNode	inputOutput	metadata	NULL	[X3DMetadataObject]	Core

Table 12.11. Field Definitions for Sound Node

XML Syntax (.x3d)	ClassicVRML Syntax (.x3dv)
```<Sound DEF="MySoundNode"` ` location="0 0 0"` ` direction="0 0 1"` ` intensity="1"` ` priority="0"` ` spatialize="true"` ` minFront="1"` ` minBack="1"` ` maxFront="10"` ` maxBack="10">` ` <AudioClip containerField="source"/>` `</Sound>```	```DEF MySoundNode Sound {` ` location 0 0 0` ` direction 0 0 1` ` intensity 1` ` priority 0` ` spatialize TRUE` ` minFront 1` ` minBack 1` ` maxFront 10` ` maxBack 10` ` source AudioClip { }` `}```

Table 12.12. Node Syntax for Sound Node

is accomplished through spatialization of sound intensity and direction. Fortunately, most modern computers include two or more speakers and sufficient computational power to handle simultaneous 3D graphics and 3D sound.

The Sound node enables sound-spatialization capabilities by providing fields that define sound location, direction, and relative intensity. This allows an author to place sound sources where they belong. For example, an opening door might squeak or a light switch might click. Because the location of a Sound node can also move, an automobile sound (for example) can move right along with the moving car geometry.

The X3D specification further defines several algorithms for determining how loudly a sound is played, based on user position and orientation in the world relative to the location of the sound source. Figure 12.3 illustrates how overall sound intensity is further reduced in the right and left channels, corresponding to what is heard by the right and left ears relative to the user's view.

Sound sources in the real world are not always omnidirectional. Often sound intensity is stronger along one direction than along another. Because browsers can automatically compute sound attenuation based on relative direction and distance, authors are also able to control sound directionality.

X3D enables further spatialization of sound by allowing authors to define two concentric 3D ellipsoids of interest that represent the inner and outer bounds of varying sound intensity. When the user's position is inside the inner ellipsoid, the sound level is constant

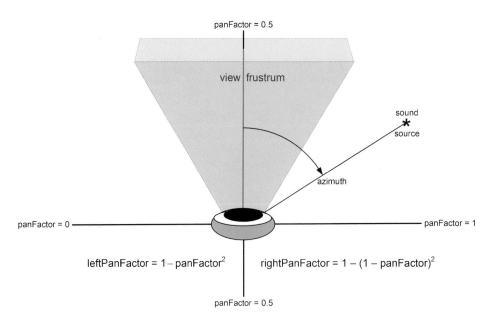

Figure 12.3. Stereo-panning algorithm for attenuation of sound intensity is based on the azimuth angle relative to the user's current view direction.

and at the defined maximum intensity level. Between the inner and outer ellipsoids, sound intensity gradually decreases and is attenuated linearly. Outside the boundary of the outer ellipsoid, the sound level is so low that a sound is considered inaudible.

One exception to the linear-dropoff relationship is specified: logarithmic-dropoff calculations are used if a maxFront or maxBack distance is more than 10 times greater than the corresponding minFront or minBack distance.

The inner ellipsoid is a good real-world approximation because minor sound-intensity variations do not matter when close by, although relative direction is still significant. The boundary provided by the outer ellipsoid is also a good approximation for how distant sounds become negligible and inaudible. The linear dropoff between inner and outer ellipsoids is a simple linear approximation of actual logarithmic dropoff effects, intended to reduce the browser's computational load. A linear (rather than logarithmic) dropoff also means that authors are much better able to define the outer boundary of where a sound remains audible. Together, these three step-ramp-step changes in intensity provide adequate realism for real-time audio rendering and user cues when navigating within a 3D scene.

Figure 12.4 shows in detail how attenuation levels and ellipsoids are defined and calculated for a sound node. The upper graph provides the attenuation (sound-reduction) response characteristic for audio volume, which varies as a function of distance

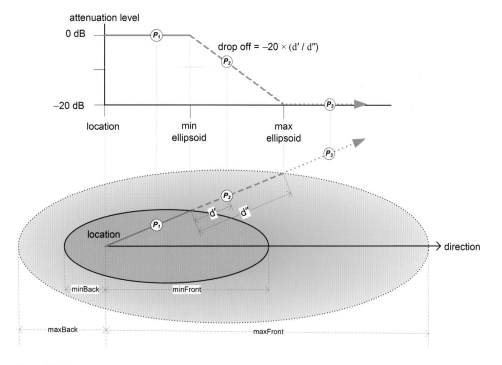

Figure 12.4. Sound ellipsoids correspond to linear spatialization boundaries for attenuation of Sound node intensity.

between the sound's location and the user's position. In turn, this upper graph directly corresponds to the red diagonal line that cuts across the maximum and minimum sound ellipses in the lower diagram.

Computation of sound-level intensity is performed along the vector connecting the user to the location of the sound source. The red-line attenuaton characteristic in the upper graph corresponds to the red-line user trajectory cutting through the sound ellipsoids shown in the lower plot.

Three example points of interest are shown in Figure 12.4: P_1, P_2, and P_3. Each falls along the straight red line moving away from the sound-source location. Point P_1 falls within the inner ellipsoid, and so receives full intensity. Point P_2 is between the inner and outer ellipsoids, and thus receives a linearly scaled reduction in intensity corresponding to $-20 \times (d' / d'')$. P_3 falls outside the outer ellipsoid and thus receives a -20dB reduction in sound-source intensity, meaning that there is effectively no audible contribution from the sound source at this distance. Each intensity level and user-view direction are further subject to the left–right panning attenuation algorithm, depending on listener orientation, as described in Figure 12.3.

Future X3D revisions may include a higher-fidelity physically based sound model capable of more realistic reflections, reverberations and aural rendering.

It is interesting to note that an ellipse can be uniquely defined by a focus point and the semimajor axis. Thus a Sound node uniquely defines an ellipsoid by providing a single focus location along with back and front distances. Figure 12.5 derives the corresponding geometric relationships, including the semiminor-axis width of the resulting ellipsoid. The

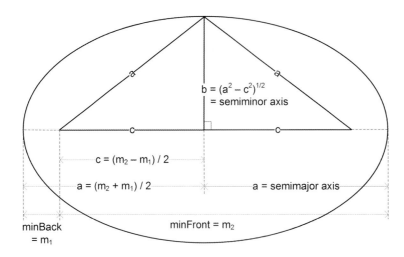

Example values for this diagram:

minBack=1 and minFront=9 produce ellipse a=5, b=3, c=4

Figure 12.5. Derivation and example values for an ellipse semiminor axis, given focus location and front/back distances. The upper plot shows intensity values corresponding to boundaries in the lower diagram.

diagram shows a cross-section of the ellipsoid, which is an ellipse that passes through the central longitudinal axis.

The derivation is based on the geometric theorem stating that the sum of any two line segments connecting the left and right foci to a point on the perimeter of an ellipse equals the full length of the major axis. This particular derivation assumes that front values are greater than back values. Similar relationships hold for the opposite condition. If front values equal back values, then a sphere results.

Further derivations shown in Figure 12.6 provide two equations for ellipsoid half width of the minimum and maximum sound-volume boundaries. These computations are based on the minFront, minBack, maxFront, and maxBack values defined in a Sound node. The minimum and maximum ellipses are calculated independently.

More field descriptions for the Sound node are given in the following sections.

3.4.2. location and direction

The location field is the local offset for positioning the sound source. The direction field is a unit x-y-z vector defining the longitudinal axis of the ellipsoids, pointing in the

$$minHalfWidth = b_{min} = \sqrt{a^2 - c^2}$$

$$= \sqrt{\left[\frac{m_1 + m_2}{2}\right]^2 - \left[\frac{m_1 - m_2}{2}\right]^2}$$

$$= \frac{1}{2}\sqrt{m_1^2 + 2m_1m_2 + m_2^2 - \left(m_1^2 - 2m_1m_2 + m_2^2\right)}$$

$$= \frac{1}{2}\sqrt{2m_1m_2 + 2m_1m_2}$$

$$= \frac{1}{2}(2)\sqrt{m_1m_2} = \sqrt{m_1m_2}$$

$$minHalfWidth = \sqrt{minBack \cdot minFront}$$

similarly

$$maxHalfWidth = \sqrt{maxBack \cdot maxFront}$$

Figure 12.6. Derivation of ellipsoid minHalfWidth and maxHalfWidth.

direction of maximum sound intensity. Because sound location and direction are affected by translations, rotations, and scaling in the parent transformation hierarchy, a Sound node is usually placed right next to the corresponding geometry of interest. This usually makes animation of moving sounds quite simple, because they simply follow along with the visible geometry of the node of interest.

3.4.3. intensity

The intensity field provides a factor in the range [0,1] that adjusts the loudness of the emitted sound. This field is useful for normalizing the relative strengths of different sound sources, each of which may vary in loudness.

3.4.4. priority

It is possible that the client browser might not be able to play all of the sounds activated by an author at a single time. The priority field is a hint for browsers regarding which sound source to choose if limited system resources or heavy computational loading preclude playback of all active sound sources at once. The priority field ranges from 0 to 1, with 1 being the highest priority. The X3D specification provides a recommended algorithm for prioritizing multiple sounds based on a combination of priority value, most recent startTime when priority is greater than 0.5, and greatest overall intensity.

If the priority value is less than 0 or greater than 1, then the appropriate browser response is undefined. This usually means an erroneous condition, although the browser is free to ignore the problem and not report an error. The X3D specification only occasionally defines a required response to error conditions, in order to help browser builders keep X3D implementations as lightweight and efficient as possible.

3.4.5. spatialize

The spatialize field determines whether full sound rendering occurs. If `spatialize="false"` then 3D directional attenuation is ignored, but ellipsoid-based attenuation and intensity effects are still calculated. By default, `spatialize="true"` and so this field is rarely changed.

3.4.6. minFront and minBack

The minFront and minBack fields define the extent of the inner ellipsoid, which is the region where sound level is kept at full intensity regardless of the distance between the sound location and the user position.

3.4.7. maxFront and maxBack

The maxFront and maxBack fields define the extent of the outer ellipsoid. Between the inner (min) and outer (max) ellipsoids, sound level decreases linearly based on the range between ellipsoid boundaries.

When the user's position is outside of the outer ellipsoid, the sound level is reduced by 20dB from the original intensity and is usually inaudible.

3.4.8. source

The source field refers to the X3D node providing audio information to be rendered by the Sound node. Usually the source field is a child AudioClip node. It is interesting that a MovieTexture node can also be used, allowing the movie soundtrack (and not the MovieTexture images) to serve as the input audio signal for the Sound node.

The AudioClip node is described in the following section. MovieTexture is described in Chapter 5, Appearance, Material, and Textures.

3.4.9. Hints and warnings

Ensure that *minFront* ≥ *maxFront* and *minBack* ≥ *maxBack*. All four distance values must be greater than or equal to zero.

Circular (omnidirectional) sound regions can be created by setting minFront equal to minBack and maxFront equal to maxBack.

Note that ellipsoids are 3D, so a user who is out of the horizontal plane might no longer be within the directional ellipsoid. Allowing generously large values for the inner and outer ellipsoids can help ensure that all users hear the sounds that are intended.

It is important to thoroughly test the response and effect of each sound node. Adding one or more viewpoints where the sound level is tested as audible is a good way to verify that a good user experience is provided. These viewpoints might then be commented out once testing is complete, or else retained as an integral part of scene design. The description field for each such Viewpoint node is a good place to note what can be heard at a given location and direction.

3.5. AudioClip node

An AudioClip node refers to an external audio file and provides control capabilities for starting, stopping, pausing, and resuming play.

The AudioClip node is in the Immersive profile and implements both the X3DSoundSourceNode and X3DUrlObject interfaces. In turn, the X3DSoundSourceNode implements the X3DTimeDependentNode interfaces. The AudioClip node includes the fields defined in Table 12.13. Node syntax is shown in Table 12.14.

Because AudioClip is an X3DSoundSourceNode and implements the X3DTimeDependentNode abstract type, it has a number of fields in common with TimeSensor. The loop, startTime, stopTime, pauseTime, resumeTime, elapsedTime, isActive, and isPaused fields are described as part of the TimeSensor node in Chapter 7, Event Animation and Interpolation. More fields are defined in the following sections.

Figure 12.7 (Sound.x3d) shows the 3D boundary between the various intensity regions. Using the notation from Figure 12.4, the P_1 region is the interior yellow sphere, P_2 is the region between the yellow sphere and the blue ellipsoid, and P_3 is exterior to the blue ellipsoid. The Sound node is located at the center of the sphere, symbolized by a speaker. It uses the parameters in Figure 12.5, enlarged by a factor of 10. Note that the straight-line edge of the ellipsoid is an artifact of the renderer. Also note that neither the Sound nor the AudioClip node generate any geometry.

Type	accessType	Name	Default	Range	Profile
SFString	inputOutput	description	""		Immersive
SFBool	inputOutput	loop	false		Immersive
SFTime	inputOutput	pitch	1.0	$[0,\infty)$	Immersive
SFTime	inputOutput	pauseTime	0	$(-\infty,\infty)$	Immersive
SFTime	inputOutput	resumeTime	0	$(-\infty,\infty)$	Immersive
SFTime	inputOutput	startTime	0	$(-\infty,\infty)$	Immersive
SFTime	inputOutput	stopTime	0	$(-\infty,\infty)$	Immersive
MFString	inputOutput	url	""	[urn]	Immersive
SFTime	outputOnly	duration_changed			Immersive
SFTime	outputOnly	elapsedTime			Immersive
SFBool	outputOnly	isActive			Immersive
SFBool	outputOnly	isPaused			Immersive
SFNode	inputOutput	metadata	NULL	[X3DMetadataObject]	Core

Table 12.13. Field Definitions for AudioClip Node

XML Syntax (.x3d)	ClassicVRML Syntax (.x3dv)

```<AudioClip DEF="MyAudioClipNode"```
``` description="an imaginary sound file"```
```url=' "HelloWorldLecture.wav"```
```   "http://x3dGraphics.com/audio/Hello```
```WorldLecture.wav"'```
``` loop="true"```
```/>```
	```DEF MyAudioClipNode AudioClip {```
	``` description "an imaginary```
	``` sound file"```
	```url ["HelloWorldLecture.wav"```
	``` "http://x3dGraphics.com/audio/```
	``` HelloWorldLecture.wav"]```
	``` loop TRUE```
	```}```

Table 12.14. Node Syntax for AudioClip

3.5.1. description

The description field is used to provide a short textual summary of what the sound is intended to signify. This text may be displayed by the browser, often in the same manner as sensor descriptions. In addition to documenting the title or intended significance of the audio file, the practice of including descriptions is especially important for providing proper user-accessibility hints. Such accessibility information assists users who are hearing impaired, as well as those users whose systems do not support audio output.

Figure 12.7. Boundary regions are shown for the Sound node. In this example, the outer region is an ellipsoid, and the inner region is a sphere.

3.5.2. isActive

The AudioClip sends an isActive true event when the node starts (or resumes) playing, and sends an isActive false event when the node stops (or pauses) playing.

While active, the current sound time for the clip being played is defined by the following relationship:

$$t_{sound} = (now - startTime) \text{ modulo } (duration / pitch)$$

3.5.3. loop

The AudioClip source repeats indefinitely when `loop="true"` and plays only once when `loop="false"`. A single play must be properly triggered by a current SFTime event to the startTime field.

3.5.4. url

The url field points to the location of the sound source of interest. The url might point to a file on local disk, an online http or https address, or to a streaming-audio protocol. More details on the url field appear in the Inline section in Chapter 3, Grouping Nodes.

Not all audio formats or streaming protocols are supported by all browsers. Such limitations may result from licensing fees or intellectual property rights (IPR) restrictions, as well as the size of related software-support playback libraries. Thus deciding on an appropriate sound format is sometimes difficult. X3D-compliant browsers are required to support at least the wavefile (uncompressed PCM) format (.wav). The X3D specification also recommends that browsers support both type 1 MIDI and MP3 compressed sound-file formats (.midi, .mp3). For special requirements, checking the browser software's technical release notes often reveals whether other formats are supported.

Format-mismatch difficulties are common for both sound and movie files. Unfortunately, translating audio files from one format to another often results in a reduction in sound quality. Such files also tend to be large. Nevertheless, providing more than one encoding for an audio source can be a good way to maintain scene and sound interoperability among multiple browsers.

If providing multiple audio encodings, it is best to digitize each from the original audio source rather than creating second- or third-generation copies of copies. Browsers skip unsupported formats and continue to look for a follow-up url resource that can be handled. It is a good authoring practice to place the address for the highest-quality audio file first in the url array, followed by an alternate address for a required encoding (such as a .wav or .mp3 file). This approach allows the nonstandard best-quality format to play preferentially while maintaining a well-supported backup.

3.5.5. pitch

The pitch field is a multiplication factor applied to sound sampling and playback. Pitch must be greater than 0 and defaults to 1 for normal playback. If pitch is greater than 1, then the audio frequency is increased, and playback is sped up accordingly. For example, `pitch="2"` plays notes one octave higher and at twice the regular playback rate, resulting in half the duration of the original audio clip. Similarly a pitch value less than 1 proportionately lowers the frequency heard and slows down playback.

3.5.6. duration_changed

The duration_changed field is an outputOnly event that provides a value for normal sound-clip duration. It is sent whenever an AudioClip node first loads a sound source, when an AudioClip is added to the scene graph, or if the sound source specified by the url field is changed. The pitch value has no effect on reported duration length. A duration_changed value of −1 indicates that audio data is not yet loaded or remains unavailable (perhaps an unbounded streaming source).

3.5.7. Hints and warnings

The AudioClip node can be started, stopped, paused, and resumed in the same manner as the TimeSensor node. Techniques for these actions are described in Chapter 7, Event Animation and Interpolation; Chapter 8, User Interactivity Nodes; and Chapter 9, Event Utilities and Scripting.

It is important to utilize DEF labels and USE copies for an AudioClip node that might be used more than once in a scene. Otherwise a browser is likely to retrieve identical sound files multiple times. This can consume significant memory and may delay operation because of excessive network retrieval operations and local-system file-buffering difficulties.

It is a good authoring practice to provide a local backup audio file in case an online audio resource is unavailable. To do this, put the address for the local backup version as the last string value in the MFString url array. Such a backup might simply be an audio file stating that the online audio resource is unavailable.

LoadSensor can be used to detect when an AudioClip url resource becomes available.

4. Summary

4.1. Key ideas

Environment sensors are powerful ways to detect and respond to user navigation without requiring direct user interactivity. Events triggered by user proximity or user visibility can trigger animation effects that pull a user further into the immersive experience provided by an X3D scene.

Because browsers are allowed to begin presenting and animating an X3D scene even while supporting downloads are still in progress, the LoadSensor node fixes a long-standing deficiency in VRML97 and enables authors to wait until external resources are ready before commencing an animation.

Properly applied, the sound nodes can greatly increase the interactivity and immersiveness of 3D scenes by providing audio streams and cues of interest, spatially located and aurally rendered in context with the 3D shapes that they support.

4.2. Related nodes and concepts

Each of these nodes directly extends possible uses of the X3D event model. Thus, they can each work well with the authoring approaches presented in Chapter 7, Event Animation and Interpolation; Chapter 8, User Interactivity Nodes; and Chapter 9, Event Utilities and Scripting.

4.3. Next chapter

Chapter 13 presents the remaining X3D geometry nodes, showing how to create shapes using various representations of triangles and quadrilaterals.

Geometry Nodes, Part 4: Triangles and Quadrilaterals

There is no "royal road" to geometry.
—Euclid, to King Ptolemy I

1. What this chapter covers

Authors have a great deal of flexibility when creating X3D content, primarily because there are many different geometry nodes to choose from when building shapes. Some geometry nodes are quite detailed, providing direct control over individual coordinates when drawing points, lines, triangles, and polygons. Often these geometry nodes are also used by 3D conversion programs that export X3D from other file formats. Because of the emphasis on low-level detail, such geometry can be challenging to author by hand and sometimes is best handled by using geometry-aware modeling software.

This book covers the diversity of X3D geometry nodes in four separate chapters. Chapter 2 presents the basic primitive shapes and text. Chapter 6 covers the fundamental polygonal nodes most used by authors and authoring tools. Chapter 10 presents the Geometry2D nodes. This chapter covers the advanced geometry nodes providing access to lower-level, higher-performance 3D graphics-card capabilities. Such advanced features include normals (perpendicular vectors) as well as triangle-based and quadrangle-based geometric shapes.

Geometry nodes contain numerous common fields, each explained in section 2. This chapter then covers the following nodes: Normal, TriangleSet, TriangleStripSet, TriangleFanSet, QuadSet, IndexedTriangleSet, IndexedTriangleStripSet, IndexedTriangleFanSet, and IndexedQuadSet.

2. Concepts

This chapter presents the primitive triangle and quadrilateral nodes that can be used to build nearly any shape. Triangle and quadrilateral nodes are specifically designed to be highly efficient on modern graphics cards. The geometric data in these nodes only needs minimal optimization preprocessing before being sent down to the underlying rendering software and graphics-pipeline hardware. Typically triangulated polygonal geometry yields the highest possible display performance, which can be important for exceptionally large or detailed geometry.

As with the other geometry nodes, each of these geometry nodes can be paired with a sibling Appearance and Material (or Appearance and Texture) combination under the parent Shape node. However, finer-grained control of composed coloring for each point, line segment, polygon, or surface in the geometry is also possible by instead using the Color and Normal nodes. Either technique (Appearance or Color node) can be utilized, but not in combination.

2.1. Purpose and common functionality

Most objects that are defined and rendered in X3D are polygonal in nature. Node definitions may be abstract surfaces from a mathematical perspective (such as Sphere and Cone nodes) but results are constructed and drawn as polygonal surfaces. This means that most X3D geometric objects defined in a scene are usually reduced to triangles and quadrilaterals by the browser software prior to being rendered.

Complex geometry using the triangle nodes is usually produced by authoring tools, scanning devices, or file-format conversion software. Nevertheless these techniques can also be used directly by authors who have the patience to construct nodes using them.

Note that the QuadSet and IndexedQuadSet nodes are ordinarily considered part of the Full profile. However, some browsers do not support the Full profile but may support adding some of the other components. An alternative way to specify browser support for these quadrilateral nodes in a scene is to require the Interchange profile (or higher) with component CADGeometry level 1.

Example syntax follows in Table 13.1.

XML Syntax (.x3d)
| ```
<X3D version="3.1" profile="Interchange">
  <head>
    <component name="CADGeometry" level="1"/>
  </head>
  <Scene/>
</X3D>
``` |
| **ClassicVRML Syntax (.x3dv)** |
| ```
#X3D V3.1 utf8
PROFILE Interchange
COMPONENT CADGeometry:1
``` |

Table 13.1. X3D Header Syntax for Scenes Using CADGeometry Component Nodes

Common characteristics of triangle-based and quadrilateral-based geometry nodes follow.

2.2. Abstract node types

Several node types are defined to properly support the X3D interface hierarchy.

2.2.1. X3DColorNode, X3DCoordinateNode, X3DGeometricPropertyNode, X3DGeometryNode, and X3DNormalNode types

The X3DColorNode, X3DCoordinateNode, X3DGeometricPropertyNode, X3DGeometryNode, and X3DNormalNode types are used to specifically identify corresponding nodes sharing common usages. Although unique, they each have the minimalist interface signatures shown in Table 13.2 in common.

The X3DColorNode interface is implemented by the Color and ColorRGBA nodes. The X3DCoordinateNode interface is implemented by the Coordinate and CoordinateDouble nodes. The X3DNormalNode interface is implemented by the Normal node.

Each of these interfaces is an example of the marker design pattern, meaning that they strictly define unique node types, and each is primarily used to ensure strong typing of node parent-child relationships. For example, only one copy each of the nodes implementing the X3DColorNode, X3DCoordinateNode, and X3DTextureNode interfaces are allowed as

Type	accessType	Name	Default	Range	Profile
SFNode	inputOutput	metadata	NULL	[X3DMetadataObject]	Core

Table 13.2. Common Field Definition for Various Geometry-Related Abstract Node Types

children inside the actual node implementing the X3DComposedGeometryNode type. Thus, a maximum of one Color node, one Coordinate node, and one ImageTexture node (or suitable substitutes) can be contained as a child node within the X3DComposedGeometryNode that is used.

2.2.2. X3DComposedGeometryNode type

The X3DComposedGeometryNode interface implements the X3DGeometryNode interface and adds many common fields, listed in Table 13.3. Essentially it can compose all renderable characteristics of a geometric shape by including Color/ColorRGBA, Coordinate/CoordinateDouble, Normal, and TextureCoordinate node information as contained child nodes.

2.3. Common geometry fields

Because the geometry nodes available in X3D are quite varied, there is only one primary X3DGeometryNode type. Geometry nodes implement the X3DGeometryNode interface as part of the marker design pattern to permit strong type checking during scene graph construction. Nodes implementing X3DGeometryNode are only allowed to be placed inside a Shape node, and cannot appear by themselves or next to other children nodes in the scene graph.

The X3DGeometryNode type does not require any specific field definitions, because of the diversity found in the variety of geometry nodes available. Nevertheless, many common fields can be found, and most of the primitive-geometry nodes defined in this chapter have common contained children: Color, Coordinate, Normal, and TextureCoordinate nodes. Common simple-type fields (such as colorPerVertex and normalPerVertex) also describe frequently used functionality and have consistent definitions. The most common combinations are included in the X3DComposedGeometryNode interface.

Type	accessType	Name	Default	Range	Profile
SFBool	initializeOnly	ccw	true		Interchange
SFBool	initializeOnly	colorPerVertex	true		Interchange
SFBool	initializeOnly	normalPerVertex	true		Interchange
SFBool	initializeOnly	solid	true		Interchange
SFNode	inputOutput	color	NULL	[X3DColorNode]	Interchange
SFNode	inputOutput	coordinate	NULL	[X3DCoordinateNode]	Interchange
SFNode	inputOutput	normal	NULL	[X3DNormalNode]	Interchange
SFNode	inputOutput	textureCoordinate	NULL	[X3DTextureCoordinateNode]	Interchange
SFNode	inputOutput	metadata	NULL	[X3DMetadataObject]	Core

Table 13.3. Common Field Definitions for X3DComposedGeometryNode Type

In addition to the fields supported by the X3DComposedGeometryNode interface, Table 13.4 lists two additional commonly occurring geometry fields. These fields are not part of X3DComposedGeometryNode because they are not consistently needed by many of the triangle-based nodes. Definitions for these fields can be found in Chapter 6, Geometry Nodes, Part 2 in section 6.2.2: common geometry fields.

Although no specific node type is defined, indexed geometry nodes also include the fields shown in Table 13.5.

Many of the concepts and fields applicable to the geometry nodes are likely familiar, having appeared in previous chapters. A particular strength of X3D is the consistency of field definitions of concepts, even when applied to different nodes. The appropriate sections on common field definitions in these prior chapters are worth familiarization and review.

- The solid field is described in Chapter 2, Geometry Nodes, Part 1: Primitives. The solid field indicates whether geometry consists of one complete shape, without internal structure or internal visibility. Setting `solid="true"` means that backface culling is turned on, and interior polygons are not drawn. Setting `solid="false"` means that both sides of each polygon are drawn.

- Chapter 5, Appearance, Material, and Textures includes a description of how a TextureCoordinate or TextureCoordinateGenerator node maps the pixels contained in texture images to specific vertex points defining the geometry.

- Chapter 6, Geometry Nodes, Part 2: Points, Lines, and Polygons explains several of the common geometry fields: ccw, colorPerVertex, convex, and creaseAngle.

The following sections contain further discussion regarding several simple-type (non-node) fields.

Type	accessType	Name	Default	Range	Profile
SFBool	initializeOnly	convex	true		Interchange
SFFloat	initializeOnly	creaseAngle	0	$[0, \infty)$	Interchange

Table 13.4. Additional Common Field Definition for Geometry Nodes

Type	accessType	Name	Default	Range	Profile
MFInt32	initializeOnly	index	[ ]	$[0, \infty)$ or -1	Interchange
MFInt32	inputOnly	set_index	[ ]	$[0, \infty)$ or -1	Interchange

Table 13.5. Common Field Definition for Indexed Geometry Nodes

2.3.1. Two-sided rendering versus backface culling, using the ccw and solid fields

As with other geometry nodes, the ccw and solid fields together determine whether one side, the other side, or both sides of all the defined triangles are rendered. The ccw field defines whether vertices are in counterclockwise order, which in turn determines the orientation of the triangles. As might be expected, the front side is determined based on normal-vector direction using the right-hand rule (RHR) when `ccw="true"`.

The direction of the thumb on the left hand can be used when the order of definitions is reversed because `ccw="false"` to determine the front side. Alternatively, the right-hand thumb points away from the back face (rather than the front face) when `ccw="false"`.

This directionality vector (meaning the normal vector) that determines which sides are front facing is also important when `solid="true"`. Setting the solid field to true means that one-sided triangles are drawn, because only the front-facing surfaces of a solid object (such as a red brick) are visible. The rendering subsystem does not generate pixels for backfaces of solid objects, leaving solid triangles transparent (and thus invisible) when viewed from behind. Another term for this process is backface culling, which reduces the number of polygons to be rendered by half. Whenever a model is considered to be a solid object, with no access to its interior, then the inside does not need to be rendered. This is an important performance optimization and is commonly used for the definition of detailed models with a high polygon count.

If `solid="false"`, then both sides of the triangles are rendered and the directionality indicated by the ccw field does not particularly matter. In effect, these two boolean values for ccw and solid are used to represent a ternary (three-valued) choice: two-sided, front-sided, or backface rendering.

2.3.2. Ordering or indexing of vertices, index, and set_index fields

Each of the polygonal geometry nodes presented in this chapter come in two varieties: ordered and indexed. The TriangleSet, TriangleFanSet, TriangleStripSet, and QuadSet nodes have ordered vertices. Meanwhile, the corresponding IndexedTriangleSet, IndexedTriangleFanSet, IndexedTriangleStripSet, and IndexedQuadSet nodes have indexed vertices and an index field.

The ordered versions of these nodes simply utilize coordinate vertices in order from the contained point values in the child Coordinate node. Thus each triplet of coordinates defines a triangle, or alternatively each 4-tuple of coordinates defines a quadrilateral. Adjacent vertices and line segments in ordered nodes must then be defined through exact repetition of coordinate values. Such repetition increases file size, sometimes significantly.

The unordered versions of these nodes instead rely on an index array to define the connectivity among point-field vertices in the child Coordinate node. Index values for coordinate-point data are integers that are numbered starting at zero, listing the coordinates of a polygon by index number. Adjacent vertices and line segments thus do not have to be redefined through repetition of coordinate values, as is the case in the ordered versions of the nodes. Instead, an index value is simply used again to point to the same coordinate value. Even with the added overhead of index values, eliminating repetition of 3-tuple vertex definitions can significantly reduce file size.

Similar to the IndexedFaceSet node (described in Chapter 6), the IndexedTriangleFanSet and IndexedTriangleStripSet nodes each have polygonal index sequences separated by a sentinel −1 value that indicates completion of each fan or strip, respectively.

In addition to possible file-size reduction, it is worth noting that both forms of each node are offered as a benefit to authors and conversion tools. Certain shapes or legacy models might be better suited to either ordered or indexed definition. Once loaded in the scene graph and rendered, however, each performs equivalently.

Of further note is that browsers may choose to further simplify geometry to improve performance once loaded. For large sets of polygons, authors can further encourage such run-time optimization by placing the parent Shape node under a StaticGroup node. This technique is only valuable when the geometry is not subject to further animation, however, since children of a StaticGroup cannot be modified after initial definition.

Because geometry is such an important candidate for such reduction, the index field array has accessType initializeOnly and need not be retained by the browser after loading. This means that a browser can reduce in-memory requirements and drop the (possibly quite large) index field once the defined geometry is created. Nevertheless, an additional set_index field with accessType inputOnly is also provided so that index values might be changed at runtime and the geometry can be animated. Such animation may also trigger recalculation of normals and shading for the underlying geometry, however, and so some author experimentation may be needed to ensure that performance of continuously changing animations remains adequate.

2.3.3. colorPerVertex

The coloring of the defined shape can be defined on a per-vertex (meaning per-point) or a per-face (meaning per-polygon) basis. The boolean field colorPerVertex determines whether the coloring is point-by-point (`colorPerVertex="true"`) or per face (`colorPerVertex="false"`). The color values are defined in the contained Color or ColorRGBA node. The colorPerVertex field has no effect when an Appearance node is instead used to color the geometry. If no Color node is provided, then the appearance properties (including defaults) defined in the parent Shape node apply.

2.3.4. normalPerVertex

The normalPerVertex field describes whether Normal node vector values are applied point-by-point (`normalPerVertex="true"`) or per polygon (`normalPerVertex="false"`).

When normal vectors are appled on a vertex-by-vertex basis, shading the interme-diate pixels between polygonal points occurs according to the governing equations of the lighting model. This can lead to interesting special effects. However, this technique is infrequently used. Normals are calculated automatically when not defined, and the cal-culation and modification of normals usually requires a special authoring tool to perform the necessary arithmetic operations.

2.3.5. Hints and warnings

Triangle vertices are always coplanar, because any triangle defines a unique plane surface. Quadrilateral vertices are expected to be defined using planar coordinate values, but might not be due to an authoring or generation error. Nonplanar quadrilaterals are ambiguously defined and so cannot be consistently rendered among different X3D browsers.

Setting `solid="false"` is a good troubleshooting technique for authors to find missing or hidden geometry, because it ensures that the renderer shows both sides of all polygons. On rediscovering such polygons that were transparent as a result of backface culling, it is often possible to reverse the value of the ccw field and then reset `solid="true"` to restore backface culling for the unneeded sides of the triangles.

Translated outputs from different formats and modeling tools can be inconsistent, so switching from `ccw="true"` to `ccw="false"` can sometimes reorient geometry properly. This technique can be especially helpful if only one side of the geometry is intended to be drawn.

Concave polygons can always be split into convex triangles, either manually or through the use of an authoring tool that splits and fixes concave polygons. Such optimization is a good authoring practice if a scene contains concave polygons. Unmodified concave polygons may render incorrectly (or not at all) on some systems.

Sufficient values must be provided for Color, Normal, and TextureCoordinate nodes to match the corresponding vertex values present in the Coordinate node.

Nonplanar polygons are problematic because there is no unambiguous way to tesselate the nonplanar vertices into planar triangles. Figure 13.1 shows 4 vertices of a

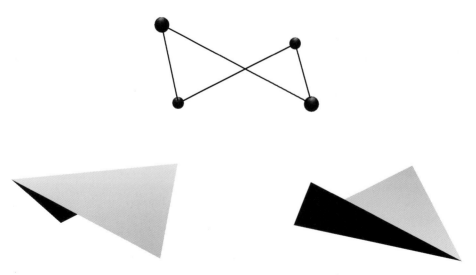

Figure 13.1. Nonplanar vertices in a single polygon are undesirable because triangulation possibilities are inherently ambiguous and unresolvable. Two quite-different pairs of triangles can be produced from a single set of four nonplanar points.

nonplanar polygon. Beneath that are two different representations of the structure implied by the four nonplanar points. Avoid defining nonplanar polygons.

3. Node descriptions

3.1. Normal node

Normals are perpendicular vectors used in lighting equations to properly color and shade geometric objects. Normals are typically computed automatically at load time by X3D browsers. Authors may precompute and provide normal values for geometry nodes by providing a child Normal node.

The Normal node is in the Interchange profile and implements the X3DNormalNode interface. Normal has the fields defined in Table 13.6. Node syntax is shown in Table 13.7.

Triangles and well-defined polygons are planar and have 2 sides. When the points defining the perimeter of a polygon are followed in order, the fingers of the right hand should be aligned to point in the direction of increasing index numbers. The thumb then naturally points perpendicularly in the positive direction of the normal vector.

Normal-vector values need to be normalized, meaning that the magnitude of each 3-tuple vector must equal 1. Failure to make normal vectors to a length of 1 is usually ignored without problems, but can sometimes lead to hardware faults on older graphics rendering cards. Unit normalization can be accomplished using the following equations.

Type	accessType	Name	Default	Range	Profile
MFVec3f	inputOutput	vector	NULL	$(-\infty, \infty)$	Interchange
SFNode	inputOutput	metadata	NULL	[X3DMetadataObject]	Core

Table 13.6. Field Definitions for Normal Node

XML Syntax (.x3d)	ClassicVRML Syntax (.x3dv)

`<Normal DEF="MyNormalNode" vector="0 0 0, 1 1 1"/>`	`DEF MyNormalNode Normal {`
	`  vector [0 0 0, 1 1 1]`
	`}`

Table 13.7. Node Syntax for Normal

For coordinate *point P* = <*x,y,z*>

$$\text{Magnitude } r = \sqrt{x^2 + y^2 + z^2}$$

$$\text{Normalized } P' = <\tfrac{x}{r}, \tfrac{y}{r}, \tfrac{z}{r}>$$

Normal vectors having zero length are degenerate and erroneous.

Note that the creaseAngle field, if present in the node of interest, influences how normals are calculated. If the angle between two adjacent faces is less than creaseAngle, then the normal vectors are generated so that edges are smoothly shaded (and visually appear rounded). Otherwise the normals are computed so that a sharp edge is visible, giving polygons a faceted appearance. When `creaseAngle="3.14159"`, (i.e., π radians or 180°) then normal values are calculated so that all edges are smoothly shaded.

Figure 13.2 shows three different normal vectors that provide differing degrees of shading.

Normals can be modified in this manner to change the appearance of objects, either while authoring or during run time. Ordinarily the normal vector remains unchanged as it interacts with lighting in the scene to produce the desired shading and specular reflections. Perpendicular normals for real world shapes do not vary either, so this stability is typical. Thus, run-time modification of normal values is a special visual effect.

Figure 13.3 shows how two identical objects appear with automatically calculated normals (top image) in contrast to specially assigned normals (bottom image). The normal vector is displayed at each vertex. Vertices where no normals are shown have normal vectors along the positive *z* direction (coming out of the page). The normals are interpolated to show possible shading variations. The example scene is Normal.x3d.

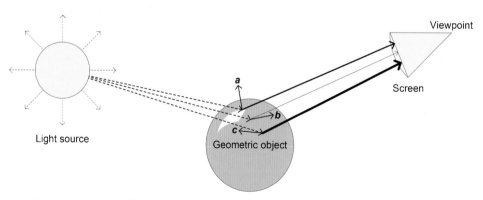

Normal vector *a*: direction perpendicular to geometry, regular shading for result
Normal vector *b*: oblique direction away from light, lower intensity for result
Normal vector *c*: near-parallel direction towards light, higher intensity for result

Figure 13.2. Varying a normal vector toward (or away from) a light source increases (or reduces) the computed intensity of a viewed pixel.

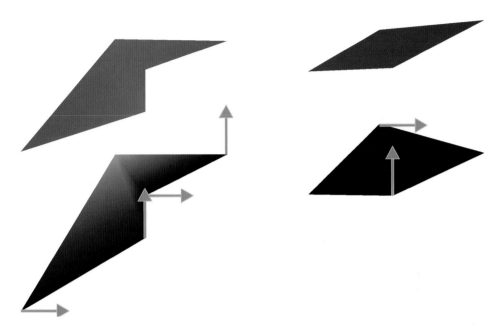

Figure 13.3. Modification of normals in the example scene demonstrates special effects that vary shading.

3.1.1. Hints and warnings

When not explicitly included via a Normal node, normals are automatically calculated by the X3D browser when loading a scene. This computation imposes a short, one-time delay at load time.

When polygonal geometry changes, normals usually must be recalculated. Such recomputation may be time consuming and reduce rendering performance if repeated every frame. Thus normal animation (as well as vertex modification) is best used sparingly for large geometry nodes.

Adding normal vectors may speed up computational preparations during loading, which is good, but they may also lead to delays because of the increased time needed for the network to download a scene. If this time factor is critical, it is a good idea to perform a few experimental measurements. Ordinarily, normal values are only added for artistic or animation-motivated display reasons and not for improving performance.

3.2. TriangleSet node

This is the most basic triangle node, defining a simple collection of triangles. The vertices of each triangle are defined in the contained Coordinate or CoordinateDouble node, where consecutive sets of 3-tuple coordinates define each vertex of each triangle. No coordinate indexing is performed because the coordinates are used in order to define the set of triangles.

Vertices can be duplicated or triangles may be disjoint (meaning unconnected). Any remaining vertex data insufficient to define a triangle is ignored.

The TriangleSet node is in the Interchange profile and implements the X3DComposedGeometryNode interface. TriangleSet has the fields defined in Table 13.8. Node syntax is shown in Table 13.9.

The example scene (TriangleSet.x3d) in Figure 13.4 shows three triangles with nine vertices. These same vertices are used throughout the examples in this chapter. The geometry is lit by the default headlight and colored by a Material node.

Type	accessType	Name	Default	Range	Profile
SFBool	initializeOnly	ccw	true		Interchange
SFBool	initializeOnly	colorPerVertex	true		Interchange
SFBool	initializeOnly	normalPerVertex	true		Interchange
SFBool	initializeOnly	solid	true		Interchange
SFNode	inputOutput	color	NULL	[X3DColorNode]	Interchange
SFNode	inputOutput	coord	NULL	[X3DCoordinateNode]	Interchange
SFNode	inputOutput	normal	NULL	[X3DNormalNode]	Interchange
SFNode	inputOutput	texCoord	NULL	[X3DTextureCoordinateNode]	Interchange
SFNode	inputOutput	metadata	NULL	[X3DMetadataObject]	Core

Table 13.8. Field Definitions for TriangleSet Node

XML Syntax (.x3d)	ClassicVRML Syntax (.x3dv)

`<TriangleSet DEF="MyTriangleSetNode"`
`  ccw="true"`
`  solid="false"`
`  colorPerVertex="true"`
`  normalPerVertex="true">`
`  <Color/>`
`  <Coordinate/>`
`  <Normal/>`
`  <TextureCoordinate/>`
`  <MetadataSet/>`
`</TriangleSet>`
	`DEF MyTriangleSet TriangleSet {`
	`  ccw TRUE`
	`  solid FALSE`
	`  colorPerVertex TRUE`
	`  normalPerVertex TRUE`
	`  color Color { }`
	`  coord Coordinate { }`
	`  normal Normal { }`
	`  texCoord TextureCoordinate { }`
	`  metadata MetadataSet { }`
	`}`

Table 13.9. Node Syntax for TriangleSet

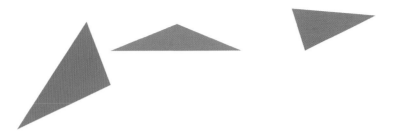

Figure 13.4. TriangleSet consisting of three triangles and nine separate vertices.

Because low-level animation control over individual vertex values is possible, the TriangleSet node can be used to *morph* one geometric shape into another. This example uses X3D animation capabilities for morphing shapes. This simple example (morphingTriangleSet.x3d) in Figure 13.5 shows a pyramid coarsely morphing into a cube. Each face of the pyramid is composed of three triangles, and each face of the cube is composed of two triangles. The image on the top left is the pyramid at the start of the animation. The bottom-right image is the cube after the morphing operation is complete. The bottom-left image shows the cube reverting back to the original pyramid.

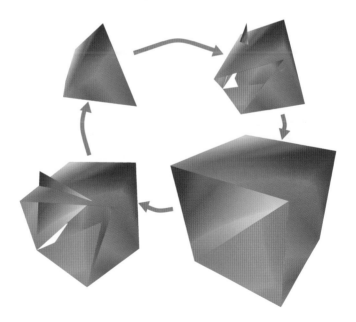

Figure 13.5. Morphing a pyramid into a cube by animating a TriangleSet. This sequence of images shows (clockwise from top left) an initial pyramid, intermediate pyramid to cube, cube, and intermediate cube to pyramid.

3.3. TriangleFanSet node

The TriangleFanSet node is an efficient way to generate geometry when there is a single vertex common to multiple triangles. The fanCount field is an array that lists the number of points to be used from the contained Coordinate node to construct each fan.

Each triangle in the fan is constructed from the latest point, the preceding point and the initial fan-center point. Thus, after the first triangle is defined, adding each subsequent triangle only requires the definition of a single point. Thus, a TriangleFanSet node can be an efficient way to define small sets of geometry.

The TriangleFanSet node is in the Interchange profile and implements the X3DComposedGeometryNode interface. TriangleFanSet has the fields defined in Table 13.10. Node syntax is shown in Table 13.11.

3.3.1. fanCount

The fanCount field is an array of integers that define the number of vertices in each triangle fan. The value of each fanCount element must be 3 or greater to define a valid fan, because the initial triangle in the fan requires three points.

Once an element of the fanCount array has been used to define a fan of triangles, the current fan is complete and a new fan (if any) may begin. The sum of all values in the fanCount array must not exceed the number of 3-tuple point values defined in the Coordinate node.

The TriangleFanSet node is illustrated in Figure 13.6 by example TriangleFanSet.x3d. It shows two fans, each colored by a Color node. Each vertex has a different color to make them easier to distinguish.

3.3.2. Hints and warnings

The fanCount field is an array containing the number of points in each individual fan. The length of the fanCount array (i.e., the number of values defined) is the actual count of how many fans are defined.

Type	accessType	Name	Default	Range	Profile
MFInt32	inputOutput	fanCount	[]	[3,∞)	Interchange
SFBool	initializeOnly	ccw	true		Interchange
SFBool	initializeOnly	colorPerVertex	true		Interchange
SFBool	initializeOnly	normalPerVertex	true		Interchange
SFBool	initializeOnly	solid	true		Interchange
SFNode	inputOutput	color	NULL	[X3DColorNode]	Interchange
SFNode	inputOutput	coord	NULL	[X3DCoordinateNode]	Interchange
SFNode	inputOutput	normal	NULL	[X3DNormalNode]	Interchange
SFNode	inputOutput	texCoord	NULL	[X3DTextureCoordinateNode]	Interchange
SFNode	inputOutput	metadata	NULL	[X3DMetadataObject]	Core

Table 13.10. Field Definitions for TriangleFanSet Node

XML Syntax (.x3d)	ClassicVRML Syntax (.x3dv)

``
<TriangleFanSet DEF="MyTriangle
        FanSetNode"
  fanCount="4"
  ccw="true"
  solid="false"
  colorPerVertex="true"
  normalPerVertex="true">
    <Color/>
    <Coordinate point="0 0 0, 0 1 0, 1 1 0,
      -.25 .5 .5"/>
    <Normal/>
    <TextureCoordinate/>
    <MetadataSet/>
</TriangleSet>
``
	``
	DEF MyTriangleFanSetNode
	        TriangleFanSet {
	  fanCount [4]
	  ccw TRUE
	  colorPerVertex TRUE
	  normalPerVertex TRUE
	  solid FALSE
	  color Color { }
	  coord Coordinate { }
	
	  normal Normal { }
	  texCoord TextureCoordinate
	    {point [0 0 0, 0 1 0, 1 1 0,
	      -.25 .5 .5]}
	  metadata MetadataSet { }
	}
	``

Table 13.11. Node Syntax for TriangleFanSet

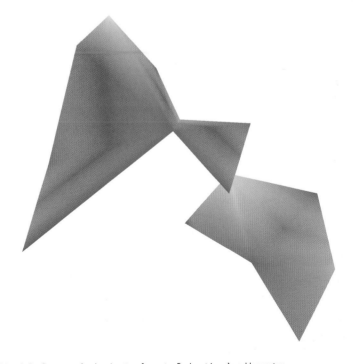

Figure 13.6. TriangleFanSet example showing two fan sets. Each set is colored by vertex.

The value of the colorPerVertex field is ignored and always treated as true.

When `normalPerVertex="true"` then the normal of a shared fan center vertex is computed as the average of all contributing triangles.

It is possible to create a fan that is self-intersecting.

3.4. TriangleStripSet node

The TriangleStripSet node is an efficient way to generate geometry when a long strip of triangles can be used to represent geometry. Each value in the stripCount array lists the number of consecutive points in the contained Coordinate node that are used to construct each strip. The strips may be disjoint.

Each triangle in the strip is constructed from the latest point and the two preceding points. Thus, after the first triangle is defined, adding each subsequent triangle only requires the further definition of a single point. As with TriangleFanSet, this is a relatively efficient representation of complex polygonal geometry that can reduce the size of large files with high-polygon-count shapes.

The TriangleStripSet node is in the Interchange profile and implements the X3DComposedGeometryNode interface. TriangleStripSet has the fields defined in Table 13.12. Node syntax is shown in Table 13.13.

3.4.1. stripCount

The field stripCount is an array of vertex counts that define the number of vertices consumed for the defined triangle strips. Each value in the stripCount array must be 3 or greater, because a minimum of three vertices are needed for the initial triangle in each strip.

Type	accessType	Name	Default	Range	Profile
MFInt32	inputOutput	stripCount	[]	[3,∞)	Interchange
SFBool	initializeOnly	ccw	true		Interchange
SFBool	initializeOnly	colorPerVertex	true		Interchange
SFBool	initializeOnly	normalPerVertex	true		Interchange
SFBool	initializeOnly	solid	true		Interchange
SFNode	inputOutput	color	NULL	[X3DColorNode]	Interchange
SFNode	inputOutput	coord	NULL	[X3DCoordinateNode]	Interchange
SFNode	inputOutput	normal	NULL	[X3DNormalNode]	Interchange
SFNode	inputOutput	texCoord	NULL	[X3DTextureCoordinateNode]	Interchange
SFNode	inputOutput	metadata	NULL	[X3DMetadataObject]	Core

Table 13.12. Field Definitions for TriangleStripSet Node

XML Syntax (.x3d)	ClassicVRML Syntax (.x3dv)
```<TriangleStripSet DEF="MyTriangle StripSetNode" stripCount="4" ccw="true" solid="false" colorPerVertex="true" normalPerVertex="true"> <Color/> <Coordinate point="0 0 0, 1 0 0, 1 1 0, −.25 .5 .5"/> <Normal/> <TextureCoordinate/> </TriangleStripSet>```	```DEF MyTriangleStripSet TriangleStripSet{ stripCount [4] ccw TRUE colorPerVertex TRUE normalPerVertex TRUE solid FALSE color Color {} coord Coordinate {point=[0 0 0, 1 0 0, 1 1 0, −.25 .5 .5]}normal Normal {} texCoord TextureCoordinate {} }```

Table 13.13. Node Syntax for TriangleStripSet

Once an element of the StripCount array has been used to define a strip of triangles, the current strip set is complete and a new strip (if any) may begin. Note that the total number of vertices in the Coordinate node must equal or exceed the sum of all values in the stripCount array.

The TriangleStripSet example in Figure 13.7 uses the same Coordinate node as the TriangleSet example. There are still nine vertices, but they form two separate triangle strips. Similar to the TriangleFanSet example, this geometry is colored with the Color node and each vertex has its own color.

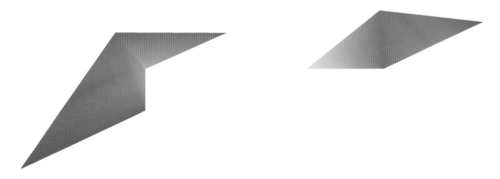

Figure 13.7. TriangleStripSet example using the same nine vertices used for TriangleSet example.

3.4.2. Hints and warnings

The stripCount field is an array containing the number of points in each individual strip. The length of the stripCount array (i.e., the number of values defined) is the actual count of how many strips are defined.

The value of the colorPerVertex field is ignored and always treated as true.

When `normalPerVertex="true"`, then the normal of a shared vertex is computed as the average of all contributing triangles.

It is possible to create a strip that is self-intersecting.

3.5. QuadSet node

QuadSet is the basic quadrilateral (quad) node that defines a collection of individual planar quadrilaterals. The set of quadrilaterals may be disjoint. The vertices of each quadrilateral are defined in the contained Coordinate node, which is also known as the coordinate field. Consecutive sets of four-point coordinate values define the four vertices of each quadrilateral. Any remaining vertex data insufficient to define a quadrilateral is ignored.

The QuadSet node is in the CADGeometry component and implements the X3DComposedGeometryNode interface. QuadSet has the fields defined in Table 13.14. Node syntax is shown in Table 13.15.

If a Normal node is not provided, normal vectors are computed perpendicular to the face of each (presumably planar) quadrilateral.

3.5.1. Hints and warnings

Noncoplanar vertices are erroneous and rendering of such quadrilaterals is ambiguous. Avoid this problem by ensuring that vertex coordinates are coplanar.

The value of the colorPerVertex field is ignored and always treated as true.

Quadrilaterals are similar to the Rectangle2D node. The QuadSet and IndexedQuadSet nodes were introduced as separate nodes in X3D V3.1 as part of the Computer Aided Design (CAD) profile, because quadrilaterals are commonly used in CAD models.

Any quadrilateral can be split into a pair of triangles, and so a quadrilateral node can be converted into a triangular node.

3.6. IndexedTriangleSet node

IndexedTriangleSet is the indexed version of the TriangleSet node. Indexing occurs for all child nodes (color, coord, normal, and texCoord fields), which allows for reuse of child nodes. The vertices of each triangle are defined in the Coordinate node's coordinate field.

Because only triangles are defined, no −1 sentinel values are used between consecutive triplet values in the index array.

Type	accessType	Name	Default	Range	Profile
SFBool	initializeOnly	ccw	true		Interchange + CADGeometry:1 component, or Full profile
SFBool	initializeOnly	colorPerVertex	true		Interchange + CADGeometry:1 component, or Full profile
SFBool	initializeOnly	normal PerVertex	true		Interchange + CADGeometry:1 component, or Full profile
SFBool	initializeOnly	solid	true		Interchange + CADGeometry:1 component, or Full profile
SFNode	inputOutput	color	NULL	[X3DColorNode]	Interchange + CADGeometry:1 component, or Full profile
SFNode	inputOutput	coord	NULL	[X3DCoordinateNode]	Interchange + CADGeometry:1 component, or Full profile
SFNode	inputOutput	normal	NULL	[X3DNormalNode]	Interchange + CADGeometry:1 component, or Full profile
SFNode	inputOutput	texCoord	NULL	[X3DTextureCoordinateNode]	Interchange + CADGeometry:1 component, or Full profile
SFNode	inputOutput	metadata	NULL	[X3DMetadataObject]	Core

Table 13.14. Field Definitions for QuadSet Node

The IndexedTriangleSet node is in the Interchange profile and implements the X3DComposedGeometryNode interface. IndexedTriangleSet has the fields defined in Table 13.16. Node syntax is shown in Table 13.17, with example values provided for the index array (but no corresponding point values provided for the child Coordinate node).

XML Syntax (.x3d)	ClassicVRML Syntax (.x3dv)

`<QuadSet DEF="MyQuadSetNode"`
`  ccw="true"`
`  solid="false"`
`  colorPerVertex="true"`
`  normalPerVertex="true">`
`    <Color/>`
`    <Coordinate/>`
`    <Normal/>`
`    <TextureCoordinate/>`
`    <MetadataFloat/>`
`</QuadSet>`
	`DEF MyQuadSet QuadSet {`
	`  ccw TRUE`
	`  colorPerVertex TRUE`
	`  normalPerVertex TRUE`
	`  solid FALSE`
	`  color Color { }`
	`  coord Coordinate { }`
	`  normal Normal { }`
	`  texCoord TextureCoordinate { }`
	`  metadata MetadataFloat { }`
	`}`

Table 13.15. Node Syntax for QuadSet

Type	accessType	Name	Default	Range	Profile
MFInt32	initializeOnly	index		[0, ∞)	Interchange
MFInt32	inputOnly	set_index		[0, ∞)	Interchange
SFBool	initializeOnly	ccw	true		Interchange
SFBool	initializeOnly	colorPerVertex	true		Interchange
SFBool	initializeOnly	normalPerVertex	true		Interchange
SFBool	initializeOnly	solid	true		Interchange
SFNode	inputOutput	color	NULL	[X3DColorNode]	Interchange
SFNode	inputOutput	coord	NULL	[X3DCoordinateNode]	Interchange
SFNode	inputOutput	normal	NULL	[X3DNormalNode]	Interchange
SFNode	inputOutput	texCoord	NULL	[X3DTextureCoordinateNode]	Interchange
SFNode	inputOutput	metadata	NULL	[X3DMetadataObject]	Core

Table 13.16. Field Definitions for IndexedTriangleSet Node

The values of the index array must be in the range between 0 (inclusive) and the length of the Coordinate point array (exclusive, i.e., less than the number of point values).

The example scene in Figure 13.8 is IndexedTriangleSet.x3d.

3.6.1. Hints and warnings

The value of the colorPerVertex field is ignored and always treated as true.

XML Syntax (.x3d)	ClassicVRML Syntax (.x3dv)
```<IndexedTriangleSet` ` DEF="MyIndexedTriangleSetNode"` ` index="0 1 2, 3 4 5"` ` ccw="true"` ` solid="false"` ` colorPerVertex="true"` ` normalPerVertex="true">` ` <Color/>` ` <Coordinate/>` ` <Normal/>` ` <TextureCoordinate/>` ` <MetadataString/>` `</IndexedTriangleSet>```	```DEF MyIndexedTriangleSet` ` IndexedTriangleSet {` ` index [0 1 2, 3 4 5]` ` ccw TRUE` ` solid FALSE` ` colorPerVertex TRUE` ` normalPerVertex TRUE` ` color Color { }` ` coord Coordinate { }` ` normal Normal { }` ` texCoord TextureCoordinate { }` ` metadata MetadataString { }` `}```

Table 13.17. Node Syntax for IndexedTriangleSet

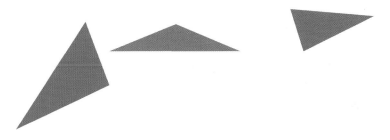

Figure 13.8. IndexedTriangleSet example using the nine vertices previously defined.

3.7. IndexedTriangleFanSet node

IndexedTriangleFanSet is the indexed version of the TriangleFanSet node. Indexing occurs for all child nodes (color, coord, normal, and texCoord fields), which allows for reuse of child nodes. The vertices of each triangle are defined in the Coordinate node's coordinate field.

The IndexedTriangleFanSet node builds one or more fans around a starting vertex, similar to the TriangleFanSet. Thus, coordinates are indexed to read the appropriate list of vertices that build each fan. The index field values for each individual fan must be separated by a −1 sentinel value.

The IndexedTriangleFanSet node is in the Interchange profile and implements the X3DComposedGeometryNode interface. IndexedTriangleFanSet has the fields defined in Table 13.18. Node syntax is shown in Table 13.19, with example values provided for the index array (but no corresponding point values provided for the child Coordinate node).

Type	accessType	Name	Default	Range	Profile
MFInt32	initializeOnly	index		[0, ∞) or −1	Interchange
MFInt32	inputOnly	set_index		[0, ∞) or −1	Interchange
SFBool	initializeOnly	ccw	true		Interchange
SFBool	initializeOnly	colorPerVertex	true		Interchange
SFBool	initializeOnly	normalPerVertex	true		Interchange
SFBool	initializeOnly	solid	true		Interchange
SFNode	inputOutput	color	NULL	[X3DColorNode]	Interchange
SFNode	inputOutput	coord	NULL	[X3DCoordinateNode]	Interchange
SFNode	inputOutput	normal	NULL	[X3DNormalNode]	Interchange
SFNode	inputOutput	texCoord	NULL	[X3DTextureCoordinateNode]	Interchange
SFNode	inputOutput	metadata	NULL	[X3DMetadataObject]	Core

Table 13.18. Field Definitions for IndexedTriangleFanSet Node

XML Syntax (.x3d)	ClassicVRML Syntax (.x3dv)

``
<IndexedTriangleFanSet DEF=
  "MyIndexedTriangleFanSetNode"
  index="0 1 2 3 4 5, −1"
  ccw="true"
  solid="false"
  colorPerVertex="true"
  normalPerVertex="true">
  <Color/>
  <Coordinate/>
  <Normal/>
  <TextureCoordinate/>
  <MetadataDouble/>
</IndexedTriangleFanSet>
``
	``
	DEF MyIndexedTriangleFanSetNode
	        IndexedTriangleFanSet {
	  index [0 1 2 3 4 5, −1]
	  ccw TRUE
	  solid FALSE
	  colorPerVertex TRUE
	  normalPerVertex TRUE
	  color Color { }
	  coord Coordinate { }
	  normal Normal { }
	  texCoord TextureCoordinate { }
	  metadata MetadataDouble { }
	}
	``

Table 13.19. Node Syntax for IndexedTriangleFanSet

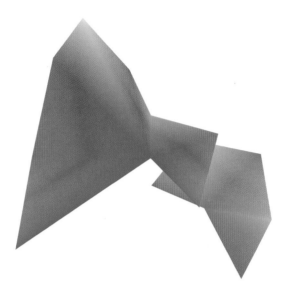

Figure 13.9. IndexedTriangleFanSet example showing two fan sets, producing the same fan sets as in the TriangleFanSet example.

The values of the zero-based index array must be in the range between −1 (inclusive) and the length of the Coordinate point array (exclusive, i.e., less than the number of point values).

The example scene in Figure 13.9 is IndexedTriangleFanSet.x3d.

3.7.1. Hints and warnings

The value of the colorPerVertex field is ignored and always treated as true.

3.8. IndexedTriangleStripSet node

IndexedTriangleStripSet is the indexed version of the TriangleStripSet node. Indexing occurs for all child nodes (color, coord, normal, and texCoord fields), which allows for reuse of child nodes. The vertices of each triangle are defined in the Coordinate node's coordinate field.

The IndexedTriangleStripSet node builds one or more strips beginning from a starting vertex, similar to the TriangleStripSet. Thus, coordinates are indexed to read the appropriate list of vertices that build each strip. The index field values for each individual strip must be separated by a −1 sentinel value.

The IndexedTriangleStripSet node is in the Interchange profile and implements the X3DComposedGeometryNode interface. IndexedTriangleStripSet has the fields defined in Table 13.20. Node syntax is shown in Table 13.21, with example values provided for the index array (but no corresponding point values provided for the child Coordinate node).

Type	accessType	Name	Default	Range	Profile
MFInt32	initializeOnly	index		[0,∞) or −1	Interchange
MFInt32	inputOnly	set_index		[0,∞) or −1	Interchange
SFBool	initializeOnly	ccw	true		Interchange
SFBool	initializeOnly	colorPerVertex	true		Interchange
SFBool	initializeOnly	normalPerVertex	true		Interchange
SFBool	initializeOnly	solid	true		Interchange
SFNode	inputOutput	color	NULL	[X3DColorNode]	Interchange
SFNode	inputOutput	coord	NULL	[X3DCoordinateNode]	Interchange
SFNode	inputOutput	normal	NULL	[X3DNormalNode]	Interchange
SFNode	inputOutput	texCoord	NULL	[X3DTextureCoordinateNode]	Interchange
SFNode	inputOutput	metadata	NULL	[X3DMetadataObject]	Core

Table 13.20. Field Definitions for IndexedTriangleStripSet Node

XML Syntax (.x3d)	ClassicVRML Syntax (.x3dv)

<pre><IndexedTriangleStripSet DEF=
    "MyIndexedTriangleStripSetNode"
  index="0 1 2 3 4 5, −1"
  ccw="true"
  solid="false"
  colorPerVertex="true"
  normalPerVertex="true">
  <Color/>
  <Coordinate/>
  <Normal/>
  <TextureCoordinate/>
  <MetadataSet/>
</IndexedTriangleStripSet></pre>
	<pre>DEF MyIndexedTriangleStripSet
	    IndexedTriangleStripSet {
	  index [0 1 2 3 4 5, −1]
	  ccw TRUE
	  colorPerVertex TRUE
	  normalPerVertex TRUE
	  solid FALSE
	  color Color { }
	  coord Coordinate { }
	  normal Normal { }
	  texCoord TextureCoordinate { }
	  metadata MetadataSet { }
	}</pre>

Table 13.21. Node Syntax for IndexedTriangleStripSet

Figure 13.10. IndexedTriangleStripSet example, producing two strips using the same nine vertices as in many of the other examples. These strips match the TriangleStripSet example.

The values of the zero-based index array must be in the range between −1 (inclusive) and the length of the Coordinate point array (exclusive, i.e., less than the number of point values).

The example scene in Figure 13.10 is IndexedTriangleStripSet.x3d.

3.8.1. Hints and warnings

The value of the colorPerVertex field is ignored and always treated as true.

3.9. IndexedQuadSet node

IndexedQuadSet is the indexed version of the QuadSet node. Indexing occurs for all child nodes (color, coord, normal, and texCoord fields), which allows for reuse of child nodes. The vertices of each quad are defined in the Coordinate node's point field.

Because only quadrilaterals are defined, no −1 sentinel values are used between consecutive 4-tuple values in the index array.

The IndexedQuadSet node is in the CADGeometry component and implements the X3DComposedGeometryNode interface. IndexedQuadSet has the fields defined in Table 13.22. Node syntax is shown in Table 13.23, with example values provided for the index array (but no corresponding point values provided for the child Coordinate node).

The values of the zero-based index array must be in the range between 0 (inclusive) and the length of the Coordinate point array (exclusive, i.e., less than the number of point values).

3.9.1. Hints and warnings

Noncoplanar vertices are erroneous and rendering of such quadrilaterals is ambiguous. Avoid this problem by ensuring that vertex coordinates are coplanar.

When `normalPerVertex="true"`, then the normal of a shared vertex is computed as the average of all contributing quadrilaterals that share the same indexed vertex.

The value of the colorPerVertex field is ignored and always treated as true.

Type	accessType	Name	Default	Range	Profile
MFInt32	initializeOnly	index	[]	[0,∞)	Interchange + CADGeometry: 1 component or Full profile
MFInt32	inputOnly	set_index		[0,∞)	Interchange + CADGeometry: 1 component or Full profile
SFBool	initializeOnly	ccw	true		Interchange + CADGeometry: 1 component or Full profile
SFBool	initializeOnly	colorPer Vertex	true		Interchange + CADGeometry: 1 component or Full profile
SFBool	initializeOnly	normalPer Vertex	true		Interchange + CADGeometry: 1 component or Full profile
SFBool	initializeOnly	solid	true		Interchange + CADGeometry: 1 component or Full profile
SFNode	inputOutput	color	NULL	[X3DColorNode]	Interchange + CADGeometry: 1 component or Full profile
SFNode	inputOutput	coord	NULL	[X3DCoordinate Node]	Interchange + CADGeometry: 1 component or Full profile
SFNode	inputOutput	normal	NULL	[X3DNormalNode]	Interchange + CADGeometry: 1 component or Full profile
SFNode	inputOutput	texCoord	NULL	[X3DTexture CoordinateNode]	Interchange + CADGeometry: 1 component or Full profile
SFNode	inputOutput	metadata	NULL	[X3DMetadata Object]	Core

Table 13.22. Field Definitions for IndexedQuadSet Node

Any quadrilateral can be split into a pair of triangles, so a quadrilateral node can be converted into a triangular node.

4. Summary

4.1. Key ideas

X3D includes many nodes that provide low-level control over large sets of triangles or quadrilaterals. These geometric representations are extremely efficient and usually lead to the fastest possible graphics rendering. Because of the fine-grained detail involved, ordinarily these nodes are used either by authoring tools when building complex shapes or else by conversion software that translates other graphics formats to and from X3D.

XML Syntax (.x3d)	ClassicVRML Syntax (.x3dv)

`<IndexedQuadSet`
`    DEF="MyIndexed QuadSetNode"`
`index="0 1 2 3, 4 5 6 7"`
`ccw="true"`
`solid="false"`
`colorPerVertex="true"`
`normalPerVertex="true">`
`  <Color/>`
`  <Coordinate/>`
`  <Normal/>`
`  <TextureCoordinate/>`
`  <MetadataString/>`
`</IndexedQuadSet>`
	`DEF IndexedQuadSetSet`
	`    IndexedQuadSet {`
	`index [0 1 2 3, 4 5 6 7]`
	`ccw TRUE`
	`solid FALSE`
	`colorPerVertex TRUE`
	`normalPerVertex TRUE`
	`color Color { }`
	`coord Coordinate { }`
	`normal Normal { }`
	`texCoord TextureCoordinate { }`
	`metadata MetadataString { }`
	`}`

Table 13.23. Node Syntax for IndexedQuadSet

Authors paying close attention to detail can use these nodes as well. The consistent definition of fields, interfaces, and concepts throughout all of X3D makes the usage of these nodes quite similar and (with practice) straightforward. Pay attention to the small idiosyncracies that distinguish each node.

4.2. Related nodes and concepts

The triangle and quadrilateral nodes are closely related to the other geometry nodes, which can be found in Chapter 2, Nodes Part 1: Geometry Primitives; Chapter 6, Geometry Nodes Part 2: Points, Lines, and Polygons; and Chapter 10, Geometry Nodes Part 3: Geometry2D Nodes.

4.3. Next chapter

The next chapter looks at the most sophisticated and powerful of all X3D extension mechanisms: prototyping. Prototypes allow authors to define new X3D nodes that are constructed from built-in X3D nodes and other already-defined prototypes. Prototype instances match a specific node type, and can then be used anywhere in the scene graph that matches the node type and is appropriate. Libraries of prototypes can be assembled for external use, making these language-extension techniques repeatable and practical.

Creating Prototype Nodes

There are more things in heaven and earth, Horatio, than are dreamt of in your philosophy.
—William Shakespeare, Hamlet Act I Scene V

1. What this chapter covers

X3D prototypes provide a way for X3D authors to create new nodes that can be used repeatedly in the X3D scene graph like any other node. First an author declares a prototype definition, building a new node made from other nodes. Then the prototype definition is used to create instances, meaning new nodes. Each new prototype instance is traversed and processed when the X3D browser repeatedly loops over the scene graph at run time. This is a powerful capability that makes X3D truly extensible.

Prototype declarations can also be reused by keeping them together in a separate X3D file or library archive, retrieving them when needed by using an ExternProtoDeclare statement. This approach allows a single master copy of a frequently used prototype to be kept up to date in one location, then reused each time it is needed. Over the long term, deliberate management of such prototype libraries makes prototype usage in large projects more practical and maintainable.

Because prototypes allow authors to define fields and even embed Script code, they are quite helpful when customizable X3D objects are needed. Frequently used node combinations and design patterns are good candidates for prototype implementation. Authors can build and incrementally improve prototypes to match their preferred authoring tasks as they become move adept and expert at X3D authoring.

2. Concepts

2.1. Extensibility

As with other XML-based languages, the *X* in X3D stands for Extensible. Unlike most languages, which have a fixed vocabulary, X3D allows direct extension of the language itself. Such extensions are accomplished by using prototypes to construct, declare, and instantiate new nodes.

The prototype approach can be thought of as a cookie cutter capability: the author first builds the cookie cutter, then can use it again and again to create new cookies, (meaning copies of new nodes). Each new node can be customized on creation by defining appropriate fieldValue values for overriding parameter defaults. In some respects, a prototype provides repeatable capabilities for a declarative scene graph in much the same way that a subroutine, method, or function definition provides repeatable capabilities for imperative software programs.

Prototype declarations can be fully copied each time they are needed, from scene to scene, and reused each time. This brute-force copying approach is often counterproductive for authors however, if the prototype definition itself changes or evolves over time. Defining a prototype declaration in a persistent scene lets the author keep a single master copy, then reference the online (or locally available) master file to retrieve the prototype declaration externally at run time.

The mechanism for creating a new copy of the node remains consistent: a ProtoInstance statement names and creates the new node, along with child fieldValue definitions.

A ProtoDeclare or ExternProtoDeclare definition must precede any corresponding ProtoInstance node used in a scene. This requirement allows an X3D browser to immediately recognize each new node, keeping scene parsing fast (and feasible in a single pass) when loading a new scene.

The only potential delay penalty involved in using prototypes might occur if an external prototype declaration has to be retrieved over a slow network link. Once the initial download is complete and the prototype is loaded, however, there are no further run-time penalties. Because the construction of the prototype definition itself is composed of other X3D nodes, perhaps even including nested prototypes, X3D run-time performance remains excellent when using prototypes as part of the scene graph.

2.2. Strong typing of nodes

Each newly declared prototype node takes on the type of the first node in the prototype body. This requirement also enforces the notion of strong typing for nodes: parent-child node relationships are strictly enforced at load time. Thus, new prototype instances are only allowed to fit in the scene graph in places where the first node of the prototype is permitted. Other nodes may follow in the body of the prototype declaration, but only the first node determines type and usability. Furthermore, only the first node is visually rendered (as appropriate) for the node or scene subgraph contained in the prototype declaration.

Strong typing requirements prevent unrecoverable (and usually self-contradictory) errors, such as a Material node being used as an X3DChild node, a Group node replacing an ImageTexture, and so on. This is a great benefit to authors and users alike. Because node-typing errors are discovered when constructing the scene graph, corrections to prototype declarations and instances can be made immediately. This situation is far superior to only learning about parent-child structural errors at load time, which leads to broken content confronting users. From the author's perspective, the worst kind of error is the undiscovered bug.

XML validation is able to thoroughly check ProtoDeclare and ExternProtoDeclare constructs for validity. Unlike other native-node constructs, though, XML validation by itself is insufficient to detect whether ProtoInstance nodes properly match the required node type. X3D browsers and X3D-aware authoring tools can check whether prototype instances properly match the node type. This is an important authoring step to help ensure that scene graphs with prototypes are constructed properly.

2.3. Comparison with Inline node

As an alternative for creating reusable content, an Inline node can be used instead of a Prototype declaration and instantiation. In fact, the Inline mechanism is a simple and easy way to copy external scene subgraphs into a master scene. However, embedded Inline nodes cannot be changed on creation in the local scene graph because there is no field definition mechanism. Thus, Inline nodes are less powerful than prototypes, and do not necessarily extend X3D as a language.

Nevertheless, Inline nodes became more powerful with the addition of IMPORT and EXPORT statements. The IMPORT and EXPORT interfaces allow ROUTE connections within a parent scene to send events to exposed fields within a contained Inline node (and also receive output events as well).

2.4. Syntax alert

Unlike most other constructs in X3D, significant differences exist between the prototype syntax used by the XML encoding and the ClassicVRML encoding. Nevertheless, each corresponding representation is functionally equivalent. This chapter illustrates both forms of syntax in detail.

The following sections provide functional descriptions of ProtoDeclare, ExternProtoDeclare, and ProtoInstance.

3. Functional descriptions

3.1. Prototype declarations: ProtoDeclare

A prototype declaration defines both a prototype interface and a prototype body. The interface defines the prototype node's fields, which are used for information passing into and out of the prototype. This capability defines a new node's fields, just as a built-in X3D node has well-defined fields that include type, accessType, and (as appropriate) default values.

The body of the prototype specifies the X3D nodes that are instantiated when the prototype is created. Any allowed X3D nodes can make up the body of the prototype, including other prototypes. Thus, author-defined prototypes can be given any capability that the built-in X3D nodes have.

3.1.1. Naming considerations

Only one declaration is allowed for each prototype node. Thus, there cannot be two prototype declarations (either internal or external) for a given node name. Because such ambiguity might lead to unpredictable run-time behavior, it is simply forbidden.

Good naming of prototype nodes and fields is important. Giving prototypes unique names that describe and distinguish their purpose leads to sensible, meaningful scene construction. Following the naming patterns already used by X3D allows others to better understand a new prototype.

A good test of a prototype name is to use it in a sentence that describes its purpose. Awkward names are revealed by awkward sentences, while good names provide clarity and a natural way of thinking about what is going on in the scene. Well-chosen names for prototype nodes and fields support good design and help authors to avoid errors when creating the prototype instance.

Perhaps ironically, the best measure that a good name has been chosen is that no one asks what it means! Sometimes this naming process takes several tries. Good naming is important and worth extra effort. Further naming considerations are provided in Appendix C, X3D Scene Authoring Hints.

Node names must be unique in each X3D scene. Do not override the definition of a built-in X3D node by writing a prototype with the same name.

3.1.2. ProtoInterface and field definitions

The ProtoInterface section defines all of the fields that make up the node signature of the prototype. Field definitions contain the field name, field type, field accessType, and (as appropriate to accessType) an initial default value.

Each protoype interface can define zero or more fields. By default, there are no required fields. Field definitions for prototype declarations are identical to field definitions for Script nodes. Thus, the author may choose to provide multiple field definitions, if needed, each with attributes summarized in Table 14.1.

Type	accessType	Name	Default	Range
[fieldType]	initializeOnly	[fieldName]	[required, author specified]	[implicit, depends on fieldType]
[fieldType]	inputOutput	[fieldName]	[required, author specified]	[implicit, depends on fieldType]
[fieldType]	inputOnly	[fieldName]	[omitted]	[implicit, depends on fieldType]
[fieldType]	outputOnly	[fieldName]	[omitted]	[implicit, depends on fieldType]

Table 14.1. Field Definition Requirements

These information requirements for ProtoInterface fields follow the same rules that apply to fields for built-in X3D nodes, restated as follows.

* The initializeOnly fields must have an initial value

* The inputOutput fields must have an initial value

* The inputOnly fields have no initial value

* The outputOnly fields have no initial value

These rules also apply to fields defined within Script nodes.

Note that ROUTE statements cannot connect directly to field definitions in the prototype interface. ROUTE statements can only connect fields of nodes that are defined within the prototype body.

The syntax for prototype interfaces is slightly different for the XML and ClassicVRML encodings. The XML version is a bit more verbose to ensure proper validation and to provide maximum clarity. In any case, the expressive functionality is exactly equivalent for each encoding.

Table 14.2 illustrates equivalent representations of a prototype interface, comparing the syntax for both the XML and ClassicVRML encodings. As usual, the ClassicVRML encoding is unchanged from VRML97 to maintain backwards compatibility.

3.1.3. XML `<field>` attributes for appinfo, documentation

Two additional features can be specified in the XML encoding for a field definition: appinfo and documentation. Because fields are used for node extensibility, these attri-butes allow the author to provide additional metadata about the definitions. The appinfo and documenta-tion definitions follow the annotation design pattern provided by XML Schema, which is often used to formally document the creation of new XML elements and attributes.

The application information (appinfo) attribute is used to provide a simple description that is referencable as a user tooltip by authoring applications. The

XML Syntax (.x3d)

```
<ProtoDeclare>
  <ProtoInterface>
  <field name="enabled" type="SFBool" value="true"
        accessType="inputOutput"
     appinfo="Whether or not ViewPositionOrientation sends output to
        console."/>
  <field name="traceEnabled" type="SFBool" value="true"
        accessType="initializeOnly"
     appinfo="Output internal trace messages for debugging this node-
        developer use only, can be ignored."/>
  <field name="set_traceEnabled" type="SFBool" accessType="inputOnly"
     appinfo="Ability to turn output tracing on/off at runtime."/>
  <field name="position_changed" type="SFVec3f"
        accessType="outputOnly" appinfo="Output local position."/>
  <field name="orientation_changed" type="SFRotation"
        accessType="outputOnly" appinfo="Output local orientation."/>
  <field name="outputViewpointString" type="MFString"
        accessType="outputOnly"
     appinfo='MFString value of new Viewpoint, for example:
        &lt;Viewpoint position="20 15 20" orientation="-0.516
        0.83 0.212 0.9195"/&gt;'/>
  </ProtoInterface>
  <ProtoBody>
    <!--ProtoBody definition goes here-->
  </ProtoBody>
</ProtoDeclare>
```

ClassicVRML Syntax (.x3dv)

```
PROTO ViewPositionOrientation
[
inputOutput     SFBool      enabled TRUE
  # [appinfo] Whether or not ViewPositionOrientation sends output to
  #           console.
initializeOnly  SFBool      traceEnabled TRUE
  # [appinfo] Output internal trace messages for debugging this node -
  #           developer use only, can be ignored.
inputOnly       SFBool      set_traceEnabled
  # [appinfo] Ability to turn output tracing on/off at runtime.
```

Table 14.2. Syntax for Prototype Interface Declarations

```
outputOnly      SFVec3f      position_changed
  # [appinfo] Output local position.
outputOnly    SFRotation     orientation_changed
  # [appinfo] Output local orientation.
outputOnly    MFString       outputViewpointString
  # [appinfo] MFString value of new Viewpoint, for example:
  # Viewpoint { position 20 15 20 orientation -0.516 0.83 0.212 0.9195 }
]
# (end of ProtoInterface section, beginning of ProtoBody section)
{

   # ProtoBody definition goes here

}
```

Table 14.2. (Cont'd.)

documentation attribute is used to provide either a detailed description or else a url for further information.

The appinfo and documentation attributes are only applicable to the ProtoDeclare and field elements. Formal support for the appinfo and documentation attributes is only provided in the XML encoding, although this information can be represented as informal comments for ClassicVRML scenes, as shown in Table 14.2. Field definition syntax and semantics in Script nodes is identical.

These attributes are beginning to be supported by X3D-aware authoring tools, further improving extensibility support for authors.

3.1.4. Field definitions for accessType and type

Defining a field requires that the author provide the field name, accessType, and type. Depending on accessType, a default initial value may also be needed.

Four accessType values are possible: initializeOnly, inputOnly, outputOnly, and inputOutput. These match the choices available for every node and field in X3D, including author-defined fields described in the Script node section in Chapter 9.

Numerous types are available in X3D, first defined with example values in Chapter 1, Technical Overview under Table 1.4, X3D Field Types. Table 14.3 lists each of these types along with default values. Note that any new field definition with accessType="initializeOnly" or accessType="inputOutput" must also have an initial value defined. Matching the original default values for a given type is typically a good choice if a special value is not needed on first declaration of the field.

3.1.5. ProtoBody definition

The nodes that make up the functionality of the prototype go in the prototype body. These nodes form a small scene subgraph that is plugged into the parent scene graph whenever a prototype is instantiated at load time.

Field-Type Names	Description	Default Values
SFBool	Single-Field boolean value	false (XML syntax) or FALSE (ClassicVRML syntax)
MFBool	Multiple-Field boolean array	Empty list
SFColor	Single-Field color value, RGB	0 0 0
MFColor	Multiple-Field color array, RGB	Empty list
SFColorRGBA	Single-Field color value, red-green-blue alpha (opacity)	0 0 0 0
MFColorRGBA	Multiple-Field color array, red-green-blue alpha (opacity)	Empty list
SFInt32	Single-Field 32-bit integer value	0
MFInt32	Multiple-Field 32-bit integer array	Empty list
SFFloat	Single-Field single-precision floating-point value	0.0
MFFloat	Multiple-Field single-precision floating-point array	Empty list
SFDouble	Single-Field double-precision floating-point value	0.0
MFDouble	Multiple-Field double-precision array	Empty list
SFImage	Single-Field image value	0 0 0 Contains special pixel-encoding values, see Chapter 5 for details
MFImage	Multiple-Field image value	Empty list
SFNode	Single-Field node	Empty node, NULL
MFNode	Multiple-Field node array of peers	Empty list
SFRotation	Single-Field rotation value using 3-tuple axis, radian-angle form	0 0 1 0
MFRotation	Multiple-Field rotation array	Empty list
SFString	Single-Field string value	Empty string, representable as two adjacent quotation marks
MFString	Multiple-Field string array	Empty list
SFTime	Single-Field time value	−1, sentinel indicating no time value.
MFTime	Multiple-Field time array	Empty list
SFVec2f/SFVec2d	Single-Field 2-float/2-double vector value	0 0
MFVec2f/MFVec2d	Multiple-Field 2-float/2-double vector array	Empty list
SFVec3f/SFVec3d	Single-Field vector value of 3-float/3-double values	0 0 0
MFVec3f/MFVec3d	Multiple-Field vector array of 3-float/3-double values	Empty list

Table 14.3. X3D Field Types and Default Values

The first node defined in a ProtoBody determines the node type of the prototype. That node type is later used to verify proper parent-child relationships when the prototype instance is created. It is interesting that, although additional nodes may follow as part of the declaration body, only the first node is eligible for visible rendering. This important rendering restriction ensures that improper behavior does not result from other incompatible nodes that may be side by side in the resulting scene graph.

As an example, a Material node might be accompanied by a Script node that modifies color values over time. Ordinarily a Script node cannot be placed as a peer of a Material node, because Script nodes are not allowed as children of the parent Appearance node. Even so, such a construct is possible inside the body of a prototype declaration because of the "only render the first node" requirement for browsers. Meanwhile, any subsequent nodes in the body of the Prototype declaration must themselves be internally valid scene-graph fragments.

Table 14.4 completes the preceding ProtoDeclare excerpt provided in Table 14.2. It illustrates equivalent representations for a prototype body, comparing the syntax for both the XML and ClassicVRML encodings.

```
XML Syntax (.x3d)

<ProtoDeclare>
 <ProtoInterface>
  <!- ProtoInterface field definitions go here ->
 </ProtoInterface>
 <ProtoBody>
  <!- ProtoBody definition goes here ->
  <!- it's a big old world out there! ->
  <ProximitySensor DEF="WhereSensor" size="1000000000 1000000000
            1000000000">
      <IS>
        <connect nodeField="enabled" protoField="enabled"/>
      </IS>
  </ProximitySensor>
  <Script DEF="OutputPositionOrientation">
   <field name="traceEnabled" type="SFBool"
          accessType="initializeOnly"/>
   <field name="set_traceEnabled" type="SFBool"
          accessType="inputOnly"/>
   <field name="set_position" type="SFVec3f"
          accessType="inputOnly"/>
   <field name="set_orientation" type="SFRotation"
          accessType="inputOnly"/>
   <field name="position" type="SFVec3f" value="0 0 0"
          accessType="initializeOnly"/>
```

Table 14.4. Syntax for Example Prototype Body Declarations

(Continued)

```
      <field name="orientation" type="SFRotation" value="0 1 0 0"
             accessType="initializeOnly"/>
      <field name="position_changed" type="SFVec3f"
             accessType="outputOnly"/>
      <field name="orientation_changed" type="SFRotation"
             accessType="outputOnly"/>
      <field name="outputViewpointString" type="MFString"
             accessType="outputOnly"/>
    <IS>
      <connect nodeField="traceEnabled" protoField="traceEnabled"/>
      <connect nodeField="set_traceEnabled"
             protoField="set_traceEnabled"/>
      <connect nodeField="position_changed"
             protoField="position_changed"/>
      <connect nodeField="orientation_changed"
             protoField="orientation_changed"/>
      <connect nodeField="outputViewpointString"
             protoField="outputViewpointString"/>
    </IS>
     <![CDATA[
      ecmascript:// scripting code goes here
]]>
    </Script>
    <ROUTE fromNode="WhereSensor" fromField="position_changed"
           toNode="OutputPositionOrientation"
                    toField="set_position"/>
    <ROUTE fromNode="WhereSensor" fromField="orientation_changed"
           toNode="OutputPositionOrientation"
                    toField="set_orientation"/>
  </ProtoBody>
</ProtoDeclare>
```

ClassicVRML Syntax (.x3dv)

```
PROTO ViewPositionOrientation
[
  # ProtoInterface field definitions go here
]
```

Table 14.4. (Cont'd.)

```
# (end of ProtoInterface section, beginning of ProtoBody section)
{
# ProtoBody definition goes here
# it's a big old world out there!
DEF WhereSensor ProximitySensor {
  size 1000000000 1000000000 1000000000
    enabled IS enabled
}
DEF OutputPositionOrientation Script {
  initializeOnly    SFBool        traceEnabled IS traceEnabled
  inputOnly         SFBool        set_traceEnabled IS set_traceEnabled
  inputOnly         SFVec3f       set_position
  inputOnly         SFRotation    set_orientation
  initializeOnly    SFVec3f       position 0 0 0
  initializeOnly    SFRotation    orientation 0 1 0 0
  outputOnly        SFVec3f       position_changed IS position_changed
  outputOnly        SFRotation    orientation_changed IS
                                      orientation_changed
  outputOnly        MFString      outputViewpointString IS
                                      outputViewpointString
  url [
    "ecmascript:
  // scripting code goes here
    " ]
}
  ROUTE WhereSensor.position_changed TO
      OutputPositionOrientation.set_position
  ROUTE WhereSensor.orientation_changed TO
OutputPositionOrientation.set_orientation
}
```

Table 14.4. (Cont'd.)

Finally, the embedded ECMAscript source code in Table 14.5 is identical for each encoding.

Thus, for each encoding, there are minor syntactic differences in establishing the ProtoInterface section and strong similarities throughout the rest of the prototype declaration. Furthermore, ECMAscript source code is identical in either encoding (as well as in an external script file, if placed there).

ECMAscript Syntax

```
ecmascript:
function roundoff (value, digits) // for local use only
{
  resolution = 1;
  for (i = 1;i <= digits;i++)
  {
    resolution *= 10;
  }
  return Math.round (value*resolution)/resolution;//round to resolution
}
function outputViewpoint ()
{
  outputViewpointString[0] =
    '<Viewpoint position=\"'+
    roundoff (position.x, 1) + " +
    roundoff (position.y, 1) + " +
    roundoff (position.z, 1) +
    '\" orientation=\"'+
    roundoff (orientation.x, 3) + " +
    roundoff (orientation.y, 3) + " +
    roundoff (orientation.z, 3) + " +
    roundoff (orientation.angle, 4) + '\"/>';
  tracePrint (outputViewpointString);
}
function set_position (value, timestamp)
{
  position = value; // save persistent value
  position_changed = position; // output event
  outputViewpoint ();
}
function set_orientation (value)
{
  orientation = value; // save persistent value
  orientation_changed = orientation; // output event
  outputViewpoint ();
}
function set_traceEnabled (value)
{
  traceEnabled = value;
```

Table 14.5. Syntax for Example Embedded Script Code

```
   tracePrint ('traceEnabled=' + traceEnabled);
}
function forcePrint (text)
{
  Browser.print ('[ViewPositionOrientation]' + text);
}
function tracePrint (text)
{
  if (traceEnabled) Browser.print ('[ViewPositionOrientation]' + text);
}
```

Table 14.5. (Cont'd.)

3.1.6. IS connections between ProtoBody fields and ProtoInterface fields

A particularly interesting and powerful capability in prototype design is the ability to directly connect fields inside the prototype body to fields inside the prototype interface. Each is referred to as an IS connection, meaning that one field *is* the same as the other. These links greatly simplify prototype construction by essentially eliminating the need to use ROUTE statements to connect prototype internals into (and out of) interface inputs and outputs.

An IS connection linking an internal field to the prototypes interface automatically passes values from one to the other, treating them identically. Each defined end of an IS connection is functionally the same as the other.

Note the differences in the IS definition syntax in Table 14.5. The XML encoding uses <IS> and <connect> elements inside a node definition to capture this information. In contrast, the ClassicVRML encoding uses the IS keyword immediately following the name of the internal field.

Note that IS/connect definitions must match both accessType and type. The accessType determines whether values are initialized or directional events are passed. Specifically, accessType initializeOnly and inputOutput fields require initializing values, accessType initializeOnly fields cannot pass events; and (finally) accessType inputOnly, outputOnly, and inputOutput fields can pass events.

3.1.7. Hints and warnings

Only the first node in a ProtoBody is visually rendered. Subsequent nodes can be used to generate behaviors or act as data nodes, perhaps utilized by a Script node.

It is a good practice to use eponymous (identically named) fields whenever possible in order to aid clarity and avoid IS connection mismatches.

As described in Chapter 1, Technical Introduction, X3D-Edit and X3dToVrml97.xslt (as well as most browsers) perform thorough checks on field definitions to ensure distinct naming, proper initialization, and type-matched IS/connect constructs. Undetected errors can lead to significant run-time problems. Table 1.5 in Chapter 1 lists the variety of error-checking capabilities provided by various tools and browsers.

Nodes within prototypes have limited scope and are not externally visible. This also applies to nested prototypes (prototype declarations within other prototype declarations).

Nested prototype declarations can be confusing and might not be implemented properly by some browsers. It is probably best to avoid them. A better practice is to define all prototypes at the top level of the scene. Using an already-declared prototype instance inside another prototype body avoids potential prototype-nesting and name-scoping problems.

The prototype's scene subgraph has its own namespace, and so USE copies of nodes cannot be referenced between a prototype body and the parent scene graph. Despite this X3D feature of independent namespaces between prototype bodies and scene graphs, it is nevertheless a good authoring practice to use unique DEF names in the parent scene and the prototype. Overloaded DEF names in a single file cause an XML validation error, because two identical XML ID types are found and the DEF names conflict. Independent names aid in clarity, so maintaining unique DEF names within a scene is a good idea (regardless of X3D scene encoding chosen) so that maximum portability is maintained.

Note that IS connections can be used for any interface field, including fields having `accessType="inputOnly"` and `accessType="outputOnly"`.

Prototype names can be the same if each is defined and used in separate scene files, then composed using one or more Inline nodes. Identically named prototypes can also be deconflicted if one is referenced and renamed via an ExternProtoDeclare url. Nevertheless, overloading of node names is not allowed directly within a single scene.

3.2. External prototype declarations: ExternProtoDeclare

As described at the beginning of the chapter, external prototype declarations allow reuse of a single prototype definition in other files. Each ExternProtoDeclare definition is nearly identical to a ProtoDeclare interface. ExternProtoDeclare adds a url field for retrieving the original prototype, perhaps with multiple candidate addresses. It also omits the definition of default values for each field, because they are already defined in the ProtoDeclare (and may change without warning to the ExternProtoDeclare author). This approach avoids the possibility of mismatched default values between ProtoDeclare and corresponding ExternProtoDeclare statements.

Table 14.6 compares the syntax used for an external prototype declaration. This example corresponds to the prototype declaration developed so far.

3.2.1. url considerations

The url field can contain multiple addresses, just as described for X3DUrlObject in Chapter 3, Grouping Nodes.

Individual prototypes can be referenced by name. This is accomplished through the use of a pound (#) symbol followed by the name of the prototype of interest.

XML Syntax (.x3d)

```
<!—Copy the ExternProtoDeclare and ProtoInstance for
      ViewPositionOrientation at the top of a scene graph to add this
      functionality into other worlds.—>
<ExternProtoDeclare name='ViewPositionOrientation'
        url='
    "../../Tools/Authoring/ViewPositionOrientationPrototype.x3d#View
          PositionOrientation"
    "https://savage.nps.edu/Savage/Tools/Authoring/ViewPosition
          Orientation Prototype.x3d#ViewPositionOrientation"
    "../../Tools/Authoring/ViewPositionOrientationPrototype.wrl#View
          PositionOrientation"
    "https://savage.nps.edu/Savage/Tools/Authoring/ViewPosition
          Orientation Prototype.wrl#ViewPositionOrientation" '>
  <field name='enabled' type='SFBool' accessType='inputOutput'
     appinfo='Whether or not ViewPositionOrientation sends output to
     console.'/>
  <field name='traceEnabled' type='SFBool' accessType=
     'initializeOnly' appinfo='Output internal trace messages for
     debugging this node -developer use only, can be ignored.'/>
  <field name='set_traceEnabled' type='SFBool' accessType=
     'inputOnly' appinfo='Ability to turn output tracing on/off
     at runtime.'/>
  <field name='position_changed' type='SFVec3f' accessType=
     'outputOnly' appinfo='Output local position.'/>
  <field name='orientation_changed' type='SFRotation' accessType=
     'outputOnly' appinfo='Output local orientation.'/>
  <field name='outputViewpointString' type='MFString'
     accessType='outputOnly' appinfo='MFString value of new
     Viewpoint, for example: &lt;Viewpoint position="20 15 20"
     orientation="-0.516 0.83 0.212 0.9195"/&gt;'/>
</ExternProtoDeclare>
```

Table 14.6. Syntax for Extern ProtoDeclare Statement

(Continued)

ClassicVRML Syntax (.x3dv)

```
# Copy the ExternProtoDeclare and ProtoInstance for
      ViewPositionOrientation at the top of your scene graph to add
      this functionality into other worlds.
EXTERNPROTO ViewPositionOrientation [
inputOutput     SFBool        enabled              # [appinfo] Whether or not
#               ViewPositionOrientation sends output to console.
initializeOnly SFBool         traceEnabled         # [appinfo] Output
#               internal trace messages for debugging this node -
#               developer use only, can be ignored.
inputOnly SFBool              set_traceEnabled     # [appinfo] Ability
#               to turn output tracing on/off at runtime.
outputOnly      SFVec3f       position_changed     # [appinfo] Output
#               local position.
outputOnly      SFRotation    orientation_changed  # [appinfo] Output
#               local orientation.
outputOnly      MFString      outputViewpointString # [appinfo]
#               MFString value of new Viewpoint, for example:
   # Viewpoint { position 20 15 20 orientation −0.516 0.83 0.212
#               0.9195]
][
  "../../Tools/Authoring/ViewPositionOrientationPrototype.wrl#ViewPosi-
      tionOrientation"
  "https://savage.nps.edu/Savage/Tools/Authoring/ViewPositionOrientation
      Prototype.wrl#ViewPositionOrientation"

  "../../Tools/Authoring/ViewPositionOrientationPrototype.x3d#ViewPosi-
      tionOrientation"
  "https://savage.nps.edu/Savage/Tools/Authoring/ViewPositionOrientation
      Prototype.x3d#ViewPositionOrientation"

  "file:///c:/www.web3d.org/x3d/content/examples/Savage/Tools/Auth-
   ing/ViewPositionOrientationPrototype.wrl#ViewPositionOrientation"
]
```

Table 14.6. (Cont'd.)

It is possible to rename an externally defined prototype by giving it a different name in the ExternProtoDeclare. This may be necessary if two different external prototypes that have the same name must be retrieved into a single scene (each presumably created by different authors).

Nevertheless this practice is confusing and can lead to errors. If possible, it is usually best to avoid the need to rename prototypes in the first place.

3.2.2. Hints and warnings

When using the XML encoding (.x3d files), it is a good practice to copy appinfo and documentation attributes, so that X3D-aware tools can provide appropriate hints to authors.

If no prototype name is provided following the pound sign (#) in the url, then the browser searches the external file for a prototype with the same name as that defined in the ExternProtoDeclare construct. It is a good practice to always refer to external prototypes by name, using the `#MyExternProtoName` convention.

3.3. Prototype instances: ProtoInstance

A prototype instance creates a new node in the run-time X3D scene graph, based on the ProtoDeclare definition of that new node. The name of the node is case sensitive and must exactly match its definition. At load time, a parameterized copy of the prototype declaration is created and initialized for use as a node instance in the scene graph.

ProtoInstance nodes can have a DEF name and USE copies like any other node. Once again, prototype instances have all the capabilities of regular built-in X3D nodes. DEF and USE constructs are explained in Chapter 3, Grouping nodes. Note that USE nodes cannot contain fieldValue initialization statements.

Table 14.7 compares the syntax of the XML encoding and the ClassicVRML encoding for defining a ProtoInstance.

3.3.1. fieldValue definitions

The fieldValue construct is used to override default field values and provide new initialization values. Such field value overrides are not necessary if the default value for a field is already satisfactory.

When appropriate, default field values can also be overridden after initial loadtime by defining ROUTE statements to pass values into the field. This capability is exactly like that available for built-in X3D nodes, again demonstrating the complete extensibility of this approach.

3.3.2. Setting node type with containerField

The node type of a ProtoInstance is set by the containerField value. This containerField value must match the corresponding field name in the parent node of the ProtoInstance. In the XML encoding, this is a field with the default value `containerField="children"` (the most common value) that can be overridden as needed. For the ClassicVRML

XML Syntax (.x3d)	ClassicVRML Syntax (.x3dv)

`<Group>`
`  <ProtoInstance name= 'ViewPositionOrientation'`
`   containerField= 'children'>`
`    <fieldValue name= 'enabled' value= 'true'/>`
`  </ProtoInstance>`
`</Group>`
	`Group {`
	`   children [`
	`ViewPositionOrientation{`
	`   enabled TRUE`
	`   }`
	`   ]`
	`}`

Table 14.7. Syntax for Example Prototype Instance Creation

encoding, the containerField value must be explicitly presented as the field name preceding the prototype name.

3.3.3. Converting existing content into a prototype declaration

It is often best to first develop X3D content as a regular part of a scene graph. Once the basic capabilities are working satisfactorily, the scene-graph fragment can be wrapped in a ProtoDeclare and ProtoBody, and then given a prototype name.

At this point, modifiable fields of interest can be identified through field definitions in the ProtoInterface section. Finally, IS connect definitions and default values for fields can be provided in the contained body, completing the prototype declaration.

3.3.4. Hints and warnings

The XML encoding for a prototype instance is more verbose than the ClassicVRML encoding. This design choice was intentional and made to maintain satisfactory XML validation capabilities. Pay close attention to syntax differences between the XML (.x3d) and ClassicVRML (.x3dv) encodings for ProtoDeclare, ExternProtoDeclare, ProtoInstance, field, and fieldValue.

4. Summary

4.1. Key ideas

Prototypes allow authors to create reusable pieces of X3D worlds. These pieces can be constructed like a modifiable "cookie cutter" so that some or all aspects of the new X3D prototype node can be changed from instance to instance.

Many prototype examples can be found in the X3D Example archives. Studying and modifying existing examples is an excellent way to learn these advanced techniques. Archives and examples can be found on the book's website.

4.2. Related nodes and concepts

The Inline node can also be used for reuse of geometry and behavior. Inline nodes cannot be modified or customized on creation, though events can be sent with ROUTE statements into or out of the Inline node via IMPORT and EXPORT definitions. The Inline node is covered in Chapter 3, Grouping Nodes; and IMPORT and EXPORT are described in Chapter 7, Event Animation and Interpolation.

The Script node is often used to provide customized behaviors for prototype nodes. Script is described in Chapter 9, Event Utilities and Scripting.

Afterword: Getting Involved

Learning X3D

The best way for you to become skilled in X3D is to build many X3D worlds. Look at worlds built by others for ideas and inspirations. Besides this book, there are many resources available to assist you with hints and solutions to your problems. Appendix A describes the material available on this book's companion web site (X3dGraphics.com). The web site includes links to all material referenced here and throughout the book. This includes links to existing worlds, online communities, tutorials, repositories and archives, browsers, authoring tools, and supporting organizations. Appendix B—Help: X3D/VRML Examples—is an extensive collection of links to X3D resources and examples. Appendix C—X3D Scene Authoring Hints—describes best practices for authoring X3D content.

Building Software

Are you a programmer? Many of the X3D browsers are open source (e.g., Flux in C++, FreeWRL in Perl/C and Xj3D in Java). Developers of these browsers are always looking for people to help produce code or test new features. Many authoring-support tools are also open source. These include Chisel (VRML97 geometry compression), NIST Translator (VRML97 to X3D) and several emerging authoring environments.

Creating Content

You do not need to create all of your X3D content. There are several repositories and archives that provide some of the content you may need to use. You can also contribute content to these archives. Displaying X3D on your Web site may require some changes to your site's Web server (namely, setting the MIME type, which is an FAQ). Your hosting company can help you with this. X3D can be used within reports and presentation to interactively show ideas that cannot be expressed in other means. X3D provides tremendous flexibility in the display of interactive animated 2D and 3D content—take advantage of this and stretch the horizon a bit.

X3D Development

The evolution of the X3D specification is an ongoing process. The specification is managed by the Web3D Consortium. You can participate in the development of future revisions of the specification by joining the Web3D Consortium (web3d.org) and participating in the X3D working group. After the initial draft of each revision, developed by the Web3D Consortium, the specification follows the International Standards Organization (ISO) approval process. Qualified individuals can be involved in that process by joining an ISO national body.

Other Web3D Activities

There are two annual conferences supporting X3D. The Web3D Symposium is a small technical conference that usually occurs early in the year, typically alternating between the United States and Europe. SIGGRAPH (www.siggraph.org) is the ACM Special Interest Group on Graphics and Interactive Techniques, and the prime mover in the 3D graphics world. Emphasizing both 3D graphics and user interaction, the annual SIGGRAPH conference attracts tens of thousands of people each summer. Both conferences include a variety of X3D-related papers, tutorials, and events. The Web3D Consortium annually publishes a Web3D Software Development Kit (SDK) DVD with material provided by Consortium members. This includes X3D browsers, authoring tools, and reusable archives of X3D content. As a Consortium member, you can even contribute code or content to the Web3D SDK.

As with any graphics technology, you will build your best work when you are having fun. Be creative, try out new challenges, collaborate with others, and produce cool X3D! We wish you the best of luck as you help bring 3D graphics to the World Wide Web.

Online Resources

Web Site Description

The companion to this book is the X3dGraphics.com web site. It contains all of the material that might normally be found in a companion CD, with links to other sites and interactive content. The site was developed to be a reference and repository for this book. This appendix describes the content and resources at the Web site. The topics can be split into two categories:

- Direct book material (e.g., examples, figures, etc.)

- Supporting material hosted by other sites (e.g., X3D browsers, X3D specifications, etc.)

The material that directly supports the book is organized into the following topics:

- Book Examples

- Book Figures

- Book Updates

- Contact Authors

The Web site is the repository for all examples, figures, and content that appears in the book. The example code can be viewed online or downloaded. If you have an X3D browser installed in your Web browser, you can also view and interact with the examples. There are more examples on the Web site than appear in the book.

Updates to X3D: Extensible 3D Graphics for Web Authors are also listed on the Web site. This section includes author signings, specification updates, and related book announcements. Selected excerpts from this book are also posted on the Web site. The authors can be contacted by direct email. Please include the phrase "X3D Book" in the subject line of your message.

Don Brutzman at brutzman@nps.edu

Leonard Daly at daly@X3dGraphics.com

The supporting material is extensive and includes the following topics:

- Browsers

- Authoring tools

- X3D specifications

- Other online reference information

- Online communities

- How to get involved

All of these sections contain links to online sources for the topic. To view any of the examples, you must first download and install at least one X3D browser. There are a number of choices, depending on your operating system and other operating environment considerations. A brief description of each browser and its capabilities is available on the Web site.

Although this book only makes use of only X3D-Edit as an authoring tool, there are a number of other tools that assist authors in building worlds. Many of these tools are not free, but most at least offer free downloads for trial use. The authoring-tools section lists these tools and their capabilities.

The X3D specification documents are the defining documents for this technology. The X3D specifications are ISO documents. Links are provided to the authoritative ISO documents and also to free online versions.

There is a large amount of other reference information available, including example X3D worlds and online tutorials. Links are provided to these resources.

There is an active online X3D community. The community is tied together via email lists, Web boards, and blogs. This community is an excellent place to ask for (and give) help, or to simply listen and participate in X3D discussions.

The Web3D Consortium (*web3d.org*) is the driver behind the X3D specifications. The Consortium has many activities involving X3D. You can join, become an active participant, and contribute to the development of the next version of X3D.

Help: X3D/VRML Examples

The online version of this appendix includes links to all online resources, and is available at *www.web3d.org/x3d/content/examples/help.html*

Applications, Players, and Plugins for X3D/VRML Viewing

Your web browser must be able to view X3D/VRML scenes to browse these X3D examples. Please load one of these player plugins if necessary.

Example test scene: HelloWorld (.x3d .x3dv .wrl .html)

Web3D Consortium Members

- Quickstart: Parallel Graphics Cortona VRML97 plugin for Netscape or Internet Explorer.

- MediaMachines Flux X3D/VRML97 plugin for Internet Explorer.

- Xj3D Open Source for X3D/VRML97, version 2.0 release, now using Java OpenGL (JOGL) rendering.

- CRC's FreeWRL X3D/VRML browser (written in open-source Perl and C).

- BitManagement's Contact X3D/VRML97 plugin for Internet Explorer.

- Octaga X3D/VRML browser with high performance and growing support.

- blaxxun Contact VRML97 plugin for Netscape or Internet Explorer.

Not (yet) Web3D Consortium Members

- Karmanaut mirror site: CosmoPlayer 2.1.1 VRML97 plugin for Netscape or Internet Explorer.

- libx3d open-source C++ libraries for X3D.

Authoring Tools

- X3D-Edit is the primary authoring tool used at NPS to create the X3D, VRML97 Sourcebook, and SAVAGE examples. Available free.

  - X3D-Edit Auto Installer is available online for various operating systems (Windows, Mac, Linux, Solaris, and other Unix).

  - X3D-Edit is available for download at *www.web3d.org/x3d/content/X3D-Edit.zip* and *www.web3d.org/x3d/content/README.X3D-Edit.html*

  - X3D-Edit Authoring Tool for Extensible 3D (X3D) Graphics provides a six-page summary of X3D-Edit features and usage.

- Flux Studio is an easy-to-use, inexpensive, general-purpose, visually oriented, 3D modeling and animating application from Media Machines.

- SwirlX3D is an X3D/VRML authoring environment from Pinecoast Software.

- Wings3D is a free open-source authoring environment with VRML export.

- Blender is an open-source 3D authoring tool that includes support for an X3D exporter.

- Rez provides an open-source framework and tools for translating planetary terrain data and images to different formats including multiresolution versions optimised for Web browsing.

- Altova XMLSpy is an XML development environment for modeling, editing, debugging and transforming XML technologies. The X3D-Edit distribution includes XMLSpy project support for X3D editing and validation, using either X3D DTD or X3Dschema.

  - X3D-XmlSpyProject.spp is an overview project for X3D specification-development work.

  - ContentCatalog.spp project files are provided with each example archive.

Authoring Support

- X3D Specifications page includes downloads and related links. (Publicly available X3D and VRML97 specifications are also bundled with X3D-Edit.)

- X3D Scene Authoring Hints provides author guidance and examples for contributing scenes to the X3D examples, VRML97 Sourcebook, Conformance, and SAVAGE archives. (Also provided in Appendix C.)

- X3D Tooltips provide hints for each node and field in X3D. Available in:
  English (online at *www.web3d.org/x3d/content/X3dTooltips.html*)
  Chinese (online at *www.web3d.org/x3d/content/X3dTooltipsChinese.html*)
  French (online at *www.web3d.org/x3d/content/X3dTooltipsFrench.html*)
  German (online at *www.web3d.org/x3d/content/X3dTooltipsGerman.html*)
  Italian (online at *www.web3d.org/x3d/content/X3dTooltipsItalian.html*)
  Portuguese (online at *www.web3d.org/x3d/content/X3dTooltipsPortuguese.html*)
  Spanish (online at *www.web3d.org/x3d/content/X3dTooltipsSpanish.html*).

- Vapour Technology provides VRML authoring tool for computing orientations (Dizzy, Peek, SpinDoctor, and Twister).

- Pellucid is a Java applet that simulates the VRML/X3D illumination model given a default view of a sphere, a default directional light with direction [−1 −1 −1], and a default material.

- The NIST Plugin and Browser Detector is used for server-side determination of VRML or X3D browser in use.

- PanoRez produces multiresolution panoramas in VRML and X3D using Rez

Conversion and Translation Tools

- National Institute of Science and Technology (NIST) VRML to X3D Translator is written by Qiming Wang and is a bundled source/jar in X3D-Edit. The X3D-Edit distribution includes an updated version of the translator (also .zip and Javadoc).

- Xj3D Open Source for X3D/VRML97 includes a command-line X3D translator between XML encoding (.x3d), Classic VRML encoding (.x3dv), and VRML97 encoding (.wrl).

- X3D-Edit includes embedded and command-line translation tools using XSLT stylesheets:

  - Conversion to ClassicVRML (.x3dv encoding): X3dToX3dvClassicVrml-Encoding.xslt and X3dToX3dv- ClassicVrmlEncoding.bat.

  - Backwards compatibility with VRML 97 (.wrl encoding): X3dToVrml97.xslt and X3dToVrml97.bat.

- Tagset pretty-printing in XHTML (.html encoding), includes cross linking of DEF/USE/ROUTE/etc.: X3dToXhtml.xslt and X3dToXhtml.bat.

- Okino Polytrans can convert many different file formats to and from VRML97.

- Chisel VRML Optimisation Tool has a new-version autoinstaller and documentation provided by Halden Virtual Reality Centre. It was originally built by Trapezium and is maintained by NIST.

- Accutrans 3D by MicroMouse Productions provides accurate translation of 3D geometry between the file formats used by many popular modeling programs.

- Project RawKee is an X3D Exporter Plug-in for Maya by Aaron Bergstrom

- Unreal Realm of Concepts is an Unreal-to-X3D exporter by Dave Arendash

Examples

More than 2600 .x3d examples are provided, available individually online or as fully complete, downloadable .zip archives. These examples are all open source and are free for any use.

Currently each example is provided in multiple file encodings: XML (.x3d), ClassicVRML (.x3dv), VRML97 (.wrl), and pretty-print XHTML (.html) form. Also available are CanonicalX3D (.xml) and Compressed Binary Encoding (.x3db) formats.

- Example test scene: HelloWorld (.x3d .x3dv .wrl .html).

- X3D Basic Examples are online at *www.web3d.org/x3d/content/examples/Basic* with compressed version (~45 MB) at X3dExamplesBasic.zip.

- VRML 2.0 Sourcebook examples in X3D are online at *www.web3d.org/x3d/content/examples/Vrml2.0Sourcebook* with compressed version (~7 MB) at X3dExamplesVrml2.0Sourcebook.zip.

- NIST Conformance Suite Examples are online at *www.web3d.org/x3d/content/examples/ConformanceNist* with compressed version (~150 MB) at X3dExamplesConformanceNist.zip. The Conformance Examples were authored by NIST and automatically converted into X3D.

- NPS Scenario Authoring and Visualization for Advanced Graphical Environments (SAVAGE) library is online at *https://savage.nps.edu/Savage* with paper and compressed models library (~600 MB) at *https://savage.nps.edu/X3dExamplesSavage.zip*.

The following known limitation applies to some .x3d scenes in the example archives:

- Scripts written in Java still follow VRML97 scripting model, not X3D Scene Authoring Interface (SAI). Meanwhile, scripts written in EcmaScript work fine and are all updated to X3D 3.0.

License

*   An open-source license is applied to X3D models and source code produced by NPS (and others) for the various Web3D and Savage model archives. Typically one of the following meta tags is included in archived X3D scenes:

```
<meta name="license" content="../../license.html">
<meta name="license"
  content="http://www.web3d.org/x3d/content/examples/license.html">
<meta name="license" content="http://savage.nps.edu/Savage/
  license.html">
```

The license is available as license.html and also available in plain-text form as license.txt for embedding in source-code files. Under the terms of this BSD-style open-source license, both commercial and noncommercial uses are permitted, and the contributing authors retain original copyright as appropriate. This license can be adapted for use by other open-source contributors, if desired. Discussion, rationale and references regarding this license are available via the bugtracker license entry.

PowerPoint Support

*   Installing Cortona VRML Browser as a PowerPoint Control (also in.html) by Don Brutzman, Curt Blais and the SAVAGE group.

References

*   Extensible 3D (X3D) Graphics
*   Extensible 3D (X3D) Specifications
*   Extensible 3D (X3D) Specification Feedback Form
*   Extensible 3D (X3D) MIME Types for proper configuration of http servers
*   VRML97 Specification
*   VRML 2.0 Sourcebook by Andrea L. Ames, David R. Nadeau and John L. Moreland
*   Don Brutzman's X3D/VRML course page

X3D Scene Authoring Hints

This appendix is a collection of style guidelines and authoring tips to improve the quality, consistency, and maintainability of X3D scenes. It is available online at *www.web3d.org/x3d/content/examples/X3dSceneAuthoringHints.html*

Authoring practices

- Actively fix any X3D-Edit [Error], [Warning], and [Hint] messages in each scene. Allowing errors and warnings to persist, even when apparently harmless, can mask further problems. [Info] messages are informational and might not need corrective action by the author.

- Keep a local copy of the X3D Specification on your system and refer to it frequently. (Local copies of all current specifications are bundled with X3D-Edit.)

- Use the X3D Tooltips. These are embedded in X3D-Edit popups, and are also available separately in Chinese, English, French, German, Italian, Portuguese, and Spanish.

- If a scene depends on having the default value of a field, it is a good practice to enter that default value in your original scene for emphasis. Note, however, that some optimizers may remove it.

- Use the correct X3D version 3.0 final specification DOCTYPE/DTD:

```
<?xml version="1.0" encoding="UTF-8"?>
<!DOCTYPE X3D PUBLIC "ISO//Web3D//DTD X3D 3.0//EN"
  "http://www.web3d.org/specifications/x3d-3.0.dtd">
<X3D profile="Immersive" version="3.0"
  xmlns:xsd="http://www.w3.org/2001/XMLSchema-instance"
  xsd:noNamespaceSchemaLocation="http://www.web3d.org/specifications/
  x3d-3.0.xsd">
```

The Transitional X3D 3.0 DOCTYPE/DTD is used by some tools:

```
<?xml version="1.0" encoding="UTF-8"?>
<!--Warning: transitional DOCTYPE in source .x3d file-->
<!DOCTYPE X3D PUBLIC "http://www.web3d.org/specifications/x3d-
  3.0.dtd" "file:///www.web3d.org/TaskGroups/x3d/translation/x3d-
  3.0.dtd">
<X3D profile="Immersive" version="3.0"
  xmlns:xsd="http://www.w3.org/2001/XMLSchema-instance"
  xsd:noNamespaceSchemaLocation="http://www.web3d.org/specifications/
  x3d-3.0.xsd">
```

When offline, the current version of X3D-Edit can only load scenes containing the proper DTD one at a time. When disconnected from the network, click on a scene (or drag and drop the scene onto the X3D-Edit icon) to launch it—the DOCTYPE will be converted to Transitional DTD on launch, and restored to Final DTD on normal exit. Alternatively, you can use a different X3D/XML/text editor or the Transitional X3D DOCTYPE/DTD with X3D-Edit.

- Preferred: X3D Amendment 1 version 3.1 specification DOCTYPE/DTD:

```
<?xml version="1.0" encoding="UTF-8"?>
<!DOCTYPE X3D PUBLIC "ISO//Web3D//DTD X3D 3.1//EN"
  "http://www.web3d.org/specifications/x3d-3.1.dtd">
<X3D profile="Immersive" version="3.1"
  xmlns:xsd="http://www.w3.org/2001/XMLSchema-instance"
  xsd:noNamespaceSchemaLocation="http://www.web3d.org/specifications/
  x3d-3.1.xsd">
```

The Transitional X3D 3.1 DOCTYPE/DTD is used by some tools:

```
<?xml version="1.0" encoding="UTF-8"?>
<!--Warning: transitional DOCTYPE in source .x3d file-->
```

```
<!DOCTYPE X3D PUBLIC "http://www.web3d.org/specifications/x3d-
  3.1.dtd" "file:///www.web3d.org/TaskGroups/x3d/translation/x3d-
  3.1.dtd">
<X3D profile="Immersive" version="3.1"
  xmlns:xsd="http://www.w3.org/2001/XMLSchema-instance"
  xsd:noNamespaceSchemaLocation="http://www.web3d.org/specifications/
  x3d-3.1.xsd">
```

- You can use X3dDtdChecker.java to convert from one DOCTYPE to the other:

```
C:\www.web3d.org\x3d\content> java X3dDtdChecker
usage:
java X3dDtdChecker sceneName.x3d [-setFinalDTD|-setTransitionalDTD]
```

- Errata-correction versions of the XML Document Type Definition (DOCTYPE DTD) and Schema are provided as part of the X3D-Edit distribution or directly online from the following links:

```
X3D XML DOCTYPE (DTD)                    X3D XML Schema
x3d-dtd-changelog.txt                    x3d-schema-changelog.txt
x3d-3.0.dtd
x3d-3.0-InputOutputFields.dtd
x3d-3.0-Web3dExtensionsPublic.dtd
x3d-3.0-Web3dExtensionsPrivate.dtd       x3d-3.0.xsd and documentation

x3d-3.0-Web3dExtensionsPublic.xsd
x3d-3.0-Web3dExtensionsPrivate.xsd
x3d-3.1.dtd
x3d-3.1-InputOutputFields.dtd
x3d-3.1-Web3dExtensionsPublic.dtd
x3d-3.1-Web3dExtensionsPrivate.dtd       x3d-3.1.xsd and documentation

x3d-3.1-Web3dExtensionsPublic.xsd
x3d-3.1-Web3dExtensionsPrivate.xsd
  X3dSchemaDocumentation.zip
```

Coordinate systems for 3D:

- Always use default scaling, with units in meters. If any content uses units other than meters, add a parent Transform node to uniformly scale it back to meters.

- Coordinate systems: $+x$-axis is nose/North, $+y$-axis is vertical/up, $+z$-axis is right-hand side (RHS)/East.

- Entities (planes, trains, automobiles, etc.) also must follow these coordinate-system conventions. Example scene links, available online: ModelOrientation.x3d (.wrl) (.html) (image).

- Position the default center of airborne, space, and underwater entities in the centroid (geometric center) or center of gravity (for physics-based models). Position the default center of ground vehicles so that the bottom touches the ground. In that way, the entity can be properly animated by a parent Transform.

- Coordinate-system example scene links, available online: CoordinateAxesNSEW.x3d (.wrl) (.html) (image).

- Coordinate-system gimbals, including DIS axis conversions links, available online: Gimbals.x3d (.wrl) (.html) (image).

- Angular rotations are expressed in radians, using right-hand rule (RHR) with your thumb pointing along the positive direction for the axis of interest and the other fingers curling in the direction of positive rotation.

Credits

- Ensure that all contributors receive proper credit for content.

- The Basic X3D Examples, VRML 2.0 Sourcebook, X3D Conformance Suite, and Savage model archives are free for duplication and further use.

- Do not add scenes, images, or audio files to the archive unless the original owner has granted permission. This means that there are clear and documented distribution rights attached. This can be meta tag information, a WorldInfo node at the top, and/or an email/document statement by the owner duplicated locally.

Dates

- Use meta tags to note the dates when a scene is created and revised:

```
<meta name='created' content='18 October 2006'/>
<meta name='revised' content='19 October 2007'/>
```

- For consistency and possible parsability, please use the date format 10 July 2007 (rather than other forms such as July 10, 2007 or 10/7/2007).

- Leading zeroes on dates are not usually used but are OK.

- Use full 4-digit numbers for years (e.g. 2007).

HTML

- Ensure HTML content is valid.
  - W3C Markup Validator Service
  - HTML-Kit
  - HTML Tidy
  - WDG HTML Validator
- Encoding values for special characters in XML/HTML files are found under Character entity references in HTML.
- Other references:
  - HyperText Markup Language (HTML) Home Page
  - XHTML 1.0
  - HTML 4.01
  - Web Design Group's FAQ Archives

Images

- Do not add images to the archive without proper permissions and credits.
- Follow naming conventions for image file names: no abbreviations, CamelCase-Naming, no embedded whitespace or underscore characters, etc.
  - Do not arbitrarily rename images provided from other sources.
  - Starting with the same name as the scene of interest helps directory alphabetization.
  - Ensure that filename extensions are lower case (e.g., CoolImage.png, not CoolImage.PNG).
- Portable network graphics (PNG) is the preferred image format.
  - Please avoid use of Graphics Interchange Format (GIF) if possible.
  - Further tips are provided by the online link about: PNG versus GIF considerations.
  - Joint Photographic Experts Group (JPG) format is acceptable, and often does a good job on photographs. Be wary of JPG compression quality, which is adjustable (best quality is usually preferred).
- Use high-resolution quality (e.g., 300 dpi or better). Try to keep image file size under 300 KB, if possible.

- An image file can be embedded inside an X3D scene by converting it into a PixelTexture node. These take up more size (often by a factor of 10) but compress well and do not require a separate network fetch. For an example, see PixelTextureGenerator.java, which was used to create PixelTextureNavyJackDont TreadOnMe.x3d in the Savage/Tools/Authoring collection.

- Use the W3C Image Info Service to check the properties of your online image.

Inline and Prototype Subscenes

- Inline scenes
  - Code with DEF and USE multiple instances of duplicate Inline, image, audio and video content. This approach is more maintainable, uses less memory, and can reduce file-transfer delays.

  - Inlined scenes ought to be interesting enough to stand on their own. If an Inlined scene is unlikely to be reused more than once, then you should probably incorporate the X3D content in the parent scene.

  - Provide well-formed urls for reliability.

  - Ensure that named IMPORT/EXPORT connections match.

  - Use inline tooltips and X3D specification

- Prototype Declarations
  - Follow X3D naming conventions for node and field definitions.

  - Provide useful and safe default initialization values for each field, rather than depending on default field values internal to the ProtoBody.

  - Include annotation tooltips for each field.

  - Avoid copying ProtoDeclare definitions into additional scenes, instead copy ExternProtoDeclare/ProtoInstance definitions.

  - Tooltips for ProtoDeclare, ProtoInterface, and ProtoBody

  - X3D specification

- External Prototype Declarations
  - For important prototypes, make a separate NewNodeExample.x3d scene that provides copyable or reusable ExternProtoDeclare and ProtoInstance definitions corresponding to each NewNodePrototype.x3d scene. This encourages

authors to avoid copying the ProtoDeclare definitions, so that a master version remains stable and improvable.

- Do not include initialization values in ExternProtoDeclare field definitions. They are illegal, because the defaults in the original ProtoDeclare field declarations take precedence.

- Copy annotation tooltips from the corresponding Protodeclare annotation tooltips for each ExternProtoDeclare field.

- Use the ExternProtoDeclare tooltips and X3D specification.

- Prototype Instances

  - Explicitly include initialization values, even if they match default values, to ensure proper operation. Sometimes a prototype can have different initialization values than expected, if it is modified elsewhere.

  - Remember to include a proper containerField attribute, identifying parent-node field name for this ProtoInstance. The default value is children. Example values are color, coord, geometry, fontStyle, proxy, sound, texture, textureTransform.

  - First debug the proper ProtoInstance operation in the scene defining the original ProtoDeclare, rather than using an ExternProtoDeclare, to make sure they work first. Browser debugging can be more cryptic for externally defined prototypes and different versions may occur in various remote url addresses, making it difficult to determine precisely which ExternProtoDeclare is being referenced.

  - Use the ProtoInstance tooltips and X3D specification.

License

- An open-source license is applied to X3D models and source code produced by NPS (and others) for the various Web3D and Savage model archives. The following meta tag is usually included in these archived X3D scenes:

```
<meta name="license" content="../../license.html">
```

The license is available as license.html, and is also available in plain-text form as license.txt for embedding in source-code files. Under the terms of this BSD open-source license, both commercial and noncommercial uses are permitted, and the contributing authors retain original copyright as appropriate. This license can be adapted for use by other open-source contributors, if desired. Discussion, rationale, and references regarding this license are available via the bugtracker license entry.

meta tags

- Follow meta-tag norms found in newScene.x3d (.html)

- Description tags are used for catalog entries. Ensure the first sentence provides a good overall description of the scene. An example is:

```
<meta name="description" value="This beautiful model of an actual
clean bedroom will impress your mom."/>
```

- Update or remove meta tags with default content descriptions.

- Remove extraneous trailing newline characters.

- Ensure you include both `<meta name="filename"/>` and `<meta name="url"/>` tags, with filename values ending in .x3d (rather than .wrl).

- Default metadata conventions are defined by the Dublin Core metadata terms.

Naming Conventions

- Naming conventions apply to .x3d files, image files, and Prototypes. It is also a good idea to follow them for DEF and USE names.

- CamelCaseNaming: capitalize each word, never use abbreviations, strive for clarity, and be brief but complete.

- startWithLowerCaseLetter when defining field names (i.e., attributes) for Prototypes and Scripts.

- Ensure consistent capitalization throughout. Of note: the Windows operating system is not case sensitive, but http servers are. Thus, mismatched capitalization can hide target files, and this error only is revealed when placed on a server.

- Use the underscore character (_) to indicate subscripts on mathematical variables. Otherwise avoid use of underscores, because they look like whitespace when part of a URL address.

- Avoid use of hyphens (-) in names, because these are erroneously turned into subtraction operators when converted into class or variable names.

- Use lowercase letters for filename extensions. Examples: .png .jpg .txt

- Be consistent. When multiple files pertain to a single entity, start with the same name so that they will be alphabetized adjacent to each other in the catalog and the directory listings. Examples: WaypointInterpolatorPrototype.x3d, WaypointInterpolatorExample.x3d, and WaypointInterpolatorExample.png

- Good choice of directory and subdirectory names can help keep scene names short.

Naming of Multiple Similar Autogenerated Files

Concatenate the following name components as appropriate. Separate components by period characters, since underscores disappear as part of a url and hyphens will break across a line.

- ConsistentDescriptiveName

- PhysicalLocation (for example .KauaiHawaii)

- SequenceNumber

- .01Month20xx

- .ext

General notes on naming conventions:

- These conventions are suitable for X3D scenes, XML tagset design, and corresponding Java classes.

- This approach matches the node and field naming conventions in the X3D Specification (and most XML).

Scripts

- Be sure to set `<Script directOutput='true'>` when using SFNode/MFNode fields.

- Use `Browser.print(...)` rather than a simple `print(...)` function when printing to the console. For backwards compatibility, X3dToVrml97.xslt will strip the preceding Browser.class qualifier when converting scripts to VRLM97.

- The preferred alternative to using the url field for Script nodes is to insert a CDATA section to contain embedded source code. CDATA can protect literals like `<` and `>` from undesirable conversions by XML parsers. Furthermore, it eliminates the need to use < and > escape-character replacements (which make script code nonportable). For example:

```
<Script mustEvaluate="true">
<field name="message" type="SFString" accessType="initializeOnly"
  value="World!"/>
```

```
<![CDATA[
  ecmascript:

  function initialize (timestamp)
  {
    Browser.print ('Hello' + message);
  }
]]>
</Script>
```

- For print-value tracing in ecmascript that can be toggled, use scripts, but first add the following field interface to the Script.

```
<field accessType="initializeOnly" name="localTraceEnabled"
  type="SFBool" value="true"/>
```

Then, at end of the CDATA section for the ecmascript, add:

```
function tracePrint(outputString)
{
  if (localTraceEnabled)
  Browser.print('[ScriptNameHere]' + outputString);
}
function forcePrint(outputString)
{
  Browser.print('[ScriptNameHere]' + outputString);
}
```

This lets the script author use trace-aware output functions as a substitute for Browser.print() as follows.

```
tracePrint('Only print when localTraceEnabled is true');
forcePrint('Always print: localTraceEnabled=' + localTraceEnabled);
```

URL Links

- Include both relative and persistent (online) url links. Use relative links first, since they are most portable and do not require unnecessary use of the network.

- Special case: use online links before relative links when updated network versions are preferred (for example, a weather report).

- Look at X3D examples and SAVAGE examples for sample usage of multiple (relative and online) url fields.

- Ensure each url link is valid. These can be easily checked manually via the pretty-print HTML version of the scene.

- Run a link checker to verify that URLs are correct. This step is performed periodically on the X3D/Savage content archives.

  - W3C Link Checker (with documentation)

  - Xenu's Link Sleuth

- Include quotation marks (")around each individual address, because each url field has type MFString.

- XML-aware editors may escape each quotation mark (") character as " for proper XML encoding. When using a text editor directly, it may be easiest to enclose the entire field in single quotation marks (') as shown next.

- Usage examples:

```
<ImageTexture url='
  "earth-topo.png"
  "earth-topo-small.gif"
  "file:///c:/www.web3d.org/x3d/content/examples/earth-topo.png"
  "file:///c:/www.web3d.org/x3d/content/examples/earth-topo-small.gif"
  "http://www.web3d.org/x3d/content/examples/earth-topo.png"
  "http://www.web3d.org/x3d/content/examples/earth-topo-small.gif" '
/>
<ImageTexture url="&quot;earth-topo.png&quot;&#10;
  &quot;earth-topo-small.gif&quot;"/>
```

- References
  - X3D url tooltips
  - X3D specification
  - Internet Engineering Task Force (IETF) Requests for Comments (RFC) 2396
  - World Wide Web Consortium (W3C): naming and addressing

Viewpoints

- Initial viewpoint is typically on the +z-axis, looking toward origin along the −z-axis. This helps provide consistent catalog viewing.

- Because the default body coordinate system is aligned along the $+ x$-axis with the $+ y$-axis up, individual entities are typically pointed to the right when seen from the default view.

- Use clear, understandable description fields. Viewpoints are a primary user tool for scene navigation.

- Use the object's name first when many viewpoints follow, so that they are more easily identified in the viewpoint list.

- Use whitespace instead of underscores in Viewpoint (and sensor) descriptions.

- Put objects in the center of a scene for default EXAMINE mode to work properly. Alternatively, use the Viewpoint centerOfRotation field to indicate local center.

- Use Savage/HeadsUpDisplay/CrossHair online prototype to put a cross-hair overlay HUD in the center of a viewpoint.

- Use development/ViewpointGroup prototype (online prototype) to hide high-detail viewpoints from the viewpoint list at long ranges. This allows scalability of many objects in a single scene.

- Use the Savage/Tools/Authoring/AnimatedViewpointRecorderPrototype online prototype to hide high-detail viewpoints from the viewpoint list at long ranges. This allows scalability of many objects in a single scene.

List of References

Alvestrand, Harald, ed. Tags for the Identification of Languages, Internet Engineering Task Force (IETF) Request for Comments 1766. Available at http://www.ietf.org/rfc/rfc1766.txt

Bos, Bert and The W3C Communications Team. "XML in 10 points," World Wide Web Consortium (W3C), Cambridge, MA, revised June 2003. Available at www.w3.org/XML/1999/XML-in-10-points

Carey, Rikk and Bell, Gavin. *The Annotated VRML 2.0 Reference Manual*, Addison Wesley, Boston, MA, 1997. Available at http://www.awprofessional.com

Foley, James D., van Dam, Andries, Feiner, Stephen K, and Hughes, John F. Computer Graphics, Principles and Practice, Addison-Wesley, Boston, MA, 2nd Edition, 1997.

Humanoid Animation. ISO 19774, International Standards Organization (ISO)/International Engineering Consortium (IEC), June 2006. Available at www.web3d.org/x3d/specifications

ISO International Register of Graphical Items. Registration authority—c/o Joint Interoperability Test Command, Fort Huachuca, AZ, 21 June 2005.

Organization for the Advancement of Structured Information Standards (OASIS). Code for the Representation of the Names of Languages, Technology Report from ISO 639, revised 1989. Available at www.oasis-open.org/cover/iso639a.html

Stone, Maureen. *A Field Guide to Digital Color*, AK Peters, Ltd., Wellesley, MA2003.

VRML97 functional specification and External Authoring Interface (EAI), International Standard ISO/IEC 14772, Amendments 1 and 2, December 2003. Available at www.web3d.org/x3d/specifications

Extensible 3D (X3D) Part 1, ISO 19775: Architecture and base components, Scene Access Interface (SAI), International Standards Organization (ISO)/International Engineering Consortium (IEC), Revision 1, July 2006. Available at www.web3d.org/x3d/specifications

Extensible 3D (X3D) Part 2, ISO 19776: X3D Encodings (XML, Classic VRML, and Compressed binary encoding), International Standards Organization (ISO)/International Engineering Consortium (IEC), July 2006. Available at www.web3d.org/x3d/specifications

Extensible 3D (X3D) Part 3, ISO 19777: X3D language bindings (ECMAScript and Java), International Standards Organization (ISO)/International Engineering Consortium (IEC), July 2006. Available at www.web3d.org/x3d/specifications

Index

Note: Page numbers followed by *f* and *t* indicate figures and tables material.